The Third Walpurgis Night

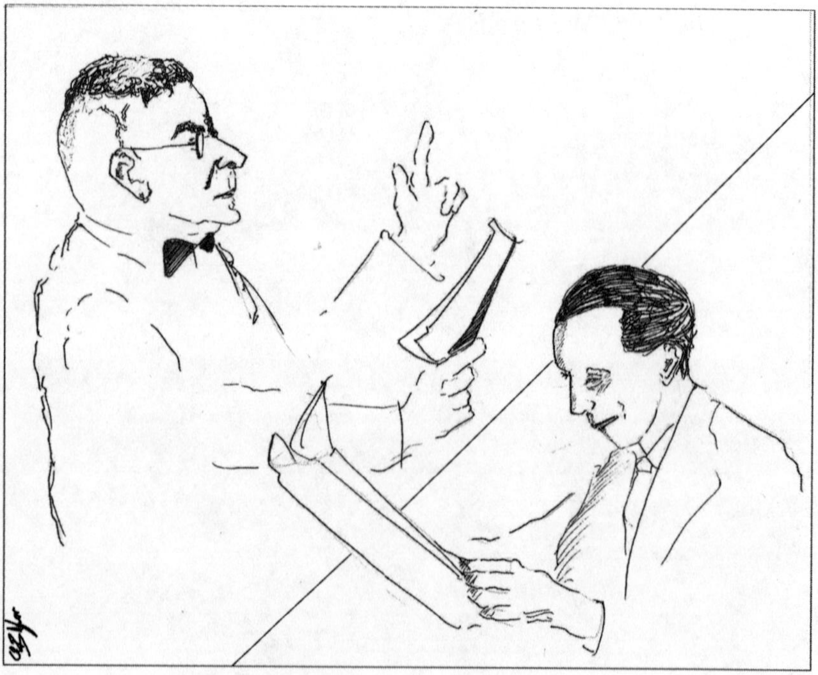

“I am still compared favorably with Goebbels—not a pleasant experience.”

The Third Walpurgis Night

The Complete Text

KARL KRAUS

TRANSLATED FROM THE GERMAN BY

FRED BRIDGHAM AND EDWARD TIMMS

FOREWORD BY MARJORIE PERLOFF

YALE UNIVERSITY PRESS ■ NEW HAVEN & LONDON

A MARGELLOS
WORLD REPUBLIC OF LETTERS BOOK

The Margellos World Republic of Letters is dedicated to making literary works from around the globe available in English through translation. It brings to the English-speaking world the work of leading poets, novelists, essayists, philosophers, and playwrights from Europe, Latin America, Africa, Asia, and the Middle East to stimulate international discourse and creative exchange.

Yale University Press books may be purchased in quantity for educational, business, or promotional use. For information, please e-mail sales.press@yale.edu (U.S. office) or sales@yaleup.co.uk (U.K. office).

Set in Electra and Nobel type by Tseng Information Systems, Inc.

Frontispiece: Printed with permission by Otto Bridgham.

Printed in the United States of America.

Library of Congress Control Number: 2019952815
ISBN 978-0-300-23600-2 (hardcover : alk. paper)

A catalogue record for this book is available from the British Library.

This paper meets the requirements of ANSI/NISO Z39.48-1992 (Permanence of Paper).

10 9 8 7 6 5 4 3 2 1

CONTENTS

FOREWORD

This, the first translation of the great political satire Karl Kraus produced in his final years, is a critical bombshell, a book that patiently and devastatingly documents the role of the media—newspapers, journals, radio broadcasts, speeches, pamphlets, even poems—in solidifying Hitler's control of Germany in the early months following his election to the chancellorship on January 30, 1933. Far from providing any sort of resistance, the German media almost immediately started providing cover and propaganda for the Nazi regime and did so with great cleverness and surprising literary skill. What we now call "fake news" (*Falschmeldung*) was the order of the day—a frightening mélange of half-truths and distortions that played on the consciousness of ordinary citizens, convincing them that the new regime was doing the right thing. In the Age of Trump, Kraus's book could hardly be more timely, although, as I shall suggest below, the differences between our time and the Nazi interregnum are also remarkable.

As the editor-translators tell us in their introduction, *Die Dritte Walpurgisnacht* was composed and typeset between May and September 1933, but Kraus put it aside, worrying that its publication might provoke terrible reprisals against the Jews of Germany (and, by extension, Austria). Kraus never witnessed the Anschluss—he died in 1936—and then the war intervened: *Die Dritte Walpurgisnacht* was not published until 1952. Translation has proved to be a major challenge because the book contains so many local and arcane references to persons and places as well as many literary allusions: it presupposes a certain familiarity with everyday life in the Germany and Europe of the early 1930s as well as with Goethe and other German writers. But, as Edward Timms, until his death the leading Kraus scholar in English, and his expert collaborator Fred Bridgham have understood, once we grant Kraus his particular *donnée*—that creative citation from documentary material can tell us more about a particular moment than can any "objective" historical account—Kraus's essay becomes surprisingly accessible, especially for a contemporary audience accustomed to conceptual writing and art. Together with Kraus's great documentary drama *The*

Last Days of Mankind, which Bridgham and Timms translated and published in 2015, *The Third Walpurgis Night* introduces us to a Karl Kraus who was much more than the author/editor of the wicked journal *Die Fackel* or the coiner of clever political aphorisms, as he is primarily known in the anglophone world. This Karl Kraus is a great Swiftian satirist.

The technique of *The Third Walpurgis Night* is almost entirely one of appropriation: Kraus gives us over a thousand excerpts from the political discourse of the first six months of 1933, interspersing hundreds of literary allusions, many of them from Goethe, but also dozens from Shakespeare, and other lyric and dramatic works. Even when we don't recognise the source of this or that citation, the impact of Kraus's satire is extraordinary, and the contemporary reader will experience a shock of recognition on page after page.

Walpurgisnacht: the first recording of the word was by Johannes Praetorius in 1668, referring to the Christian feast day of the eighth-century abbess St. Walpurga, a feast traditionally celebrated with bonfires and fireworks on the eve of May Day (April 30), to ward off witches and demons. Kraus is of course referring primarily to the famous *Walpurgisnacht* scenes in *Faust* 1 and 2, but Goethe's treatment of the demonic has none of Kraus's ferocious political animus: Kraus once remarked that a second Walpurgis night was World War I, whose catastrophic outcome he predicted immediately in 1914 and satirized mercilessly in *The Last Days of Mankind* (1922).

The third Walpurgis night, in any case, is a scene of *writing*—the "writing on the toilet wall", as Kraus put it, initiated immediately upon Hitler's assumption of power. The book's famous opening sentence, "*Mir fällt zu Hitler nichts ein*", is meant quite literally: Kraus's focus is not on Hitler's *Mein Kampf* or on the Führer's own speeches—that would be too easy—but on what appeared, day by day, in print, on the radio, and in public forums. From reports in provincial German newspapers, to the seemingly liberal Austrian *Neue Freie Presse*, to the commentary of Hitler's famed Minister of Propaganda Joseph Goebbels as well as the rhetoric of respected thinkers like Martin Heidegger and Gottfried Benn, the Nazi ethos—and especially its virulent hatred for the Jews—was relentlessly and carefully promoted.

The case of Goebbels is especially interesting. In American war movies of the 1940s Goebbels and Goering (Hitler's deputy) were usually represented as sinister versions of Laurel and Hardy or Abbott and Costello. But Goebbels was no clown. The top student in his high school class and the holder of a Heidelberg doctorate in Romantic literature, Goebbels was a failed *littérateur* turned bank clerk, who had joined the Nazi Party as early as 1924. Well educated and just clever enough to be extremely dangerous, he paid lip service to avant-garde notions of "Making It New", assuring his readers that "Things are on the move". Radio, Goebbels is quoted as declaring, "should never only play the ideological card", nor should "art always beat the big drum". Appealing to educated readers, he vigorously denounced kitsch: "no more electoral slogans on everyday crockery" or "the misuse of the Nazi symbol on every sheet of rolls of paper in places where the walls are already covered with the same symbol". The campaign "against kitsch" is then twisted to justify the call to arms against the "un-German spirit", although in fact that campaign could hardly have been kitschier as when, for the Reich Chancellor's first visit to Berlin's City Hall, "on both sides of the vestibule heralds in historical dress were to be lined up".

Kraus's portrait of Goebbels, a collage from various texts, especially his Reichstag Speech of 8 May 1933, is a small masterpiece:

> [Goebbels] has attitude and empathy, he knows about stimulus and impetus, application and implication, dramatic presentation, filmic transposition, flexible formulation, and the other aids to radical renewal, he has experience and perspective, indeed for both reality and vision, he has zest for life and world-philosophy, he approves of ethos and pathos but also mythos, he supplies subordination and integration into the living-space and working space of the nation, he embraces the emotional realm of community and the vitalism of personality ... he acknowledges fluidity, accessibility, and significant form and can distinguish between the expansive and the convulsive ... at all events he recognises potential for development and defines emotionally the type that, inescapably, in the final analysis must surely eventuate in trend-setting hegemony and knows that ... the goal is totality, though in the first instance steely romanticism— in short, you can't fool him about anything that was previously to be found in the cultural ragbag of the *Berliner Tageblatt* or *Berliner Zeitung* and that, whether modern German or modern Jewish, denoted a world sucked dry by those who saw the rest as suckers.

Note how this passage moves from the seeming praise for Modernist techniques—I say "seeming", because the very first word, "attitude", is ambiguous, as are "stimulus" and "impetus", and "vision" is qualified by being coupled with "reality"—and makes its way to the "world sucked dry" by none other than "modern Jewish" writers. Indeed, all the buzzwords of avant-garde "radical renewal" are slightly skewed, creating absurd parallels, puns, and double entendres. The phrase "he approves of ethos and pathos but also mythos", for example, conflates Aristotle's argument in the *Poetics* that mythos (plot) is the heart of tragedy with the *Rhetoric*'s analysis of ethos (the presentation of self) and pathos (the appeal to the audience). In Kraus's sentence, mythos becomes sheer myth—the lies the people are told by the Nazi press—and hence distorts the ethical and pathetic arguments. The whole absurd catalogue culminates in the phrase *trend-setting hegemony*, which in fact means that the new "trend"—or law!—is the hegemony of the state, whose "goal is totality", posing as a "steely romanticism". To make the critique palatable, Goebbels places the blame on "modernism", "*whether* modern German or modern Jewish", but it is the latter—those urban "bloodsuckers" from Berlin—who are bleeding our people "dry". And complaints lodged against the "cultural ragbag" of the Berlin (i.e., Jewish) literary press is essential under the new "trend-setting hegemony"!

But it is not only politicians like Goebbels who distort the language this way. Kraus has a few astonishing pages on Heidegger's Inaugural Address as Vice-Chancellor of Freiburg University in May 1933, commenting on the passage where the philosopher defines the "spiritual world of a people" as "the power of profoundly preserving its earthly and blood-based strengths as the power of the innermost arousal and utmost upheaval of its existence". "The attachment to a combination of blood and soil", Kraus responds in an absurdist twist, "which these unfathomable advocates of violence now eagerly expound, could remind us of another hazard, not philosophical but medical, arising from such a combination: tetanus. Thus the psychosis might be traced back to an epidemic of national spasms characteristic of those who strut their stuff on parade grounds or lecture platforms or are capable of doing both at once." The "tetanus" mentality is everywhere: Kraus cites the following comment by Gottfried Benn:

> You claim that what's happening in Germany today [violent upheaval] constitutes a threat to culture, to civilisation, *as if a horde of savages* were threatening the very ideals of mankind, but let me ask you in return: what do you imagine the twelfth century, say, was like, the transition *from Romanesque to Gothic sensibility*, do you think it would have been up for discussion? . . . That a vote would have been taken: round arches or pointed arches? The apse: circular or polygonal—a matter for debate?

Of course not! And so intellectuals should make an effort "to see only what is elemental, thrusting ever forward to its inevitable outcome".

Kraus juxtaposes these highbrow appeals to German tradition—its *völkisch* past or great Christian architecture—to accounts beginning to appear in the local newspapers detailing the torture and murder of this or that Jewish shopkeeper who refused to give up his shop or leave town. In these early months of the Third Reich, even the German Jews themselves were eager to advocate "converging with the German national character so as to develop characteristics that do not form part of the primeval Jewish racial heritage". Dismissing talk of atrocities committed against Jews, the "Honorary President" of the National German Jews declared that such "spontaneous" actions have nothing to do with policy: "[we] are absolutely convinced that the resolute will of the government and the leadership of the National Socialist party is to maintain law and order". One business firm that had hired a number of Jews went on the record to protest that "there has not been a single case of persecution or attacks on people who think differently or on members of foreign states, specific races, or religious communities." Indeed, in the words of Hitler's Vice-Chancellor Franz von Papen, "We must move from a nationalism that divides our peoples to an international security system that unites them." That system turned out to be none other than the rule of the SS, the armed wing of the party whose later role would be to carry out the Final Solution.

The newspapers continue peddling the peace doctrine: in the May 1933 issue of the Jewish-owned *Neue Freie Presse*, the declaration is made that "The anti-German atrocity propaganda will spontaneously dissolve into nothingness through the power of truth." The very same month (May '33), an invitation was sent out to the faculty of the Johann Wolfgang Goethe University in Frankfurt:

> The Student Volunteer Corps invites all professors to the burning of Marxist and other pernicious writings, which will take place on the Römerberg on the evening of Wednesday, 10 May.
>
> In the light of the great symbolic importance of the ceremony, the students would welcome the presence of the entire professorial body.
>
> *Accordingly, I invite colleagues to attend in large numbers.*
>
> The procession, with musical accompaniment, will march from the University to the Römerberg on Wednesday evening at 8 pm. The student fraternities will participate in uniform, as will the SA battalions.
>
> Signed: Krieck
> Vice-chancellor

The burning of the books! Here "other pernicious writings" is, of course, just a code word for Jewish material. "An age of barbarism begins", as Nietzsche has it in a cruel aphorism Kraus quotes, "the academy will do its bidding." No professor, it seems, raises the slightest objection (by May the Jewish professors have all been purged). Nor do the media question the following commentary made by Hitler's deputy, Rudolf Hess:

> In some foreign countries, the *propaganda aimed against Germany* has recently seized on the *untrue assertion* that the National Socialist Ger-

> man Workers' Party *aims to annex* parts of *Switzerland, of Holland, of Belgium, of Denmark, etc. Nonsensical* as this *imputation* is, there are nevertheless *some who believe* it. The Leadership of the Reich accordingly considers it *of the utmost importance to state* that *no one in Germany seriously thinks of laying a finger* on the independence of other states.

"The 'etc.'" Kraus remarks wryly, "presumably refers to Austria and Czechoslovakia". But even as Hess could protest that the Third Reich had no designs on other nations, Nazi propaganda was quietly undermining Austrian resistance to the upcoming Anschluss.

The first step—a favourite Nazi ploy—was to reverse the roles of aggressor and victim. As Kraus notes, "The headline 'Heimwehr assault'—based on the mere appearance of broken bones—makes it possible to denounce as a lie the frivolous assertion that defenders of the Austrian homeland were attacked by Nazis. For nowadays it is always the perpetrator who is attacked, assuming the role of victim at least in the sense that he was forced to use violence." Thus there are daily complaints that German diplomats or agents are being abused in Vienna. On radio, there's a complaint that "a German journalist was made to share a cell with an Austrian homosexual." Or again the Austrians are portrayed as hopeless troublemakers, as in this item from the *Völkischer Beobachter*:

> If the responsible men in the government continue *to trample the rights of the people underfoot*, a *terrible awakening* will bring it forcibly home to them with indisputable certainty that, on the day of the coming insurrection, no one *will go unpunished for ruling a people through despotic acts and prohibitions.*

The reference is to Engelbert Dollfuss, the Austrian chancellor (1932–34) who defied Hitler and was determined to avoid Anschluss: his own authoritarian rule—he had dismissed parliament on grounds of treason and was hence attacked by the Socialists as an Austro-Fascist—was a perfect target for the Nazi attack machine. Instead of directly attacking Austrian Jews, the Nazi press could condemn the Catholic Dollfuss and thus sow sedition. "While Germany under the rule of Adolf Hitler is heading for an economic boom, Austria under the despotism of Herr Dollfuss is facing ruin." Or: "Harmless tourists, visiting a kindred people, are exposed to such [brutal] treatment." Or again: "Germans love Austria but increasingly feel at risk: Germany wants to remain at least inwardly linked to Austria, with which it is inseparably linked by *ties of blood*."

There are those ties of blood again. Step by step, the Dollfuss regime is belittled and attacked, so that when, on 25 July 1934, Dollfuss is assassinated by the Nazis in cold blood, right inside his Chancellery office, the public has been primed to condone the crime. Even translation (from the British and French papers) is used to cement the fake news. When the *London Times* notes that "In Great Britain there has never been very strong public support for the possible merger of the Austrian and German peoples", the German translation reads: "In England there has never been *strong opposition* to the question of a possible *unification of Germany with Austria.*" Such faux translation goes hand in hand with another device: the "re-vindication of the content of a proverbial expression", in cases "where an originally bloody or violent content has long since been transposed onto the plane of intellectual conflict". When we say "an eye for an eye", for instance, we mean revenge, not that we are literally going to pull out our enemy's eye. But in Nazi rhetoric, the situation is reversed: metaphor is turned into hyperbole:

> We don't say: an eye for an eye, a tooth for a tooth. No, if someone puts out our eye, we'll cut off his head, if someone knocks out our tooth, we'll shatter his jaw.

Similarly the metaphor "rubbing salt in the wound", which has not been taken literally for centuries, is suddenly enacted as a necessary punishment for this or that troublesome Jew:

> When the old comrade inflicted a deep cut on his hand while peeling potatoes, a group of Nazis laughed mockingly and forced his heavily bleeding hand into a sack of salt. They found the old man's cries of agony a great joke.

Indeed, one can take "the people" at their word; when they claim that "they won't harm a hair on the head of any Jew", says Kraus, "it's evidently the only treatment that wasn't inflicted, while many a Jew lost the skin off his scalp or had his head shaved so as to be branded with the sign under which the Nazi idea has conquered". And so the most blatant atrocities can be justified. Even the simplest phrase, like the address "Meine Damen und Herren" (Ladies and Gentlemen) becomes "Meine Männer und Frauen", a phrase with a very different valence, "Frauen" referring either to wives or to women who are *not* ladies, and "Männer" stressing physical capacity based on gender itself.

Throughout the book, Kraus maintains his distance, seemingly doing nothing but put before us documents that speak for themselves. But in Section 29, toward the end of the book, he speaks more personally:

> Now I ask myself how I was able to find my way through this dark labyrinth, while the German language—my language—was led astray by the hypocritical urgings of a mischievous will o' the wisp; stumbling over

> roots and snags even more treacherous than the linguistic minefield of the World War, while I was both encouraged and deterred by well-meaning readers demanding clear views as visibility deteriorated after the political landslide? Posing such questions to myself is to query in the same breath the moral justification of questioning the Nazi seizure of power, an event of elemental force whose workings provide a link between the press and my bias against it. . . . I go about this with a greater degree of responsibility and with insight into the connection between both evils. For *National Socialism has not destroyed the press; rather, the press has created National Socialism.* Apparently only as a reaction, but actually as a fulfilment of its true nature. (emphasis added)

As mentioned earlier, Kraus did not live to see the Anschluss and World War II; he died in 1936. Would he have softened his view of the press? I doubt it, but most readers, myself included, will find his conclusion that the press *created* National Socialism, rather than the other way around, exaggerated, if not just plain wrong. Press iniquities were Kraus's monomania, and one can point, as Walter Benjamin did in his famous essay on Kraus, to "the strange interplay between reactionary theory [the trust in traditional bourgeois individualism] and revolutionary practice that we find everywhere in Kraus".[1] True, Kraus had no *theory* of Fascism: indeed, he avoided all larger theoretical formulations. But what he understood is that, whatever the sources of Nazi ideology, once on the scene, it was the media that were able to gain *acceptance* for the Nazi agenda, and to do so much more rapidly and easily than would seem possible. And if this was the situation in 1933, think of our own social media world and its avenues of dissemination and control.

How do the two moments of history—the 1930s and the 2010s—compare? Much has been made by recent commentators of the parallel between the fall of the Weimar Republic and our own now-shaky democracy, and Trumpian doublespeak is regularly compared to that of the Nazis. The president's "Fascist" ideas and undemocratic executive orders are roundly deplored, with fake news becoming the byword of the day.

At one level, of course, the differences are more profound than the similarities. Today it is precisely the media—CNN, MSNBC, *The New Yorker*, *The New York Times*—that practice Resistance, that question each and every statement President Trump makes and that call out his abuses of racism and sexism. The government takeover of the entire press that occurred in the Germany of February 1933 is thus unthinkable in the contemporary United States or, for that matter, in Western Europe.

The press situation thus seems to be the opposite of Germany's in 1933. But not quite. Fake news is by no means confined to the right; left news outlets are just as likely as the right to make statements that are blatantly false or at least biased—statements that are never questioned. I recall that during the fabled Arab Spring, CNN's Anderson Cooper regularly pointed at the large numbers of protesters in Cairo's Tahrir Square as evidence of the revolution's widespread popular support. Interviews with politicians and ordinary citizens seemed to confirm Cooper's optimism. We regularly heard, on this and the other major networks, about the unstoppable new drive toward democracy in the Middle East. Then when the Egyptian movement utterly failed and the military dictatorship took over, no explanations were given: Egypt simply disappeared from the CNN radar screen, and attention turned elsewhere. The wrong news is no news.

Kraus had an uncanny understanding for this state of affairs: he understood that it is the reporting of events, not the events themselves, that shapes our thinking. Nothing comes to us unmediated. His *Third Walpurgis Night* can thus be read not only as brilliant satire but also as cautionary tale: "Breaking News"—and everything now seems to be "Breaking News"—is less true story than attention-getting device so that whatever is or is not the case, the media come out on top. However wrong their predictions, they are never penalized for them, and however negative their assessments, they are still seen as providing a valuable service. A year into the Trump presidency, CNN, which attacks and ridicules Trump from morning till night, was able to hire more than a dozen new reporters on the strength of the profits the network had made in its exposé of the president's iniquities. In media-speak, nothing succeeds like the success of having a clearly defined object of attack, a scapegoat. In its brilliant and cruel dissection of the Nazi media of 1933, *The Third Walpurgis Night* is thus a truly prophetic work.

Marjorie Perloff

TRANSLATORS' PREFACE

The difficulty of translating such a complex text means that only short excerpts have appeared in English. Following their first complete English translation of *The Last Days of Mankind* (Yale, 2015), FB and ET have devoted two years to tackling the complete text of *The Third Walpurgis Night.* Coded passages that often appear hermetic to readers of the original German are contextualised for greater transparency, reflecting the findings of recent scholarly research. "Having spent many years thinking contextually about Kraus, and in certain ways getting inside his mind", ET understands "Kraus's angular, refractory style, his allusive intertextuality, his determination to make the reader struggle every inch of the way" (ET 2, 538). Struggle we did, with FB providing a first draft, notes, and glossary and ET polishing the main text until an agreed-upon version emerged. The aim was to achieve clarity and impact where Kraus had good reason to be cautious and obscure: he did not want the Neanderthals to understand him.

Resisting the advice, attributed to Dorothy Parker, not to toss such a book aside lightly but to throw it with great force, our challenge was thus to render passages of deliberate intricacy transparent while recognising the underlying subtext of this pioneering anti-Nazi polemic, beginning with that defiant statement of speechlessness: "As to Hitler, I have nothing to say" (alternatively, "Hitler brings nothing to my mind"—both perhaps closer to the German than our reluctantly rejected "Mention Hitler and my mind goes blank"). Elias Canetti was reportedly so incensed that he tore the issue of *Die Fackel* containing that extract to pieces before Kraus's eyes.[1] But when the brain is paralysed by events that defy explanation, Kraus's response oscillates between Goethe's invocation of "the indescribable" ("Das Unbeschreibliche, / hier ist's getan"—*Faust* [12108]) and Shakespeare's painfully consoling principle that "the worst is not / So long as we can say 'This is the worst'" (*King Lear,* IV, 1).

A French version of the text, *Troisième nuit de Walpurgis* (Agone, 2005) by Pierre Deshusses, provided encouragement for our project, suggested solutions to some textual difficulties, and offered tentative interpretations to many of

Kraus's allusions while taking a generally literal approach. We are also indebted to mini-biographies available on Google of persons in positions of power yet often overlooked in the standard histories and otherwise difficult to track down, an obviously ever-expanding field of research into the Third Reich. We would be happy to acknowledge more fully these assiduous if anonymous contributors. Of the voluminous literature on the period, two masterworks have thrown further light on virtually all the issues Kraus addresses (and, one might add, vice versa—though Kraus's analysis has hitherto remained largely unknown): Michael Burleigh's vividly compelling *The Third Reich: A New History* (Macmillan, 2000) and the now-standard, comprehensive introduction to *The Coming of the Third Reich* (Allen Lane, 2003) by Richard J. Evans. Thanks are gratefully owed to Nicholas Jacobs, who encouraged and followed our collaboration at every stage, and to Raymond Hargreaves, whose meticulous reading of our draft text and suggested improvements would surely have earned Kraus's approval. As with *The Last Days of Mankind*, our collaboration with Yale UP has again been a privilege and a pleasure—with Ash Lago, Jeffrey Schier, and Martin Schneider.

Goethe's *Faust* Part 2 has been translated many times, but we have confined our consultations to one pioneering classic, by Bayard Taylor (Osgood & Co., 1875), and two more recent efforts: by David Luke (World Classics, Oxford University Press, 1994) and John Williams (Wordsworth Classics, 2007); however, occasional attributed borrowings aside, we have attempted to provide versions of our own, with line references in square brackets.

Cross-references to the text and within the glossary are extensive, though not individually tagged unless the headword for persons, organisations, events, concepts, etc. is uncertain. Glossary entries are mostly restricted to the weight their subjects carry in Kraus's text. References to Kraus's journal *Die Fackel* (1899–1936) are designated with issue and page number (e.g., F 811–19, 21). References to Edward Timms, *Karl Kraus, Apocalyptic Satirist*, vol. 1: *Culture and Catastrophe in Habsburg Vienna* (Yale, 1986) and vol. 2: *The Post-War Crisis and the Rise of the Swastika* (Yale, 2005) are given as Timms 1 and Timms 2.

Sadly, Ted did not live to see the publication of this book but was fully involved until shortly before his death. Without his expertise, fertile imagination, and unflagging enthusiasm, the project would have been unthinkable. For both Kraus and his unrivalled champion, the great polemic marks a painfully fitting closure.

FB

INTRODUCTION

The original German text of *Die Dritte Walpurgisnacht* was composed and typeset between May and September 1933 as a polemical response to the Nazi seizure of power. Kraus was encouraged in this project by his friend Bertolt Brecht, who wrote from exile in Denmark: "You have disclosed the atrocities of intonation and created an ethics of language".[1] But in the autumn of 1933 Kraus put the project on hold, fearing not only for his own safety but also that such a publication by an Austrian Jewish author would provoke brutal reprisals against Jews trapped in Germany. After his death in 1936, followed two years later by the Nazi annexation of Austria, the proofs of *Die Dritte Walpurgisnacht* with his handwritten corrections were preserved and taken by his lawyer Oskar Samek to New York for safety, but it was not until 1952 that this great satiric essay was finally published by the Kösel Verlag in Munich, edited by Heinrich Fischer, Kraus's literary executor. It is this edition, divided by Fischer into twenty-nine sections, that forms the basis for this first English translation.

In the famous opening sentence, which appeared in his journal *Die Fackel* in 1934 together with other short excerpts, Kraus declared: "Mir fällt zu Hitler nichts ein" (As to Hitler, I have nothing to say). Behind this opening ploy lies the idea that individual protest has been silenced by the horrors of Nazism. Hence Kraus's decision to configure *Die Dritte Walpurgisnacht* as a cacophony of competing voices, measuring the ideology of the Hitler regime against the testimony of German humanism from Kant to Freud. If the argument appears to lack a progressive logic, this, too, reflects the author's awareness of the limits of language in the face of catastrophe. A poem from September 1933, with Biblical, apocalyptic allusions, spells out the fate of the Word—the *logos* at the root of western civilisation:

Don't ask about the actions I've been taking. I'll not speak out, nor say what it's about.	Man frage nicht, was all die Zeit ich machte. Ich bleibe stumm; Und sage nicht warum.

And there is silence when the earth's been quaking. No word that fits; You speak with drowsy wits, And dream of smiling suns when morning's breaking. It cannot last; Later it all was past. The Word expired on Hitler's world's awaking.	Und Stille gibt es, da die Erde krachte. Kein Wort, das traf. Man spricht nur aus dem Schlaf. Und träumt von einer Sonne, welche lachte. Es geht vorbei; Nachher war's einerlei. Das Wort entschlief, als jene Welt erwachte. (F 888, 4)

The intertextual framework for this modern Witches' Sabbath is provided by motifs drawn from the mediaeval German Walpurgisnacht scene in Goethe's *Faust*, Part 1, and much more extensively from the weird and phantasmagorical Classical Walpurgis Night section of Part 2, which are often set against scenes from *Macbeth*. Using modernist collage, Kraus juxtaposes these motifs against the witch hunts of the Third Reich and its leader's aggressive self-righteousness, the beguiling doublespeak of Goebbels with his weasel word *Gleichschaltung* (alignment, meaning coercion to toe the party line) and the raucous chanting of the stormtroopers, while a poignant counterpoint is provided by the plaintive cries of their victims: Jews brutally tormented, socialists and communists dragged off to concentration camps, the livelihood of lawyers and shopkeepers destroyed. Goethe's hero is a time-traveller whose longing for authentic being takes him back to the realms of myth, while modern Germany has embarked on a similar journey in search of its Aryan ancestry. The impact is heightened by a range of further discordant registers, from the exalted tones of intellectuals like Heidegger to advertising slogans and popular songs. These polyphonic techniques—over a thousand excerpts from the political discourse of 1933 interwoven with more than two hundred literary allusions—enabled Kraus to express not simply his own opinions but also the ongoing struggle for the soul of Germany.

Faust's redemption rests on his ceaseless striving, indeed his crimes appear to be legitimised by the energy with which they are committed, but Kraus is far from drawing a parallel between Faust's escape from eternal damnation and Hitler's activities. Rather, the question of whether the natural world originated in a single violent seismological event that so fascinated Goethe—the "Vulcanist" position (represented by Anaxagoras in the play), as distinct from "Neptunist" gradualism (represented by Thales)—became connected in Kraus's mind with the Nazi seizure of power. He repeatedly alludes to *Faustnaturen* (*eine Faust* is a fist), and identifies the vitalism portrayed in the play as one of the ideological antecedents of fascism. For example, the aptly named Manfred von Killinger (who in his memoirs described thrashing a young woman with a horsewhip and was subsequently appointed prime minister of Saxony by Hitler) prompts the thought: "a Faustian nature, perhaps, but a superman?" Faust's deluded arrogance and existential quest for knowledge and beauty ultimately prove less telling than the moral framework of Shakespearean tragedy—the nemesis awaiting Lady Macbeth's defiant "What need we fear who knows it, / When none can call our power to account?" The fact that Macbeth is defeated by an army assembled in England is also prophetic, reflecting what shocked Kraus in 1933: the failure of Britain, France, and the United States to take a stand against Hitler. But though the final sentence of *The Third Walpurgis Night* anticipates retribution, it is wishful thinking rather than a restoration of moral order providing Shakespearean closure, such as Horatio proclaims to "the yet unknowing world" in the final scene of *Hamlet*, and which Kraus had still felt able to use in 1918 to conclude *The Last Days of Mankind*.

After his election victory of March 1933, and to international relief, Hitler, echoing Bismarck, adopted the stance of the statesman, an "honest broker" in world affairs (10 May), who insisted that everything in Germany now depended on "channelling the released current of revolution into the safe bed of evolution" (6 July). By the summer of 1933, the Four-Power Pact seemed to have made Germany great again, but Hitler shocked the world when he proceeded to take back control by withdrawing from the League of Nations and boycotting its Disarmament Conference. Kraus's aim throughout was to expose the gulf between "creeping fascism" and the continuing "seismic eruption" on the streets. He foresaw that the revolutionary violence of the stormtroopers would inevitably clash with Hitler's desire to consolidate his power by evolutionary means, as would indeed happen in June 1934 with the massacre of Ernst Röhm and his confederates. Since—at least until *Anschluss* in 1938—a further gulf yawned ever wider between defenders of Austria's independence and advocates (right across the political spectrum) for a Greater Germany, Kraus was fighting simultaneously on several fronts. His guarded admiration for a more radical Socialism in 1932 as "a final hope", born of despair after the dismal failures of the Social Democrats, turned into eventual support for Dollfuss's authoritarian regime (one he thought mercifully free of "racial mania", its "vigour and resolve unprecedented in Austria") as the "lesser evil"—a pragmatic choice which Kraus's ethical radicalism had in the past ruled out. Based on his absolute priority, "Anything but Hitler", it cost him the respect of left-wing friends and readers, while Dollfuss's assassination on 25 July 1934, on Hitler's orders during a failed Nazi putsch, virtually silenced him as a political commentator.

Kraus's assault on the failings of Austrian Social Democracy—after its all too law-abiding allies in the Weimar Republic had been so swiftly sidelined—may seem unduly harsh but derives largely from the irreparable polarisation "when the patriots are not democrats [My country, Right or wrong] and the democrats are not patriots [Workers of the world, unite!]". "To oppose violence by democratic means" [the Social Democratic credo], "which violence can then be used to destroy democracy all the more effectively, leaves us with the same old ticklish question: 'Now the Party's over, what shall we do with the rest of the evening?'"[2] In the broader historical context, Dollfuss, "the saviour of Austria . . . undervalues himself when he compares the national emergency of today with that of 1914. At that time, Austria would have done better not to rise up, but to remain as lethargic as ever; only now, twenty years later, is it entering upon what the standard textbooks recognise as a 'sacred defensive war.'" The enemy is at the gates, indeed already within, threatening to turn Austria into a "vassal" state, so "Freedom [the war cry of Social Democracy] is safer in the hands of the [Austrian] Fatherland than the other way round". Dollfuss's reception of the propaganda visit to Austria of Hans Frank along with Nazi fellow jurists Roland Freisler and Hanns Kerrl as "not especially welcome" leading to their prompt expulsion delights Kraus, with his love of ironic understatement.

The idea of a "synthesis" between Austria and Germany, let alone coordination or alignment, has become the more undesirable, the greater its growing popularity as an insidious Nazi slogan. The Movement prides itself on being a synthesis of "tradition and innovation", meaning an alliance between Nazis and traditional elites, not only von Papen, Hugenberg et al. but, more publicly, the staged meetings of Hindenburg and Hitler as prominently hailed in the Nazi press. Kraus's verdict: "What an abdication of the marshal's baton before the knapsack!" Already there is no synthesis possible between a chancellor publicly dedicated to peace and a Führer secretly intent on war, when the progressive to whom the future belongs has acquired the archaic aura of a tribal chieftain. A race to split the atom will soon coincide with the modern equivalent of burnings at the stake. As for the synthesis proclaimed by the National German Jews (see Glossary), "convergence" of character traits with those of the host nation is beyond satire. They will soon be the victims of Nazi violence presented as if they were its perpetrators through a process of inverted causality that Kraus had already diagnosed during World War I, when Germany was seen as the "innocent instigator" and Austria its victim. "Wars begin when diplomats tell lies to journalists—and then believe them when they see them in print".

Then, Kraus's main target had been Vienna's liberal *Neue Freie Presse*. Now, journalists "are unable even to fake it, which can to some extent be construed as—for them—a cultural advance". (Kraus had picked up subsequently deleted clues from the first edition of *Mein Kampf* about the need to "fake it" to win over the masses.) Alignment of the press signifies no more than its final phase and true nature: prostitution. Moreover, "the highly intelligent Propaganda Minister has made explicitly clear that all attempts to comprehend the New Order intellectually are misguided, since Soul is the only thing needed". Kraus returns to this point repeatedly, that—in the summer of 1933 at least—"the strength of the National Socialist Movement has hitherto been its lack of programme, arising from its ethos". "Those who weave its deceptive web start every day afresh, remembering nothing and ashamed of nothing . . . the uncertainty principle on which the machinery runs facilitates this irruption of the irrational." Oddly enough, it is "the intellectuals who have cottoned on to this" (the "rapturous enthusiasm of the thinking heads for the headhunters"—a fatal *trahison des clercs*) "rather than simple minds, who continue to brood on it", while "the number of those dissatisfied with the implementation of the programme as broadcast is growing by the day, talking of a second revolution". As the party bosses start to fear the embittered revanchism of the "brown plague" of stormtroopers, its days are numbered.

Though the "immutable sanctity of the Word", the "inviolability of language", is under threat, Kraus does not abandon his first principle—that language is the defining feature of the human condition. In analyzing the proliferation of new acronyms, for instance, culminating in his own despairing SOS to the USA, he anticipates the insights of Orwell's Principles of Newspeak, and, more crucially, the definition of "doublethink" as "the power of holding two contradictory beliefs in one's mind simultaneously, and accepting both of them. [. . .] The essential act of the Party is to use conscious deception while retaining the firmness of purpose that goes with complete honesty". However, Orwell predicted that traditional concepts "such as honour, justice, morality" would cease to exist under totalitarianism, whereas Kraus shows how the new rhetoric infuses reassuringly familiar words of "oldspeak" with new force: thus *Wille* no longer means free will but the submission of the individual to the authority of Hitler—the *Führerwille*.[3]

In fact, Kraus has little to say about the mind of the Führer, whose view of the world has been shaped by the adventure stories of Karl May. Instead, he focuses on the "satanic humbug" orchestrated by Goebbels, the quintessential Berlin journalist and paradigmatic spin doctor with a background in liberal journalism that has been merely "aligned" to the new ideology (notably the leading Jewish-owned liberal *Berliner Tageblatt*, for which Goebbels had once aspired to write). Now Goebbels is peddling primitivism through modern terminology, appealing to the spiritual values (the "new man", a spiritual renewal very different from that invoked by Expressionism) that sanction bestial vindictiveness against the enemy within—socialists, pacifists, Jews. Kraus exposes the forgotten physical origin of metaphors now condoned: when "the empty husk of a word suddenly fills again with the blood that was once its content", such as "running the gauntlet" or "rubbing salt in the wound"; he lays bare Goebbels's genius for propagating euphemisms such as "protective custody" (*Schutzhaft*—even of the German language, Kraus adds); or the sinister implications of "hit tune" marches (*Schlagermelodien*) and the implementation of the boycott of Jewish shops "at a stroke" (*schlagartig*); or the repetitive emphasis on "fanatical" (*fanatisch*) behaviour as a virtue.

The blood myth—from religious sacrifice to the adulteration of "racial purity" (a nonsense, since it was precisely from "the Kashubians, Obotrites, Polabians, Sorbs, Wends, Veleti and other Slav peoples that the Prussian blood sprang")—becomes a daily evocation of blood greater than any mention over a whole year in other countries; bloodthirsty metaphors create a climate that encourages the infliction of real wounds. Kraus exposes this "miracle of transubstantiation", the eruption of empty phrases, of subliminal sanguinary thoughts, into violent actions, as a reversal of the whole process of civilisation. He predicts that by the time Germany finally does awake from such rabble-rousing slogans as "Deutschland erwache! Juda verrecke!" (Germany, awaken! Jews, exterminate 'em!), the second half of the slogan will have been shamefully fulfilled. He (psycho-)analyses the hidden agenda behind newspaper solecisms and misprints, as when Goebbels declares that the national revolution is intensified "when viewed through the *prison* of fanatical popular conviction"; "*Clinch* your fists! Be prepared!"; "Germans, *pursue* only Aryan newspapers!"; "Germans, take pride in your *notional* identity!"; "Follow instructions as *proscribed!*" He spots arrangements for special bathing hours for Jews "apart from the communally shared bloodbath" and slips in puns so poignant that we don't know whether to laugh or sigh as we confront "a political reality that talks of action and actually means what it slays". He demolishes the idea of *Volksgemeinschaft* as "virtual reality" with its essentially fictitious implication of both political solidarity and biological homogeneity. His eschatology culminates in the simplest of throwaway phrases: "letzten Endes" (at the end of the day; in the final reckoning)—a leitmotif, repeated with or without scare quotes, to make it clear that the "final end" of National Socialism is annihilation, echoing the Biblical "End of Days"—a combination of journalistic cliché and cataclysmic violence that signifies unprecedented catastrophe.

In spite of everything, laughter in the dark cannot be totally suppressed. To solve a tragic conflict between principle and tourism in Oberammergau, where "people who rent out rooms and dress up as apostles are allegedly conscience-stricken at having to portray Jewish types", the Nazirene with his divine mission is mooted as a more fitting blond, blue-eyed hero of the Passion Play. Gentlemen are already required to prefer blonds. Blacker still: "the opening of concentration camps for women surely proves that it is primarily the toughening up of this generation, rather than its reproduction, that is the aim". If everything in the world happens because people are incapable of imagining that it could happen, then satire is outrun by its subject. While absurdities and self-contradictions are allowed to speak for themselves, Kraus fills the final sections of his polemic with a savage indignation that may surprise readers hitherto unaware of its startlingly prescient existence.

The Third Walpurgis Night

1

STUNNED BY THE SEIZURE OF POWER

As to Hitler, I have nothing to say. I am aware that as the upshot of extended reflection, of repeated efforts to grasp the phenomenon and the forces driving it, this falls far short of expectations. They were, after all, pitched higher than ever before at a polemicist who is popularly—but mistakenly—expected to take a stand; and who, when confronted by any evil that appeals to his temperament, has indeed been prepared to "stick his neck out". But there are evils which not only make the neck cease to be a metaphor but may also prevent the associated activity of the brain from formulating a single idea. I feel stunned, and since—before this actually occurs—I don't want to give the impression of having been struck dumb, I still feel compelled to give an account of this failure; to explain the dilemma into which such a complete upheaval in the German-speaking world has plunged me, the paralysis caused by the awakening of a nation and the establishment of a dictatorship that now controls everything apart from language.

Perhaps I may justify myself to intrepid readers by confessing that the attempt at an intellectually adequate treatment of the exhausting impressions arising from this inexhaustible spectacle, from this momentous, indeed overwhelming dilemma, might also involve the impulse for self-preservation; the more so as this would help to preserve certain intellectual options, perhaps even more important than direct comments on the phenomenon itself. For what does this signify other than the danger of seeing the very act of thought itself subordinated to the swastika, the writing on the toilet wall that haunts every horizon and blocks every escape route, leaving only the awareness of an arbitrary power that practises what it proclaims.

Verbally sensitive writing that might resist this power is caught between the compulsion to speak and a feeling that it is all in vain. Such writing carries a heavier burden and runs greater risks than the daily assaults of irresponsible journalists, which tend to be overtaken by events and thwarted by the effects of their volatile fighting spirit. It is entangled in a hostile web of convergent yet unpredictable forces, an intractable conflation of the verbal with the real. For the reports of the daily chroniclers of history contain only the horror—the horror of the message and of the messenger who should bear responsibility for it; they make their report and awaken a desire for expiation of the deed through the word. Now it is time for the unsayable to be said, but this would never get beyond an attempt to demonstrate the inadequacy of the powers of the intellect. For this reason those who are calling for an individual "voice" should be aware that, even as a scream out of suffocating chaos, it must still rely on language; and that a shaping impulse which by nature tends to be mastered by its materials cannot take a stand but is searching for a foothold amid the multifarious assaults of an evil that would deal with him far more easily than he with it.

Is the damage inflicted on the human mind something our minds can absorb? Does not the crux of the seizure of power, its uniqueness, lie in the stance adopted towards the mind: assailing the "intellectuals" while itself remaining unassailable? Are we not disempowered more by the mindlessness of the movement than by the physical danger it poses? And is it a question of courage when confronted by this eruption of geodynamic nature, does it allow—beyond the idea of the misery of earthly life—any other idea than the safeguarding of thought itself?

Supposing that this elemental eruption had its sights fixed especially on exposing oppositional thinking, or indeed any semblance of thinking at all, then surely it would not be cowardly for an author to heed the warning not to spit into the crater but to reserve the right to form other plans. Even the poet of the nation whose awakening makes such caution advisable, even Schiller would not survive as a poet if he dared to imply today that the tiger's jaws are child's play compared with this horror of horrors—the people who share his nationality regard their birth certificate as a mark of distinction, and have no passport apart from the special peculiarity: of being Germans.[1] There is so much to cause amazement that it's not easy to find words. In order to say what happened, language can only come stammering along behind. For a moment has arrived in the life of nations that is not lacking in grandeur, insofar as people who benefit from electric lighting and all the resources of radio technology are being reconnected with primal being, causing a disruption of all life relationships, frequently through death. For man is arrogating his rights from heaven, from which may God be preserved! Blood proves itself by shedding blood; a servile system of command, to which people's beliefs and birthright are answerable, attacks life, liberty, and property. It happened in a single night, and every subsequent night you'll wait for what is coming. "Once violence has been overcome, you'll settle in a lovely home", sneers Mephisto [11,280].[2] The chosen few prevailed over the many who were called, and by no means was everyone satisfied, but they invoked ideals to ennoble their enterprise. Rising from the depths, they will sink even deeper, as social relations are reshaped by some mystical surge. Order is being restored; put your hands over your ears and you no longer hear the groaning.

A cleansing of the juices, a bloodletting has taken place, an upheaval that certainly affects commercial interests without actually prioritising them, ignoring the reaction of envy not unmixed with malicious glee in the outside world. This earth-shattering eruption leaves mere onlookers dumbfounded by the overnight transformation of the most zealous supporters of the civilising process into fire worshippers and adherents of a blood myth—an incredible spectacle. This cataclysm, brought about by ideas as simple as the egg of Columbus before he discovered America, mobilises symbols, flags, and firework displays on a scale previously unknown and unimagined in historical evolution, combined with a superabundance of spoken and printed clichés that saturate the airwaves and almost exhaust the capacity of the paper mills. It sweeps everything away like an epidemic of cerebral concussion that affects all those who live and breathe, making the detached onlooker feel as tactless as someone who fails to take his hat off at the funeral of mankind.

But since humanity is supposedly experiencing a resurrection, we must do justice to feelings that far transcend the messianic fervour of prehistoric eras saturated by religious symbols. Having witnessed women in public gatherings rending their garments, how can we remain unmoved? Have we not heard how "all of this great nation, the greatest on earth", celebrated a birthday—a forty-fourth birthday which has no special significance—in the following terms, as the day "the good Lord sent us a saviour in the hour of greatest need":

> On the threshing floors of the granaries in the wilds of East Prussia, barely clear of snow, as in the isolated farms in the valleys of the Karawanken Alps, the country folk came together, and as their thoughts turned to Adolf Hitler the taut furrows in their *gnarled* peasant faces relaxed, and from their ardent hearts they sent a prayer to the Lord above to preserve their Führer for years to come. On the storm-battered Halligen islands in the North Sea, the Frisian fishermen gathered and put their salt-racked hands together, thanking God for sending the Reich a ruler in its hour of need.

Since there were similar observations in the Alps and on the plains of Lower Saxony, in the uniformly grey and grimy shacks of the Westphalian miners and on the summit of the Erzberg in Styria (as seen from Vienna), let us take a more sober view, for it looks suspiciously as if the journalistic plague has not yet been completely eradicated, despite the racial purge. Happy the man who retains his enthusiasm for such hyperbolic observations and who, while we are seized by radical doubts, couches his blithely religious confidence in the credo:

> The divinely ordained regeneration of the German character, German spirit, and German blood would not have created National Socialism and its Führer, this most glorious phenomenon of all time, nor permitted his victory in the Reich, if it had not also been its wish and its will for this force of nature, this instrument of heaven, to cleanse the whole world of parasites—the cause for more than two thousand years of almost all the tribulations and catastrophes that divided, sapped, and enslaved the peoples of the earth.

However compelling this perspective, a backward glance makes it even clearer that it should be taken with a grain of salt—that the parasites only succeeded in the division, sapping, and enslavement of the peoples of the earth after the invention of printer's ink, thanks to a profession in which members of their host nations also make an adequate living, albeit with less proficiency. The notion that "Germanness shall heal the world's distress" was always contested.[3] The idea becomes all the more questionable for the foreseeable future, now that the German press, far from being eliminated, has merely been "aligned" (*gleichgeschaltet*).[4] Is it is not rather the case that in Germany today, thanks to the journalistic propagation of ideas predating the invention of printer's ink, a certain sapping, enslavement, and perhaps also division is already noticeable. Be that as it may, for the time being the natural phenomenon, given its intensity and especially its organisation, elicits not only respectful astonishment but also those misgivings the human instinct for self-preservation entertains when facing all divinely ordained events. This raises the question whether it wouldn't be insane rather than audacious to go head-to-head with the impossible that has occurred, exerting an impact far greater than any previous political absurdity. Would not such a venture only be legitimate and pertinent if it could resist reality, rather than helplessly raising rational objections to the ferocious elemental force unleashed upon the world? Would not silence signal the expectation that nature, the great arbiter, will avenge the insurrection against her? Take a stand? Rather, keep your distance!

> It is of no avail, so come!
> Flee, flee from this phenomenon! [7507]

Nevertheless, no argument advocating restraint under duress has the power to negate one's innermost convictions. Nor would it be possible to silence someone determined to confront an evil that defies all opposition, unless that evil, as a power inaccessible to thought, could impose some inner inhibition, a form of mental paralysis. Such a power infects even those furthest from its source by a process of osmosis, leaving them with a sense of incommensurability that trumps every intellectual impulse to resist, every attempt to regroup one's forces. That is in truth the pale cast of thought, sicklied o'er by the native hue of resolution, and there is no help to be had even from the encouragement of one's readers, whose friendly request for some sign of life doesn't seem to have been thought through. It could in no way be held against them if they didn't dare take up the issue of *Die Fackel* they are calling for. And some of them are so impetuous that I recoil from them more than from the danger, for they storm the bookshop and leave with regrets accompanied by the insinuation that he "is probably too scared to publish". Not a bad guess, insofar as the thought of appearing before such followers at such a moment is indeed inhibiting, given the risk of being misunderstood by both sides. Would they realise that everything in the world happens because people are incapable of imagining that it could happen? If, unwilling to be put to shame by the courage of my readers, I nevertheless overcome my inhibition, granting those who have put their coin in the slot the delivery of an opinion together with a glimpse of the machine's inner workings, the project, measured against the magnitude of the unspeakable, can hardly produce more than an expression of the constraints encountered, the meagre though not unworthy return on efforts to understand the whole phenomenon. Giving an account of one's reasons for hesitation might certainly provide an incentive to begin. Once the right words have been found, even the phenomenon of Hitler could not withhold its significance. But at the end of the day it is difficult to reach that "final analysis" which some demon has unfailingly worked into every specimen of German speech and writing.[5]

For what has happened is truly designed to restore mankind to its condition before the Fall (albeit retaining the apparatus responsible for its degeneracy) and to reduce the life of the state, the economy, and cultural practices to its simplest formula, namely annihilation. And the sceptic who longs to relax feels himself drawn into this miracle of simplicity. He feels how unjust it is that the gift of willingly succumbing is given only to the faithful and to converts, to whom it comes naturally—in huge numbers, growing by the day: the enviable ones who—according to the *Völkischer Beobachter*, which misses nothing—

> *like us learned to renounce all intellectual differentiation* in our veneration, nay love, of *such a Leader.*

They've had an easier time of it than the likes of us, but even someone who can rouse himself sufficiently to check what has been achieved instinctively tends towards that kind of renunciation. It's a thankless task: the investigator, faced with the most simple enquiry, comes up against all possible problems of logic and morality—they take his breath away, he can't see straight, has to stop his ears, forgets how to laugh, loses his zest for life. And the words that come to mind get lost in a labyrinth of innumerable antitheses and thematic confusions, one word leading to the next. Language loses its way, to its shame, and if it is fortunate enough to recover, it still lags behind a reality from which it is separated only by chaos. Oh for a Leader, a guide you can trust! To be spared all that and just lead the simple life, like them! For

> that is the great miracle: the fact that the new *Germany's* creator

(which is at least flexible enough when inflected as a genitive)

> possesses the compelling power of *restoring even our most complicated fellow human beings to folkish simplicity.*[6]

And I am supposed to immerse myself in the problem of whether the commandment "Germany, awaken!" would have been carried out so fanatically, and so smoothly, had it not been accompanied (and swiftly implemented) by the simpler instruction "Jews, exterminate 'em!" True, I once stood rooted to the spot listening to the merry battle cries of street-vendors—"Maaatches!" "*Berliner Zeitung* midday edition!" "Fragrant spring flowers!" while "*Fridericus!*" and "*Der eiserne Besen!*" struck a more aggressive note.[7] A raucous female voice rose above the melee, insistently asking: "Why does the Jew make a packet slicker'n'quicker than the Christian?" Eureka! I'd got to the root of the matter, intuitively grasping what would otherwise be difficult to put into words.

How could I succeed where the whole world fails, try as it might! This indescribable phenomenon, so slickly accomplished that the world can only shudder at the countless victims, soothing its humane instincts by professing incomprehension; the transformation of a linguistic community, still safely intact though it has lost its soul, into a thing of horror; the failure of a solidarity that was once aroused by a simple case of injustice. This indescribable phenomenon, which makes one's livelihood dependent on renouncing all previous beliefs, projects one's race back unto the third generation! Any attempt at description would inevitably fall short, incommensurate with what has taken place. "The Indescribable, / Here it is done" [12,106]. Indeed, the polemical effort involved would quite rightly be as ineffective in practical terms as when the polemicist was taunted by those irrepressible rascals of an earlier period who proved invincible.[8] Such villainy could only flourish because it had the power to satirise the satirist. Is an author who can only destroy, yet didn't manage even that, to capitulate when faced with a monstrous challenge that calls for absolute mastery? There is a mysterious collusion at work between things that exist and those who question their existence: they produce satire of their own accord by material that assumes such grotesque forms (forms I once had to invent in order to transmit it plausibly, however implausible it was). So I am no longer needed, and my mind goes blank. For the brain does not awaken as the nation does, it feels slighted by nature, and if it envies, say, plants for their vitality—nature not having abolished springtime even in this most godforsaken year—its only thought is of fellow human beings compelled by this awakening to spend their days in torture chambers. It is impossible to think of anything complex. One adapts. Indeed, part of what makes these astonishing events so calamitous is that one cannot articulate even the simplest ideas that might wring sympathy from those who have succumbed to bestial instincts: that is, those who do not kill but are incapable of believing what they haven't experienced.

For they can sleep when the spirits reawaken, and it is a joy to be alive.[9] Certainly, the yield of unproductive nights, when the most insistent and incomprehensible materials make sleep impossible, would be rich enough if silence were the form of expression I had chosen for my response to the end of days. But even this would be presumptuous. For it would not be a silent repository of knowledge but merely conceal the horror of recognition: an anguished dream of cultural corruption and decay, a nightmare in the Nazi colours of black, white, and red, the spectre of bloodstained paper—all reanimated in their deadliest form. This diagnosis of an endemic insanity, dressed up as a programme and put into practice by force; the horrified glimpse of an airless room where the actions and reactions of social beings are constrained by a modern bed of Procrustes; the reappearance of those familiar "innocent victimisers", the unity of guilt and deception when the crime becomes its own alibi and people glory in gruesome acts—"You think I'm capable of that?" the perpetrator asks, and persecutes the witness for spreading propaganda: cumulatively, this shows that the problem is not susceptible to reason. For even if the rational mind were not obstructed by the delusionary nature of the Nazi project, it would repeatedly be tempted to doubt its own sanity, haunted by visions of an alternative reality that would hardly exist on the Dog Star if it were suffering from rabies. Only in a febrile delirium could the fantasies of fascism acquire reality and its illusions be transformed into actions, which are then dissolved into hot air by a dissimulating machine which they call the Wolff Bureau. They manage—by a further projection—to find themselves encircled by a world of enemies who only want peace. This is the same pernicious vicious circle as before, one that inverts cause and effect, self-obsessed, never reflecting on what the world thinks of it. Thinking that has strayed into this labyrinth, where centaurs—half-man, half-beast—size themselves up in racial terms, will never extricate itself again.

What situation could be more difficult than that in which the mind finds itself at this conjuncture—even if conditions were not further complicated by plans for territorial expansion. Especially a mind committed in good faith to a specific timescale in *The Last Days of Mankind!*[10] A mind that is still more receptive than productive has to come to terms not only with the monstrosity of war but with the astonishing thought that it could be repeated, risking even greater destruction. Vainly, the mind once again seeks support from the Shakespearean formula that so eloquently links suffering with consolation:

> O gods! Who is't can say, "I am at the worst?"
> I am worse than e'er I was.
> And worse I may be yet; the worst is not,
> So long as we can say, "This is the worst". [*King Lear*, IV, 1]

And yet such thinking does not mitigate the helplessness that my mind is struggling to express. It conveys a calamity exacerbated to the point that satire is outrun by its subject, which unwittingly assumes its finished form, trumping all efforts to compete. Satire as imitation is no longer possible, representation fails, and the creator is blamed for its implausibility.

Such sensitivity to events is a curse that at least prevents a numbing of the senses and leaves one feeling more fully alive to a hundred different stimuli every day, though without any day being long enough to complete the required catalogue of linguistic, moral, and social outrages. Being able to diagnose the evils of the world by contemplating the dregs of humanity and construe the ultimate fate of active, suffering mankind from the most inconspicuous surface phenomena—a mind thus endowed thinks of itself as a victim and its wealth of impressions as a defect; it envies simple souls the redemption they scarcely needed. Dependent on the most negligible stimulus, spellbound by every single droplet of this deluge of sin—who can blame it for wanting to be, for once, like those who do not see what is there to be seen, who assume that what is inconceivable cannot be happening, or to whom it is granted *not* to say what they suffer![11] Is such a mind to be denied the means to defend itself by amplifying in all its grotesqueness what it has already seen and denounced: the atrocities and the lying excuses made for them, the shameful distortion of truth in language infused with an aura of saintliness, the prostitution of life and death when both serve some alien purpose, the daily deadly sins against nature and the spirit, barriers erected against understanding what is happening, against artistic creativity? While I was silent, I restricted my reading of the press (from which, after all, I derived all my evidence against the world it had corrupted, resisting the impulse to dissect a living body nurtured by that impious mother. And I have preserved a hundred thousand documents attesting to its direct or indirect guilt: an unexploited reserve every bit as capable of illustrating these misbegotten times as any polished article. But how could I do justice to the material if ever I managed to see this nightmare of action and reportage through to the bitter end, this ultimate alignment of destruction and awakening, this most bloodcurdling triumph of platitude with its unprecedented world-historical ramifications? Even if it did not paralyse the creative urge but gave it wings—how could it master the myriad forms of this third Walpurgis Night? If all that political life teaches us is that in the end we die, how could this transformation of cliché into experience stimulate creativity? Could astonishment at an innovation that destroys fundamental principles with the elemental force of some epidemic of brain seizure (as if the bombs of advanced bacterial warfare were already being dropped) reanimate someone who had been rendered speechless when he discovers what a world looks like that practises what it preaches?

On all sides, nothing but stupor, people spellbound by the deceptive magic of an idea which consists of not having any. From an initial impetus that led straight from no starting point towards no destination. From the inspiration for a four-thousand-year plan, with the human paradise to begin just beyond the hell endured by one's neighbour—and with everyone suffering from some mysterious system operating with concepts like money transfers and rediscounting—to culminate in illuminated chaos, in the chiliastic dream of unleashed millenarians. The synchronicity of electro-technology and myth, of splitting the atom and burning at the stake, of the innovative and the archaic!

All around, nothing but wonder at the miracle of a state whose institutions—down to the last legal paragraph—derive from a delirium, and whose economy consists in boycotting Jewish businesses, guided by gurus from Norse mythology who regulate all existence, such as the Norn Verdhandi. How can such an upheaval, I ask myself, fail to weaken the residues of mental resolve that have survived the hardships of the war years and its aftermath. At the end of the world I'll retire into private life.

2

THE SATIRIST'S DILEMMA

Meanwhile time marches on, and I see younger polemicists emerging who have taken up the torch, displaying a courage that remains anonymous even when it appears over a byline, while I brood like some Hamlet forever missing his cue for passion and action because the evil is so impenetrable. But one cue is provided by examples of journalistic presumption explicitly designed to damage my reputation and even to align my ideas with those of National Socialism, placing me in a hazardous position while trusting that I will remain silent. One evening paper, the *Wiener Allgemeine Zeitung*, appears on the streets early enough for me to run the unwelcome risk of encountering a Prussian chief of police.[1] This paper, subsidised by those cosmetic products that don't need any of the ornamental epithets its theatre critics scatter around, has suddenly recalled my existence. Normally, this would have interested them far less than the existence of the most insignificant celebrities, now that I seem to have vanished from the realm of cultural activity. That I have my doubts about the pretensions of this type of journalism (or progressive intentions, as they would say) should nevertheless be common knowledge, and I have distanced myself from them without fear or favour, not least because of their leftist leanings. But I am happy to dwell on its chosen theme, seeing it as more significant than they imagine, for to reach the apex of global despair I start from the bottom rung.

When I gave a radio talk, for instance, the title and name of the presenter had to be removed, providing an example, at the height of the opposition to the Emergency Powers, of how a liberal-minded editor preferred to follow his own instinct, sacrificing freedom of speech. But this hard blow—and I speak as someone accustomed to adversity—was offset when I saw my work linked with the intellectual vistas of National Socialism. A comparison was drawn between its destructive activities in the realm of culture and my early satire *Die demolirte Literatur*, memories of which have evidently overshadowed my satirical work of the following decades. The comparison with National Socialism was decidedly in my favour, for my demolition was said to distinguish itself from the current amateurish destruction of literature in Berlin by its "unprecedented intellectual verve" and "tremendous satirical power", though it was veritable child's play compared with my subsequent critique of the direction German writing has taken. The idea that I had already "risen to be the implacable arbiter where the German spirit and the German language are concerned" in that satirical début is certainly exaggerated when you consider all that I have had to say since then about a print culture that is in the hands of people who have failed in other professions. But that's exactly why they give precedence to *Die demolirte Literatur*—praise for which counts as an alibi for the generation of writers it left unscathed. My deadly enemies were charmed by it, and a connoisseur of satire like Monty Jacobs thought that since then—that is, over thirty-five years—I've had nothing more to say. Today, for all the appreciation of that exemplary work, the parallel with National Socialism is thought to be that its targets "survived being sentenced to demolition". Still, it remains to be seen whether their fellow writers will survive the judgement passed on them over the years in *Die Fackel.* While I am still compared favourably with Goebbels—not a pleasant experience—the same paper in another article considered the problem of my intellectual connection with Hitler from a different angle, from which, thankfully, I do not emerge in such a favourable light. For here a polemical life's work is assigned more weight, and the writer takes up my battle against the press through which I forfeited my youthful laurels. So now I am perceived as still standing in the front line but as one who reaps the credit for the energy and success of others. Namely in a leading article that tries to demonstrate the influence of Jewish thinkers on Hitler, "spiritual ancestors" who provide the following precedents:

> Indubitably the ideas of compulsory labour and the state's obligation to feed people were already pioneered by Popper-Lynkeus. One could extend the list of pioneering Jewish thinkers up to Karl Kraus, whose boldest dreams have been realised by Hitler. There is no longer a *journaille* in Germany, all the enemies of *Die Fackel,* from Reinhardt to Kerr, have been eradicated!

One would like to think this is no time for teasing. So let us take seriously what a journalist has written here, demonstrating no small courage vis-à-vis both Hitler and his forerunner. If the latter is being praised for prioritising the ideas and the former with their realisation, I must nevertheless reject the priority I'm credited with, insofar as it seems to refer to public awareness of the danger of a "*journaille*"—the term being ostensibly attributed to me. This is just as unjustified as its attribution to me by the National Socialist press, which uses it unselfconsciously, though without any reference to its source in *Die Fackel,* the language of which in other cases it has certainly besmirched for its own ends. This is due to a mistaken alignment of my intentions with its intentions, which is now adopted by the liberal *journaille*. I am indeed the source; however, as made clear at the time, I am unfortunately not the creator of this brilliant coinage. It was an occasional contributor to the *Neue Freie Presse*, an insider who talked a lot of good sense and spurned those who had a stranglehold on public opinion, refusing to make his heart a den of thieves. This was Alfred von Berger, another author lacking the racial qualification to be cited as a source, who once presented me with the word, prophesying that it would one day take wing. As for my anti-journalistic thinking, which covers more than just disseminating such expressions, its priority over any Hitler idea is self-evident.

This leader writer (whose surname, Deutsch, at least suggests the language his paper should use) sometimes hits the nail on the head, as he does here.[2] But his suggestion that my dearest dreams have been fulfilled by Hitler is wrong, not least because even in Germany, let alone Austria, there is still as much of a *journaille* as ever, indeed a much more active one than in the moderate era which gave birth to the term. He should be aware that my struggle, which has nothing to do with the expropriation of opinion-forming organs and their root-and-branch replacement according to racial criteria, will outlast such tomfoolery. My salutary initiative is something this journalist, who intends the comparison to disparage it, should at least recognise from the time he received permission to trace in back numbers of *Die Fackel* specific instances of the *journaille* concept as applied to the *Neues Wiener Journal*, a paper with which he was in dispute.

The notion that "all enemies of *Die Fackel* have been eradicated" fails to recognise that they are the targets—not enemies—of satirical animus; and the idea that I could henceforth live in peace, since my thirst for revenge seems to have been sated, reflects the horizon of the leader writer rather than that of the satirist. The former underestimates the profound dilemma persistently faced by the satirist, who cannot count the removal of his targets as a success even when he himself is finished with them, let alone when death or some devilish political power has snatched them from his grasp. Certainly he wishes to achieve a degree of detachment from the motifs that stimulate him, not letting himself be diverted from his objective by some random journalistic intervention that might disrupt the satirical formulation which is his primary concern. But it is painful to see the guilty party escape before the example has played out, when it is not only the formulation that is lost but also its intellectual and moral significance. Even greater than the satisfaction of removing an evil that has not been totally disempowered by one's polemic is the desire to see it still in place, and only the shallow-minded could believe that the satirist is not genuinely sad when deprived of a public personality who is equally at the height of his powers.

For it is one thing to pursue a journalistic action which is required to replace a criminal case, and which consequently needs to end in practical success, such as chasing someone out of Vienna, but it is something else again to produce satirical proof that someone is the greatest scoundrel in the land (though it was an exaggeration, and we would be glad to have both of these characters with us today).[3] Let alone the possibility of repeatedly taking the measure of our age as reflected in some shoddy theatrical display to which it has succumbed! That the principals involved, "from Reinhardt to Kerr", have been deprived of power may be a welcome result; but irrespective of the fact that I would refuse to touch anything deriving from such a repulsively idiotic source, it will turn out that my loss as a satirist was greater than that suffered by the world of culture.

Yet I tell myself what statesmen tend to say after a setback: "I am an optimist." I think many will find their way back home, even if they still have to assure their interviewer now that it wasn't a case of flight, since they travelled by train. At any rate, I don't give up hope that a retrospective summary of what I experienced in Berlin (and have already noted down) regarding the collusion between the theatre, the press, and the law may not be lost to posterity and may also be accessible to the present generation; I even believe that, in spite of the decline in the publisher Paul Zsolnay's fortunes, the time will come when I shall be able to do justice to Emil Ludwig's view of Mussolini and of me. But as far as Reinhardt is concerned, I cling to my opinion that he will reemerge as an almost indestructible phoenix. The tendency of other countries to be taken in by German cultural products can only be increased by Nazi cultural policies fanatically designed to reach an even lower level; Oxford, too, has followed suit with its honorary doctorates.[4] (Even in Paris, where tolerance thrives regardless, those who found Berlin's civil law too hot for their liking and consequently think of themselves as refugees can set up their stall and entertain hopes.) The very paper that circumscribes my mission so narrowly—and in the midst of depicting the panic still had the presence of mind to establish that Reinhardt, the great magician, had hastened to Vienna merely to see his dentist—will take every conceivable precaution to ensure that every trace of his earthly life will be preserved. After all, the cleansing of the German stables, itself a cheerless task, also led incrementally (and excrementally) to a breathtaking surge of gossip in the press about backstage anxieties here in Austria. Hence the unprecedented expansion of celebrity culture in the daily illustrated news, inflating minnows into maestros, which would be catastrophic if the manufacturers of fashionable trench coats were not continuously intent on covering them up.

No, there are no easy answers, for I cannot respond to this situation simply with malicious glee. I must mourn a loss that is unfortunately not irrevocable, about which—if it were irrevocable—I could still not complain. It's hard to explain. I cannot complain that I've lost certain figures from intellectual life since I could not honestly say I didn't want that to happen. But on the other hand, I do complain because I intended something quite different, and above all because I have given it more mature reflection.[5] And especially because it's the natural inclination for a satirist never to be totally reconciled to a shrinking of his material. After all, he is not concerned with settling individual cases but rather with preserving an exemplum which enables him to present the evil of the whole category to which it belongs—a task he will never complete nor wish to complete. For as long as some idiot rings a bell with him, so long as some swindler provides an appropriate model, he must be concerned not to lose them, and no one can imagine the unending trepidation that satirists have on this score. Many are called to be targets, certainly, but few are chosen, and there are reasons why someone becomes a celebrity. Just as no one wants the bison to become extinct, so, too, the satirist keeps watch in the thickets of politics and culture. Losing his targets on account of his own polemical touch—something fortunately out of the question today—is a cause for regret, and it is a common error to suppose this was his intention or even his dearest wish. On the contrary, he is intent on protecting them from interference by some more active power that shares his aversion, though wrongly and from a totally different perspective. No, never have Mortimers died more untimely deaths—cursed be those responsible![6] And expect no gratitude from Shakespearean kings who order assassinations—and then wish their victims were still alive.

So if the reason I have to mourn a loss which I cannot complain about, and vice versa, is a complicated one, it turns out—and this is no dilemma at all—that winning gives me no pleasure. For the simple reason that I haven't won. But getting to grips with this material does seem to make for heavy going, and it should be clear how cautiously I have been manoeuvering between apocalyptic and journalistic dimensions, landing squarely in a void that will feature in the annals of German cultural history as blank blood-sealed pages. The positive outcome of this is first of all a recognition that the fundamental decision to destroy life's values has turned the dross that has been brushed aside—the literary émigrés—into undeserving martyrs or brought them an otherwise unattainable respect in foreign eyes that naturally incline to confuse every victim of German proscription with talent, or at least character.[7] As for character, this misunderstanding was corrected by the behaviour of those concerned; it was no small surprise to discover at the time of the book burnings that the great moment has involved such Lilliputians.[8] How unworthy of such a favour, both before and after the event, an honour so rarely bestowed on modern writers, many showed themselves to be—if they deserved it at all! Even if awarded a Nobel Prize, I wouldn't want to be burnt at the stake together with Tucholsky, but if ever there was a classic example of fortune distributing her gifts indiscriminately and unfairly, it is this Blacklist, the sight of which turns one green with envy.[9] Where is the justice in this, when one has dedicated one's life's work to subversion: weakened army morale, advised against annexations, recommended loyalty to the Austrian fatherland only as protection against the German alternative, with the oft-repeated (though seldom attributed) verdict that Germany is the home of barbarians with electric lighting, and the Germans the nation of judges and hangmen?[10] And how frustrating to be a mere onlooker as many others are allowed to burn who lack the mission "to sing songs and tell tales"![11] But who knows, perhaps even the National Socialists still have some feeling for legitimate opinions, or perhaps their hand is stayed by knowledge, and misunderstanding, of the credit I deserve in the matter of *journaille*, by a debt of gratitude for the stimulus they reproach me for. As for the National Socialisers themselves, one could hardly claim that my work has not had a subversive effect there too, that I have failed to focus on themes that speak to the heart of the *Volk*, without the least desire to enter into that way of thinking. Certainly, the opposing camps can both provide me with pathetic opponents as well as wayward followers, which might account for the special dilemma which the National Socialists have with me, comparable to the dilemma I have with myself. They dislike my race, but perhaps they are impressed by so categorical a refusal to form alliances of any kind.

And so (at the end of the day) it would be advisable to avoid the risk of finding favour. But perhaps one should fear neither favour nor hatred, for the suspicion might also spread that a party with an inbuilt fondness for beating people to death could, exceptionally, resort to the more drastic reprisal of cutting someone dead—by ignoring them—a tactic the other side has adopted with some success. Of course, that still leaves one diabolical way of curbing the effectiveness of my satire, indeed nipping it in the bud: by constructing a hallucinatory realm that leaves my mind blank. After deeds of heroic resurgence which catch people unawares by their very novelty, the tried and trusted German tactic would be to wear opponents down and after protracted but persistent tedium finally disarm them. An outcome due to the losses inflicted on the satirist by removing his favourite stimuli, and worse still by compensating him through providing substitutes that make a mockery of any description satire could devise: thus the nationalist movement, manoeuvring deftly, threatens the satirist's very existence by removing his customary targets and offering intractable alternatives, even if this was not its express intent. By victimising him not through the Blacklist but through an infinitely darker cunning, using refined techniques of which one would not have thought them capable, given their lack of sophistication, the nationalists would fulfil the mission so many contemporary figures have already attempted. By their own activity they would erase all trace of me, leaving them free to whistle their way happily through the last days of mankind.

3

AND WHAT ABOUT CULTURE?

The national movement includes one of the most capricious figures ever to frolic at the forefront of German culture, a journalist who is still permitted his freedom thanks to his nimble manoeuvrings. Our first encounter occurred several years after the World War. The man in question is Bernhard Diebold, better known under the name Bernhardo Dieboldo, which he adopted and which I don't allow him to forget.[1]

In the *Frankfurter Zeitung*, rather more effectively than that joker from Vienna, Diebold draws parallels between National Socialism and my own activity, prompting them to take stock of my work and encouraging me to take the movement seriously. This I am reluctant to do since I prefer, on the contrary, to occupy myself with the German language, adapting it to the French libretti that inspired Offenbach's operettas—a task that is far more rewarding. At the end of the day this is more important than occupying oneself with a movement so completely unaware how barren it is that even the abyss separating us cannot avoid yawning. But I've also always liked to avail myself of the press as a spur to heroism; it may not love me, but it stimulates me to undertake "new deeds"—as Wagner advocated.[2] Diebold, as we shall see, is intent on promoting Wagner as Offenbach's polar opposite in order to make Goebbels suspicious of me while at the same time ingratiating himself. But Nature decreed that he should be a political opportunist, making him both quick-witted and thick-skinned. He is one of the most difficult cases I have encountered, among the most likely of my patients to suffer a relapse (in whatever journalistic situation he finds himself) and succumb to the paranoia people feel towards me, masquerading as criticism: now that there is great pressure to denounce others with aggressive popular backing, he has seized the opportunity to let off steam against a target where he can show his real mettle. For a long time Diebold passed for the leading expert on German theatre until I got wise to him, and when one day, his confidence already shaken, he let himself go and tried his hand at humour, I seized the initiative and painted him life-size as the joker who—when a travel agency leased the *Frankfurter Zeitung* for an advertising supplement—supplied German honeymooners and wine merchants' buyers with all kinds of droll stories about Italian topography. The map I reproduced in *Die Fackel* served as his visiting card, and while the tourists had a jolly time traipsing around on Vesuvius, I revealed to the rest of the thinking world the rubbish behind all his bragging about the philosophy of art. His essential banality was thus exposed. Dieboldo, who already tended to lose his composure both publicly and privately whenever my existence impinged on his awareness, did what all hysterics do when their situation is exacerbated by an awareness of their impotence: he struck out in a different direction. His response was a critique of Offenbach's incomparable *Brigands*, whose title was found offensive even before the reaction in contemporary Germany. I had incautiously drawn the attention of a Berlin theatre director to this fine work. Diebold consequently launched into a tirade of ignorance, denial of artistic and intellectual content, and misplaced venom. At the time, only an even greater outpouring of lunacy induced me to leave well alone. A letter setting the record straight was ignored by the *Frankfurter Zeitung*, which had once promised me it would stop anyone smearing Offenbach who was suspected of vilifying the dead satirist in order to discredit the living one.

Under the new regime the *Frankfurter Zeitung* has had to adapt to the decree that it should not have any opinion at all, though its strong financial backing seemed to have spared it formal "alignment" and to have allowed it to retain some of its integrity, a poor compensation for the ideological mutability of newspaper publishing as a whole, which I have vainly tried to expose to the wider world. For I was far from illustrating this ideology as successfully as the daring Nazi coup managed to do—at one blow!—when it turned the tables by extorting conformism from the extortionists—an action that forced many a buccaneer to relinquish shares in a publicly reputable family concern and abandon the stolen ship to political corsairs. For a while the *Frankfurter Zeitung* got by as best it could, and it couldn't help feeling the "Annunciation of the Third Reich" by Hanns Johst "made one's heart leap with joy". Wearing its heart on its sleeve, it soon declared that it no longer felt there to be any dichotomy between its liberalism and the new "implacable lifestyle" of National Socialism, although in discussing a play by Goebbels it did have to acknowledge:

> Art as a way of looking at life objectively, *as Goethe understood it*, is *not the author's aim.*[3]

While the paper's policy was to avoid recognition of Goebbels's actual aim, a hundred years after Goethe, it allowed Diebold, a valued collaborator, to express himself more programmatically. But when he promptly showed the new powers what he was capable of, it wasn't for the trivial purpose of self-preservation but rather with the more moral intention of drawing their attention to an author he found uncongenial and hoped to silence, so as to increase his own sense of security. He hoped that a simple hint would suffice but only succeeded in achieving the opposite. Diebold had no reason to fear the determination of the New Order to "counter the rampant trend for denouncing people", nor the other individual initiatives currently encouraged. So he came up with an article whose title was a tentative question:

> *And what about culture?*[4]

But instead of flatly answering in the negative as a man of culture—a role he can play after all, as befits a former extra at the Burgtheater—he gave the political upheaval a welcome only slightly tinged with scepticism, an exception being the regret he felt over the victimisation of Reinhardt,

> that theatrical genius who staged exemplary poetic reinterpretations of the German classics for generations to come.

Accordingly, since future generations have been provided for, Diebold can devote himself to the merits of the reform of national culture, and here he plunges into the issue that is really troubling him:

> The Reinhardt problem *too becomes a totally secondary one* compared with the *question of culture in general*, which currently looms large. And when Commissioner Hinkel accuses "Jewish caricaturists and Marxists" of mocking such German luminaries as Schiller, Goethe, and Kant, *we must ask ourselves* whether, *in critical terms*, the justification for such a *serious accusation* (*in which it is certainly not only Jews who are implicated*) can be readily denied. *And when we recall* how a giant like Richard Wagner was *breezily dismissed* in *certain radical circles*, while *a Jacques Offenbach*, who *in comparison* stands there *looking like a tiny, comical, porcelain figurine*, was *trumpeted forth as an all-conquering genius—then* the *problem of cultural confusion* over these last few years appears *in a well-nigh tragic light*.

The fact that Herr Reinhardt not only staged reinterpretations of the German classics for generations to come but also made a hash of Offenbach and yet was capable of turning precisely that staging into the means of postponing the bankruptcy that came before the fall—this may be no less secondary than the lamented fall itself. But what is of prime importance is the way the problem of cultural confusion appears to Herr Diebold in a well-nigh tragic light, and what symptomatically justifies his action to save the intellectual honour of the nation: he has to resort to swindling. For no one in Germany, myself included, has actively agitated for Offenbach while at the same time breezily dismissing Wagner, though I can assure Herr Diebold that a generation capable of surviving such folly will owe more to the tiny, comical, porcelain figurine who was the greatest music dramatist of all time, indeed the creator of a whole theatrical world, than to the giant to whom the cultural hypocrites and now also the nationalist upstarts allege they can listen entranced for six hours at a stretch. (And although I'm of the opinion—reluctant as I am to turn to Nietzsche for support—that even the French libretti so despised by Herr Diebold—of little significance when separated from their context, of great significance since they cannot be thus separated—contain more organic life and flow than all the wagalaweias and hojotohos that perhaps plumb the depths. These profundities are, alas, inaccessible to language, music, and the "total work of art", but they certainly contain something quintessentially German to which Wagner's masterly prose naturally inclines.) But although I am in no doubt myself that German Radio over twenty years of *völkisch* nationalism will not replace the absolute delight it afforded the nation in the two years of the Offenbach cycle—

> German Radio has nothing more beautiful and more effective to offer in the realm of culture

is how one nationalist writer puts it—even this point becomes secondary compared with the question of culture in general.

The question is whether Diebold will use this climate of terror to avenge himself against a proponent of cultural trends not currently in favour, someone he need not even mention to expose him as the object of a "serious accusation", one in which "Jews are certainly implicated". We "must ask ourselves, in critical terms", how this Diebold conducts cultural criticism and why he chooses this as the moment to present it. For he knows that Offenbach is as unpopular with the nationalists as I am with Diebold, and since he is used to targeting him when he means me, he hopes, as it were by association, to kill two birds with one stone. This is all the more obvious when he does name me in person, in order to substantiate the suspicion of cultural bolshevism. It would never have occurred to him to hate Offenbach if he hadn't hated me, but what could previously only be read between the lines can now be openly articulated, and one recalls who is actually responsible for a problematic development that would otherwise have left Diebold cold. Of course, the roundabout way by which he reaches his goal is wearisome. First, he lists all the sufferings the *völkisch* soul has had to endure prior to the "momentous political upheaval", which "necessarily also transformed cultural awareness". Diebold portrays the dissipation that, until salvation arrived, had dislocated "social forms"—not people's manners (which should never degenerate into hysteria) but their morals. The worst kind of defaulter was tolerated, there was no such thing as being "cut dead in the street"—Diebold quickly translates this as *mort civile,* lest the Nazis get the wrong idea—no crime could any longer result in ostracism. Pearls of wisdom about conditions that, though they cannot directly be attributed to Offenbach, are still bound to make a man like Diebold hot under the collar.

> Even in the behaviour of the public towards the press, indifference was transformed into total lack of discrimination.

Here Diebold does not mean the arse-licking enjoyed by certain influential theatre critics, nor the respect they continue to receive even when unmasked as the pseudonymous authors of amusing advertising features; rather he means the blackmailing, muckraking journalism in rags that were "now permitted to be bought quite openly at kiosks or in cafés, thus sparing the buyers' blushes". But was there no defence against this? Yes, there was:

> A feeling for public dignity certainly existed *in certain individuals.*

Not in those who did not participate in the "social consensus" (Diebold spells this "con-sensus" to make his meaning plain), which would have consolidated the wisdom from *Tasso,* permitting only "what is right and proper".[5]

> *The passionate efforts of individuals* could achieve but little against the fragmentation of moral attitudes.

Up to this point, one would think Diebold wanted to do justice to the impact of *Die Fackel,* even without naming it. But it turns out that it is himself he means as a passionate advocate of moral standards, while he names me, on the contrary, as responsible for the process of fragmentation, the spread of muckraking journalism, the toleration of defaulters, the prevention of *mort civile.* For immediately following this we read:

> *Oppositional authors,* such as Karl Kraus and Tucholsky, who were *forever* passing *a "No" verdict on others, never a "Yes" to the momentous future;* destroyers of culture like the ambiguous dramatist Brecht *were able to confuse the widest range of educated people.*

And there was me thinking whatever fascination I exercised did not extend beyond my "partisans", the circle of readers of a "little magazine"! But Tucholsky and me—never me without him, except at the book-burning: him without me—how can one possibly compare the impact, irrespective of the difference in talent? The two of us, an inseparable pair, obviously fill the role of those "disobliging demons, forever gleefully screeching their resolute 'No!,'" according to Diebold, our yes-man playing the role of Elpore.[6] Brecht, another author I've evidently damaged in the eyes of our genius of the positive, is a better German poet than Johst, better even than the favourites whose talents Diebold commends to the protection of the nation—Brecht's "ambiguity" is obvious:

> In *Mahagonny no one in the audience knew for certain if he should pay for his whisky*, or whether it would be more "ethical" not to pay.

This problem seems to have occupied Diebold throughout the whole period of cultural confusion more than Brecht's poem "The Lovers", with its cranes and clouds, which forms part of the same play.[7] Then, unfortunately, he even links me with Bernard Shaw, whom I can understand the civilised bourgeois regarding as a *terrible old man*, concluding:

> The uncertain, the relative, the ambiguous became interesting in art and in life.

Moreover, this trend, to which I together with Tucholsky appear to be totally devoted, can be ascribed to the "American-style magazine" which I have increasingly allowed to supplant the literary journals.

> *It's certainly true* that one also went to hear the *Missa solemnis* and celebrated Goethe and Wagner jubilees.

But only "between two film showings", of course. Diebold's support for the momentous future made no impression:

> *Our jeremiads*—against a society that fluctuated between cultural braggadocio during the *Goethe celebrations* and an undignified whimper at every crisis—*were greeted with a condescending smile*. Anarchy among the *most insignificant personalities* destroyed the *authority of the truly great*.

The classics had been deprived of their spiritual grandeur, and people were in thrall to libertinage. But in my case this reproach is wide of the mark, since I opposed the bourgeois diversions provided by Bekessy every bit as much as the denigration of Goethe, but also, above all, the use of Schiller quotations for tourists travelling to Italy, admittedly at the risk of offending (if, alas, not completely destroying) the authority of one of the truly great.

> *Someone had to put a stop to this!*

So Goebbels was born, ready to regulate times that are out of joint—with his own writings and with those of Johst, whose

> *spiritual approach to artistic nationalism*

Diebold acknowledges. It is of course true that, looking to the future, he ventures to warn against the national perspective in the realm of art "becoming confused with military and folkloristic phenomena":

> It's quality that counts, also within the realm of national art.

So perhaps it's not what you think, gentlemen: quantity alone is not enough. Diebold expects from Goebbels—whom he credits with what he himself possesses: "a remarkable courage in the face of his own party"—not only demolition but also construction, "the promotion of distinctive individual achievements". As for the past—forget it!—he would like to preserve Piscator and his "stimulating ideas" and of course the "spiritual goal" of our own Unruh, of whom they have simply no right to deprive the *Frankfurter Zeitung*—in all some five Frankfurters with an honest attitude to culture, which unfortunately could not prevent the destruction of the "mythic" German past, now linked—under the new dispensation—to the blood myth. But the cultural confusion that must have prevailed becomes clear in the following complaint:

> All too frequently and *wantonly* the *variety* and revue arts of the *demimuse* have been equated with the true muses, though *this was not necessary* given the purity of the cultural convictions of a *Thomas Mann*, the revelatory naturalness of a *Käthe Dorsch*, and the *sound and solid constructions* of modern *architects*.

In future times, however, culture will no longer be confused with "ideological rhetoric, oppositional criticism, and naked sensationalism". Except that the concept "German" is to be widened to include Reinhardt as well, and attention paid to the fact that not only folk song and Germanic saga but also "those most mysterious creations of a Goethe or a Beethoven" have "arisen from the spirit of the countryside and a shared language". Diebold makes urgent and wide-ranging demands, but he remains confident:

> A *creation of the will* that aims at a *popular unitary culture* has no reason to renounce the *highest intellectual forms*.

How the creation of the will might do this, he doesn't say, but "that beard's got potential", a barber once told me in confidence, besides bolstering my polemical courage with the saying: "Spare the brush and spoil the shave". And here Diebold arrives at the point he's been aiming for—namely for Hitler and against me:

> All willing towards unity is of more benefit to the community than the sort of individualism that only recognises its own goal. Really great per-

> sonalities always think of the good of their community as a whole, and act accordingly.

A classic case of how German thinkers like this drone on about such terms as creations of the will, willed unity, cultural development, unitary culture, spiritual formation, and all the rest of it, with only rubbish to show for it at the end of the day. I should like to think Diebold considers the will to brag of more benefit than anything else he has in mind. To me at least, it seems stronger than his heartfelt conviction about Hitler's thinking. But since it is a case of a literary figure's words becoming deeds, one cultural question needs answering. Is it not a matchless vision of a momentous future when someone throws himself into the arms of a mere imitator in order to demonstrate to him that his precursor is the real culprit for the cultural evil? And doesn't Diebold prove the Viennese joker a liar for saying there is no longer any *journaille* in Germany? And is not this disguising of rancour as public opinion a model of its kind? It is only impaired by the candour with which a person reveals to all who know his case what is actually troubling him, and where the shoe pinches: it's a large one, he is really putting in the boot, a boot of Italian dimensions. Thus Dieboldo undertook a desperate step which leaves him one last chance.

Oppositional authors are not always reduced to saying "No!"; sometimes they can also be constructive. There is a vacant post that needs filling. That greatest scoundrel in the land he was compelled to leave, Alfred Kerr, could still render it an invaluable service. The denunciation to the court in Berlin concerning my position during the war, the appeal to the anti-Semitic Tyrolean League, might have earned him the right to remain. He suffered a great injustice at the book-burning, which didn't include *Die Fackel* evidently because it contains his war poems.[8] But what a man of honour Kerr is compared with the type who has sold his soul to the devil to keep him supplied with dirt! Diebold will not have to leave the country if he points to his article which answers the question "And what about culture?" with expectations of a general and a personal kind.

As for the personal ones, there has already been one practical success:

> *Offenbach prohibited in Germany.* The management of German Radio has received instructions not to transmit any works by Offenbach in future.

As if the aether, which has room for a "casual entertainment with internees in protective custody", needed any such instruction! As for the general expectations, only a thoroughgoing pessimist would not support them with a momentous future-oriented "Yes!", since we have learnt that Johst's "spiritual approach to artistic nationalism" brings in an average of no less than seven marks.

Just as I make use of a statement in a journal as a hook on which to hang cultural history, so too, in order to make sense of this century, I spurn nothing that the daily news throws up, revealing among other things how a tendentious theatre politics is coping with one insolvency aligned to another. Since theatre life at a national level is more a question of honour, it is self-evident that we can't forgo *Ball at the Savoy* by Abraham and Grünwald, admittedly not without this creation having been "thoroughly nordified, both musically and textually" (erasing the names of its creators).[9] At least, so one of these new theatre managers assures us, though he has also declared his intention of staging *The Flying Dutchman* in the near future, since he "feels especially drawn to it as a former seaman himself". But since he also intends to cultivate classical operetta, the feelings of those who count in cultural matters could be more broadly accommodated if a decision were made to turn back to Offenbach's *Brigands* after all, which was such a big draw at Berlin's Städtische Oper.

4

GOEBBELS, MANIPULATIVE MODERNISM, AND BUCOLIC JEW-BAITING

Things are on the move. "Everything that motivates and inspires the German people", prescribed by Goebbels as the products of the nation's creativity, is beginning to take shape. The leadership was well advised when it chose as Propaganda Minister a man who (like only Diebold before him) seems capable of stimulating tourism (currently the prime objective) as well as intellectual reconstruction. Goebbels is familiar with all the fashionable terminology which rootless intellectual authors are no longer able to use. He has attitude and empathy, he knows about stimulus and impetus, application and implication, dramatic presentation, filmic transposition, flexible formulation, and the other aids to radical renewal, he has experience and perspective, indeed for both reality and vision, he has zest for life and world philosophy, he approves of ethos and pathos but also mythos, he supplies subordination and integration into the living space and working space of the nation, he embraces the emotional realm of community and the vitalism of personality, he professes loyalty to kith and kin and international solidarity and favours synthesis, he transmits stimuli and tentatively explores parameters before arriving at the central modality, in order to fathom latent potential and accentuate the problematics of intellectuality, he knows all about fossilised tradition and burgeoning creativity, he values willpower, recognises purposive achievement, such as the artifice inherent in artistry, he acknowledges fluidity, accessibility, and significant form and can distinguish between the expansive and the convulsive, indeed I suspect that he is oriented in the cosmic; at all events he recognises potential for development and defines emotionally the type that, inescapably, in the final analysis must surely eventuate in trend-setting hegemony and knows that when the build-up of will-power precipitates willed conformity and hence collective action and cultural symbiosis, dynamism and rhythm form prominent parameters, and that then the goal is totality, though in the first instance steely romanticism—in short, you can't fool him about anything that was previously to be found in the cultural ragbag of the *Berliner Tageblatt* or *Berliner Zeitung* and that, whether modern German or modern Jewish, denoted a world sucked dry by those who saw the rest as suckers.[1]

> Words connote their origin,
> Old and new are kith and kin [7094]

Except that one would never have credited them with the dynamism displayed by those rooted in the soil, nor has any journalist previously had an authentic prince as his adjutant.[2]

Such slickness in the way they've got the show on the road (and opened their "box of tricks") amazes even the shrewdest culture vultures, who always managed to wangle things somehow. It puts to shame all those directorial wonders of the theatrical world, now dethroned; but it also prompts representatives of a loftier cause to regret losing such a force of nature when he became Minister of Atrocity Propaganda. And yet there has been no actual change of tone within the German-speaking world. The same manipulative thought processes are used to impress on the minds of the people whatever potential is still latent; "vision" is a cliché; "rhythm" a relic of the syntax Expressionism assigned to collective experience; and even repressed complexes, which are indubitably of suspect origin, can be accommodated. After all, the powers of expression of the Führer were not honed in the school of Gundolf, and his worldview seems to owe less to Freud than to Karl May. But even the Führer has lamented the inferiority complex from which the nation is suffering. And what has the theatre done up to now?

> It carried individualism to an extreme, putting the repressed complexes of some sick person or other on the stage. *This they called art for art's sake.*

The man in charge of culture has it all at his fingertips, he's a master of all the literary buzzwords, those arcane abstractions every typewriter in Berlin spews out, and on occasion he even knows how to hit the polemical-satirical note (though I generally preferred the targeted object itself), for instance when stigmatising double shirt-cuffs as outmoded, picking to pieces the "full beard" (also known as the "patriarchal beard" or "big bushy beard"), and ironising "pathos" as soon as it "stirs man's blood". This is the tone of tedious flippancy capable of saying things like "Here comes the bogeyman!" in a way that makes you feel even the original version of this was the lesser evil, so that you prefer the outmoded traditions that are being mocked with the occasional "Aha!", "Hmm!", or "Oho!" Let alone the satirical "Forsooth!" that is much worse than when it's meant to be taken seriously, or even the enervating "dia*bol*ical!", though thus enunciated it does gain its full resonance. This kind of prankster, himself the epitome of constant busy-ness, also sees through the whole business of "dealing" in some commodity that ought to remain intangible, especially in the sphere of "ideology". In his book-burning speech of 10 May the satirist Goebbels had already stigmatised "the great scholars lurking behind bundles of dusty documents". At this point he brings himself to concede that radio should never

> *only play the ideological card*

or again, that

> *this does not mean that art should always beat the big drum.*[3]

Which makes him sound sympathetic, apart from the dishonesty of knowing that art has no option but to do precisely that, and must be manipulative, even if, by its nature, it could do otherwise. It is even more surprising to hear that Goebbels also rejects all "patriotic kitsch", hearing which, spoken in a Berlin accent, is enough to make one favourably inclined towards it. But the sophisticated intellectual cannot dispense with the satirical cliché, even though it reflects a movement whose very essence is kitsch and blood, for he is essentially unconnected to all the resources at his disposal. So while it's true there has as yet been no decree issued against the blood, he has denounced kitsch, on the mistaken assumption that something better might emerge. For the man whose features in fact bear witness less to the new reality than to old-fashioned irony, and who perhaps even saw through the innkeepers and cigar sellers who used to roam through Berlin's Grunewald dressed up as Cheruscans, hasn't given up hope.[4] Like Moses, he seems to possess a magic staff that can draw water from stone. He summons authors, directors, and publishers, gives them directives, orientations, goals, and scares them by vowing that "writers and other creative elements in the *Volk* will be confronted with so many problems that they will still be working on them a hundred years from now". To which those unfamiliar to such thinking can only reply: A hundred years it is, then, and happy is he who finishes sooner! Meanwhile, all aspects of life are storming forward at a frantic pace. As the illustrated magazines show, two months were enough for girls to grow tresses three feet long, and the Führer has acquired a bodyguard of men over six feet tall.[5] Like Faust in the classical underworld, one might exclaim:

> I feel fresh life, my heart is beating fast,
> Remembering the grandeur of the past. [7189]

If, accordingly, Frederick the Great is being widely honoured once more—as top soldier, if not for his principle that gazettes should be left undisturbed by censorship—the link is also being made with a more recent heroic past by no means lacking in thoughts and memories.[6] Someone recently called himself an "honest broker".[7] This was obviously aimed at those other brokers going round the Stock Exchange in uniform. There are also picture postcards showing Hitler beside the founder of the German Reich, the difference being that although "we Germans feared nothing in the world" then either, we did at least fear God.[8] By contrast, exaggerations of another kind are expressly taboo: for example, inscribing electoral slogans on everyday crockery, or when a butchers' guild exhibited portraits of heroes made of lard, or, especially, the misuse of the Nazi symbol on every sheet of rolls of paper in places where the walls are already covered with the same symbol. For we are dealing with

> a full-blown spiritual awakening of the German people, which should embrace the whole of public life *as well as the private life* of every German.

The campaign "against kitsch" derives from this trend, though in fact it runs counter to the call to arms "against the un-German spirit", for kitsch often comes close to being the most genuine expression of national traditions. German film, too, which after all tends towards kitsch by its very nature, was ordered to provide "more of the ideas of the new epoch" rather than merely its symbols, which of course leads to the question of where to get such ideas from if one couldn't bring oneself to steal them—a reluctance one might well overcome if only there were something worth stealing. While the battle against kitsch continues, it was arranged (as a precautionary measure) that for the first visit of the Reich Chancellor to Berlin's City Hall, "on both sides of the vestibule heralds in historical dress were to be lined up". This innovation breaks with the tradition whereby the *Berliner Herold* was customarily remembered only for pronouncements beginning "Have you heard", continuing with the news that the celebrity Gert Rut Sadinsky was recently spotted disappearing with the lawyer Wolf III into a hotel in the Kantstrasse, and wondering what the lawyer's good lady, who is sometimes herself to be seen with the film star Fred Neppke, would have to say about that.

As for other forms of productivity, some of the nation's creative writers—those who have not exhausted themselves writing on the windows of Jewish shops on Boycott Day—have made a promising start. Polemical writing has been given a fresh impetus, and topical verse that employs biting satire to get to grips with grievances is encouraged. Take one noble gentleman's furious lampoon entitled "Jewish capital flees abroad".[9] From the very first stanza it strikes home with its demand to settle accounts with the Jews once and for all:

> *Unbelievable*, how that gang *behave!*
> Lying and agitating and subverting,
> At home and abroad, above board and hidden,
> Their aim is to win back total control.

Oh these poor fools, if they think they can.
For your time's up, *you fine gentlemen!*

The free rhythm, with a certain casualness in syntax and punctuation, aims more at an acoustic effect, of course. He's a Junker from east of the Elbe, giving vent to his natural emotions in the big city, seeing that

Germanic blood with this alien race might fuse—
These bloodsuckers, who *unbelievably* bled our people dry.
Begone, you *Jews!*

True, they seem to have found little nourishment:

This herd of aliens on German *sand.*[10]

But they were still to be found everywhere, as a simple backward glance shows:

'Twas what you saw *on all your German travels*
In cities, hamlets, palaces, or hovels:
Crooked noses everywhere....
Jews shooting upwards into positions of power.

More than that. There are graphic descriptions of how Aryans found all the positions they aspired to already taken by Jews, who were simply slicker'n'quicker:

In trade and commerce—Jews everywhere,
In press, theatre, film—without compare
It's the Jew who's *playing* the lead.
Soon every privvy, if you're in need,
You'll find occupied—Germans take heed!
A *puzzle picture*—soon things were so bad,
The whole world now wonders, it's gotten so mad,
Why the German awakes, shakes this scourge from the land?
It's enough! No more! Let the world understand!

Hence the demand:

Kick the Jews *out of* the civil service!

And above all:

No German woman shall give her money to a Jew either!!

Such liaisons are improper in any case, since the Jew etc. etc. Let them try it in the outside world:

If to that sort of thing other nations consent,
Fair enough—haggle *to your hearts' content!*

It's obvious that the flight of Jewish capital abroad is here treated somewhat indulgently. For the author grasps all sides of the problem, and since he only wants to express what is troubling him, he is well aware that it is not polished poetry, but indignation pure and simple that has gone into the verse:

I'll make it simple, so everyone understands,
Plain and simple for these German lands,
For today I'm *not much interested in style.*

It would certainly be interesting to see how he writes elsewhere. But sometimes a rhyme does come to him that hits the mark:

Words, words, words, yet it all was shit,
We Germans don't mince matters, no, not a bit!

So what is aimed for is far from the stilted literary German of those who are being given their marching orders:

Jabber away and scribble as much as you want,
Till *the world* catches on that, while you rant,
You're all of you totally depraved!

But if the world is to understand, the following defiant ditty might certainly help—you can really feel the poet finally losing his patience:

Reconstruction's our task! We've no time
For whining Jews, they're swindlers—the swine!
Roosters crow it from the rooftops for all to hear.

Diebold's exacting demands have not been fulfilled. We are dealing here with a bucolic form of arts and crafts, but the undoubted aim of strengthening the will of the nation can only be accomplished by sacrificing aesthetic refinement—and what punctuation there is comes from the typesetter. That goes for the following song, too, a further response to the dictates of the hour, with the title and the refrain "Jews, begone!"—a demand that of course directly contradicts any opposition to the "flight of capital". In this song, the German people are bluntly described as

Slaves to the Jews, and *to the curse of money*

but

The peasant behind his *arrow* would fain
Have a clear view of the sun again!

An arrow the size of an aeroplane would be needed to block the sun (most peasants use a harrow). On the other hand

The German businessman cannot look forward any more

Clearly this doesn't mean that he cannot look forward to more money, since the Jew has of course etc. etc., but that the businessman, too, and for the same reason, has no clear view of a rosy future.

You seek proof?—look at the millionfold proofs!
Jews, begone!

They have even coloured the syntax of our German poet, and grammar in general:

German art and culture no more was seen to be

There's only one thing for it:

Consult the *German* businessman
Is he to be ruined? *Is that their plan?*
Jews, begone!

It's a clear-cut case:

The Jew has declared war on us,
The German nation, 65 million strong,
Who want to live free, for God ordained it thus.
Jews, begone!

In days to come we will thank God

that we have been finally *cleansed* of these exploiters of the people

If they "don't come to their senses at once", he concludes,

Then Jews, begone!

No one can claim there is any element of uncertainty, relativity, ambiguity here. Nevertheless, we're hardly dealing with Diebold's conception of folk song and German saga, sharing the language of Goethe's writings. I don't believe the poet has any special relationship with *Pandora*, for instance, even if the crude fist he makes of things is clearly Faustian, and he may well be familiar with that most indispensable utterance from *Götz*.[11] The poet's refrain even echoes Cato's *Ceterum censeo*.[12] But the demand that the Jews must be gone, if they don't come to their senses, misses the mark inasmuch as some have already come to their senses, while others can't get hold of an exit visa, even if they did have the financial wherewithal to be gone. This radical war cry has been dispersed abroad by our brave boys in the SA, its targets rather less so. Even in this essential point of the programme we sense the discrepancy between theory and practice, a striking feature of the fine speeches that accompany the work now proceeding on its merry way. Hitler can readily assure Americans trying to protect the Jews:

> We would willingly give every one of them a free steamer ticket and a *thousand-mark note* for travelling expenses, if we could get rid of them.[13]

He can't have imagined how many would rush to say "Done!" (or "It's a deal!"), hoping to take a German man at his word and longing, when once out, to see that "the slanders about barbarism and terror should cease". How nice it would be, for example, if leaving Germany for Austria would bring you the thousand-mark note that an exit visa costs. Every creature on God's earth wants to live as free as God ordained, but they can't always do so, even if they're not yet in a concentration camp.

The songs that give expression to the thought of liberation were very popular in Berlin when spirits were still high from the satisfaction provided by Boycott Day, whose economic success didn't come close to its effect on morale. At that time there was also still a demand for the official party postcards, like the one depicting the brave SA man in pursuit of his onerous duty, standing in front of a shop window inscribed:

> Jewish pig, may your hands rot off!

Or a disabled trade union leader and war veteran, heart of gold, shame, dread, and resignation in his face, being pulled along in a dog cart, followed by a mob of civilians and armed men. Or a Munich lawyer, who had enquired at the police station about the arrest of a client, being escorted by spectral figures on bicycles, with his trousers in tatters and a placard around his neck declaring

> I am a Jew, but I will not complain about the Nazis

(He was taken to a concentration camp and then shot "while trying to escape".)[14] This picture was acknowledged to have had a publicity value—especially abroad, where it was entitled "Return to the Middle Ages"—similar to the group photograph surrounding Battisti's corpse.[15] Consequently, the exhibiting of national trophies is said to have been restricted after it was realised that they were partly to blame for the spread of atrocity propaganda. Not only must kitsch be eradicated, they say, but also the serious consequences of photographs of isolated incidents liable to project the wrong image to the world at large. Forms confirming that nothing has happened to torture victims are routinely available in the Brown House to all who succeed in leaving the building.[16]

5

POLITICAL LEADERSHIP AND ARTISTIC TRANSFIGURATION

As for the literary expression of the public mood, including such vehement outbursts as those against Jews for both staying and running away, the gallows humour about stringing 'em up undeniably seems excessive. But words have no less right than deeds to be judged with a tolerant eye that distinguishes the storm and stress of a fledgling movement from its core values. In giving it the benefit of the doubt, we must not overlook its benefits, and we should also acknowledge the stance of a leadership which has explicitly told us time and again that it disapproves of the violations it has authorised. For surely no one could seriously believe that words bluntly affirming impulsive action could accord with the taste of a man described by Gauleiter Kube, himself an aesthete, as follows:

> It is the will of Adolf Hitler that the political struggle should be ... *ennobled* by the nurture of German art. We close collaborators know that he is *the most sensitive and discriminating art lover ever to have led a great nation. I remember him* approaching *the steps of the altar in the Pergamon Museum*—it was *before the great decisive struggle* about the Schleicher cabinet—in order to refresh once more *his innermost mortal longings* at its monumental beauty.

So after the days of harsh struggle the German people should again reflect on their spiritual values, for "the soul's reawakening is what is urgently needed". Up to now the arts, which are actually the more powerful sphere, were given far too little attention, and even the literary expert would be amazed at the secret longings of the man of action, of whom his own newspaper, which is surely well informed, drew the portrait of a Maecenas undreamt of by Horace under the title "If artists only knew ...":

> *If artists only knew* how much Adolf Hitler *embodies the quintessential artistic personality,* none would oppose him—*this axiom, coined by Baldur von Schirach* at the time of our fiercest struggles, illuminated even our darkest hours like a shining star auguring a bright future.

So it was not Hitler's aura in itself, it was how Schirach perceived and expressed it that uplifted us. Even when, alas, we were on the point of despairing—

> this talisman of hope *fortified us* against ever faltering: *If artists only knew. . . .*

A charm with the secret power of depriving someone of favour with God and man? On the contrary! The *Völkischer Beobachter* confirms the insight of this prophet whose very name sounds like something out of the *Edda* crossed with the Pentateuch:

> If only they knew *what we were destined to experience early on,* namely that a political leader *need by no means necessarily and in the natural course of things be without understanding of art,* but given toughness of heroic conviction and an uncompromising assumption of command, can *very well be open to all artistic transfigurations of existence*—had they known, as we knew for certain *right from the start,* they would have joined the *host* of those who, like us

"learned to renounce all the sophistication of the intellect", in order "to love him unconditionally".

> If only they knew—this thought took possession of us, it almost tormented us.

How the staff of the *Völkischer Beobachter* must have suffered! Its office is not far from Dachau. But:

> They *should* know it, they *must* know it!

This is why "prominent, artistically creative personalities from the world of theatre and film" are summoned to the Kaiserhof Hotel:[1]

> So now I heave myself with all my might
> Up from the very depths towards the light,
> And summon into life a joyful band
> Of creatures who will populate the land [7570]

which results in an unconstrained but animated exchange of views, a friendly confabulation of statecraft with the Muses, echoing the journalistic clichés of earlier days! Many a one whose talent I moulded is there, sunning himself. There's the UFA star Willy Fritsch, achieving his goal with a handshake, and the actress Maria Paudler (whose toeing the party line also leaves me cold) entering into the Third Reich; we hear sweet little Liane Haid exclaiming: "Tremendous what you've done, Herr Hitler, keep it up and good luck!"; and Goebbels, always laughing, like Mephisto among the lascivious spirits of the underworld:

> With whom the satyrs can rejoice,
> A cloven hoof is spoilt for choice. [7232]

And now:

> *no longer does that painful "If only they knew" flash through our mind; rather we delight in the certainty: Now they know!*

That, in the context of the arts, is only one step away from what the *Deutschösterreichische Tageszeitung*—the *Dötz*—established: that the public cheered the composer of a Goethe symphony dedicated to the Führer because it celebrated

> together with the maestro *those great geniuses* whom his work serves: *Goethe and Adolf Hitler.*

The music critic who wrote this is one Heinrich Damisch.[2]

> *Only thus* can it be, *must* it be

was the apt verdict of his colleague on the *Völkischer Beobachter* when the artists finally got the message.[3]

Everywhere things are stirring. Poets summoned to the Kaiserhof by their art-loving masters come in on cue:

> And now Apollo joins the blessed choir
> Of Muses there, to charm them with his lyre [7566 (Williams)]

—doing the honours to the Muses at the tea table, as Nestroy would say. Soon little ditties spring to the lips, impulses of a folksy creativity to match not only the heroic mood of the times but also its fondness for the idyllic:

> Under a birch tree the lovers gay
> Were standing, lad and lass, blond-curled.
> The sky was blue, 'twas early May
> And the sun was shining on the world.

And as "two blond hearts trembled aglow", and while

> In the treetops a songbird sang
> And nodded its happy little head.
> Then upwards the blood of the lassie sprang,
> To the roots of her blond braids it spread

—even the bystander feels swept away. And if the *Völkischer Beobachter* dismisses as "kitsch" such a dumbing-down of the blood myth, it only proves that the paper underestimates the range of Germany's natural endowments and may unduly restrict reflections on its primal instincts to Richard Billinger's archaic visions of blood and soil. It is not true that the German soul finds complete satisfaction in battle; through hardship the path always leads to heaven, and the cultural momentum already achieved promises to soar beyond Breughelian scenes of horror into the realms of True Romance. Folksy literature, purified of its dross, will fulfil the aims discussed at the Kaiserhof, and we can imagine it advancing as far as Körner, where the lust for battle is concerned, and matching Baumbach's affirmation of the pursuit of pleasure (both elements being combined in the military farce). The lassie's braids will continue to grow, the Lorelei will comb her golden hair, not a single strand of which will derive from Heine, nor will the corpses in the calmly flowing Rhine. The civilising process has been thrown violently into reverse. After the wheat has been separated from the chaff, the grain burnt and Jews beaten to death with the winnowing shovel, the literary treasures left behind will be preserved as cosy parlour tricks.

6

HEIDEGGER AND THE VERBAL ACCOMPLICES OF VIOLENCE

It goes without saying that philosophy cannot lag behind when it comes to the construction of a lifestyle that Seneca must have had in mind when he proclaimed that "to live is to fight as a soldier" (*vivere est militare*), all the more so if that philosophy, essential to the "ideological superstructure", is designed for a fully-functioning Walpurgis Night,

> For when phantoms take their places,
> The philosopher their presence graces. [7844]

But how is he to do it, and where on earth is he to be found? That in itself may be difficult, given what one hears of the circuses being performed nonstop in barracks and camps, while the problem of bread supply has not yet been solved: given the use of steel rods and whips made of rhinoceros hide, with stiff joint exercises for cripples, the transformation of naked bodies, female ones too, into bloody lumps of flesh, ordeals often inflicted to the accompaniment of merry marching songs, while victims chant slogans, or blood relatives are forced to join in or to beat each other up—in short, things that have no precedent in the momentous actions of high tragedy, let alone in a revolution. It must be difficult to connect such barbarities to the act of thinking, let alone to discover if any learned men have devised formal instructions for carrying them out. For even if the pen balks at depicting these things, a duty we owe to the memory of all these martyrs, as well as to those who had to endure only fear of death and bestial mockery at gunpoint ("Y'afraid, Yid?"): the game of execution promised for the morrow—even if description is impossible, one simply cannot conceive of a writer, someone with ethical responsibility for the survival of humanity, who would advocate such a means of purging a body politic. To be sure, lest we despair of man's essential innocence, and as protection against going mad oneself, one would like to cling to some meaning inherent in the events themselves. But the impulse to derive it from philosophy would surely only make sense if one recognised the context as pathological. For to assume that the blood fever of this now frenzied world springs from a more natural or heroic impulse than that of perverted sexuality; to assume that this blood wedding and its pairing with filth, that the naked pursuit of economic ascendancy, whatever its idealistic trappings, could be rooted in primal instincts other than lust for power and enslavement, sheer greed, and envy; to assume that bestial acts of retribution which have never before erupted in a community in dire straits, even in panic at starvation; to assume that all these could only be conceivable from some metaphysical perspective, on account of their exceptionality—*that* could only be a philosophy which has ripened into its "most German" form and which this nation claims for its own species as distinct from those of other peoples. And here, as elsewhere, it comes directly into conflict with representatives of its own better nature. Goethe was opposed to such claims; he did justice to this incommensurability with his observation:

> A comparison of the German people with other peoples awakens in us feelings of embarrassment which I try to avoid at all costs. *Has our people truly awakened?*[1]

And Wagner absolutely refuses to have anything to do with this most German of virtues, one that it claims for itself incessantly; a propensity, especially now that it has the airwaves at its disposal, to put the idea into the heads of other nations that they should think of themselves, first and foremost, as French, English, Italian, Czech, and, now especially, as Austrian. True, Bayreuth would not today include in its programme notes the view that the more powerful a people, the less it seems to care about

> addressing itself with such awe and reverence. In the public life of England and France it is far less common to speak of "English" and "French" virtues: the Germans, on the other hand, tend to refer continually to "German depth", "German seriousness", "German fidelity", and so on. *Unfortunately, it has become clear in very many cases that such appeals were not altogether warranted.*[2]

One shudders to think what a certain eminent visitor to Bayreuth would say if he came across the view:

> While Goethe and Schiller poured out German genius over the whole world without even mentioning "Germanness", these speculative operators fill all German bookshops and picture galleries, all so-called "people's" theatres—meaning joint stock companies—with coarse, totally insipid and trivial products, invariably defiled with the glowing recommendation, "German" this and "German" that, to entice the complaisant throng. *The German people will soon be almost completely fooled by this*

> *nonsense—we really have reached that stage.* The national predisposition towards indolence and complacency is beguiled into becoming *a smugness quite divorced from reality.* The greater part of the German people is already playing its part in this shameful comedy, and it is *not without horror* that any thoughtful German can contemplate *those absurd rallies with their theatrical parades, idiotic ceremonial speeches, and pathetically feeble songs,* all aimed at fooling the German people into believing it *is becoming* something exceptional without needing to make any special effort.[3]

Still, Bayreuth has been ordered to abstain from the Horst Wessel song, which would after all be incompatible with a cast of mind daring enough to find

> that it is the *simple fear* felt by those peoples previously influenced by German genius which has *now totally estranged them from us* and led them to devote themselves wholly to French civilisation . . . since they at least quite rightly prefer the genuine article to the fake.

The fact that it is now actually obligatory to declare one's faith in someone who has said such things, someone who is even taken for the embodiment of patriotism itself, is all the more unimaginable since he has himself called it into question:

> As patriotism opens the citizen's eyes to the interests of the state, it leaves him blind to the interests of humanity at large.[4]

Consequently, Wagner would be rejected out of hand in any search for a philosophical custodian of National Socialist thought. In fact, one would be hard put to find any such thing; rather, it's still something in the making, spawned from the intellectual potential of a life that reveals the mass-produced article in all its organic forms. It has long been evident that the new German book trade has nothing worthwhile to offer, either in its sales pitch or in its window displays: nothing but "action" and "will", "blood and soil", every catchphrase a hand grenade, a direct hit by authors whose fixed stare is indistinguishable from that of their readers; the bleak optimism of a generation that has heard something about "having looked death in the eye" and hence feels a compulsion to repeat this while terrorising its fellow men. Romanticised white-collar projects for wars of liberation designed to enslave others. A seething mass of useful idiots: aesthetes, faith-healers, and now those stooges deftly turning their hand to transcendentalism in university faculties and journals, converting German philosophy into an introductory course on the Hitler Idea.

For instance Heidegger, the thinker who has made his fabulous blue-sky thinking conform to the prevailing brown-shirted trend and begins to perceive—as clear as daylight—that the spiritual world of a people is

> the power of profoundly preserving *its earthly and blood-based strengths as the power of the innermost arousal and utmost upheaval of its existence.*[5]

I always knew that a Bohemian shoemaker comes closer to the meaning of life than an innovative German thinker.[6] Why a people has to be aroused and undergo upheaval of its earthly and blood-based strengths, and how that might lead to the green shoots of national recovery—these are naturally questions of faith rather than of reasoning. Still, one can't help recalling the objection made to an agitated pedagogue in Gogol: Certainly Alexander the Great was a great man, but why start smashing the furniture?[7] Heidegger, dutifully promoting "Intellect on Active Service", does not fail to tell us how we should act:

> *We should act in the spirit of questioning, unsheltered resoluteness amid the uncertainties of existence as a whole.*

Fortunately, the newspaper which quotes this promptly provides a clue:

> *Take a bite—only the best will do: Berna Cheese.*

But we're still in the dark. The attachment to a combination of blood and soil, which these unfathomable advocates of violence now eagerly expound, could remind us of another hazard, not philosophical but medical, arising from such a combination: tetanus. Thus the psychosis might be traced back to an epidemic of national spasms characteristic of those who strut their stuff on parade grounds or lecture platforms or are capable of doing both at once. But what would be the use of such an insight, since the movement is not something to be healed but to be hallowed. "It's somewhere I don't dare to go", Homunculus confesses to Mephisto:

> I'll whisper in your ear the goal to which
> those two suspect philosophers will lead.
> I've heard the Power of Nature is their creed! [7834]

Nietzsche? No, surely not! For all his shifting allegiances between cultures, he would hardly have sided with those advocating a return to nature by subhuman methods, as cruel as they are unsavoury, given his liking for southern and Semitic forms of life. True, he called for "twentieth-century barbarians", but when he actually encountered them, he repudiated them most emphatically. It is also true that, time and again, like Thor, he "philosophised with the hammer"; and he caused much mischief with the Superman he "proclaimed unto you"—a figure that, even with regard to those future aeons into which he projected his thought, remains merely a conjecture, to be greeted in its present incarnation, as Faust was in Goethe's play, by the Earth Spirit's scornful words:

> What pitiable fear
> Seizes you, Faust the superman!
> For truly:
> Where is the call
> Of your creative heart, that carried all
> The world and gave it birth, that shook with ecstasy,
> Swelling, upsurging to the heights where we,
> The spirits, live? [489–494 (Luke)]

Hitler's enforced conformity falls far short, and Nietzsche, who rejected racial breeding, would have found little Hellenic joy in implementing the axiom that man is something to be transcended. For what monkey is to man, and man should be for superman—"an object of ridicule or bitter shame"—is precisely what today's superman is to man. Behind the "magnificent blond beast in lusty pursuit of his spoils and victory", an ideal in which a literary generation revelled, he would recognise only the very "herd morality" he deplored, that of contemptible underlings now revelling in the thought of power. Is this fulfilled by the recourse to lies in order to conceal the spoils, with headhunter's scalp consisting in jobs for the boys? Would Nietzsche's blond beast have been this type of marauder:

> The Jewish chemist Georg Grünwald had his shop in Prenzlauer Allee in the north of Berlin. One day soon after the Reichstag Fire, another chemist set up shop opposite Grünwald.
>
> In mid-April a troop of Brownshirts stormed into the shop. "You, Jew, pull down your shutters and close your shop, or it could go badly for you!"
>
> Grünwald replied that he had been established there for twenty years, so he wasn't the competition but the other one.
>
> The night after this dispute Georg Grünwald vanished from Berlin without a trace. His wife raised the alarm at the local police station. Two days passed. On the third day the station rang the apartment of the chemist's wife. She could fetch her husband's body from the city morgue for burial. The woman ran to the police station. "What happened to my husband?" A shrug.... Frau Grünwald thought of the new chemist....
>
> Two private detectives took up the hunt for the murderers. The same night Frau Grünwald was found poisoned in her apartment. The police

> report said: suicide. As far as the police were concerned, the case was closed.
>
> In Prenzlauer Allee there is now only one chemist, a German one.

And does the following example show how "the triumphant monster recovers the innocent conscience of the beast of prey":

> A Swiss gentlemen's account of a journey: I arrived in Hesse. In an old inn a couple of stolid churchgoers laughed as they told me of the fun they had on the day of the boycott with a small shopkeeper whom two SA men had driven into the village square at rifle point. The Jew had begged for his life, whimpering since he believed his final hour had come. Then they let him go. Now no one uses his shop. Another Jewish shopkeeper on whom the writer then called told him there were still good neighbours who brought him food at night, so he and his children wouldn't starve.

Perhaps the Antichrist would have preferred them to the churchgoers. Or are the guards in the concentration camps representative of the "master morality"? Does the "noble race" liberate itself from communal constraints by allowing cowardly monsters to get their revenge for the erotic cross they have to bear at home? When they "went to women", they couldn't forget the whip:

> The camp was divided into different classes. The worst off were the communists and radical socialists in the third class. The Jewish prisoners, it is true, were supplied with food by the Jewish Community, but they had to do the most menial tasks, clean the toilets, polish the boots of the SA men, if ordered *kiss their feet or lick their boots.* If they objected, a rubber truncheon provided assistance. I saw their hair being torn out, taking pieces of the scalp with it. They were also forced to hit themselves in the face or to box each other. "Let 'em have it, you dogs!" Otherwise the truncheon did its work until blood spurted. Many had nervous breakdowns, others fell ill. The doctor visited once a week, but it was always the same: Next, next—without listening to what anyone said. Someone beside me said: "It's my lung, I'm spitting blood"; the answer was "castor oil".

No, surely no philosopher could have wanted that.

> In one night, Thales, you I think would fail
> To make from slime a mountain on this scale [7859 (Luke)]

Or did Nietzsche's concept, which cannot be blamed for outrages committed by subordinate functionaries, originate from the conduct of those who practise power but deny what they preach, and those who preach power but deny they practise it? Did it originate from the fervour of vindictive murderers, newly promoted? Or from the heady pronouncements about law and order by police chiefs whose contingency plans envisage "a pogrom, the like of which the world has never seen", promising "St Bartholomew's nights" followed by "days of national resurgence" and "hours of retribution", compared with which previous episodes will be child's play?

> The peaceful flow of Nature's living powers
> Needs no constraint of nights or days or hours.
> She moulds and rules all forms, and even on
> The greatest scale no violence is done.
> But it was done here! [7861 (Luke)]

For instance in the literary confession of one Killinger, whose deeds match his name, and who under the title *Reminiscences Both Serious and Amusing of Life during the Putsch* was responsible for the following amusing example:

> A *female* is brought before me. Arty bohemian type. Short straggly hair, shabby clothes, an insolent, wanton look on her face, hideous rings under her eyes.
>
> "What's up with you?"

She scowls and spits (can you blame her?) in the face of one of his noble band.

> "Horsewhip. Then let her go", say I bluntly. Two of *my henchmen* seize her. She tries to bite. A slap round the face makes her see reason. In the courtyard they pin her *over the shaft of a carriage*, then lay into her with whips *until there wasn't a single white patch left on her back.*
>
> "She won't be spitting at any more members of our brigade now. First she'll *have to lie on her belly for three weeks*", says Sergeant Herrmann.

As done and described by one of the highest dignitaries of the state, with executive power to punish reports of atrocities with penal servitude. A Faustian nature—perhaps; but a superman? If Hitler's induction into Wagner's world was already an error of judgement, perhaps it was even more careless to have drawn his attention to an intellectual affinity with Nietzsche and a terrible gaffe to have photographed him amidst the Weimar Circle in front of Nietzsche's bust. A French paper published the photo and an English scholar points out the inappropriateness of the connection with an author whose most thought-provoking wordplay was precisely about Germanness, such as "Horneo and Borneo" applied to the racial problem.[8] It was Nietzsche who asserted, almost as a "maxim":

> Have nothing to do with anyone who connives in this phoney bunkum about race!

And indeed Nietzsche in *Ecce Homo*, a work which itself admittedly borders on the psychopathic, whose millenarian approach not only forms the time frame he deemed necessary to vindicate his ideas but also prompts the observation:

> The Germans have all crimes against culture over the last four hundred years on their conscience.

And who also wrote:

> The Germans are a rabble—whoever keeps their company cheapens himself.

Such declarations would have earned him a thousand years of concentration camp in their company.

> A Jew among Germans: what a relief!

according to Nietzsche.

> Supposing one lives among Germans, it's a relief to meet a Jew. The Jews' shrewdness protects them from our type of idiocy, for example from becoming "nationalistic".

Moreover:

> I'm no admirer of the most recent speculators in idealism, the anti-Semites, who these days roll their Christian-Aryan-hypocritical eyes, and with their misuse of trite rabble-rousing—a moralising posture which exhausts everyone's patience—seek to stir up all the most bovine impulses of the German people.

A sentence which, incidentally, serves as an exemplary instance of German polemics. And this Nietzsche can be frankly personal:

> Shame on those who now importunately offer themselves to the masses as their saviours.

Thus speaks the bust in the photograph. What can the Weimar Circle have been thinking of? How could Goebbels have so misled the Führer as to recommend him to be photographed next to such a graven image? They showed more tact and sense of precedence in Geneva when they placed Goebbels himself behind the Chief Rabbi of Australia.[9]

■

Nothing doing with Nietzsche, then. A more suitable philosophical sponsor might be that second one I'm tracking: Spengler, who let it be known that it bestows "high rank on man as a breed that he is a beast of prey", and who even provided an explicit intellectual justification for events in Dachau and Sonnenburg, in the Hedemannstrasse and the Papestrasse: by praising the "actively intelligent" ability to pounce on the weak and by endorsing the spirit that

> *knows that feeling of intoxication when the knife* slices into the body of the enemy, when *the smell of blood and sound of groaning penetrate the triumphant senses.* Every true man in the cities of late cultures *still sometimes feels the dormant glow of this, his primordial soul.* No trace . . . of those toothless feelings of pity, of reconciliation.

You can certainly believe him when he declares:

> *No one could have longed more urgently than I have* for the national upheaval of the past year.

They offered him the professorial chair in Leipzig. He understands those "undergangsters" of the Declining West, and the *Untergangster des Abendlandes* understand him. His simple precept for people's dealings with each other—which is compatible with his complaint about the harshness of the Treaty of Versailles—in itself justifies an unprecedented awakening of the primordial soul. Among living philosophers, no one else fits the bill. Spengler could be their man. Unfortunately, he too seems to have let them down since he distinguishes between "being well-bred" and "the breed to which one belongs"; only the former relates to "ethics", the latter to "zoology".

7

GOTTFRIED BENN AND THE SACRIFICE OF INTELLECT

That leaves Gottfried Benn. As a late convert to the Nazi movement, he has made a complete about-face from left to right and been attacked on that score by the émigré intellectuals. About them I did indeed have my doubts, but he always struck me as a prime suspect. For the convert provides even more valuable service than the philosopher whose belligerence predated the breakthrough of the Hitler Idea. Benn's support carries weight as evidence of the seductive power of National Socialism, as an exemplary sacrifice of the intellect, documenting the mindless opportunism that epitomises the current situation. To the outside observer it also reveals the depths to which any literary hack can sink. It has long been recognised that such authors lay it on thick when they are of Aryan descent, but we shall see that Benn, despite his radical rejection of the intellectual lifestyle, does not disown the formal tools of his trade, carrying the complete set into his new home. The speech in which he was obliged to explain himself was squeezed between reports barked out on Radio Berlin and subsequently printed in the *Deutsche Allgemeine Zeitung,* which is known for occasionally daring to flout authority. The same issue carried on its masthead the motto "The starry heavens above us and the moral law within" as proclaimed by Kant, who through a regrettable misunderstanding has likewise been enlisted as a philosophical pillar of the Third Reich but who conceived the categorical imperative as something quite different from "Perish the Jews!" Or did he envisage it as the basis for the Gauleiters' decree, on pain of an immediate three-month prison sentence, requiring "the raising of the right arm at the first and fourth verses" of the Horst Wessel song?

The propositions advanced by Gottfried Benn are even more categorical than those of Immanuel Kant. He represents the most extreme example of writing subordinated to the frenzy, apparently so passionate about it that he has completely lost track. And if the SA murder squad *Mord-Sturm 33* understands this philosophical interpretation of its activities anywhere near as well as Goebbels, then—assuming the author of *The Seventh Ring,* Stefan George, is elevated to poet laureate of the Third Reich—Benn is its emissary in prose. For he is more authentic than Diebold, more powerful than Mirko Jelusich, whose "global repute" as a poet was recently established by our *Deutschösterreichische Tageszeitung*, and who, after a novel eulogising Mussolini's power and a novella doing the same for Dreher's Beer, is indisputably "Austria's greatest writer". If it is not immediately obvious that Benn surpasses the author of "Jews out!" as a polemicist, this is perhaps because he has "an eye for style" and presents his intellectual message in an infinitely more nuanced way, not forgetting to lace it with a copious supply of philosophical, historical, and even geological erudition. You'll hardly find a sounder intellectual basis or a more graceful formulation for what, at the time of writing, the men of action are putting into practice. For Benn is well aware that he has a hard task as an intellectual serving the party whose thinking he represents, but he seems imbued with the hope that resolute fanaticism can make up the deficit. So he lets fly from the very start, refusing to "discuss events in Germany" with refugees who accuse him of being a turncoat, arguing that one can speak of such things only with those who have experienced them inside Germany.

> Only those who have lived through the tensions of the last few months, who from one hour to the next, from one day's newspaper to the next, from one upheaval to the next

—he means mass rallies, not the disruptions experienced by individuals changing their address every night for fear of intruders—

> *from one broadcast to the next, experienced this runaway progression*

—he means: they chose to stay put—

> at close quarters, *struggling with it* day and night.

Only such people count, only with them can Benn speak. But not with refugees! For they (in his words) have

> missed the opportunity *to feel growing within themselves, not as an idea but as lived experience*, not abstractly but *as a rude force of nature*, the concept of the *Volk* which is so alien to them; missed the opportunity to grasp the . . . concept of the "national" in its authentic, convincing manifestations; missed the opportunity to see history at work in its myriad forms and *images, a tragic force perhaps*, but at all events a manifest destiny.

But of course they've missed the opportunity! That's precisely what choosing to be a refugee means. Those who didn't miss the opportunity, for whom it was lived experience, were hauled from their beds at night by a rude act of nature. If few of them got to see the myriad images of history in the *Berliner Illustrierte*, many did experience the impact of its tragic force, while more than a few are no longer in a position to do so. ("National" in Austria still denotes a criminal record.) But Benn means the others, those "initially resistant onlookers", who were nevertheless

> carried away by the creative momentum reconfiguring mankind.

He was reconfigured, the others merely carried away, which is why a mutual understanding is hardly possible. He implies that on problematic issues his opinion always diverged, notably on the concept of barbarism. He does not mince words:

> You claim that what's happening in Germany today constitutes a threat to culture, to civilisation, *as if a horde of savages* were threatening the very ideals of mankind, but let me ask you in return: what do you imagine the twelfth century, say, was like, the transition *from Romanesque to Gothic sensibility*, do you think it would have been up for discussion? . . . That a vote would have been taken: round arches or pointed arches? The apse: circular or polygonal—a matter for debate?

Of course not; and the intellectuals should make an effort

> to see only what is elemental, *thrusting ever forward* to its inevitable outcome

and not as their "bourgeois nineteenth-century brains" see history. Thus Benn implies that blood must flow so that architectonic questions can finally be resolved, questions which—as art historians have insisted—were already being calmly discussed at the time by Councils of the Church, taking special account of the plans of master stonemasons who were not yet guided by Uhland's challenging precept, "Mix your heart's blood" (and that of others) "with the mortar to build German liberty". If we now set aside the objection that, in cultural history, a worldview that doesn't involve bloodshed may also be an achievement, one the "bourgeois nineteenth-century brain" owes to a revolution, albeit a French one, let us draw another point to Benn's attention: architectonic developments, like all living things, may be influenced by revolutionary change, war, and pestilence, and if there are ruins there is also sometimes new life sprouting from the rubble; but it is also true that the architecture of the future, a style which is probably already causing the genius of mankind to bury its head in shame, would cost too high a price in precious human lives—some of which are known to me. Benn believes in history as an ineluctable destiny, although in truth it is as malleable as the writings of a literary opportunist; he places his trust in a necessity which seems less a matter of inevitability than the chance product of human organisation; but only a man who has kept his head by dodging falling bricks can explain things in this way. One day he will have to square his conscience with the question of whether this narrow escape was the right moment to hold forth on the philosophy of history, and whether someone making a pact with chaos was justified in hailing its progenitors—personalities of the stature of Berchtold and Hindenburg Jr.—as the instruments of Providence. Even if we could follow the popular orator onto a plane so elevated that things again become intelligible, his faith can surely not have blinded him to the threat now faced by the remnants of culture that are worth preserving; nor to the question whether the twelfth century, for all its aversion to Jews, would actually have abandoned its intellectual advances and beaten up its scientific benefactors. To be sure, Benn does not mean that such actions will just reignite a problem like that of round or pointed arches: the choice is more fundamental. For history, echoing the jargon of the Berlin literati, is planning nothing less than "a new human type"—a type to be

> sent forth from the teeming womb of the race, which must fight its way through adversity, which must absorb the idea of its generation and its species within the fabric of the times, ever resolute, active, and anguished, as the law of life decrees.

So far we are only confronted with prefabricated literary verbiage, though it does bear a strong resemblance, both in word and deed, to the tirades of *Der Stürmer.* His "conception of history", Benn says, is neither rationalistic nor humanistic but "metaphysical". The former claim is true, the latter highly debatable. And he accepts the intellectuals' reproach that he is "fighting for the irrational". How odd that these Germans have to fight even when they're thinking (fighting is indeed their forte). At last we get to the key. For:

> irrational means close to the wellsprings of creation and capable of creativity.

You there, he calls out to them, "can't you get it into your heads, down there on your Latin shores" (an inferior landscape):

> What is happening

—in Germany—

> is *the emergence* of a new biological type, history *is mutating, cultivating a new race.*

Cultivating? Hold on! I'm convinced that some of those involved confuse it, both practically and etymologically, with castigating—just as Viennese politicians, when there was a threat of the plague (but only because of an accident in the lab), were once heard to say that it was wrong to castigate bacilli. (And just as I also suspect that many who welcomed the book burning derive auto-da-fé from author, if not from automobile.) As for history mutating, it seems best illustrated by the photo of an atrocity showing a callow youth asserting his power, the kind of snotty little brat we know so well, looming large as a result of the angle from which the scene is photographed. He is curling his lip and pointing his rifle at seven men with chalk-white faces, forced to stand in front of a wall with their arms raised for hours on end. They were then chased up and down steps and flogged by petty officials as they ran the gauntlet, until collapsing, covered in blood. If this horrific trophy symbolises the defencelessness of a people in relation to its armed minority, then our Gottfried is probably right in his interpretation of what we are seeing as the emergence of a new biological type. Nothing could emerge more clearly than the mutating spectre of this photographic nightmare: phantom of a whippersnapper who has unmanned German manliness. . . .

Now, according to Benn, the idea of *cultivating a new race* is based on the view that man is "admittedly a rational being",

> but *above all he is mythical* and *deep.*

"With regard to his future", we should think in these terms:

> *that he must be grafted onto the base of the ancestral tree,*

for he is "older than the French Revolution, more multi-layered than the Enlightenment ever thought". There follows an intellectual-cum-mythical, unfathomably shallow load of waffle: one is allegedly felt to be "largely a creature of nature, close to the source of creation", and

> *we know from lived experience* that he is much less *free, much more bonded through his wounds to original Being* than the barely two-thousand-year-old *antithesis* of Idea and Reality proclaims.

Of more recent vintage is the dualism that emerges from Benn's lifeless newspaper metaphors. For we do know from experience how the new biological type threw off his bonds, inflicting many wounds in the process. Benn does not think along these lines, however, but rather irrationally:

> *Actually man is at home in a perpetual Quaternary, long before the most recent ice ages, whose roaming hordes were the florid fantasy of journalistic*

> *hacks, an* atmospheric diluvial web, *bric-a-brac from the Tertiary*; actually man is primal alertness, living for the moment, loosely attached to reality, vision: embodiment of the rhythms of concealed creative ecstasies.

Whatever next! The geological expert is amazed, while even the layman is right to be puzzled by this display of the irratio-national. For who could have guessed that a Berlin publishing house, close to the wellsprings of creation, has already used such terms in its blurb, even if it has now collapsed or, worse, been forced to toe the party line! Is atrocity propaganda to be refuted by this verbiage? Brutal murder by an ideology that would never have occurred to anyone born on Latin shores, where the events are simply explained as "a return to the Middle Ages"! How irrationally man can think, if he's a German; how distant he can roam without getting dizzy—as might be expected closer to home! A philosopher of Walpurgis Night advises:

> Yield to your laudable temptation
> Seek the beginnings of creation!
> Be poised to act, don't hesitate!
> Move onward by eternal norms
> Through many thousand thousand forms,
> *And reach at last the human state.* [8321 (Luke)]

Well, there is quite a lot to be said for going back to primitive man to explain the course of events, while selflessly relinquishing any claim to be classified as *homo sapiens* oneself. That's the latest trend, and since the intellect has failed, we follow the precept: throw the baby out with the bathwater. Benn wins the philosophical race: he is not popular, but he is mythical and deep; he truly can read the runes. One would have liked to consult Keyserling (telegram address: Cleverclogs), he's also on the move but only wants to go back a thousand years or so to revive German culture. Benn simply ignores such trifles as a waste of time. He even goes back beyond the Deluge (*après lui*); for if you can see connections at such a distance, the intermediate stages are unimportant, and since the movement is in any case setting itself up for a thousand years, we can simply tack on the millennia already completed. As regards a past of which we have virtually no knowledge, an act of faith is best. Benn surmises that the Quaternary, whose reactivation he envisages for the Germany of today and wishes for its future, can be traced back beyond "the most recent ice ages", a period we can still recall, although he seems to associate its denizens with journalistic hacks. And certainly back beyond the Tertiary, the period known for the awakening of the mastodons. Supposing the mastodons are capable of listening to the radio and reading the papers, nothing would surprise them, although the approximate sequence of these periods is already known, while as to the present we are still groping in the dark. Benn could not say with certainty if there were already Germans in the period he confuses with the Late Quaternary, nor does he even seem to be sure what bric-a-brac means (it's not exactly a native term). But to glamorise happenings which in Chicago would qualify for police protection, he presents them as the embodiment of the rhythms of concealed creative ecstasies, which he distinguishes from the fantasy of post-Quaternary Ice Age hordes, actually followed by a diluvial web of florid journalese. In reality, Benn seems more rooted in the Ice Age than in the Quaternary, unless he's mixed it up with the Iron Age, and this in turn with the World War period when people gave gold for iron, and blood was the currency of feature articles. Be that as it may, if an impressionist like Ullmann had swallowed a dose of geology, he would have given the Third Reich a more solid foundation, while the astrological data of Nestroy's Knieriem would have provided a more reliable indication of its future. It seems to be a case of germanogibberish, rarely seen even in postdiluvial writing. Having taken the precaution of consulting the encyclopaedia before delving into such uncharted epochs, we ourselves may also have somewhat irrational tendencies. In pursuit of things which are (at the end of the day) unknowable, we would be willing to accompany Benn back as far as the troglodytes—but the path leads to Neanderthal, a region of Germany not only imagined as close to the wellsprings of creation but also equipped with all the comforts of modernity, including radio.[1] Of course, Benn goes further and formulates the following hypothesis: opponents should "finally get it into their heads" that

> *it's not at all a question* of forms of government but of *a new vision of the birth of mankind.*

During the war, mankind allowed the bullet to go in through one ear and out through the other.[2] Is it really possible that all those wartime motifs are coming back to life? Are they dreams, are they memories? "The business of this revolution is—" "Just so, the business of this revolution is business!"[3] A new vision of the birth of mankind, then, nothing less. "Perhaps an old one", Benn goes on, for he's open to negotiation. Be that as it may, it does explain the commitment and unanimity with which those easing the birth pangs of the Third Reich are currently lining up behind Hitler. It is not yet time for its gravediggers, but the zeal of these midwives is probably due not only to the manifold eugenic possibilities which have now opened up but also to the ban on promoting birth control, imprisonment doubtless still being the most reliable method. (The only reform, incidentally, with which its sister nation has aligned itself, since it rightly wants a growing Austrian population to resist annexation.) But Benn, knowing apparently that a birth, like every beginning, tends to be difficult, places his most exalted hopes on the rebirth of mankind, continuing his prediction of the promise involved:

> *perhaps the final magnificent conception* of the white race, *probably one of the most magnificent realisations of the World Spirit imaginable*, a prelude to which is the hymn

"Jews out"? No way!

> Goethe's poem "To Nature"....

For surely the most shocking aspect of this turn of events is that it not only intoxicated plain idiots but also deprived intellectuals of their senses, as in the World War. The German press chief noted with satisfaction:

> The day before yesterday all the flags were sold out—proof positive that we now have the whole people behind us.

Even stronger proof is the sellout of language. Certainly, no concept could be so elevated, no value so sacred that it would deter today's scribblers from applying it to any conceivable ornamental purpose; but this rapturous enthusiasm of the thinking heads for the headhunters seems to be an inner compulsion! Benn, speaking in tongues, also wants to convert those who have fled to save themselves from the fantasy of the current hordes, a fantasy that has converted him into a visionary. He preaches his ecstatic message to those refugees who have decamped and thus avoided one of the most magnificent realisations of the World Spirit ever, missing out on the birth of mankind, though they may be in at the death. He tells them that "it is not success which determines this vision", for

> if ten wars should be unleashed from East and West to annihilate this new German man, and if the Apocalypse were approaching over land and sea to break open his seven seals, this vision of mankind would remain in our possession, and whoever wishes to realise it must *cultivate it*....

In a word, we are finally beginning to recognise that the outcome of the World War—the termination in civil law of a criminal prosecution before the court of world opinion—has profited us nothing, since it left behind no symbol of that outcome designed for minds oriented towards the swastika emblem, nothing to restore German thinking to itself, to its values, to its language. For that outcome could not be construed as a victory, but neither was it visible as a defeat with a moral impact. "Reparations"—a rendering of accounts in an illusionary realm which the other side also occupied—were meant to make amends for an irreparable deed; but they only bred an irreparable resentment. As a nation founded on the principle of victory, the Germans inevitably felt cheated.

Not believing in a defeat they hadn't really seen, they colluded with a spirit that fabricated guilty men: the guilt was displaced from those who had declared war to those who had signed the peace. A civil war of revenge began, which the Social Democrats were no more able to prevent than they had once been able to resist voting for war credits. Responsibility for the war was denied by those who started it, and the terrible consequences of war were blamed on making peace. External enemies had provoked the war, while its humiliating outcome was the fault of the "enemy within". Nothing could appear more plausible to the next generation than the "stab-in-the-back" theory, since no decisive victory was evident in the field, while defeat on the home front resulted in deprivation. The phantasm of reparations, which would never have made up for the real damage: an arsenal of lies, alleging that even paying off an absolute minimum of reparations would cripple the national economy. But the thought of what conditions—material, let alone cultural—a German victory would have imposed on the world is unimaginable, even in the most distant geological era, for it would have been a final victory, terminating in Paris.

So a nation has now fallen victim to the satanic humbug which has conflated the uniformly disastrous consequences of the war with the consequences of the peace, the harshness of which would still afflict the defeated state even if it was right in mobilising its historians to fabricate a theory of war innocence. Over and above the conclusion that the others started it, this investigation has advanced the claim that the losing side made sacrifices from which the others gained and is therefore entitled to war indemnity. It was above all Austria-Hungary that felt the impact of the victorious Allies' mistake, their failure to differentiate between criminals and those who had been led astray, Austria-Hungary that suffered most from the assumption that nations can be carved up without any knowledge of ethnography. What Germany is suffering from, more than the enemy's arbitrary use of power, is its own ideological fabrication of an enemy within, a fantasy that turned the heads of the wholesome part of the population into the bargain. (Not without England's connivance, something it now regrets; not without the hawkishness of people in the West who represented the idea of humanity.) What a bleak thought that the failures of the first group are to be compounded by the attempts of the second to remedy them! Nationalism—never a help when it comes to thinking—truly teaches a nation how not to learn from its mistakes, and its legacy is the irreparable inversion of all that is hale into a hectoring *Heil!* For not every nation's culture thrives on victory, on greatness, on ostensible unity, and it is a tribute to such a nation when an Austrian politician says that Germany, which has always been great, "reached its full flowering when it was oppressed". Such an opinion, for the benefit of a specific segment and indeed the whole of mankind, accords with the idea that victories are suffered and defeats gained; that defeat at Königgrätz was more beneficial for the Austrians than the Prussians, whose culture was further eroded by their military triumph at Sedan. Such insights are now trumped by the prospect that even a repetition, an intensification, of the disaster of 1914 would be to no avail. For even if the apocalypse were upon us—and its horsemen have been sighted here and there—we could still not hope for any intimation of the last trump. That, alas, is the driving spirit, once defined as the postwar "mentality", to whose points and barbs more civilised Germans are now exposed and against which one of them recently objected with unprecedented insight. We need not go back to the Quaternary, from which I digress, but only to the start of the war, to grasp the contrast apparent in the following statement:

> It was not least this arrogant assertion of unbridled power, born from scientific and scholarly advances and poured out in books and lectures, which provoked in Europe that fateful image of Germany, projecting into the wider world a totally distorted view of the essential nature of the German people, *a terrible mistake which precipitated the world war.*

If this insight, albeit in a more reader-friendly form than usually characterises the national press, is how the *Reichspost* puts it today—a paper that viewed the World War partly as a retaliatory measure initiated by Austria, partly, given its special relationship with Germany, as a dastardly act perpetrated by those countries encircling it—then it surely must be true. Provided it adds that the terrible mistake which precipitated the war also implicated those who promoted that distorted view by pouring the spirit of militarism into militaristic literature and thence into military action; and provided it recognises as the tragic outcome that it has proved impossible to reverse the process. Unperturbed by this nerve-racking, exhausting, interminable cult of Siegfried the warrior, which haunts Europe like a vampire and results in the construction of a fortified Siegfried Line, this is a world that wants a full complement of devils, as if there weren't enough on earth already. It still upholds the childish precept "more foes, more fame", as if the commercial practices of an isolated ruffian could be applied to economic relations worldwide. The human community is astonished that one of its members insists on isolating itself, an isolation splendid only in the sense that it is achieved at the expense of others. All the diplomatic precautions, all those increasingly ludicrous conferences expecting to make progress by continually changing their location—they're like a pygmy's staff against the steely delusion which traces the development of a body politic back to the Quaternary and measures it in the thousands of years. What price the norms of mankind? This is irratio-national!

8

PAPEN'S TWO-FACED POLITICS AND THE MILITARY TRADITION

To turn now to the problem of the "Numerical Strength of the Auxiliary Police".[1] This fades into insignificance compared with the question whether—with every German civilian recruited—the quota may not already be exceeded, judging from the "Ten Commandments of the Defence Catechism" which are based on the principle:

> Every German man must be morally and physically prepared to take up arms in defence of the Fatherland.[2]

The very first commandment pulls no punches:

> You must be capable of marching thirty kilometres nonstop with a heavy kitbag on your back.

This ignores the possibility that life might have created you with completely different purposes in mind. But a specific strategic contingency is also envisaged:

> You must perfect yourself in the *arts of running* and shooting.

Moreover, the art lovers currently promoting these priorities make further demands:

> You must be as *continuously alert* as if you were preparing a *running commentary*

with special reference to developments in the armies of neighbouring countries. Having mastered map-reading, you must hike through our border regions with the General Staff map in your hand, and when you are abroad you must

> attempt to follow the military manoeuvres of the states concerned.

Clearly, the conception underlying this vision is capable of realisation, for it amounts to a training programme for espionage. Above all:

> You must read at least one systematic study of military strategy every year and subscribe to a defence journal.

In short, ten commandments that have obviously been written by the editor of some such journal but are at odds with one in particular: "Thou shalt not kill". But when in addition we read:

> The claim that Germany is preparing for war is grotesque

and that the responsibility rests with those

> who are using such tactics to combat a nation that is doing the world no harm

then we might conclude that the following commandments would suffice: "Thou shalt not tell lies" and "Thou shalt not bear false witness against thy neighbour", nor indeed falsely claim that he is doing so. Admittedly, the discrepancy has promptly been resolved through the reassurance provided by one of those officials whose earlier profession still permits them a sphere of activity:

> The protection of our frontiers is entrusted to our SA.

Above all, we now have that speech by the inimitable Franz von Papen, who was already carrying out those commandments (apart from the one about the kitbag) at his wartime diplomatic post in Washington. His recent unforgettable proclamation was designed to whet the world's appetite for "the most beautiful death in the world"—being slain by the enemy.[3] He also made no secret of the "ancient Germanic abhorrence of dying on a bed of straw":

> As if *a peacetime corpse* would make a more aesthetic impression, as if it did not rather depend on *the spirit* in which a person dies, rather than on the *appearance of his mortal remains.*

But it must have been reassuring for the wider world when Papen reserved the following special praise for the Führer:

> At the end of his life he will be able to say: I have restored *the German military tradition* with its immortal qualities to its *central position in the thinking* of the German nation.

And above all the precise announcement that

> since 31 January 1933 Germany has *erased* the concept of *pacifism from its dictionary.*[4]

That shouldn't surprise us since it is after all a foreign word, but in this dictionary, amid the frolics associated with all those Francks, Fricks, and Freislers, we don't find "Friedensliebe" (love of peace) either. Fortunately, to continue in this vein, we were then confronted by one of those remarkable contradictions that characterise the Nazi movement, not only between actions and speeches but between one speech and the next. On the very next day the Führer read out the impressive declaration in which pacifism was solemnly restored to the German dictionary and the central position in German thinking exclusively reserved for civilian life.[5] Underlining this point, he assigned to the SA and the SS the "status of a fire brigade or a security firm", even though no fire brigade has ever been seen throwing paraffin on a blaze while security firms are responsible for protecting not frontiers but domestic business premises. Of course, neither of those organisations could lay claim to the praise bestowed by the same speaker on the SA in Kiel, shortly before (or immediately afterwards):

> You represent the *greatest organisation* that Germany has ever known, an organisation not only of the *Will* but of *Strength and Force*.

And certainly there can be no pastor who has ever addressed fire brigades or security firms as "pillars of the state" that "must have regained the sense of Christianity as a heroic faith". We are evidently caught up in a never-ending circle of contradictions, and the world is at a loss to know what's what, sensing in speeches devoted to pacifism more pugnacity than veracity. The underlying meaning appears to be: If you want war, prepare for peace (*Si vis bellum, para pacem*). Thus the world should be grateful when Papen finally succeeds in reconciling the divergent standpoints through the happy formulation:

> We must move from a *nationalism that divides our peoples* to an *international security system* that *unites them.*

"There you have it", as Kerr used to say, whose politics also proved thoroughly two-faced. Not that this Papen is having an easy time, even though he too has now deleted nationalism from the top spot in the German dictionary that it surely deserves. As the statesman who undoubtedly hit the jackpot of world history by brokering the seizure of power, he now has to sweat it out as Hitler's Vice-Chancellor. But the inside knowledge he possesses, above all about the history of the movement since the Reichstag fire, enables him to survive despite all the pressures. For many a pronouncement by his allies must grate on his ears, like the promised Day of Reckoning "when guys like you will be cleared out"; or when, as President of the Association of Catholic Artisans, he was assured that clerics attending its Congress would be purged, a threat that was in part carried out.[6]

But we can have no sympathy for a politician who, having supposedly taken a prisoner, discovers that the man could easily send him to a concentration camp.

If the tribute expressed in the phrase "You've come a long way" ever rightly applied to the vagaries of human experience, it applies to these barons, above all to that compulsively robotic Konstantin von Neurath, who as Foreign Minister applies a veneer of cosmopolitan elegance to criminal activities. Not to mention the misfortune of veteran organisations like the Stahlhelm, now suspected, as is the case with every organisation in the land, of harbouring communists in disguise. Such tragic ironies are encapsulated in the Jewish anecdote about the boy who is desperate to become a soldier, whose worried father points out a passing Prussian general: "Just look, that's how you'll end up!" ("Siehst du, das wird dein Soff sein!"). Admittedly, no one could have predicted at the cradle of all these aristocratic Guards Officers and Junkers that they would end up—on the orders of an Austrian corporal—having to kowtow to the rank and file. Not to mention Hindenburg as Head of State: what a capitulation of the marshal's baton before the knapsack! But then again, what a fine sight it must be when princes become the lackeys of men who have worked their way up by their bootstraps! Goebbels has a scion of the Schaumburg-Lippes not simply as his adjutant but "as his most passionate admirer"; Goering, Tsar of all the Prussians, is already completely at home with traditional dynastic connections through a prince of Hessen whose brother is the son-in-law of the King of Italy.

> On the telephone the young man simply introduces himself as: "The Minister's office". Never once his own name and rank. For the sons of these venerable families are fantastically proud of being merely the secretary of a National Socialist minister.

Or rather, merely the office! Not forgetting the newspaper baron Alfred von Hugenberg, who came from an earlier Walpurgis Night held at Harzburg (not the Harz Mountains).[7] He is experiencing the disillusionment that physical difficulties caused Mephisto in the classical version:

> Here I must clamber over rocky rubble,
> gnarled roots of ancient oaks make me bend double!
> I miss the tangy smell of my own Harz,
> the stench of pitch that's lacking in these parts,
> above all sulphur. . . . [7951]

Lots of that here, but still:

> For what we've left behind we pay the price,
> the customary was a paradise. [7963]

Yes, it's easy to get lost amid the confusion; even for me, "confronted by stumbling-blocks" [7804], though very different from those of the World War. Maybe, as I grope my way forward, it will all vanish and even Papen, long since liberated from the dignity of office, will be imprisoned somewhere on the slopes of the Upper Pineios.[8] Perhaps it may all end well, with those gentlemen from the Herrenclub still allowed to retain their titles of nobility, exempt from taxes on wealth they owe to Jewish brides. Thanks to those liaisons, they may finally continue in a function that was not exactly their forte: as liaison officers with a "wider world" that places a premium on social forms of whatever kind, provided they are formal; so that indigenous traditions may be preserved which had not hitherto been their primary concern. This might smooth the transition to a cosmopolitan ethos, behind which unconstrained German tribalism and German assertiveness can run wild. The kernel may be rough, but the shell is sweet.

A revolution that consists of side effects may even demand "intolerance as the order of the day"; but then it is all the more essential that the medicine is carefully dosed and made palatable to Germany's enemies, so as to counteract their hypocrisy. For now they are even becoming agitated about passages of dialogue by our national poet, Hanns Johst, such as the following:

> "The causes *promoted by the brothers over there*, of *world community and humaneness* ... of international peace and so on—they simply don't add up."
>
> "The German people are calling for priests brave enough to shed *blood, blood, blood, priests who slaughter.*"
>
> "*We must drive a wedge through international reconciliation* ... then we can *put ants in the pants of the French.*"

(There are ants in the Classical Witches Sabbath, too.)

> "Justice or injustice—for me that's all *bullshit!* I'm a soldier and I'll always be a soldier!"
>
> "No, I wouldn't touch all that *philosophy-of-life garbage* with a ten-foot pole—here we use live ammunition! *When I hear the word Culture, I release the safety catch on my revolver!*"[9]

And that's what they have the audacity to compare with our manifest love of peace! This is what they call "a horrifying image of the spiritual state of Germany"! Are they not Pharisees? But we've unmasked them:

Council of the League of Nations Reveals Its True Face!
All State Delegates Support the Jews!

Yes, precisely! And they even find it ill-judged that Papen's speech renouncing nationalism was delivered in the Teutoburg Forest, which they assumed no longer existed, having long since been converted into newsprint. But they're mistaken, on the contrary robbers are lurking there among the bushes, calling for "fair play" the moment a traveller attempts to defend himself. And if he becomes utterly confused, the Minister of Culture intervenes—that Bernhard Rust who in an outburst of enthusiasm liberated the fatherland from the thralls of science, and who now

> *repudiated pacifism* in the sharpest possible terms and declared to great applause that the climate of international affairs could never be healthier than *when the individual nations confront each other with mutual respect for the existential rights of the other side.*

Responding to the dilemma caused by this happy blend of contrasts, the *Vossische Zeitung* managed to find a solution by explaining

> that Germany, although *attuned* to patriotism and self-assertion, still wishes to maintain *a cosmopolitan outlook which, rightly understood, places the peaceful community* of peoples on a higher plane than all ambitions arising *only from a nation's blind hunger for power.*

So the contradictions only need to be rightly understood, making special allowance for the small matter of constructing a philosophy of life when a state has been placed on new foundations; above all when here, as so often, it is unclear who is responsible, so that newspapers never know who will give them the next kick up the backside or when they can expect it.

9

NATIONAL GERMAN JEWS

While current developments still allow journalism to be neither fish nor fowl, adapting naturally to the claims of cosmopolitanism, other Jewish spokesmen have succumbed to repeated bouts of intransigent Teutonism, which earn no gratitude and scant respect from the racial disciplinarians. The most astonishing aspect of this phenomenon is the total failure to realise that it might actually be better to show some courage, given that submission is of no use anyway; and the complete and basically aberrant inability to calculate the limited payoffs of cowardice. To be sure, every individual act of self-preservation is forgivable when under duress and where fear prompts someone to evade, if possible, an anticipated threat; and many reports of individual or communal acts of charity, quite apart from the manifestly tragic distress involved, might even count as expressions of altruism. But consider a solidarity more abject than that of German National Jews, proponents of a mission which even in peacetime was surely already an oxymoron, like the nonsense rhyme: It was pitch dark, the moon shone bright, a coach crawled by as fast as light! To do justice to both German identity and an inverted variant of their own, they call themselves "National German" Jews, and have indeed published a whole book, in several languages, under the title

Atrocity Propaganda Is Based on Lies![1]

which is moreover recognised in a press release by the Public Information Service of Greater Germany as "the honorable fulfilment of a natural duty":

insofar as one can speak of Jewish honour at all.

To such impartial assessments they respond with the resilience due to their being German, so that being spat in the face is attributed to the rigours of the climate. They have also heard—for nothing is impossible in a lunatic asylum where the inmate can assault his carer and promptly become Prime Minister of Prussia—they have also heard from another of these monsters that "Jewish doctors are the incarnation of falsehood and deceit".[2] Confronted by such an orgy of confusion about moral concepts and aware that many a Jewish doctor has saved the life of many an Aryan morphine addict—what response does the "executive committee" of the National German Jews recommend?

> Although we are currently treated by *our fellow Germans of non-Jewish origin*

(whose rights we fully recognise, don't get us wrong)

> in a way we can only consider extremely unjust, we *must not let this divert us from the straight and narrow path*, and this path *leads us right into the German community.*

Right on! But such forcefulness is unlikely to impress the SA, and the situation of wealthier Jews also demonstrates that such methods are quite unnecessary. It's always hard to avoid confrontations if you keep to the straight and narrow, and persistence will probably make little impression on those for whom the recognition that we owe to the Jews

> the invention of the microphone, the radio valve, the extraction of nitrogen from the air, the discovery of the pathogen responsible for pneumonia, of the gonococcus bacterium that causes gonorrhea, of measures to combat syphilis, vascular ligatures, experimental pathology, paediatrics, the discovery of cathode rays, galvanoplasty, individual treatment of mental illness etc. etc.

means damn all. Especially when efforts to treat mental illness have proved fruitless, often actually being hindered by the spread of radio technology. However, the view that Jewish genius, no less than German genius, is not determined by racial origin could call both concepts into question. And you would be risking your life if you claimed that if ever the adage "unto the pure all things are pure" applied to a vital issue, it applies to purity of race, though physically it scarcely exists and conceptually it has forfeited its place in human thinking.[3] And it could be fatal to suggest that it might be no bad thing for those faces reflected in today's illustrated magazines to be more hybrid, for then something better might emerge. (Although hybridity has brought no advantage to the Kashubians, Obotrites, Polabians, Sorbs, Wends, Veleti, and other Slav peoples, since it was precisely from them that the Prussian blood sprang, which now makes such stringent racial demands. But of course one mustn't generalise, and who would think of endorsing racial theory on the grounds that Jewish blood has often been adulterated, when such mingling has demonstrably resulted in the most intelligent, most beautiful human beings.) But Jews who feel the urge to identify as National Germans are combining two types of inferiority complex, both of which should be repressed. In the *Berliner Tageblatt*, which is allowed a certain leeway (if only in exceptional cases) such that, to satisfy a cosmopolitan readership, it has even highlighted the achievements of Jewish scholars, those National German Jews advocate

> *converging* with the German national character so as *to develop characteristics* that *do not form part of the primeval Jewish racial heritage,*

that is to say, to do something they are under absolutely no obligation to do. But this is not required, not called for, not appreciated, which is why they should even shed that characteristic pushiness which does tend to be seen as part of their primeval heritage. It's quite a challenge to converge with a national character whose representatives either shout "Jews out!" or frustrate the attempt to comply when they burst into your railway carriage at the frontier, like bloodhounds on the scent of a newly detected crime, snarling: "Are you a Jew?" If so, you have to remain in Germany, only to be deprived of your citizenship and probably also your food rations. To show a willingness to "converge" any further, rather than feel abhorrence and shame for a debased humanity, almost makes the supplicant a suitable case for treatment. But arrangements for special bathing hours—apart from the communally shared bloodbath—have perhaps reinforced the insight of the "Honorary President" of these National Germans that they are dealing with

> *isolated incidents,* committed by people such as are to be found in any nation and in any organisation, who have *used the opportunity* to settle in their own way a *personal* desire for revenge against *individual* Jewish people with whom, *for whatever reason, they have minor disagreements.* ... In any case, *we German Jews, irrespective of our specific sympathies, are absolutely convinced* that *the resolute will* of the government and the leadership of the National Socialist party *is* to maintain law and order.

He would further like to "make it absolutely clear" that the protest against atrocity propaganda

> was *not* a result of *duress of any kind* but *quite spontaneous,* since we were convinced that this *smear campaign* greatly damaged *our German homeland* and was *meant to* do so. There is a further, subsidiary issue—and I *stress emphatically that this factor is of only secondary importance for us:* this smear campaign, allegedly carried out in our interest, has *done us Jews living in Germany an exceptionally great disservice.*

Is this documentary evidence of a deep conviction, is it the outcome of brute force cunningly applied, or is it both at once? If it is a Jewish document, it is surely also an official German communiqué: explaining things away until the opposite emerges, swamping the facts in slimy words, standing justice on its head, making a mountain into a molehill and murder into a difference of opinion, and presenting the armed incursion into Austria by Bavarian National Socialists as a brief exchange of gunfire, which, according to the Wolff News Agency,

> for reasons as yet unknown occurred on the German-Austrian border between *members of the Austrian* Defence Force and a *group* of hitherto *unidentified persons.*

It is hard to gauge the global impact that these types can achieve by presenting the situation of a country under siege as an "internal affair". This is the method pioneered by wartime military commanders and leader writers: a Berlin lawyer alludes to the PEN Congress as a "squabble among littérateurs", the compulsive liar speaks before the court of world opinion about a brief exchange of gunfire, and the Jewish "Honorary President" mentions minor disagreements. He even takes up the cudgels for "indigenous Bavarian traditions", of all things, and ends up assuring us that he

> *always objected to* Professor *Einstein being categorised as a German scientist.*

He had always made it clear that

> *the leading German Jews would welcome it if he moved his desk and his observatory to Jerusalem* or somewhere in America, *since science could lose nothing by this change of location and German culture could only gain.*

Max Naumann is his name, and he wrote it in the *Neues Wiener Journal.* This attitude justifies ten times over the anti-Semitism whose existence it denies. But the discovery that atrocity propaganda is based on lies remains unappreciated, however well it may succeed in assimilating to a morality that brands truth as lies—and to the new variant of the double liar. But these meretricious types, who deny the suffering of others to protect their own skin, are integral to this time and place. One solitary hope remains, constituting a possible justification: that the French bishops take the testimony of German Jews not to refute but rather to confirm—indeed accentuate—a peril that might yet be resolutely resisted.

10

TURNING HEADLINES INTO LIES

Here in Austria, where the crisis does not yet exert such coercion, they still insist on continuing the battle of the liberal soul for "Greater Germany", disregarding momentary difficulties. You see how far I have digressed from the Quarternary when I ask: What do you think about the *Neue Freie Presse?* About an enterprise whose shares had fallen below 25 cents and which suddenly received from somewhere a boost for its hope of national survival. We haven't yet reached the stage of a complete takeover, but a readiness to make concessions can be observed, suggesting that Hitler's irresistible moustache is taking precedence over Cleopatra's nose, which—as we recall from the World War—was one of her most beautiful features.[1] We mustn't take offence at the natural depravity of Lippowitz's *Neues Wiener Journal,* at its tendency to deny, suppress, and if need be falsify the facts and even turn headlines into lies. But what do those true believers who regarded the *Neue Freie Presse* as their bible have to say about that paper's initiatives? It is already prostrating itself so as to stay ahead of the game. Unlike its liberal colleagues in Berlin it does not want to be taken by surprise. Being one of the old guard, it surrenders but never dies—surrendering even before the battle has begun. It was the *Neue Freie Presse* which assured us in print that "tranquillity and order prevail" in the Third Reich and that "every German citizen of the Jewish faith can go about his business" at any time and even after the exclusion of Jewish doctors and lawyers from public office; and which on 31 March, on the eve of the boycott, printed the announcement by one firm that in their sphere of operations,

> which extend across the whole of Germany, there has not been a single case of persecutions or attacks on people who think differently or on members of foreign states, specific races, or religious communities.[2]

Yes, even on 2 April it reported having received "such a large number of telegrams and letters" that it was not in a position to publish them all, but still found space for the declaration that

> business activity has *so far* at no point encountered any disruption or obstacle arising from the political upheaval. Even the Jewish business world has *up till now* been able to conduct its affairs *unimpeded.*

The irrepressible frankness of these reports was admittedly qualified by the comical reservation

> *(These reports all derive from the period before the imposition of the boycott.)*

Could a more satanic insult ever be added to nonexistent injury than by the events that intervened on 1 April? Yes, by the symbolism of enclosing the truth of the matter in parentheses! Those telegrams derived from 31 March, long after the announcement of the boycott. But it was precisely after that announcement that such reassuring documents had to be produced, though even the *Neue Freie Presse* was no longer shameless enough to print such a mockery of the truth. Admittedly, the day before the boycott it was shameless enough to end its editorial with the prophetic words:

> *The anti-German atrocity propaganda will spontaneously dissolve into nothingness through the power of truth.*

How those prophets value a concept of truth that varies from day to day was revealed by the opening words of an editorial published a few days earlier:

> *What we wrote yesterday proves to be completely true.*

This is one of the most priceless statements it ever published. In addition it carries an announcement by the *Kulturbund* that none of the "intellectual personalities" associated with it has been affected in any way; and from the Touring Club stressing how happy its Jewish members are, especially in Chemnitz (where they were all already at Nazi Party Headquarters).[3] Atrocities are reported as if they were civil murders and without any indication of the milieu, as if the murderers were not "SA men" but simply "men"; political offenders in Austria get away with being identified only by their initials; when members of the Catholic Centre Party are maltreated, they are not even mentioned (a tactic the paper used to apply to me); the only thing it criticises, amid the bloodstained thuggery, is the dismissal of the conductor of the Dresden Orchestra.[4] A fraudulent report by the Wolff Press Agency it duly calls a "modification"; after a speech by Hitler it stresses the "Universal Approval of the German Press", including even the *Völkischer Beobachter*; and the *Neue Freie Presse* can hardly wait to assure Hitler that he has already achieved so much that he can now afford to be a little more tolerant. What golden words when the paper writes:

> In these tempestuous times there are *not only expressions of weakness, servility,* and rapid changes of opinion, *which we would prefer to ignore as*

> *we proceed to the business of the day, albeit with pained feelings,* but also proclamations *that betray true male courage....*

even though it probably doesn't mean the cases where, drowning the hurricane, it itself gave voice to protests such as

> (This Prussian spirit by no means precludes forbearance.—Ed.)
>
> (Such attacks are deeply to be regretted.—Ed.)

But this Jewish method falls short of the German madness, and the editorial, whose style alone belies the pro-German stance, shows that the intellectual vacillation so characteristic of Ernst Benedikt's moods now verges on panic. Admittedly this panic sounds muted rather than shrill. His words go pussyfooting around the hot potato hoping that it will cool down. Bomb attacks are not conducive to the national cause; radio propaganda disturbs brotherly relations with Austria instead of arousing sympathy; if despite all promises this propaganda continues, the task will be to avoid completely disappointing the expectation that new grounds for friction can be avoided, for sensitivity has grown; abusive pamphlets dropped from aeroplanes are counterproductive pinpricks. Such methods, the paper fears, will not advance the aims of the National Socialists in Austria but will only strengthen those who view Germany with suspicion and cast doubt on the peacefulness of its policies. On no account would the paper wish to be one of those, even if this means risking "naive questions" about the commercial advantages of taking the path of least resistance. It ventures to express regret

> that the popular agitation is *overshooting the traces.*

Never would the paper itself kick over the mark; and to this very day it sticks to the version that the assassination of Theodor Lessing "may well have been" politically motivated. Toscanini's refusal to conduct at Bayreuth merely "gives pause for thought". Many of its subscribers are also thinking again, scratching their heads and wondering whether it might not be simpler to take the *Deutschösterreichische Tageszeitung*, which is also written in bad German but produces far more atrocity propaganda. And they don't even notice the hidden subterfuges it practises in order to be tolerated in the Third Reich longer than Lippowitz. It has good reason to repudiate the "fake news" that "in a special edition for Germany it omits news items that might cause offence there and substitutes others". This it already does in the edition for Austria, not simply by omitting such items but also by faking them. For example, what does it make out of this sentence from *The Times:*

> In Great Britain there has never been very strong public support for the possible merger of the Austrian and German peoples. . . .

It conveys the opposite meaning, using emphatic type:

> *In England* there has never been *strong opposition* to the question of a possible *unification of Germany with Austria.*

A further passage from *The Times:*

> *The acts of violence* and *neglect of standards of conduct on the German side* and the *firm resistance* of the Austrian government have united British sympathies on the side of Dollfuss.

is toned down for the benefit of readers in the Berlin financial sector:

> *The attitude in Germany* and the *understandable opposition* of the Austrian government have brought English sympathies to the side of Dollfuss.

The speech at the Paris Socialist Conference by Hugh Dalton, formerly British Under-Secretary of State, is falsified so that the following passage:

> *The contempt* with which the Hitler government is regarded throughout England is on a scale hard to imagine. In England, despite the other grave antagonisms between parties and classes, there is on this question only one opinion, a single unified voice of revulsion.

is reduced to the simple sentence:

> The Hitler government receives *condemnation* throughout England.

But the paper won't escape the consequences of the correct version any more than the Hitler government will. Are the editors, like the German Jews, motivated by the wish to go about their business unimpeded? Without a doubt; but also by the outlook with which my Commercial Counsellors responded to the World War: "We've had a bellyful of them atrocities".

11

MURDER WITH MENDACITY

Using such set phrases as a form of exorcism satisfies the social needs arising from impoverished imaginations, never blaming the perpetrators but rather the victims and invariably those who report the deeds. Once again we experience the greater atrocity that people "can't credit it" and only believe those who, as chance observers, pass judgement on a segment of complexity which, however extensive it may be, cannot possibly cover the whole public sphere and certainly not everything at once. Unshakeable credit is given to people travelling through Germany who conclude from the fact that they've "seen nothing wrong" that nothing has occurred and everything is in order. Moments free of violence have been witnessed by many a traveller who is then able to give plausible eyewitness testimony, and that he has seen nothing can be confirmed by others who were in the same position. In times like these, people disregard the most basic logical question: whether that which is happening must always be visible everywhere or even visible at all; quite apart from the ethical question: whether it might not on the contrary be more correct deliberately to multiply a single case by a factor of ten, if this is the only way to draw attention to this particular case and, assuming it is done with conviction, to alert people's conscience to the possibility that ten times as many cases have in fact occurred. Doesn't what they say and what they deny suffice to convince us about their actions? Haven't the perpetrators of atrocities, which at one and the same time they photograph and deny, already admitted them by calling them a "reaction to propaganda"? Don't they, at least retroactively, make what were at first "lies" come true? (And retroactively almost legitimise the propaganda of the World War.) As if it were at all possible to tell lies on a large enough scale to counter the truth, and as if "telling lies" were a charge that systematic mendacity could level against others! How can someone stoop so low as to justify the denial of a murder on the grounds that it was merely grievous bodily harm and present this as an all-purpose alibi! What a base piece of knavery to allow this to allay our fears: taking it as proof that a just cause is being vilified by allegations about one of its victims being dead, whilst he seemed to horrified eyewitnesses to be lying there "as if dead"! As if there could be a formal record of the panic caused by such violence, or even the possibility of "reliable information" about it, when those affected are compelled to maintain the silence of the grave, even the wives and mothers of the victims:

> On the 16th of the month my dear husband passed quietly away.
> The funeral took place very quietly.
> *Through a misunderstanding* my husband has been snatched away from me. Silent sympathy is requested. . . .

Grief beyond words! How is "exaggeration" possible in a sphere where testimony, sympathy, and enquiry are precluded and the terror prompts fears that sufferings will increase and the infection of this preposterous danger spread further? Could there be a more ethical action than "propaganda" where there is even the faintest suspicion of "atrocities", a more mendacious, disreputable fiction than its denial? Naturally, such things are "beyond belief" and everything sounds invented, whether the reported atrocity is simple or sophisticated. But events too plain to be invented are authenticated by name, place, time, and circumstantial detail:

> A furnace worker was to be fetched from his flat. His wife asks for him to be allowed to stay at home and be interrogated there. Two blows round the head lay her flat on the hallway floor. The children come in, an eleven-year-old boy and a nine-year-old girl, kneel down, and raise their arms imploringly on behalf of their father and mother. An SA man takes his rubber truncheon and starts hitting the children.

Such reports become even more incredible when the action originates from the inventive fantasy of sadists:

> An unremarkable Jew supports his five children through the rag trade. Members of the SA come to his place and demand five hundred marks. He cannot give them this sum because he does not have it; he has probably never seen so much money in one place at the same time. They beat him until he lies whimpering on the floor. Finally he groans: "In the dresser there are 30 marks for the next rent instalment". They take the money. Then they force him to drink a full liter of castor oil, shove him inside a hessian sack, tie it round his neck, and drag him down into the cellar.[1] The oil has its effect. The man is left literally crouching for four days in shit and urine. His screams are heard from the street. A butcher releases him. When he emerges from the bathtub, his body has been eaten away by the filth as if he had been lying for hours bound hand and foot in an ant heap.

Merely one of the cases where it is still permitted to "impede an economic agent in his freedom to make decisions". One of the thousand cases where not a butcher but the European police should have intervened. One of the thousand cases which should prompt not only the audience that heard it but human beings of all races and religions to burst into shrill cries of outrage. Only this would give full weight to the comment:

> Many women were crying.

But the others don't believe it, and those who realise it is possible are appeased by the official explanation that it was a dispute between a few individuals and a rag-and-bone man, which they simply settled in their own way. And that he would have been spared if he had done a deal with such scoundrels, for he would then have had more than thirty marks in the dresser. "Regardless of any specific emotional proclivity"—as if such people had emotions or proclivities—they denounce atrocity propaganda as a tissue of lies and place their trust in tranquillity and order, now that the highest Prussian authority, Hermann Goering, has proclaimed:

> Every shot fired by an SA or SS man is *a shot fired by me.*

But worse than murder is murder with mendacity, and worst of all is the mendacity of those in the know, providing a pretext for ignoring the facts and believing the lies; the willingness to act as dumb as the violence demands; a cruel idiocy. No, there could not possibly be anything more deceitful and stupid than this conception of "atrocity propaganda", and whenever it crops up you can be sure that no atrocity could be as clumsily invented as the tactic of repudiation by guilty consciences; an ignominy only exceeded by the impulse to disbelieve what they know to be true, by the determination to treat what is unimaginable as if it were unreal, and by the sacrifice of any lingering sensitivity to the manipulative headlines that have hollowed out their hearts. And such blunted feelings, inured to horrors by clichés, further strengthen the practice of the manipulators. Thus reports that could cause anyone to lose his composure are composed in the following terms:

> *One can safely say* that millions of people in Germany are in danger of starving to death.

How then could any lingering sensitivity be capable of comprehending a murderously male system of oppression whose narrative is interrupted by alluring adverts for "Femina"? How could one imagine the bloodstained orgies of carousing mercenaries when on the very next line the rehabilitation of a nightclub follows, which—in contrast to an SA barracks—is rightly praised for "not being a cabaret for sadists"! How could the audience of this unbridled reportage feel pity for an elderly rabbi who has been tortured when on the same page they are distracted by the voluptuous experiences of a youthful company director? The correlative for this journalistic conception of humanity, which prostitutes misfortune as a marketing slogan and tells lies even when it speaks the truth, is the habitual response of readers who would only regain contact with mankind if they experienced one thousandth of what they refuse to believe. In case of doubt, blows on the head will teach them the truth about violence!

12

PURVEYORS OF CULTURE AND THE PEN CONGRESS

The purveyors of culture have completely adjusted to this situation, ignoring everything that doesn't concern them directly lest they endanger what does, helpless against what has already cost them dear in the expectation that everything will still turn out for the best. Faced by the strong-arm tactics of a coercive force that compels people to abandon their honour, no revolt seems conceivable within the restricted world of German politics, either by the nominal representatives of an imploding civil society or by a Social Democratic movement that was feeble and contemptible in its exercise of power, but every one of whose members now deserves sympathy. (Still, among the exceptions one needs to differentiate between workers who die under torture rather than pay lip service and leaders who are "fighting" after taking refuge abroad.) No protest was to be expected against the clampdown on journalistic prostitution from those engaged in it: why should something nonexistent—character and principles—not be made to "toe the party line"?

Some voices have been raised against the subjugation of a more significant intellectual life, voices at least powerful enough to put the silence to shame. Scholars and scientists like James Franck and Walter Johannes Stein, Max Planck and Wilhelm Koehler have courageously stood up against the insane agitation to turn universities into shooting ranges and politicise their seminars. Artists like Max Liebermann and Ricarda Huch have refused to follow orders to turn the Muses towards hero worship. Then there's the example of Thomas Theodor Heine, who finally withdrew from a milieu that had compromised itself at every turn after his discredited gang of fellow graphic artists had mobilised the powers that be against him. (Little good did it do Olaf Gulbransson: "Alexas did revolt . . . for this pains / Caesar hath hang'd him", as the bard puts it, while "Canidius and the rest that fell away have entertainment, but no honourable trust".)[1] Wilhelm Furtwängler, who wanted to keep his options open abroad by entering into dialogue with the Tyrant of the Muses, doesn't count since he has become a Councillor of State. Gerhart Hauptmann is said to have put his trust in the tyrant without too much soul-searching, and is now reconciled to the possibility of a brutal bricklayer like Mattern becoming Provincial

Governor of Silesia.[2] But when the literati demand that the German intelligentsia protest against the mistreatment of their peers, this comes from overestimating literature's ethical concerns and underestimating the scale of the calamity, its impact on the book trade being the least of its consequences. It was not the fate of people who write but of people in general that should have been opposed in word or deed: accompanied by public resignations from a position of honour which it would be contrary to human dignity to retain. (How I now regret not having been admitted to the Literary Section of the German Academy of Arts!) When a poet such as Hauptmann "holds his tongue", that's still better than when a journalist like Stefan Grossmann speaks; but it was to be expected that Hauptmann would distance himself a little from officialdom, lest he be taken as an official spokesman. For the sake of the intellect, whose eradication may not be apparent in every professional sphere. For eradication is certainly under way, though in literature less through demolition than through inflation of reputations. Over and above the parlous state of their profession, the intelligentsia has had to confront an oppressive force that threatens the whole human realm with capricious cruelty. What is the use of all the journalistic babble about the difficulties of defending a culture which has revealed its weakness by not mobilising either in self-defence or for a higher cause, either in the interest of literature or for the welfare of mankind, which has been robbed of more than just reading. For many, defiance took the form of distancing themselves from the outrage by anaemic language. Nor do any of these exiles demonstrate the ultimate courage of their convictions when they promptly pay their respects to Heine, himself not a genuine exile. But it is certainly touching that Grossmann, on returning home, cannot suppress his nostalgia:[3]

And I *found myself murmuring* those lines by the greatest German emigrant:

> Thinking of Germany at night,
> That's what puts my sleep to flight.[4]

Fortunately I've never quite lost my foothold on Austrian soil. . . .

Even the soil congratulates itself, while not ceasing to envy its German counterpart, which has dispensed with many who had no business to be there. Their efforts were in vain, for troglodytes are beyond reform. The worst thing about the cultural loss is the price paid in human lives! A mere trifle, even an hour snatched from the most insignificant of human lives, is worth a whole library destroyed by fire. The bourgeois intellectual enterprise, even as it collapses, is deluding itself if it devotes more column inches to the losses it has sustained than to the martyrdom of anonymous victims, the sufferings of a working class whose existential value has proved indestructible, both in its struggles and its readiness to provide mutual support. What a contrast to an enterprise which replaces solidarity with sensation and can nevertheless, to the extent that the atrocity propaganda is true, still turn it into lies! Journalism has a poor grasp of existential issues and fails to realise that when the simplest private life is a victim of violence, this is a more pressing intellectual concern than the whole discredited culture industry. And above all the sellout by journalists who shape the cultural horizon by glamourising theatrical wheeler-dealers and indulging in deep psychological analysis of their financial backers.

The evening edition of a Viennese daily may be agonising over the fate of Austria, but have they reported what Otto Preminger is planning to stage this autumn? All hell may be breaking loose, but the question still arises whether Max Pallenberg's guest appearance has been confirmed, and alongside reports of torture chambers we're kept informed about Kurt Robitschek's chamber theatre. Max Reinhardt, perennial fetish of enlightened thought, dazzles our eyes and ravishes our ears more than ever, and we read enraptured reports about the hocus-pocus of some nonentity with "genius worthy of the Führer".[5] All this may derive from the urge to find a substitute for what the Aryan cult has found under Hitler's direction. But it is still tragic that such trash should distract people from seeing what these Nazi spectaculars are leading to. The culture shmucks have got themselves a profitable sideline, now they've learnt to combine the spheres and give a political twist to backstage gossip. The cult of theatrical values, which you would have thought incapable of any further escalation, it is now intensified by auditions for the Third Reich. Fail on that score, and you forfeit any chance of your talent being overvalued, while the racial watchdogs on the other side are not to be trifled with either. That is why Herr Werner Krauss, magus of the north (and back there is where he belongs), a demon of middling talent whose journalistic celebrity in Vienna would have turned the head of a hundred Mitterwurzers, leaves in his wake what our high priests of culture are pleased to call "a rumble of ecstatic disgruntlement". This style of journalism, which defies all prescribed norms and is peculiar to Vienna, claims an advanced knowledge of the most invidious competitive practices and of the hatching of commercial plots normally intended for intellectual consumption only after the event. Quite apart from making you want to puke, there is nothing to gain from a systematic study of expectations in the theatrical world (including actresses who are expecting), even if the existential pressure in Berlin had not reached the current level of blackmail, to which critical reprisals in Vienna can now be added. The celebrities, who worm their way in wherever they can earn wages and reviews, do not change their convictions but adapt to those of their directorial and journalistic superiors. Besides the mediocrity formerly sanctioned by the press and now based on race, besides the motley throng milling round in full daylight to snap up roles from their colleagues, the upheaval in the theatrical world has also affected some who showed more courage and helpfulness than the journalists who make a living from their cares. Even if a bold decision had not restricted the impact of its headlines but permitted a tenfold larger type, journalism could never take the measure of any catastrophe since it is implicated in them all. Its complaint about damage to the cultural patrimony—a total distraction from the main issue—derives from a concept of solidarity in which the claims of humanity are reduced to special interests. This type of journalism is guided by instincts that ignore fundamental values and show no respect for misfortune. That's why, while revealing horrors that challenge the imagination, it still finds space for "piquant details", for instance the fact that a writer without talent, though capable enough as a man of the Left, was able to escape "without his toothbrush". But the damage to culture is infinitesimal, measured against the calamity that has overwhelmed the members of less problematic professions, faced with desperation and death, with the extermination of so many lives, both social and physical. Cultural damage claims attention through the tactics and resilience of professional survivors, an insurrection of bit players and dilettantes now making outrageous claims for compensation. Compared with the national festival that marked the boycott of Jewish businesses, the book-burning was a pantomime that made the whole of Europe laugh, being clumsy in its methods and counterproductive in its effects, since it revealed the barbarity of the perpetrators while generating publicity for the victims! It was certainly a good way to stir up the emotions of fellow authors, not to mention those directly affected. But the way the literary world that had been spared the flames profited from the panic; the shrewdness with which it responded to the damage others had suffered; the way it did its utmost to retain its dishonour—that could have aroused the suspicion of the vandals (were their instincts not so godforsaken as they are primitive) that they had got hold of the wrong victims. Although the calamity did not only affect the intellectuals, the responses they ventured in print were merely those of the burnt child who dreads the fire—or of the child yet to be burnt. Celebrities whose careers prompt them to proclaim convictions they may not actually hold have always occupied more space in the public sphere than society requires.

The situation becomes more dispiriting when the celebrity remains silent just when a statement would most urgently be needed, when one begins to detect secret panic and public cowardice, and when belated explanations are needed to make confusion more confounded. You will have guessed that I'm referring to members of the PEN Club, who followed their President, Felix

Salten, to Dubrovnik. A short time earlier he had carried out the daring idea of organising a tombola (with dancing) on behalf of German intellectual freedom:

> *There was great excitement at how Fortuna would decide the outcome.* Members of the *Ladies' Committee* chose the winning numbers from the wheel of fortune, and *great was the delight of those lucky enough to claim* one of the beautiful winning numbers their own. But even those who had drawn blanks *didn't let it dash their spirits.*

In a word, this is the milieu from which a manly protest against the moral and physical mistreatment of one's fellow authors was supposed to emerge. The Honorary President, "creator of celebrated animal stories" (*Bambi*!), a man sensitive to all living creatures when not out stalking them, had himself photographed "among his hunting trophies". A further photo showed him "at his writing desk" holding a gold balance, whose purpose is made clear by the inscription:

> "A true writer must weigh his words with the utmost care", says Felix Salten to his wife.

Which is why he chose not to make any statement in Dubrovnik, brushing off all requests for him to do so with the pretext:

> I am a Jew, and have never yet been interrogated on that subject in Germany!

So—just the opposite of the placard (promising never again to complain to the police), which some less fortunate than himself were forced to wear on their chest.[6] Evidently, this happy Felix does not want to complain about the Nazis, either. He doesn't interfere in Germany's internal affairs anymore that they do in his, so far. He doesn't want to get involved in the kind of controversies that created such trouble for Arthur Schnitzler, for whom he acted as a lifelong mentor. He has insured himself against fire damage; but the awkward question arises whether one can be assured that the policy will be recognised. And whether there is not at least an Index of members of the Jewish religious community and what will be the reaction of that community, to which this pedlar of innumerable allegiances has always belonged, having now even had his literary vocation confirmed by a carpet salesman.[7] The Jewish community was doubtless reassured when he "finally had to vote for the more hard-line resolution". How that came about, and what had gone before, in short "The Truth about the PEN Club Congress" was harder to make out from the hundred clarifications of the topic than the substance of a debate extruded by the fishwives of Dubrovnik, who would doubtless argue with greater style, logic, and linguistic verve, as befits their profession. One thing alone was clear: that even the "more hard-line resolution" expressly avoided any reference to those authors compelled to suffer torture for their convictions, while a lack of convictions enables others to travel to Dubrovnik. Both groups, in different ways, are open to the advice which Salten, once safely home, echoing Goethe, enunciated:

> "Happy the man who can shut himself off from the world without hatred. . . ."[8] To *shut oneself off* from the world, from the world as it is today, *at least for a time, to recuperate*, the better to reflect, *to regain* one's breath a little, and *a vestige of courage*, to cut oneself off time and again—*that's of prime importance*. And: *without hatred. Above all without hatred!* First, and foremost, that is what is required.

The repudiation of hatred is surely directed at me, but it is more important that the vestige of regained courage has led to his decision "not to take part in a debate against Germany" but rather seek out a "shared platform" based on communal destiny, indissoluble brotherhood, linguistic kinship, and all those similar notions extending from Walther von der Vogelweide to Grete von Urbanitzky, the much-publicised comrade-in-arms in Dubrovnik, who stormed off to consummate her Anschluss with the fatherland. Salten may have faltered, but he then regained courage. But though every word by a true writer must be weighed, like gold, with the utmost care, his stammering attempt to restore honour documents the moral and stylistic disposition of the literature over which this Goethean presides. How heart-rending his declaration must have been:

> That is the death-knell of the PEN Club!

"Speak for yourself!" would have been the response of Peter Altenberg (whom Salten claimed to have introduced to the wider world, but whose memory he compromised through his tacit support for Bekessy). For no one has yet discovered who benefited from the PEN Club banquets, nor how its members differ from the Rotarians, and these in turn from members of Berlin's elitist Schlaffaria Club, of whom it is rumoured that some are now toeing the party line, with the result that in future only Aryans may greet each other with the catchphrase "Lu-lu". As for the PEN Club, there is at least the recognition in the *Deutsch-österreichische Tageszeitung* that

> the president of the Viennese group, Felix Salten, *although a Jew, stood up against the way Germany was being treated. . . .*

On the other hand, he seems to have disappointed the Social Democrats, who made the creator of that woman of the people, Josephine Mutzenbacher, a

Viennese citizen, and the literary world too, which chose him as its spokesman; and there are many similar cases of people accused—unjustly—of abandoning principles they never possessed.[9] There has never been more absolute proof that a representative body becomes redundant the moment its clubbable stooges are faced, for the first and probably the last time, with defending the values they claim to represent. Embarrassed by all the pressure and turmoil, those stooges did finally reach a "resolution" but thanked their lucky stars that they didn't have to take a firmer stand than their feeble natures allowed. It would be futile to require such people to rise in revolt, even against the imprisonment of the former Radio chiefs Hans Flesch and Alfred Braun, against whom—after their arrest—suspicion of being true Europeans intensified, and whose awareness of cultural diversity is held against them by the ignoramuses now in power.[10] What contrasting images they are: those seeking a platform in Dubrovnik, and the six victims of torture, beset by wolf-like concentration camp guards and publicly humiliated by a sordid violence with which the platform-seekers collude. How that whole gang of wordsmiths and cultural freedom fighters, former flatterers of those now toppled from their posts, are put to shame by the action of General Ferdinand von Bredow, who with a single sentence rehabilitated what it means to be German by identifying with the victims and exposing his person to the barbarism which dishonours all things German.[11] That the barbarians were amused and Goebbels responded with a joke truly characterises the black mass of which we are speechless witnesses but makes it difficult to shut ourselves off from the German world "without hatred". Be that as it may, there are people who remain attached to that world by language, and the Teutoburg Forest, from which I have digressed during this wide-ranging review of events, will be hosting some strange hunting parties.

As for Benn, we left him behind in an even more primitive period of German history when there were not yet any featherbeds for refugees to lounge on, nor feather-brained philosophers trying to fool us. Even for Benn it's all finally becoming too much, so he says:

> But let's leave philosophy and go on to politics. . . .

But that doesn't produce anything sensible either, although he is expressly determined to turn from visions to the facts of experience. Here, too, he exaggerates. Acknowledging that the state is in a difficult position internally and externally, he nevertheless maintains

> that it would require *Iliads* and *Aeneids* to do justice to its destiny.

That may be, but it's doubtful if they will get written. And at this point, in view of all the difficulties of the situation, Benn speaks from the heart, reproaching the stateless ones for appealing to the international community and wishing upon a German state beset with difficulties

> a war to destroy that state, bringing collapse and ruination.

And yet:

> It is the nation *of which you are citizens,* whose *language* you speak, whose schools you attended ... *whose industry published your books,* whose theatres staged your plays ... and which would *not have done you much harm,* even now, *had you remained here.*

Certainly not grievous injuries, nothing worth mentioning. And given the guarantee that Benn tacks on, they might well have stayed, had not citizenship unfortunately failed to lull them into a sense of security. But if it is easy for someone to give advice from the safe harbour in which he finds himself, it is definitely more cowardly to advise others against seeking a safe haven themselves. Benn seems to think it was out of sheer arrogance that the refugees preferred hunger in Paris to a life of luxury in Berlin. One needn't necessarily share Goebbels's view that life as an emigrant is "ignominious". Exile, while more honourable than dancing to his tune, certainly gives no pleasure to those who, while tactfully sympathising, also begin to feel an aversion to their homeland. For it is sadly the case that other countries see exiles not merely as victims of political oppression but often also as representatives of a specific ethnicity. One can well imagine that many will succeed in reinforcing a prejudice against that ethnic group: their very presence will be responsible for propaganda running counter to German interests and repudiated by Germany. Is it not likely that Berlin literati will lay it on too thick in Paris, exploiting their hosts' magnanimity to the point where they themselves are regarded as "les greuel"?[12] One hears, for instance, of comparisons with "our German style of interior design" from which that of the host nation "comes off badly". At all events, the outside world would be far more impressed if Germany had not designed a lifestyle that caused emigration, for the new arrivals can be relied on to keep the outside world informed. But even if the homeland must bear responsibility for the consequences of flight, it unquestionably also had individual motives. The argument about the books produced by German industry is scarcely persuasive when they are put on the Index or burned outright, for which their authors might indeed have been prompted to feel grateful for reasons of publicity, though hardly likely to induce a sense of patriotic ardour. But German industry should not complain about the ingratitude of the emigrants, rather about the actions of the patriots who destroy their products and reduce their sources of income. As for linguistic kinship, Benn may be right to the extent that the writing of the refugees can be correlated with the speech patterns of those who remain behind (feeling at home without necessarily being retarded). For both the German written language and colloquial spoken German fall far short of the full potential of language. I believe that on the basis of this phenomenon I would be in a much better position to explain the essence of the German upheaval than Benn with his windy geognostic, indeed geomystical nonsense and his attempt at a metaphysical explanation of matters that are all too physical.

13

VERBAL IMPERIALISM: "GERMANY, AWAKEN! . . ."

A literary man sensitive to fine writing might even understand my position and recognise that, in the journalism and rhetoric of the new creed, we have not seen or heard a single German verbal expression that has not belied its purported content. Among the many neologisms inspired by the upheaval, this is already indicated by "Nazi", the concept on which a revelation of the World Spirit is supposedly based, together with other phrases that could never have been conceived or formulated before the onset of the new order. I don't mean those egregious formulations we encounter (in the Jewish press too), where, as a matter of principle, the handling of every word is inflected and distorted by twists and turns; nor the misuse of the dative, consistently treated as if it were the only grammatical case (*cassus*), thus revealing the war footing (*belli*) on which German journalists operate with their own language; nor the inability to convey the most undemanding intellectual content logically and maintain the simplest construction consistently; nor do I mean the persistence with which every propagandist for Greater Germany "*prescribes*" interference from abroad. Not even the muddle when Germany's National Socialist press exhorts its readers:

> *Germans, pursue* only Aryan newspapers!

Misprints, admittedly, can be revealing:

> *Germans*, take pride in your *notional* identity!

Nor do I mean the modest contribution to Anschluss made by the sister paper of the German press in Austria:

> Follow instructions as *proscribed!*

It is certainly shameful that on account of such exertions, which alas do not extend to any primer of German grammar, nationalistic German journalism must endure mockery from the most prominent illiterates on the other side. But for those living every day from hand to mouth, such lapses are not easily avoided, especially while the imperative is in force:

> *Clinch* your fists! Be prepared!

even though one of the incendiary slogans heard at the book burning was

> against the mangling of the German language! For the preservation of the most precious asset of our people!

Easily said, less easily done. If I were bold, I'd have foretold that if people whose linguistic sensitivity and grammatical knowledge enabled them to gain power and wealth by demanding that "Germany arise!" and "Every Jew dies!" were examined about the construction of those very phrases, they would have struck (or, as they insist on saying, "stricken") difficulties. They certainly don't know that a comma is needed here, since each of the named nations is being hectored not in a second-person address, but in the third person, so that the action called for—arise or die—is not an imperative but an optative, merely expressing a wish, which particularly in the case of Jews would scarcely be appropriate. If, for example, in a comparable passage from Schiller's *Fiesko*, we were to read "Verderben, gehe deinen Gang!" ("Perdition, take your chosen path!") without the comma, it would be an address not to perdition but to some political leader on whose path perdition might well follow. The exclamation mark does not in itself signify a command, it could simply intensify the wish. Still, we can accept that the punctuation error in the quotation about Germany and Jews has some justification, given that those brusque demands would be weakened were they expressed more carefully. After all, the Caesars were always above grammar, so better for those campaigning for autarchy to speak bad German than to use foreign words they can never really understand. (For example: "dynamic" or "synthesis".) It is precisely the attempt to replace them that has led to that enrichment of German vocabulary which is the envy of other nations. But this enrichment also results from the expanding needs of trade and commerce, a development which—at the end of the day—justifies the unthinking adoption of Jewish idioms and an acceptance of the inflated patois of profiteers already in vogue among republican authors. So now all variants of the primal soul's awakening can claim to be "one hundred percent guaranteed"—with "expedited delivery". What is exceptional, however, is the ability to continue in this creative spirit with true-to-type neologisms that adapt language to the needs of the regime's profound duplicity and accentuate its sanctimonious bent, the tendency to draw a veil over ignominious actions. Virtually every communiqué adds further examples of violence disguised as the norm, as when forcible entry into someone's home is described as "rehabilitation". Or when failure is presented as imminent success and someone stretches the facts by reporting that a rival militia has been "deconstructed". Even I have no choice but to register the new atrocities of word and deed that are embedded every day, such as "Reichskulturkammer", "Gaukartei", "Reichsschaft", "Fachschaft", "Reichfachschaftsleiter", "Gaukulturwart", "Werberat", and all ranks down to "Blockwart".[1] As ever, I turn to Goethe for a response:

> A new word irks you? But how narrow-minded
> To ban all but the old familiar kind! It
> Shouldn't matter, there are more in store.
> Surely you've heard the strangest things before. [6265]

The most disturbing feature of the massive expansion of hallucinatory idioms is surely the use of innumerable "disguised" expressions, which German nationalists would attribute to the guys from the ghetto were they not using them to conceal heartfelt German impulses. Or consider "schlagartig" ("at a stroke"), suggesting an astonishing and indeed shattering blow, used to signal both the start and the end of a boycott. And—not to forget the central issue—that weasel word "Gleichschaltung" (alignment), that coercion to toe the party line which cannot even promise to spare us the sight of VIPs. It's true that Goebbels, with his profound knowledge of the journalistic vernacular, imposed a prohibition on reporting formal state occasions in language "appropriate to former times", for instance by referring to "the cream of society", which might offend those who are now on top (foremost among them Goering, who repeatedly uses such phrases for that very reason). But now that newspaper reporters have to toe the party line, the resultant language will be a poor substitute for what was once "an object of love and delight to the human race".[2] There can be no doubt that, in all matters of substance, this language signifies a compelling disruption of nature's harmonising tendencies, a plenipotentiary power as inventive as that which dispatched "human raw material" to the trenches in the World War.

This procedure, which makes short shrift of human lives, already encompasses the syntax and stylisation of the ideas which constitute this system of violence. Primarily the terminology, of course, which must adjust to the pressure to save time and gain space. The subversion of language, its enrichment through abbreviation, to which we owe such phantom phonemes as Hapag and Wipag, Afeb and Gesiba, Kadewe and Gekawe, and all the magic formulae promulgated by the same law that now gives us Osaf and Gausaf.[3] One no longer knows what is more ominous: intrusion by the Gestapo, the Fepo, or the Uschla, protest by the NSBO, or compliance by the DHV; while the writing on the wall, *Mene Tekel Upharsin*, prophesying the destruction of a kingdom, could only be a Metufa film. But since the inception of the SA and the SS, an SOS to the USA is our only option.

So long as these techniques for the exclusion of language do not reduce us to reading the runes, they offer ample scope for "alignment". But sometimes it is as if Germany's expansionist drive were also asserting its entitlement to annex further living space for the German language, disrupting the very boundaries of thinking in words. One can see that such verbal imperialism strongly resists usages which seem, from its perspective, to contain traces of the suppleness and informality of the hated âme latine, which since the war have indeed been relentlessly subjected to a punishing process of "Germanisation". Consequently, "Monsieur" as a title is reduced to "Herr", but, in more ill-bred times, public conveniences, even those reserved for expressions of the âme latrine, came to be designated "Männer" and "Frauen". (It is a personal idiosyncrasy of mine that, here as elsewhere, I reject Nietzsche's no less German diminutives "Männlein und Weiblein"—likewise the "Hojotoho!" and "Wagalaweia!" of Wagner's whooping Valkyries and Rhine maidens.) But when the two sexes are gathered together in public, they are still customarily addressed as "Meine Damen und Herren"—on the model of "Mesdames et Messieurs". The possessive pronoun lightly hints at camaraderie, not the aim of seizing possession. That sense was first enacted in the German Reichstag, when—at a stroke—we were confronted with the inscrutable formula:

> "Meine Männer und Frauen!"

Since the plural "my wives" is hardly compatible with possession as normally understood, at least in the West, we are left instead with a retinue of henchmen and henchwomen, fully compliant with the Führer Principle. Whether we call this expansionist drive or verbal assault—new linguistic territory would be conquered.

14

SELF-REFUTING RHETORIC AND THE PRICE OF BUTTER

But Benn may believe that polished German is not required, now that the enemy is once again being addressed so bluntly, since one should be no more scrupulous with language than with anything else. Perhaps he subscribes to the significant principle recently proposed by a leftist thinker:

> Belief in the immutable sanctity of the word, the inviolability of language

(is not advocated, quite the contrary)

> *seems to me to be a prejudice* favoured by the powers that be and calculated to eliminate the poet as the creator of living form.

I certainly don't think that any powers that be would have much time for my conception of language. My view, on the contrary, is that any creation of living form capable of challenging those powers would be inspired by the belief that language is indeed inviolable. I admit, however, that to journalists this belief must appear an even greater prejudice than the rule of law does to burglars. Sadly, the prejudice repudiated by journalists, unlike that scorned by burglars, cannot be judicially upheld, since the powers that be are infinitely less interested in intellectual property than material property. Think what recognition and protection a man of property would have if the state took the following statement to heart:

> Intellect is not something metaphysical. Intellect is rooted in *reality*.

A thought that is surely worth its weight in gold! I suspect that if I drew Benn's attention to an ungrammatical construction, he too would wave the prejudice aside and stress only the creation of living form as his goal. But even on the basis of some syntactically inoffensive sentences I could demonstrate the refutation of his thought by his language. Its fraudulence extends right through to his invocation of the terrors of the Apocalypse.

Hence, he can't resist the kitsch of a sentimental appeal to homegrown patriotism either, imagining that the following scenes will be revealed to refugees encamped on the Mediterranean coast:

> Just cast a glance at the sea stretching away towards Africa. *Perhaps at this very moment* a battleship *is ploughing through* it with Negro troops, some of the six hundred thousand colonial troops of the notorious Forces d'Outremer to be mobilised against Germany, perhaps also at the Arc de Triomphe or the Hradčiny Castle in Prague, and swear an oath against Germany, a country, that has no political objective but to secure its future ... an oath of revenge.

Of course, what he means—except that "perhaps" is the wrong link—is that another group of refugees is looking at the Arc de Triomphe and yet another at the Hradčiny Castle in Prague—something you can't readily do from the sea, except in Shakespeare's *Winter's Tale.* Be that as it may, even in warlike dealings with those Negro troops there may—perhaps—be greater guarantee of safety than Benn has promised to returning refugees, given their doubts about Dachau. As for the active treatment of Negroes, one can cast a fairly confident glance at the Colonial Exhibition in Berlin, which has just opened under the slogan:

> "German lands in foreign hands!" Always remember—and always work for what we have lost.

Memories are on display of a heroic colonial army and its "brave black Askaris", who now revert to their savage origins "in foreign hands". We must

> *educate* our youth *in the colonial idea.* To become worthy successors to our pioneers and first settlers of the land, whose work and achievements

(disregarding the brutal occupation of Cameroon under Jesco von Puttkammer of "Putkamerun" fame)

> stand alone, untarnished and exemplary, in the colonial history of the nations.

For self-righteousness is at work, in spite of judicial reform; and the Colonial Exhibition is

> a monument with a message for its visitors: We shall never forget you—*we must get you back!*

Which actually leaves it unclear whether it is only the Germans who want to get the colonies back, or also the colonies who want the Germans back. So we may revert to language, which I believe is better cared for in France itself—if not in the French colonies—and similarly under the Hradčiny Castle, than by German newspapers and their readers, irrespective of their political affiliation.[1]

I'm speaking of these nations' own languages but also of how sometimes even German is spoken there. The claim that the sole aim of Germany, where language is treated as if it were in protective custody, is to secure its own future—something that seemed impossible to the refugees, for their part—that at least sounds more modest than envisaging one of the most magnificent revelations of the World Spirit.

But Benn is promptly off again into some prehistoric past, for the arguments of his opponents sound "as if they come from another geological era", which would actually bring them closer to his own. As for present-day society, to which he returns his attention, he's been told, and can

> therefore confirm that the German worker is better off than before.

Benn cannot repeat this often enough, and though he doesn't specifically talk of nutrition, he assures us that workers now

> enjoy the feeling of being alive in all its shifting forms.

That may be literary journalese (and none the better for that), but he urges his opponents to rest assured that the struggle continues, for the German national community is something which I would never have guessed, namely

> no vain delusion.

Indeed, he goes so far as to avow that this year of 1933 has

> reaffirmed a fundamental segment of the Rights of Man

which is only credible insofar as this segment has permitted the destruction of another. He also passes over his opponents' appeal to his "radical feeling for language", something I might challenge more effectively by reference to the phrasing he uses to do so. Then he addresses his people, as they clear a path for him, in emotive terms spawned by the high and mighty, but which today even the aged Attinghausen from Schiller's *Wilhelm Tell* would have disdained:

> Who am I to stand apart, am I then wiser—not at all!

Such pathos leaves me cold, however familiar I am with the language of his people. But he has his people to "thank" for it, people from whom his ancestors have descended and to which his children will return. He is resolved to guide them according to his powers, and were he to fail, his people would still be his blood brothers—his "Volk":

> "Volk"—that's saying something!

For there are moments when this whole anguished world sinks out of sight, and there remains only:

> "Volk".

Sounds great, but misses the point that other nations also exist, and if each were to think of itself as the chosen one, the Apocalypse would be child's play compared with the worst that is yet to come. But what does Benn care for Europe! He feels only scorn:

> This Europe! It may have values—but when it can neither bribe nor *shoot,* it's pitiful to behold!

That's exactly why every German must learn to shoot. Benn goes on to compare Hitler with Napoleon, preferring Hitler since he is indistinguishable from his movement, while Napoleon was merely an individual genius. He embarks on character studies of great men, who have in common "an abnormal lightness of being in all things, notably in their organic functions". In support of this, he then argues that the "principles underlying his interpretation" are the same as those of Fichte, Burckhardt, and Nietzsche—Hegel also gets a mention—but above all recalls his own "fanatical purity", to which the refugees, too, have appealed. One wonders how long he will sustain this purity as he fights for the cause, especially with such intellectual ammunition. But it is not without interest to turn the page of the newspaper in which he makes his appearance, for there an editorial warning turns the tables on his irrational confidence and insight into the Quaternary:

> In politics one *should not underestimate everyday things* either, things that are of immediate concern to the people.

Certainly not! But haven't we heard that the German worker's feeling of being alive exists in all its shifting forms and that he is better off than before? Yes, we have, but nevertheless:

> In recent weeks, following the margarine directive, a rise in the price of all fats has been recorded. The price of butter rose from a low of 84 marks to 120 marks per 50 kilograms.

There follow examples of the "effects" on consumers.

> In some places, notably in southern Germany, prices have risen even higher; in Munich some 200 traders have *been dispatched to the Dachau* concentration camp, *moreover* on charges of profiteering.

This lapidary phrase "moreover" is like that in Kant's essay *On Perpetual Peace*; but the method is more reminiscent of Shakespeare's irate monarch whose Fool recommends as a remedy:

> Cry to it, nuncle, as the cockney did to the eels when she put 'em i' th' paste alive. She knapped 'em o' th' coxcombs with a stick and cried, "Down, wantons, down!" 'Twas her brother that, in pure kindness to his horse, buttered his hay.[2]

But he couldn't afford butter now, even if all the traders in Dachau were to be beaten with a stick. For the reduction of butter and milk prices will hardly be as successfully implemented as current plans have been for the reduction of consumers or indeed, to a certain extent, of the unemployed, of whom it is officially stated:

> The solution of the unemployment problem, on which *all efforts* must now be *concentrated*, is *at the end of the day* decisive for the success of the German revolution.

It is also reported that northern fishermen (putting their salt-racked hands together to thank their god for sending the Reich a ruler in its hour of need) are already complaining about their daily wage of 20 pfennigs. But the *Deutsche Allgemeine Zeitung* also cites otherwise unwelcome revelations about the economy, which as early as 25 May led it to conclude just how imperative it is

> for the measures taken to be *hammered out* both in a technical and a psychological sense.

That is to say, not merely in the physical sense that is the movement's strong point. Once again, Benn's principles are more of a philosophical and geological nature. But I would have been more than satisfied with his account, which is such an incomparable eye-opener, were we not experiencing a plethora of volatile formulations and distortions that defy any attempt to describe them.

15

RUBBING SALT IN THE WOUND

Responding to the prospect opened up by Benn, I would rather derive my insights from a vision that deals not with the birth of the new man but with the destruction of language as touchstone for authentic being, capable of exposing the vernacular spoken by the Volk today, for which the Volk will one day be held responsible. From whatever spiritual underworld—remote from the World Spirit—that vernacular may emanate, its analysis will carry more conviction than attempts by the Office for Racial Purity to establish "whether there is any trace of Jewish blood". Verbal analysis will trace those bastardised linguistic forms back through the world of commerce to the point where venerable metaphors are betrayed by a new reality. And for someone intimate with language, what revelation could be more astonishing, what spectacle more striking than the sight of the empty husk of a word suddenly filling again with the blood that was once its content? How welcome if this blood were indeed merely a metaphor: a sanguinary thought attesting to the authentic circumstances in which the word was born; but as terrifying as the Gorgon when an outpouring of physical blood starts to flow from within the protective linguistic crust. (In the new faith, though its followers don't yet realise it, it signifies the miracle of transubstantiation.) Look how the renewal of German life has enabled an old phrase to return to its origin in some dire event in the past, losing its figurative applications! For the true philosophical sense of this process: when, for the first time in political history, the core meaning discards later accretions and something like bloodstained dew remains as a coating on the verbal bloom—this also applies when we see the metaphor retracted into the realm of reality. When these politicians sworn to violence still use phrases like "holding a knife to an opponent's throat", "shutting his mouth", or "ruling with an iron fist"; when they are forever "making a fist of it" or threatening "a bare-knuckle fight": the only really astonishing thing is that they still use such expressions for actions they are not actually carrying out. The government that "will crush anyone who opposes it with all necessary brutality"—does just that. "Throwing someone out" of the German Workers' Front denotes a throat injury, inflicted by the leader concerned, while total renunciation of any figurative sense is evident in the promise made by the President of Württemberg:

> We don't say: an eye for an eye, a tooth for a tooth. No, if someone puts out our eye, we'll cut off his head, if someone knocks out our tooth, we'll shatter his jaw.

Such things also occur without any precondition. And this re-vindication of the content of a proverbial expression infuses all turns of phrase where originally bloody or violent content has long since been transposed onto the plane of intellectual conflict. There is no variant, however subtle, that is immune to this process—not even the terrible "rubbing salt in the wound". It must once have happened, but people had forgotten it and renounced all thought of physical violence, so that this completely faded from consciousness. It was applied to the aggravation of a sense of loss, of some form of spiritual suffering. The idiom is still with us, while the action from which it derives no longer comes to mind. Until now:

> When the old comrade inflicted a deep cut on his hand while peeling potatoes, a group of Nazis laughed mockingly and forced his heavily bleeding hand into a sack of salt. They found the old man's cries of agony a great joke.

It is unimaginable, but since it happened, the phrase can no longer be used. Or take "to get off with a black eye". Nowadays, not everyone manages figuratively to escape so lightly; some don't manage it literally either. It was a metaphor, once. It only remains one if the other eye was blackened as well, or not even then. And the obsolete phrase "fits like a fist in your face", used for taking someone's measure, has turned up again, for fists have flattened faces so often as to become commonplace. The hackneyed phrase revives and dies by the same token. In every area of social and cultural renewal one observes this awakening of cliché into action. Defying technical progress, it survived a world war in which swords were drawn and gas warfare was balanced on a knife-edge. Such figures of speech won't survive the losses of this revolution.

> That's why we have no choice but *to plunge in the knife*. Mere *pinpricks* hold no terrors for us.

The knife, destined for the Nazis' former German-Nationalist allies, has long ceased to be a metaphor. The pinpricks remain metaphorical as a means of resistance not yet used against the oppressor, although anything is possible. They have everywhere reinstated the full reality of "running the gauntlet" and especially of the pillory, which since the Middle Ages has been no more than a crumpled piece of paper. Those who "trample corpses underfoot" actually do so. It's all there, down to the last crumb, except there's no bread. Otherwise, one can safely take them at their word: they'll keep it. They can, of course, claim that "they won't harm a hair on the head of any Jew", since it's evidently the only treatment that wasn't inflicted, while many a Jew lost the skin off his scalp or had his head shaved so as to be branded with the sign under which the Nazi Idea has conquered. Among the rich supply of atrocities it has devised, one statesmanlike imagination expressly denied the possibility that anyone had

> had their fingernails extracted or an earlobe nipped off.

This is unlikely to be contradicted by reality; indeed, "a prize could safely be offered" to anyone establishing instances where it has occurred. Such a fantasy prize will just as difficult to win as the Olympic prize for a poem on Liberty, Love, Beauty, and God.

16

POETS AND BARBARIANS

Still, the groundwork has been done, the soil loosened, the asphalt removed! And there can be no mistaking the professional competence of a programmatic purge that reflects the anti-Semitism of Adolf Bartels, whose discontent with the modern era is reciprocated. There are sensational developments in every economic sector of the Nazi movement: fists appear from nowhere, dealing out occasional punches and grabbing anything that is not screwed down, in a tragic farce that extends to the cultural sphere. The fate of Philemon and Baucis is played out afresh every day in summerhouse colonies, allotments and smallholdings, and the expropriation of their little property at the hands of Mephisto's three burly henchmen occurs in the form of legalised criminality or naked theft.[1] But the rule of law by decree tolerates other arbitrary instances of metaphor coalescing with hard facts: a dilettante dreaming of laurels during sleepless nights grabs a handful from land seized with the help of the SA. In literature, too, there have been reported cases of unscrupulous competition ending in bloodshed. Authors who use their elbows, sometimes quite literally, to thrust aside Jews suspected of coining it quicker'n'slicker quite rightly define themselves as the "Kampfbund" (Fighting Unit). The new order operates as violently as the seismic force in Walpurgis Night:

> My forbears, Night and Chaos, saw
> Me help the Titans in their war.
> Ossa and Pelion like balls we used
> And hurled, like children much amused,
> Till, tiring of our game, we smiled
> As wanton boys do, while we piled
> Those twin peaks up—a wicked jest—
> Now Mount Parnassus' godly crest. [7558]

The "Kampfbund" are bloody amateurs! They too have turned a catch phrase into a reality.

At last the book market will be opened to aspiring authors whose entitlement arises from their previous failure to gain access to it—this is the purpose of the

"Blacklist".[2] Actually, the hope of gaining access is an even more fatal misconception than that commonly harboured by those who had monopolised the market. The intention to discredit the latter and satisfy the former was precisely what led to a Blacklist in the first place—the Index of books prohibited from crossing the threshold of the Third Reich, though it should not be thought of as some Leviathan which has devoured every Jew. Instead, it is an assortment of works that have struck it lucky, including those that were burnt, which are marked with a star and will consequently survive as objects of curiosity. But into this list, which I calculate to contain no more than 191 authors and two anthologies, stray Aryans have also found their way, apart from individual works that are in any case destined for oblivion.[3]

Naturally, it puzzles me why Waldemar von Bonsels, who rushed to join the bandwagon, has been given approval for "everything except" *Maya the Bee* (and two other works); and why Franz Werfel's *Barbara*, of all books, has passed muster—something Sigrid Undset appears to have misunderstood, since she has expressed her pleasure at that decision. One can't help noting (without gloating) that Alexander Lernet-Holenia's *Poems* have been spared. On the other hand, it is a source of genuine satisfaction that, despite his tribute to Horst Wessel, Hanns Heinz Ewers ("Hah! Hah!" for short) could not save his erotic shocker *Alraune*. The French press had already trumpeted:

> A pornographic author, literary dictator of the Third Reich!

His best work, especially that which links him with the sexologist Magnus Hirschfeld, is now dependent on the Austrian book market. Since it has become advantageous to denounce people, I could seize the opportunity to harm him further by revealing that he once extolled Jewishness, and in particular Heinrich Heine, whose name has recently been removed from a street sign in Chemnitz for reasons made quite explicit:

> It may be appropriate to draw the public's attention to the fact that Heinrich (Harry) Heine (1798–1856), after whom this street has hitherto been named, was a Jewish poet ill-disposed to all things German. The idea that one should "revere all that is noble and sacred" was . . . unknown to Heine . . . and he dragged all things German in the dirt.

But Ewers has asserted that the heart of this poet was nothing less than

> A singing lute! . . . It was a jewel of the Holy Grail,
> That still today and in distant times to come
> Shall sing in glowing colours of the world and all its glories.

And if that's not enough, I could also reveal that he adapted a poem from the Yiddish, a veritable curse against the persecution of the Jews:

> Though he wander the world, and live where he might,
> The blood libel taints the haunted Semite.
> So Russia, God grant you—never respite!
> And woe to all nations with whom you're allied,
> And shame on the man who *may have fought* by your side!

Obviously, I only cite this because of the clumsy subjunctive—bad grammar in a good cause. And it is, after all, directed against Russia:

> A curse—of pains and groans and dread—
> Let this curse strike you—and strike you dead!

In this context he could always quote August von Platen, a good German who composed even better poetry, not merely adaptations. Although he's not referring to the Jews, Platen too is writing about Russia:

> Though we be crushed and ground to dust,
> Their legions are but slaves,
> New flowers shall bud and grow—a host!—
> From the rotting wood in our graves.
> Then, when the last sword is shattered,
> Happy the man who dies!
> *From our bones that now lie scattered*
> *The avenger shall arise!* ('Gesang der Polen')

The avenger arising from his grave ("exoriare ex ossibus ultor")—how easily that can be made to rhyme in German! But more than that:

> Come now, one and all,
> You men, draw near!
> You alone do I call,
> Only outcasts should hear!
> Flee from the land
> Of your birth! Let each one
> Put a burning brand
> To his house and be gone! ('Eamus Omnis Execrata Civitas')

Exactly the attitude that Benn finds so reprehensible! And this is what Platen's refugees say:

Onto our huts the driving snow descends,
So gather round the fire outside, my friends,
Feel free to sing, by way of consolation,
A song to curse the cause of all our tribulation.

. . . .

You laurel wreaths, when forebears won the day,
Are you in truth so withered all away?
What once we watered, tree of liberty,
Your shoots no longer rise to make us free?

Were we not once a Volk like any other,
Do we deserve a tombstone ere we wither,
Buried by the fiend beneath that stone?
So he can, like a thief, steal all we own?

. . . .

Guilt-ridden conqueror, inflicting yet more damage,
Even on our children's thirst for knowledge?
Their history book lessons no longer free,
Their treasures sealed under lock and key?

. . . .

But to heaven we raise our lamentation,
And poets shall think it their vital vocation,
Through lands near and far, to make our case,
And inflict on you—brute!—eternal disgrace.

Man's soul is armed, that is quite plain,
Else God had made the world in vain,
A globe to crawl on—so defined,
A worthless plaything for you and your kind!

But though under your heel we were made to groan,
Your sons and their sons shall surely atone.
A golden-maned lion shall one day smile
And smash the teeth of the crocodile! ('Klaglied der Verbannten')

And this:

The enemy split asunder, many are now content,
Yet all the while Nemesis swirled
Round the victor's tent.

Triumph turns to disaster when
Its fruits are the lamentation of men
And *the boundless hatred of all the world.* ('An einen deutschen Fürsten')

And this:

Is your shoulder not breaking,
Your weary shoulder aching?
For the hatred of all Europe
Weighs upon you, Autocrat! ('Monolog an einen Selbstherrscher'),

And this:

He played at God,
That he could do,
Honoured by the many,
Magnificent, too—
An achiever through and through.
But every law he undermined,
And though all-powerful of his kind,
One still must add—
He was so bad!

Temples he built
to the very Devil,
but now let his guilt
bear the mark of his evil,
And brand stigmata
On the back
Of the man who put others on the rack—
A torture he devised.
But he's been recognised.

. . . .

He wove a tangled web of shame,
Atrocities and horror.
Unravelled, now they bear his name,
The cause of constant terror.
A villain he has ever been,
A heartless villain, quite obscene,
Unlike any ever seen.

So, Furies, fill his bitter cup
To the brim, fill it up! ('Unterirdischer Chor')

Even Benn will surely not deny that our language can express such emotions, although here the cause of Poland is being defended against Russia. But there is comparable power in the text cited by a French newspaper, when an American officer dedicated the lilies he laid on a London grave much visited by foreigners:

> If the unknown English soldier could speak to the American recruit, he would say that he prefers this simple flower to the crown of a murderous dictator that tarnishes this memorial.

But Platen at times felt that silence was the stronger answer when defining his response to his own people:

I'll pack up all I have,
Heart's treasure put in store,
What the kindly god gave
Me, avails me no more.

. . . .

Dissemble, then, Muse,
Bewilder the foolish crowd!
Though the tyrant's henchmen accuse
Me, I pass by, head unbowed.

The censor has cast a murderous glance
At the book that lies on his knees,
My songs he's perverted, at every chance
Destroyed my harmonies.

Though I perforce must hold my tongue,
I now see it was silly
To show a public face among
A *people bent on folly.*

So, poet, you should not complain,
The loss to the world is small,
To be German born—earth's old refrain—
Is the worst thing of all. ('Epilog')

His fatherland preferred Heine, in spite of his race—Heine, who piled ignominy on Platen by attributing to him a sexual disposition which today would be considered normal, and which perhaps explains his sultry fusion of mysticism and manly self-control. Platen, in one of his noble sonnets, makes do with "Let better ones be crowned" (not that this includes Heine), but that he be allowed to depart:

> Yes, let my fatherland be scorned!

And he asks:

> On the Rhine and the Danube, what would you choose
> To compare with the acme of Ancient Greece?
> Journals, newspapers, and their reviews,
> Tobacco and beer and chiefs of police?
>
> What you never knew, in mutual reflection:
> Freedom and art, where the sun ever shines,
> Each bestows on the other the crown of perfection,
> And you think yourselves Greeks, you Philistines!

Such is the level of culture of those who "botched all they attempted", but:

> From an ocean of fools a few swimmers
> Of genius are exempted. ('Sonette 76')

Like Goethe, he knows how distant the German language is from the language of Germans and the poets from the German people. He can express this in patriotic language without being a compatriot of the others:

> Ingratitude severs the bonds at last,
> Combined with hatred to rebuff
> My honest love: the die is cast,
> O my country. Enough is enough! ('Sonette 77')

Platen knows whereof he speaks, like Hölderin's Hyperion with his curse on the Germans: "Barbarians from time immemorial, grown more barbaric still through diligence and science and even religion".[4]

> Land of trouble and bitter
> Self-denial, I'll leave you now without a sigh,
> Escape constraint by thousandfold fetters,
> The scourge of drudgery until you die.
>
> . . . .
>
> If you hate what is base with all your heart,
> And your fellow men begin to spout
> Their servile praises, it would be smart
> To renounce your homeland, and then get out!

From this infantile race you had better depart
Than stay yoked to the hatred of some thuggish lout! ('Dies Land der Mühe, dieses Land des herben Entsagens')[5]

A hundred years later German professors stand to attention as the treasure chest of books is sealed up and follow the stormtroopers to the celebrations of a servile people:

> *Johann Wolfgang Goethe University,*
> Frankfurt
>
> Frankfurt, May 1933
>
> *The Student Volunteer Corps invites all professors to the burning* of Marxist and other pernicious writings, which will take place on the Römerberg on the evening of Wednesday, 10 May.
>
> *In the light of the great symbolic importance of the ceremony, the students would welcome the presence of the entire professorial body.*
>
> *Accordingly, I invite colleagues to attend in large numbers.*
>
> The procession, with musical accompaniment, will *march* from the University to the Römerberg on Wednesday evening at 8 pm. The student fraternities will participate in *uniform, as will the SA battalions.*
>
> Signed: Krieck
> Vice chancellor

What does Nietzsche say? "An age of barbarism begins, the academy will do its bidding!" And "Turning towards things beyond the German realm has always characterised the most capable of our people".[6] Platen was already convinced of this; like Hölderlin, he spoke "for all who live in this country and who suffer, as I have suffered". This is how he took his leave:

You, whose malice renews the paste
That mixes foolishness with bad taste,
So that only vulgar people thrive,
Daily more rabid and prone to survive:

so when "once the mischief these lying rogues deploy has stepped over every conceivable line", it would be too late to ask back one whose soul had already become estranged. He would decline:

"The Alps he'll nevermore traverse
His mission among us is complete!"
Silence shall be my revenge, my curse! ('Sonette 86')

But one cannot assume that he would have remained at his post, silently, in today's academy!

Ewers, however, who like Platen gave voice to his rage against tyranny, even if he took a different line on Heine, now writes in the preface to his confessional *War Primer*:

> That *old warhorse*, who even in his duelling fraternity days wielded a mean blade, is one of nature's *exemplary, inspirational, potent, colossal, blond, blue-eyed, ever-helpful, kindly, almost wise*

(I'm almost out of puff!)

> *Teuton*, who the instant *truth takes up cudgels with lies and hypocrisy, rises up like a giant*, and *with impassioned, exuberant, unshakeable conviction, defiant in the face of death, reaches for his sword.*

Given such aptitude to be one of Hitler's Praetorian Guard, it required—since at the time he was in America—

> the entreaties *of his mother and friends* ***to deter*** him from a daredevil attempt ***to embark*** *on* a voyage ***to reach*** his homeland.

His use of the German language is less exemplary than his German sentiment—these three infinitives!—for

> the sabre-fencing scars from his student years would have only too easily *disclosed* to the *vigilant British the true nationality* of the pseudo-American.

And yet he would dauntlessly have risked the journey had he not preferred to stay put and devote himself to propaganda activities, both spoken and written. Combating the anti-German atrocity propaganda that was already making itself felt. He opposed it by singing:

> Blood cannot be gainsaid,
> Through blood we must wade,
> Till it spills over our boots!

More specifically:

> Scared to bits, Brits!

That is: Britain should tremble before him, not the other way round.

Lies, deceit, delusions galore
I shall tolerate nevermore!

This is just how the German is expected to address the world. At rallies in New York, too, every time an American, an Englishman, a Belgian, or a Frenchman gives an anti-German lecture, you "can count on seeing"

> a tall, blond gentleman in impeccable evening dress (*not every German knows* that in America *this is not merely a formality*)

rising from his seat, a man who has already "shot down" many a speaker, as if he were actually on the battlefield, but at the same time resembling that iconic effigy familiar from advertisements on the home front. There, just at the start of the war, the question asked was

> Why do *cultured people* groom their hair with Javol?

and the poet replied with verses, accompanied by an illustration:

Javol's a product I must praise,
I've used it now for many days
My scalp is blonder, but even better,
It helps refresh the old grey matter.
A poet feels it's just the thing
To groom his hair and cleanse his skin.[7]

Jawohl, indeed! This is the poet who—making allowances for *Alraune*—is the spiritual gatekeeper of the Third Reich. But he is also on the supervisory board of Berlin Laundry Ltd., and not every German knows that this is not merely a formality.

17

TRANSLATIONS FROM THE HEBREW?

There is a ready explanation why some authors pass muster—even foreigners, who are naturally suspect:

> Not every Russian author is a cultural Bolshevist. Dostoevsky and Tolstoy are rightly not on the Index [*without Dostoevsky there could be no Moeller van den Bruck!*]

That Dostoevsky fellow must have some merit, after all! But the accompanying commentary, in which the Prussian Ministry of Science, Art, and Popular Culture ratified its Blacklist and declared it "mandatory for all official book advisory boards nationwide", goes on to state explicitly that "not every Jewish author embodies 'asphalt literature.'" You would never guess—wait for it!—which Semite is the chosen one, the sole survivor from the flood of iniquity. Emanuel bin Gorion! A name that few contemporaries have ever heard. The crew of Noah's ark may have escaped the deluge, having fled abroad, but one man pokes his head out and calls across to those standing in amazement on the shore: "*Who* are you?" they ask, for they don't quite follow. Actually, "Bin" is a forename.[1] The official commentary (which really is needed here) explains that the criticism which Bin Gorion, as a Zionist, "consistently directed at assimilated Jewish authors, exemplifies the Jewish-racial principle". And since the surname too is heard for the first time, so that something nonexistent and truly unprecedented now exists, I feel compelled to make the following proud admission: among the assimilated Jewish authors Bin Gorion has consistently criticised, I myself hold pride of place, so I'm hoping that a crumb of recognition may also come my way. It's not too late to draw attention to the "polemic" he launched against me—the quotation marks give me goose pimples, but it will have had the Zionist hawks crowing, insofar as they got wind of it at all. The hardliners of the Third Reich, who have no sense of humour, remain stony-faced. There is no denying that this is not a polemic I have included in my bibliography since I deplore self-aggrandisement, both in myself and others. Nor would I have commended it for any other reason since, on principle, I allow such essays to speak for themselves. But, were I prompted to include it in a public reading "From My Own Works", it would certainly be quite a showpiece. Then you would doubtless hear the cry of the courtier Alvarez as he makes his exit in Offenbach's *Bluebeard:* "I've been binned!" ("Je suis *bien* perdu!") But now we have a sensation that will leave an indelible mark on literary history: Goering, of all people, is a fan of Gorion. Admittedly, there is a danger of confusing Bin with Benn, but it is surely good to hear that there is a place for someone like Bin within one of the most magnificent manifestations of the World Spirit.[2] This will leave its mark on cultural history. To think that the most renowned Jewish coreligionists have been persecuted and their books burnt; that thousands who have practised a useful and honest trade have been maltreated, ruined, or murdered; but that this one exception, whose relationship with the German language amounts to an act of retaliation, that Bin Gorion of all people should be proclaimed as standard-bearer in the struggle against the anti-German spirit—even to imagine such a thing is tantamount to atrocity propaganda! All those who were hitherto unaware of his existence must now brief themselves about a rank outsider who has won the jackpot under the Third Reich and reflect on how he thinks, how he writes, undaunted by the strain of deciphering the letters of the old German script.[3] I, too, must reexamine this exceptional case, having previously ignored him just as people ignore me, never dreaming that I would encounter him again at such a historical juncture. Bin Gorion! One can only surmise that nationalist students think him the only author who no longer has to be translated from the Hebrew.

Feeling that I counted for nothing when faced with this excess of positives and negatives, to both of which I have significantly contributed, I readily seized the opportunity when it arose to offer my services, however indirectly, to the authority now entrusted with policing the German language. With Berlin Radio I no longer have the slightest connection, or let us say just two contracts: to produce Offenbach's *Journey to the Moon* and to give a reading of Goethe's *Pandora.* Given the uncertainty prevailing in German jurisprudence, where the fundamental principle is that the national interest overrides every principle, it would be difficult to argue against the objection—also applicable in international law—that a contract is only a scrap of paper. Besides, a trip to Berlin now seems as utopian as one to the moon, and the longing to meet Pandora in person is surely more plausible than the wish to give voice to Goethe's vision in the Germany of today. The official conception of legality, as interpreted by high-ranking judges and laid down in the law journals, tends to credit cutthroats and bombers with a nationalist motive, not only as a reason for suspending or even abolishing punishment but also for their appointment to public office and lifelong enjoyment of the fleshpots in the halls of fame. Under these circumstances, it might be especially difficult to enforce a legal claim of a cultural-bolshevist nature. I imagine that in a civil case one would be directed to take one's claims to the criminal court and promptly receive a hiding from the usher. So I was all the more surprised when Cologne Radio decided to enlist my services, and pleased not least because Offenbach and Charlotte Wolter were born in the city—two geniuses who dominated the stage and whose Jewish origins—certain in the case of the great French musician, and perhaps also in that of the great German tragedienne—might well be no secret there either.

The invitation from Cologne Radio related to its unexpected wish for permission to discuss the sonnets of an Englishman that had just appeared, freely rendered into German by a Jew, for a—now somewhat restricted—series of talks entitled "The World in Books". It arrived just at the time the student body in Berlin had launched its crusade against the anti-German spirit, aiming to draw a clear distinction between the German cultural heritage and that of Hebrew origin. It also occurred to me—believing, as I do, that world events are essentially dictated by chance, though equally convinced that all things are connected—it occurred to me that this rendering of Shakespeare's sonnets—the first, after many "translations", to appear in German—is in fact also the last work in this language, appearing as it did in a world in turmoil after the Reichstag fire. It was announced, after order had erupted, in the already totally Nazified *Börsenblatt* of the German book trade, as a final and certainly most inopportune and unprofitable return on intellectual labour that has become redundant. Since in any case the book then fell victim to the Reichstag fire, it was spared the official book burning for which the Nationalists admitted responsibility.[4] Even without such distracting events, German booksellers and German literary journals, their subscribers and readers, would hardly have shown much interest in a work imbued with the spirit of their language, any more than Austrian literary circles, which were scandalised to see the *Sonette* published instead of *Die Fackel.* For they were by no means misled by the explanation publicised by a bookshop on my behalf: that you can find "all today's events" in Shakespeare, including my own actions. And now Cologne was evidently concerned to include my version of Shakespeare's sonnets in a World in Books. They didn't need to ask me twice, a sign of life being what I wanted from myself, and this was my modest contribution to the discussion:

21 April 1933

To:

West German Radio Ltd.

Cologne

In response to your kind request for two volumes of Karl Kraus, *Shakespeares Sonette* to be made available from our publishing house for discussion in your programme "The World in Books", we express our thanks and beg to advise you first, that as a matter of principle we do not supply complimentary review copies. Further, we feel it is our duty in the present case to warn you against an error of judgement which might run counter to the directives now in force in Germany governing the critical assessment of culture. We draw your attention to the fact that, though the renderings of Shakespeare's sonnets by Karl Kraus are indeed in the German language, they lack the statutory indication that they are actually translations from the Hebrew. Should you prefer a direct translation into German, you might fall back on that by Stefan George—if indeed you really think it appropriate to include the original English author in your series.

Yours most sincerely,
Die Fackel Publications

18

SOUNDBITE-HOOKS AND FOREIGN POLICY

These, however, are mere pinpricks, as the leader writers of the World War were wont to declare in that age of grandeur. They don't do justice to the struggle against the anti-German Spirit in its deeper sense. It would be surely better to investigate the extent to which this struggle is German in origin. My "Prayer to the Sun of Gibeon", misinterpreted by the dimwitted when it appeared in 1916, highlights the absurdity of a world of power politics in which the pan-German present uncannily converged with an Old Testament narrative fraught with atrocities. The reflection "On the Sinai Front" of 1917 pointed to the concurrence of two ethnicities, as expressed by Schopenhauer's definition of a nation that "worships a God who promises it the lands of its neighbours". During the World War the Old Testament and modern German ideologies of being "chosen peoples" had already reached a point of convergence—of alignment before the event. Is not the endlessly reiterated motif of "root and branch extermination", of vengeance unto the third generation (even if only retrospectively!) conclusive proof? Seen in this perspective, if the story of the sacrifice of Isaac is deleted from the German curriculum for being un-German, there should be no objection to the Book of Joshua. And could not the national resurgence so accurately charted by Schopenhauer invoke another German thinker, Georg Christian Lichtenberg, even more readily? Not, of course, his observation that he would

> give a great deal to know for whom exactly the deeds were done which are publicly described as having been done for the people.

Here, he is only pretending not to know, for he clearly recognised that the deeds were done to line the pockets of a minority of scoundrels, who had already pocketed the rights of the majority they had outwitted. Equally unacceptable is his proposal: "Make those in charge sleep on top of a powder keg—that might put an end to war". But one of his attempted translations is noteworthy, for with it he does full justice to the demand that, in the field of language, we should go right back to the original Hebrew:

> It is no credit to the Germans that to "*lead people on*" [*anführen*] is practically synonymous with "*to deceive*". Surely this *comes from the Hebrew?*

How tempting to construe leadership in this way, when one recalls a similar passage about leading people on, admittedly only in the first edition of Hitler's autobiographical reflections. This is unlikely to be reinstated by those of his followers recently credited with the ability to reconstruct many details

> which he himself had *forgotten* or at least omitted to mention in his autobiography

of which so many editions have appeared. That revealing passage in the first edition, relating to the need to "fake it" to win over the masses, may however have referred to the Communists and thus subsequently been misunderstood. More forthright is the position of a subordinate who misleads people into believing the programme only to disabuse them with the words:

> They come along with their Party manifesto and with Hitler's *Mein Kampf* and ask: Why hasn't this been carried out yet? Why haven't the banks been taken into public ownership? *And they think that could influence us!*

But the statement that

> Anyone who *insinuates* that the government intends to plunder the interest received on investments and pensions *is a liar*

makes it crystal clear that the liars are those who believed it was the truth, when they tried to deny that a twenty percent surcharge was being imposed. Has redemption from the slavery of extortionate interest rates really ceased to be an ideal simply because it hasn't happened? Just the reverse! Has the promise to close rapacious department stores lost its validity now that they are being recapitalised, with the sole consolation that—wherever the Jews have been thrown out—the Nazi bosses are digging in? How idiotic to put your trust in a promise and fail to see the joke when it is broken!

Those who thought something definite was on offer, without realising there would be a price to pay, might seek enlightenment about the essential function of being led astray from a poet regarded as German in the most superlative sense, if such a one exists. To understand the National Harvest Festival, staged in Hamelin of all places, where five hundred thousand agricultural workers were herded together on a hillside levelled into racial conformity with a plateau, which placed everything in a false light, we should listen to Eichendorff:

THE NEW PIED PIPER

Tally ho! Tally ho! Playing this tune
I'll lead the field astray.
Radical change can't come too soon,
The system's had its day!

You say we're poor, you're riding high,
But we'll cut you down to the ground.
Reduced to rags, *you'll* find out why
It's misery then all round!

I shall revive an ancient song,
All dance with one accord.
It's called "My country, right or wrong"—
Oh, give us wisdom, Lord!

No chance, as long as the spell cast by the dynamics of change persists! Every one of the thousand explanations for a thousand actions, all seeming to contradict the thousand promises made, has contributed to this intellectual stupor—a certain something, always shifting, fluid and flickering, a continuous slippery relativising of meaning running off the tongue, all the more attractive for affirming the Absolute, the all-embracing epitome of totalitarianism. A fluctuating phenomenon that insists on hard facts where none can be pinned down, strikingly reminiscent of the technique prefigured in the newspaper baron Imre Bekessy's more localised and bloodless dictatorship. Inherent in this multiple-entry bookkeeping, which uses soundbite-hooks to trap the mind, is a devious cultural politics designed to conceal contradictions.[1] The capacity to turn sense into nonsense and back again, to transform a debacle into a sensation—in short, what used to be called talking bunkum—this is something at which National-Socialist communiqués excel.

Take for instance the response of the *Kampfbund*, after Toscanini had cancelled a guest appearance at Bayreuth in protest against Hitler's racial policies. Committing itself to culture through thick and thin, the *Kampfbund* declared:

> The Kampfbund for German culture, which *from time immemorial* has concerned itself with the protection and promotion of all aspects of the German cultural heritage in Bayreuth, *has established* that none of its responsible spokesmen *has ever spoken out against the artistic participation of Arturo Toscanini*, and that in particular the head of operations in Prussia and Member of the Reichstag [Hans Hinkel], . . .

"From time immemorial"? The logical explanation is that more lies have been told in the last three months than in the previous three centuries. But the whole thing is plausible in its totality, and no one conscious of his German identity can any longer doubt that everything is in working order and freedom of movement permitted even to those of foreign blood. Someone more logically inclined, who did not know that Toscanini had cancelled because other artists had been banned from participation, would have to reconstruct the facts along the lines that Toscanini applied and now falsely claims that he has been rejected; or: he was invited but fears an unfriendly reception. For no one would suspect that after spurning a gift out of repugnance for the giver, he would be told in reply that they really wanted to give it to him, so why is he complaining? Someone who has received a good kicking confirms with a clear conscience that he has not kicked anyone. He suppresses the fundamental argument in order to foreground some side issue—the familiar subterfuge adopted by the innocent aggressor in all situations. Transposed into Nordic terms, the intrigue seems to involve not the courage of Baldur but the cunning of Loki, who—at the end of the day—brings about his downfall. That the gift intended for Toscanini would have been extremely beneficial to the giver—since, according to a Bavarian minister of state, Bayreuth without him is as "totally bankrupt" as Germany is today—is not mentioned in Bayreuth, where they know they have received a kicking but pretend not to. Our friends at the *Deutschösterreichische Tageszeitung*, which had already got over the loss of Bruno Walter as one of the "great" conductors, found consolation in the conviction that

> the German people, *drawing on their own cultural strength, will bring forth German conductors to erase* all memory of Toscanini.

You may place your hopes in eugenics, but by the time they are fulfilled, Bayreuth is likely to have closed its doors. In the interim, this world has only brought forth Herr Richard Strauss. But when he, or Herr Furtwängler, raise their right arm, it's not immediately clear that they are about to conduct. Still, the "*Dötz*" knows that in the Third Reich such matters have an accelerated tempo.[2] It goes on to say:

> German cultural politics will *quickly ensure* that the suppression of talented German conductors by the Jewish press and its circles of influence will be neutralised, and *in the shortest possible time* German music *will certainly have an adequate supply of really famous conductors* to fulfil the mission of German art as it scales the heights.

Well, it might be easier to eradicate sweaty feet, the traditional mission of the men rooted in blood and soil. Didn't the "*Dötz*" do its utmost to refute the superstitions to which the sufferers used to cling, a plausible explanation for much that has become all too obvious today. Even at a time of national exaltation, the day of the Reichstag election, the paper had to pacify one disgruntled reader:

> *Sweaty feet.* It is *impossible* that you could have read here that the eradication of sweaty feet *causes other illnesses,* for we do *not* write *such* nonsense. It is impossible for you to have contracted *multiple sclerosis* by curing your sweaty feet.

That was its final word. It may regret today that such clear insight into the real world should have been restricted to a single subject, however fundamental.

The urge to force the issue is really out of place, for success in the field of cultural politics cannot possibly come as quickly as economic, or especially diplomatic, success. One can understand why the *Völkischer Beobachter* was so enthusiastic for the Four-Power Pact, given the relatively short time it took for the party's foreign policy demands to be realised. There are actually only seven of these, drawn up by the statesman Wilhelm Kube, an impassioned lover of the fine arts:

> 1. All responsibilities imposed upon Germany by the infamous treaty of Versailles are *rescinded.*
> 2. The predatory French state undertakes *to pay reparations to Germany* for the infamous deeds committed by its white and coloured hordes in the Rhineland, the Ruhr, Upper Silesia, and elsewhere.
> 3. The German minorities in *Poland, Czechoslovakia, Denmark, Belgium, Italy,* and *Yugoslavia* are accorded the right to declare themselves, by plebiscite, part of *Greater Germany.*
> 4. German-Austria, Alsace-Lorraine, German-speaking Switzerland, Liechtenstein, Luxembourg, Danzig, and the so-called Memelland shall be reunited with Germany in accordance with population distribution.
> 5. Low German–speaking Flanders shall be separated from the French-speaking Walloons and accorded the right to attach itself to Holland.
> 6. *Leadership* of this European league of nations is accorded to the *only* nation which *can claim a right to it on the basis* of the size of its population, its history, and *its culture:* Germany.
> 7. The Dawes Plan is terminated with immediate effect and the payments extorted from Germany by the so-called "victorious powers" [more accurately: predatory powers] shall be *repaid* to Germany.

These far-reaching, indeed utterly far-fetched demands sum up the Führer's most deep-rooted aspirations, to which he most likely pledged himself on the

Pergamon Altar. Of course, not everything could be fulfilled at once, the realm of things abounds in harsh constraints.[3] But if we assess the realities, raised to the power of three by Kube's predictions, we can surely say that one of the party's fundamental principles is beginning to assert itself:

> Unlike other parties, we refuse to adapt our programme on grounds of expediency to the so-called current situation. It is this very *situation* that *we shall master*, thereby *adapting it to our programme*.

At the stroke of a pen! And now this author is called upon to master such real-world situations as the economy. Anyone who still asks awkward questions can simply be told that he is lying; and if that doesn't satisfy him, every issue can be clinched by quoting the familiar adage: "that it shall be through Germanness / that we will heal the world's distress".[4] In addition, we have the utterly irrefutable declaration:

> The *strength of the National Socialist Movement* has hitherto been *its lack of programme*, arising from its *ethos*.

That ethos is so powerful that even mentioning it might be defamatory, should someone believe what one is saying. Admittedly, our fourth demand includes German-speaking Switzerland, but that seems to us so absurd that a dash is needed—giving pause for thought—to distance us from such a desire:

> For instance, the foreign press has recently begun to wage a polemical campaign, *asserting in all seriousness* that Germany is stirring up agitation in the Confederation, aimed at—annexation of Switzerland. *Nothing seems too wildly fanciful* to be disseminated and believed *these days*, provided a way can be found to exploit it against the New Germany.

If the situation were not so serious, all Hell would break out in satanic laughter. It is true that (in the words of the folk song)

> boldly we shall conquer France.

But Goebbels cannot understand why other countries accuse us of wanting war when Hitler has plainly stated

> that we have absolutely no warlike intentions; and "are telling the world the truth".

Obviously, malicious people are confusing plans that will take a thousand years to realise with what must be done immediately. It is true that the Führer (once) envisaged:

> *Forty-eight hours after* National Socialism *has seized power,* the Treaty of Versailles will lie in shreds at the feet of the French people. In particular Clause 231, which refers to Germany's war guilt and forms the basis of the Treaty of Versailles, will immediately be declared null and void. This is an obvious task, which the Weimar "system" couldn't face because they were too cowardly and pacifist, or wouldn't face because they were bribed by France, together with the unpatriotically treacherous Marxist International, rather than pursuing exclusively national interests.

Thus spake Hitler. But what does it prove? At most, that the seizure of power is not yet complete, because otherwise the task would obviously have been carried out already. After all, Article One of the party programme declares:

> We demand the *union of all Germans* in a *Greater Germany,* based on the right of all nations to self-determination.

This is supposed to be "irrevocable". But thus spake Hitler's Deputy, Rudolf Hess:

> In some foreign countries, the *propaganda aimed against Germany* has recently seized on the *untrue assertion* that the National Socialist German Workers' Party *aims to annex* parts of *Switzerland, of Holland, of Belgium, of Denmark, etc. Nonsensical* as this *imputation* is, there are nevertheless *some who believe* it. The Leadership of the Reich accordingly considers it *of the utmost importance to state* that *no one in Germany seriously thinks of laying a finger* on the independence of other states.

The "etc." presumably refers to Austria and Czechoslovakia. At any rate, it would follow that no serious thinker in Germany belongs to the NSDAP—or maybe they do—or maybe not—. And thus spake Goebbels to the representative of Switzerland in Geneva (Neurath "readily concurred"):

> *The doctrine* and policies of the German Government are *in no way directed at Switzerland.* The Reich *would be guilty of highly irresponsible adventurism,* which would bring it into conflict with any number of states, were it to lay claim to the annexation of *all racially and linguistically German* populations.

So those instigating the irrevocable programme are irresponsible adventurers—or maybe not—or maybe they are—"What-the-hell, snotty-nosed Yid!", as the Viennese comedian Ludwig Gottsleben used to say when his partner wrong-footed him by pinching his impromptu punch line. Logic is at a loss.

Foreign policy disputes can be easily resolved by pointing out that, internally, the people are being all the more closely "welded together", and that anyone still complaining may end up with the Marxists and the butter profiteers; for carping critics arrangements have already been made. As if the highly intelligent Propaganda Minister had not made explicitly clear that all attempts to comprehend the New Order intellectually are misguided, since Soul is the only thing needed and the realm of feeling must first be absorbed before formulating ideas. Oddly enough, it's the intellectuals who have cottoned on to this rather than simple minds, who continue to brood on it. At the Ullstein publishing house they're already immersed in prayer:

> *Let us become quite simple and human again*.... Let us *cast off the onerous burden of the intellect.*

No more cheeky *chutzpah*, then, just hacks, pure and simple. The Gentiles have an easier time of it. Just as Benn the Romantic has decisively committed himself to faith in the absurd, so Rudolf Binding (a rather different Bin this time) is cautiously feeling his way towards veneration for the Brown Flower.[5] Previously, I was only aware of his leftist leanings, while his attempt to imitate my version of the triptych of one of Louise Labé's *Sonnets of Unrequited Love* caught my special attention. It was particularly the third section that he took as his model under the aegis of that great Jewish newspaper which has now also veered to the right. He is confronting Monsieur Romain Rolland, who has become disillusioned with Germany.[6]

Now, Binding declares, now at last a voice must be raised for Germany, now silence is no longer an option, and he intends to "speak frankly about German affairs". His vacuous inner turmoil and obsession with the Volk puts one in mind of Benn but is expressed more fluently:

> We deny nothing, nor do our leaders deny ... any of the things you hold against us. We do not deny "our own statements, our incitements to violence ... the racist proclamations that must offend other races like the Jews, the childish bonfires of books, the intrusion ... of politics into academies and universities"—we do not deny instances of emigration and ostracism.

Well, one has to ask, what does that leave to justify the sacrifice of intellect that Binding has made for the fatherland? What drove him to submit to the Führer cult? The bonfires are certainly child's play compared with all the rest; even if his invocation of the pious, cheerful innocence of a Matthias Claudius is perhaps somewhat different from the "SA spirit". However, religious belief is always stronger than rational cognition, and an intellectual can sacrifice everything without losing his trump card:

> But all of these things, however *terrible* they might *seem* and however momentous their impact on the one *or the many*, are

Unfortunate incidents? Unavoidable concomitants of the revolution? Isolated individual actions committed by subordinate elements? Unauthorised operations by irresponsible authorities, although there are no responsible ones and nothing occurs that is authorised? More of the same, spawned by lies in a war of attrition on the brain? This man of letters has found a new formula:

> Marginal phenomena, which never impinge on the *authentic sovereignty* of *events*, their *core truth*.

Binding, who has penetrated from the margins to the essential core, feels no need to repudiate anything when there is so much to affirm. Indeed, he is fired with indignation. So, Rolland thinks the Germany of today is a denial of the real Germany, does he? Doesn't that suggest that

> you, Monsieur Rolland, feel an obligation to teach Adolf Hitler and the whole nation what it is to be German. *Goethe*, whom you ... cite as one of the great citizens of the world ..., *is every bit as irredeemably German as Goering or Goebbels or the SA man Müller or me*—though we're all quite different.

Binding himself might well be the most irredeemable German of all, binding the others together. But perhaps he hasn't yet discovered that nationalist editors, serving the cause to which he is himself devoted, write such irredeemable German that the Nazi organ in Vienna, noting Einstein's departure for America, crudely ejaculated:

> That *would be* another unpleasant Hebrew we've *gotten riddance of.*

So what! Having gotten riddance of Einstein, we've now gotten something far more significant in Binding's eyes:

> The world *cannot adequately* grasp *just how* deeply rooted this revolution is in *religion:* with its processions and sacred symbols, its banners and solemn vows, martyrs and fanatics of all ages, even children, its prophecies and promises, its unshakeable belief and the *deadly* earnest of the people. Oh, we well know all about the outer trappings.... But a people now believes in itself which had lost that belief. And its belief lends it beauty.

The unbelievers can't fool Binding! Consistent in his muddleheadedness, he was already working towards a "religion of armed resistance" back in 1915 (a point he emphasises), putting "all peoples" in their place, which would mean that

> no nation, nor any alliance of nations, would be a match for us. Armed resistance would become our sacred mission.

In a word, a German poet. Now his prophecy has been fulfilled. He knows that the nation must first deal with the most pressing issue of blood: not the blood that's to be shed—that's a marginal phenomenon—but its own blood, the core truth that defines authentic sovereignty.

Here are anxieties undreamt of in earlier days. While the "racial screening of 350,000 postal workers is in full swing", many a citizen may perhaps imagine he can ignore these most vital issues. But in this they are mistaken, as the *Berliner Lokalanzeiger* informs us:

> The national resurgence of the German people has *for obvious reasons* also brought about a powerful revival of interest in genealogical research. *Many hundreds of thousands are* now *required*—notably since the passing of the Law for the Restoration of the Professional Civil Service—*to answer the question: Who were your ancestors*, and *which race* did they belong to? *Many are already nonplussed by the question (a crucial one today): What were the maiden names of your grandmothers?*[7]

A strange occupation for a nation whose leaders appear to believe there must be some connection with the price of butter. The hope of tracking down a Jewish grandmother is what anyone with a grain of sense might cling to—a stroke of luck that would leave this generation with some prospects for the future. Only unmixed blood breeds those delusions that expose a people to the mockery of its neighbours. What a clever cultivated woman she must have been, living perhaps in the Berlin of the 1860s. But no, now she's exposed as a stain on the family's good name, and woe unto you for being her grandchild! Her mere existence will cost you your job, but first you must track her down. Some who have already found her have not yet been found out themselves, though their colleagues are already muttering. Sooner or later the truth will out, and the *Lokalanzeiger*, which compares this quest to a scavenger hunt, is doing its bit. It suggests a way out, if it costs too much to consult a genealogist:

> *First the Aunts....*

They know a lot and have it all stored away. That way madness lies, according to Shakespeare? But no, the quest takes a Faustian turn:

Goddesses reign in solitude,
Enthroned beyond all time and space,
Don't speak of them but hide your face. [6213]

Except that we are now concerned, not with Goethe's mothers, but simply with aunts.

To reach them, you must plumb the dread abyss.
And if we need them, blame yourself for this. [6220]

In short, as Faust tells Mephisto:

It reeks of that old witch's noxious brew,
Which long ago assailed me—thanks to you. [6229]

Although the chill of dread is Man's best quality [6272], many of his leaders would nevertheless be well advised to avoid the path to the aunts—Herr Goebbels and Herr Ley, for instance, for whose names an extra consonant and an extra vowel might be found which they were keeping concealed. Apropos aunts: the New Germany that reads the *Lokalanzeiger*, especially the younger generation, associates "aunts" with something quite different and, for present purposes, unhelpful—the "uncles" of lonely-hearts magazines.[8] Such figures are no relation, and consequently unable to give information about kinship, but avuncular friends and advisors. So it is often the case that a young man spoiling for a fight has an aunt in this sense, but that she has no nephew. These are German specialties which may be somehow connected with the peculiar phenomenon currently astonishing the world. To the extent that politics has a human dimension, it might turn out that this is what led via back stairs and easy stages to an elevated position.

Perhaps this very phenomenon also explains a mind-set that has inserted between action and responsibility the concept of Aryan truth, which switches masculine to feminine roles in all questions of guilt, a sophisticated technique for shifting blame for anything from the World War to everyday brawls. The difficulty of distinguishing between active and passive roles in, say, "student assaults", the ambiguity inherent in the phrase, might imply that National Socialists were beaten up by Jews—a not totally implausible scenario since on one occasion in the Judengasse it actually happened. It may sound somewhat farfetched that Jewish students from the Anatomical Institute in Vienna pelted zealous Nazis with skulls, but at least it shows what tactics a peaceable Aryan majority has to resort to, responding to those projectiles with the bombs they love. National Socialism's favourite weapon is to reverse the roles of aggressor and victim—just as bourgeois society defends itself by invoking law and order.

The headline "Heimwehr Assault"—based on the mere appearance of broken bones—makes it perfectly possible to denounce as a lie the frivolous assertion that defenders of the Austrian homeland were attacked by Nazis. For nowadays it is always the perpetrator who is attacked, assuming the role of victim at least in the sense that he was forced by others to use violence. Nestroy, yet again: "Mama, I blame Constanze, the way she behaved forced me to call her a silly goose".

This unabashed appeal to inverted causality, pioneered by Bekessy, fully restores the concept of German honesty—albeit by default. How deeply entrenched must a moral code be for it to offer a prize of 200 Austrian schillings for "the best and most appealing examples of fake news", be it for spreading economic panic, reporting a hoax, or merely one of those atrocity reports used by the opposition to spread their notorious propaganda? Take the schooling of Nazi cadres in Austria, fed on Nietzsche's *Gay Science* that all morality is a function of the "will to power": does that not conjure up the image of those good times when Bekessy's *Die Stunde* was setting the tone of public life? The difference being, of course, that the knavish tricks now seem to be in the service of a more heroic politics of extortion. How impressive to see a world of felonies, treacherous assassinations, and authorised denunciations imbued with the aura of indisputable truthfulness and swathed in the insignia of moral glory! Thus at the end of the day it is legitimised by that venerable symbol for Nazi loyalty, towards which Johannes Schober, despite the extreme vacillations he epitomised, was infallibly leading us. (In this world abounding in phantoms, Schober's shadow recently re-emerged between those of Steffi Richter and Lord Rothermere, who wished to lay the Polish Corridor at her feet. The oath he has sworn to protect democracy he will doubtless keep with unswerving loyalty to National Socialism.)[9]

How the human condition must be purged before a celebrity is thought fit to appear on a postage stamp! A black mass calling the faithful to their devotions is unique in the history of civilisation, sustained by an unshakeable cult whose high priests accuse each other of treason before the whole congregation, only to reach a compromise with protestations of mutual respect leading to a done deal.

> Reich President von Hindenburg has appointed Diplomingenieur Gottfried Feder Undersecretary of State in the Ministry of Economic Affairs. -- Feder is an enemy of Hindenburg's. During the electoral campaign for the Presidency he created a stir in a speech he gave in Kassel on 12 March 1932, the day before the first ballot, accusing Hindenburg of *six breaches of his oath:* at the dismissal of Ludendorff; at the flight of William II to Holland; at the strike of munitions workers; by cancelling a visit to Ludendorff on Tannenberg Remembrance Day 1925; by signing

> the Defence of the Republic act and expelling the ex-Kaiser; and finally, in the period 1925–1932, by not carrying out the duties of his office as willed by the electorate (this, incidentally, was also true for the period after his second election). Feder said in conclusion that one can never be too old to keep one's oath.

I make that seven. But taken together, they add up to loyalty:

> Reich President Hindenburg and Reich Chancellor Adolf Hitler have given the whole German people a shining example of unity by the *bond of trust* they *sealed* in Neudeck, compelling all Germans to do likewise in service to the new state and through *loyalty* to those called upon to lead it.

According to a detailed account:

> Finally the interview was abruptly ended by Hindenburg. Hitler had hardly left the Reich President's study when, doubtless affected by the emotional impact of the audience, he [Hindenburg] collapsed unconscious. After medical consultation, it was decided that he should be urgently advised to retire forthwith to his castle at Neudeck. According to reliable sources, the doctors were directed to give this advice on the express orders of Hitler. Hindenburg has been a prisoner of the Hitler regime in Neudeck ever since.

Who was it said:

> So with such types you're now allied,
> That's always made me terrified.
> No good can come from sorcery [10,693]?

As for loyalty, another version was doing the rounds not long ago:

> Reich President von Hindenburg, who coined the phrase "Loyalty is the soul of honour", has never kept faith with anyone in his life.

A man of his word; but no foreign words anymore, such words shall no longer be allowed to stand:[10]

> The representative of supreme power in the state, i.e., the Reich, is the Führer, who will doubtless soon be known as Reichsführer. *The foreign word Reichspräsident will later disappear.*

On the same day, the Reich Press and Propaganda Office of the Reich Federation of German Hoteliers publishes a warning against the use of foreign words on restaurant menus. New word, same recipe. The man's already gone—transformed into a foreign word. But just how unfounded the rumour is that his discussion with the Reich Chancellor had an unfortunate effect on the Reich President, is proved by the variant account in the *Norddeutsche Allgemeine,* which retains its reputation as an official mouthpiece: "Hindenburg's Remarks about Hitler", conveyed to the paper by a reader whose words will in Germany certainly not fall on idle ears:

> Working together with the new Reich Chancellor is a *daily source of delight.* The relationship I enjoy with Hitler is *a beautiful one—that between a grandfather and his grandson could not be more beautiful.* It is touching how *considerate* he is towards me, old man that I am. *He is always anxious to help me, whether to sit down or stand up,* wherever it is. I *never fail to be amazed* at the *vast range of general knowledge that he has acquired.* He is a man of *great intellectual gifts.* In addition, he is a *deeply religious* person and very *kind-hearted,* someone who will always be a simple, modest man of the people.

Who was it said:

> A loathsome fellow who offends
> Me with his creepy raven friends [10,701]?

No, nothing can surprise us anymore; or at most that supermen still use good and evil as their yardstick. "What need we fear who knows it, when none can call our power to account?—Yet who would have thought the old man to have had so much blood in him?" "These deeds must not be thought on after these ways. So, it will make us mad", says Lady Macbeth, spurring her husband on. They weren't so squeamish in those days—"if it were done when 'tis done, then 'twere well it were done quickly".[11] Nor in the late Roman Empire, where blame for fire-raising got pinned on the Christians; where belief in symbols was not even shaken by a horse being appointed consul; where, at the end of the day, a ruler on his way out, dressed as a woman, was murdered by the Praetorian Guard.

19

"WHEN JEWISH BLOOD . . ."

The only difference lies in the "ethical instrumentation" of criminal actions—something unknown at the time when Macbeth murdered sleep. Our world, which still retains certain established modes of thinking, feels shocked and apprehensive as it follows the contest between words and deeds, deeds and words, and anxiously awaits the outcome. If it attends more to the words and their bellicose meaning, it is told to judge the Reich by its deeds; if it refers to deeds, Hitler's conciliatory Reichstag speech is cited in refutation. Point out this contradiction, and they dismiss it as a side issue which bears no relation to the kernel of the revolution, legally invested with power. Moreover, evolution lies ahead, for the revolution is now complete, its tremendous achievements command respect, but it is in its infancy and what we've achieved so far is mere child's play. First we must get rid of the Marxist commissars, and if irresponsible elements interfere, watch out or we'll eliminate you and have no qualms about it! Thus the world once more prefers to heed the words, downplaying atrocity propaganda in the light of the official explanation that the Party has so far been magnanimous—something interpreted by its enemies as weakness. The deeds that now follow are merely an understandable reaction to the world's anxiety about such deeds. This leads to new misunderstandings causing further confusion, which in turn gives way to greater clarity facilitated by daily briefings.

The basic position is that everything that has taken place was done to save us from the Communists, starting with the Reichstag fire, for which they were responsible. There follow warnings against isolated individual actions, from which the leadership distances itself while admitting that it may have prompted them and then attributing them to their opponents. Does this all not sound like satirical exaggeration? But it stems from the real world, where the cult of action, enflamed by morphine, lets rip in sentences like these (from Goering):

> If many now allege that in my speech in Essen

(where every shot was authorised!)

> *I gave the signal* for undisciplined behaviour, that I even gave the signal for looting and pillage and the like, *I must protest!* But I am *not such a*

> *coward* as *to distance myself from what* they did, *rather I approved of it.* And if under the intoxication of events they overstepped the mark, *we in the leadership* are to blame. For *it is what we preached.* We shall continue cleansing, implacably! – – exterminating – – [1]

And all without harming so much as a hair on anyone's head! The Brownshirts go on the rampage, seizing brown shirts that enable them to commit further offences, doubtless including the incident that exposed the subterfuge. Atrocities occur, as disclosed by the spoils on display, generating propaganda which is "officially retracted" on the very day it begins. Confusion of the senses, confused perceptions of the boycott of Jewish stores as a day of national honour—and its abrupt termination as no disgrace.[2] And from every single setback to the triumphant deception of all the senses—always the same apparent contradictions, revealing at a deeper and more comprehensive level the bipolarity inherent in the notorious assertion "that it shall be through Germanness / that we will heal the world's distress".[3] In the Germanic realm there can be no suspicion of collusion between words and actions, for there are anomalies within every announcement. They are integral to an ideology whose manifestations may be modified by morphium or alcohol. This Aryan, essentially contrarian, attitude towards the facts—identical with the "mentality" already observed during the World War, the tendency to deny the obvious—would be incomprehensible to any outsider reluctant to invoke the irrational and accept its indubitable source in the Quaternary. A solitary voice has challenged this mind-set, which within the broad sweep of its terrors amazes us less by what it does than by what it simultaneously denies. An unknown civilian has been quick-witted enough to turn the tables on this mendacious form of physical intimidation:

> Stormtroopers recently burst into a well-known store on the Kurfürstendamm. They behaved in an extremely threatening manner, and the son of the owner ran to fetch police protection while his father was held captive in the store. He shouted out to the police patrol that Communists had forced their way into his store. In front of the SA men he repeated that he took them for Communists in disguise and provocateurs, since official reports maintain that the SA have good manners and act in accordance with the law. After conferring for some considerable time, the police had no option but to take the SA men to the police station.

What incomparable presence of mind! If everyone had the wit to take their lies at face value, the German world would appear in a different light and the adherents of Irrational Socialism would avoid the devastating revelation that their truth was a lie.

We would have been spared that sense of the earth shifting on its axis from one day to the next, from the glorification of death in battle to the view that "all war is madness" (Hitler).[4] From the totally bloodless course of a revolution—and the protest against "false rumours of barbarity"—to the authentic version:

> *When Jewish blood spurts from the knife,*
> *We'll be having the time of our life.*

True, this turned out to be a fallacy, but it continues to circulate as a marching song embodying Coué's optimistic autosuggestion that "day by day, in every way, we are getting better and better"—supposedly the quintessence of what is called the "SA spirit". The song, understood partly as charisma, partly as a lethal threat, inspiring apprehension both among the defenceless and among those in power, may intrigue philosophers of religion like Benn and Binding, but doesn't actually captivate them. Are we to assume that the singers are merely bragging about shedding blood without any practical consequences, that it was only a harmless threat of persecution since we're not having the time of our lives while Jews are no worse off, indeed, that our frustration is proof that the talk about knives is mere sabre-rattling? These mendacious singers, who should be able to restate their theme as if they were explaining some catchphrase from the official news agency, cannot be seen as mere dupes, for that would be to cast doubt on the only part of the National Socialist programme which has been honestly and consistently carried out. It is precisely those anti-Jewish measures that the liars would like to conceal from the eyes of the world, which they accuse of shedding "crocodile tears" (such as have really been seen at Hitler's rallies) for a small criminal minority which deserves its fate a hundred times over.

That same world must have felt comforted when it was simultaneously, on 6 August 1933, given the assurance:

> *In the course of the National Socialist revolution, fewer than twenty persons have lost their lives.*

If this were true, the catchphrase about Jewish blood would be mythical and Germany's economic plight comprehensible. But since I personally know of one family, five of whose members make up at least a quarter of that total, and of some ten other individual cases, my knowledge would almost coincide with the actual figure for the whole nation. This leaves further possibilities out of account and assumes that figures from official sources (the Wolff Bureau, the "Conti" Programme) were lies concocted by anti-Nazi atrocity propaganda. It also implies that none of the thousand cases of death announced via London is true and that even the bloodbath of Köpenick, which in itself accounts for the number, did not actually take place.

For America, the task of monitoring the figures is even harder, if it relies on information received from the Führer which offers only an authoritarian guarantee. What it *could* easily monitor, however, is the reliability of another concrete assurance, one which concerns not a fact, but a promise. The Führer, whose divine mission has now also been recognised by a Catholic cleric, the Führer to whom a mistaken assertion—say, false information spread by subordinates—but hardly a false pledge may be imputed—the Führer, we learn, has already once declared to the Americans that he is prepared to pay the thousand-Mark tax imposed on those Jewish corrupters of the people willing to emigrate; who have not taken up the offer to leave the fatherland and are hanging on—at the risk of a hanging. Now, once again in an interview, he has added a further, apparently binding, declaration to the already crystal-clear formulation that he finds the world's attitude towards Germany as baffling as "Germany's rebirth appears to be to the outside world":

> Let me *say again, we will pay for transport and expenses*, and add to that *a small bank account*, if you will have them!

Immigration poses a serious problem for the States, testing to the limit what humanity can do for a hundred thousand lives saved but cut off from their livelihood. Will they disdain to take this magnanimous butcher at his word? They could do so with a clear conscience, since the small bank account was deducted in many cases from a larger one that didn't leave the country. One cannot simply concede that nothing remains of this solemn, concrete pledge, not only not to hinder but even to expedite escape, except the subterfuge of the man who made it, and that any hope held out was mere mockery of misfortune. Whether the world understands Germany or not, it must not tolerate deception where its own interests are at stake. The details that the Wolff Bureau did not report must be made good! *Out* with transport, expenses, and small bank accounts! *Out* with the Jews! Let metaphor become reality—with no return ticket! The world takes at face value what it's told directly. Of course it's true that our Bundesleiter, Alfred Proksch, who escaped without a small bank account, put the matter in a nutshell:

> *When the value of words is measured against deeds, they don't always turn out to express the truth.*

Along with the semantic value, the cash value of your salary often disappears as well, together with your pension. But why not at least test this out with Herr Ley, certainly a man of action, but one who answered the accusation in Geneva that "tens of thousands of German workers were languishing in jails and concentration camps" by refusing "to descend to such depths"; but who nevertheless took up the point and said:

> You *don't know Germany. So I'll happily invite the whole group* to Germany at my expense to inspect the concentration camps and *form their own opinion of Germany.*

Why don't they take this up, naturally under the condition that such an inspection is not announced in advance? Of course, even Gauleiters are dignitaries who have to keep in step, and if the opening lines of that bloodthirsty marching song should happen to be on the agenda, they might well be indignant, should an adversary "go so far as to declare that blood flows in German prisons". But words cannot be denied as deeds can—deeds that one's adversary did not see for himself. Try to deny words, and they can be quoted back at you. The evasive answer of those with no blood on their hands might be met with the quotation:

> Our Movement has brought in its train death, blood, wounds, and tears. Do not let it degenerate into kitsch!

Compare this to the Seventh Commandment! But no, it is not a confession by nationalist murderers, merely evidence that nationalist martyrs cannot speak German, for they certainly don't mean that the movement "brought" blood in its train, but that blood was "shed" for the cause. Whichever way you read it, they also boast of what they deny, and "Thou shalt shoot" is now a commandment.

For the Commandments cannot prevail against the irresistible urge to update them, and a halo reeking of blood rises up like a seductive fata morgana. At the spectacle of the coordinated ranks of SA and Stahlhelm, the modern Nibelungs and Huns, marching together through the sunlight, the sun cannot refrain from laughter.[5] For the attempt to align night with day strikes it as implausible, like a brain wave lacking in brainpower. But dwellers upon earth are wrong to be sceptical about what is taking place in their midst. Has "celebration of the primitive" ever reared its ugly head more ominously? Does something so elemental need a first cause? The world looks at this nation in astonishment: no wonder the nation looks back equally astonished. When the world catches the perpetrators red-handed, they gaze back at it wide-eyed, like the wolf when it hears tell of the wolf in the fairy-tale. For they meant no harm when they did something wicked, and they can't understand why the world so badly misjudges them. At the risk of appearing to abandon their commitment to the slogan "Every Jew dies!", which was at least interpreted as a heartfelt wish, they protest that nothing of the sort has actually happened. It was a lie, but now they're telling the truth. Yes, it surely must be a misunderstanding, and perhaps one that could be cleared up by recognising that the character thus revealed with such brutal honesty is not naturally bad, but simply equipped with a sensory apparatus peculiar to the species, which enables it to justify every action it commits. If Blood Brother X does not believe in things of which he may once have heard, this may still be put down to the psychological blockage imposed by changing circumstances. But if he doesn't believe the things he has seen, either, nor even those he has done; if he doesn't know what he is doing and promptly exonerates himself for that very reason, that points to a disposition insensible to falsehood, someone whom those differently constituted should avoid but not mistrust. Given the ability never to tell a lie, let alone the overwhelming multitude of lies required by the facts of the case, he must possess some hypnotic faculty that enables him to absolve himself of the things that illusion created in the first place. It seems rather stupid to seek systematic revenge for political differences, where retraction does not lead to pardon, let alone facts of birth for which nothing can make amends, no matter how much someone might regret being born a Jew—such intransigence is surely proof enough that there is no plan in operation here but rather some vague yearning for open spaces, probably for that place in the sun that has to be seized from someone else.

> Incomparable, unrestrainable,
> They are always yearning,
> With desire and hunger burning
> For the Unattainable! [8202 (after Bayard Taylor)]

And then there's the touching inconsistency, not only in the guidelines themselves but also in how they are carried out: for instance, if a Jew gets beaten up on Spandau Bridge because he didn't salute the flag, and another Jew in Neue Friedrichstrasse gets beaten up because his salute was an insult to the German nation. What *is* consistent is one's amazement that whatever one does, it must be wrong. An SA man beats someone up when he happens to be abroad:

> The perpetrator was immediately seized and imprisoned. When the police arrested him, he was *extremely perplexed*, for he had *only done what is normal in Germany.*

At home, diplomats are beaten up and asked "what they were doing in Germany as foreigners". It's instinctive, not planned. It would be a primitive psychology indeed that assumed the shape-shifting dislocations of one's dream life to be consciously calculated. In the whole sequence of visions conjured up before our mind's eye, from the Reichstag fire to the successful missions of Rosenberg and Habicht, the attempts to win over England and take possession of Austria, we were left day after day with the impression of something weird, rather than something terrible: the only explanation is that they mean well. When the world, remembering the Armenian atrocities (which it could have intervened to prevent), takes offence at tortures which required far more imagination to dream up than strictly necessary, it is told:

> Please believe that *we are all pained* by *the degree of incomprehension our measures* sometimes encounter.

They meant no harm; just the reverse. They feel outraged when credited with the deeds they perpetrate. They then tend to call such deeds "alleged", a succinct but well-chosen way of expressing the decision not to address such accusations, derived from the undisputed authority of a public morality based on boasting about what is alleged not to have happened. In order to free up an official post for someone unqualified for the job, pickpockets accuse the official of acting for personal gain, and since transfer to a concentration camp is preferable to conviction in court, the suspicion is reinforced that he was capable of combining his duties with innumerable malpractices.[6] And so what is alleged becomes real, while real deeds are merely allegations: that is the real meaning of the breakthrough to the "new type of civilised man" as formulated by the literati. Thus when the murderer is also a liar, he is no longer a murderer, and the more cowardly the deed, the more heroic the aura he acquires. This is the strategic alibi provided by the little word "alleged", which we see cropping up again and again in commentaries on what has occurred. Naturally, the world is aware of atrocities that stink to high heaven, and it has to live with this knowledge. But it evidently also enjoys the spectacle of a defiant morality which continues to speak of "alleged atrocities", without eliciting the response: "Enough! Away with you! Be gone from the planet!"

20

AUSTRIAN INDEPENDENCE AND THE INNOCENT AGGRESSOR

The Nazi leadership has adopted the opposite strategy by protesting against "Austrian atrocities". Against the way their *agent inspecteur* has been treated here. Against the trivial penalties imposed on their loyal servants. They adduce photographic evidence of real, not just alleged, arrests. They complain on the radio that a German journalist was made to share a cell with an Austrian homosexual (something that here might be glossed over as a courtesy). Bomb throwers have been hunted down, though they were merely holding instruction classes; and idealists, who have done practically nothing except pour sulphuric acid into postboxes and stuff excrement into vending machines. And so they hit back in an outraged tone:

> *And the world's conscience is silent?*

And with the documentary film:

> *Deeply Shocking Images*
> *of an Oppressed People in Desperate Straits*

And that's why they had no alternative but to close the border, issue travel permits to would-be assassins, set up an Austrian Legion, and foment revolt in a country of which it can be said:

> *The policies of the Austrian government have provoked widespread international concern.*

But it shouldn't be thought that unravelling the intricate web of this spider with the crooked cross on its back can be achieved in the twinkling of an eye, and that unravelling would restore to life the flies it entrapped. A hundred interlocking threads make up a mesh of fraud and deception, lying and cheating. They know nothing and change the subject; they've done nothing but somebody else is the culprit; nothing happened but he's done it; when caught out telling a blatant lie, they blame those who speak the truth. They take a dim view of what is done when someone else does it, or even when they do it themselves. Accordingly, they inform on political conversations overheard in the telephone exchange, and in the papers deplore the "growing scandal of phone-tapping"; they call "an armed attack from a hidden position a cowardly, low-down murder" and then commit the crime themselves. If you're accused, dig in your heels, blame someone else, and see how he feels: as with the propaganda dropped from aeroplanes. The armed incursion into Austria is an internal German matter and "the deterioration of the mood in England can be attributed to the English public's inability to understand Germany's intentions towards Austria"; consequently, there is an alleged conflict between Germany and Austria and alleged interference of Germany in Austrian affairs by the alleged dropping of leaflets on Austrian soil, while the real dropping of leaflets on German soil has contributed to alleged aerial rearmament in Germany, which accounts for the alleged démarche of the powers. Clearly, Austrian independence must be guaranteed—declares the Wolff Bureau to its sheepish confreres—but its infringement continues and the alleged breach of promise will not be noticed if the communiqué containing the promise is falsified as well. If the world still doesn't understand us, it is asked "if the Reich Chancellor's great speech in May about peace has already been forgotten". At the same time General Epp reclaims the colonies, and to the pacifist insight that, because of Versailles, the government cannot support this struggle, he appends the statement:

> *However,* the national associations are *not constrained by the German government's cautious approach to the issue.*

When the Bavarian state government then announces, with respect to friction on its border with Austria, that neither it nor the SA leadership has "the slightest knowledge" of any such difficulties, and that "no one in Bavaria has the slightest intention of interfering with Austria's internal affairs", the national associations are once again not constrained by this cautious approach. Not even the Bavarian minister, who from the outset countered the terror of the Austrian government with his decision "to ensure the freedom of our blood brothers in Austria", and had the same General Epp "restore order"—Epp, who knows very well the difference between a government's constitutional obligations and a national emergency. The world is confused. That it swallowed all that has been perpetrated over the last six months can probably be attributed to the paralysing effect of horror. But how did it get over the actual words without a brain seizure? And there's always more to come. While insidious cunning has no scruples about using the public media, a guilty conscience boldly faces up to its accuser using the most bare-faced forms of impudence available to the dialectic of power, with a bewildering effect that defies comprehension. (We shall call this procedure "Uschla" and reserve explanation of this no less enigmatic term.)[1] Slippery arguments are used to justify deeds committed on Austrian terrain by appealing to the German Spirit, enabling the perpetrators to slip away across the fraternal border. Evasive reasoning, then evasive action, relying on a judicial lethargy which has fortunately been replaced by emergency decrees.[2] Here in Austria, those implicated in the bomb throwing could juggle with alternative alibis, ranging from the concrete allegation that it was the Communists "using Matuschka methods", to the gruesome supposition that the unfortunate Viennese jeweller Futterweit hacked himself to pieces out of hatred for the party, to get his name in the papers, or out of hysteria:

> Are they afraid of evoking *another Meller scandal* in which *some bombs were used rather than a kitchen knife?*

So asked the satirist from a popular rag specialising in explosive reports, a notorious character who—far removed from all fiction—had been convicted of burglary, robbery, fraud, and embezzlement and sentenced to four years' hard labour, as it later emerged, and who continued on an emotional note:

> *We need not fear the truth.* We shall *ourselves help establish* it, *leaving no stone unturned to expose the actual perpetrators.*

The argument advanced as to why it could not have been National Socialists is not without a certain ethical flavour:

> *We are not in the habit of endangering Aryan customers* or *innocent Aryan passers-by by throwing bombs at Jewish shopkeepers.*

Since the conviction of party members as murderers is imminent, the population is

> *understandably very disturbed* by *irresponsible elements whose identity* has *still* not been established.

When the actual perpetrators were unmasked with no further effort involved:

> *As long as the police* have *not* released the names of those imprisoned, it remains *impossible to check the rumours and assertions.*

When it turned out (as this notorious character already knew) that most of them had got away:

> In all of five cases the *police did not manage to capture a single perpetrator.* ... *Where are the perpetrators* who shot at Steidle? *Where are the perpetrators* who planted an infernal device in the doorway of the depart-

> ment store Auf der Wieden? *Where are the perpetrators* who placed an explosive charge in the Stock Exchange?

One of them has written from Bavaria that he now has a fabulous trainer:

> Either I do physical training or I laze around and swim.

Another one they only caught when he was returning home to Austria, with a false passport, to have another go. As for the extradition and conviction of all bomb throwers affiliated to the party—what would the outcome be?

> *Impossible to prove participation of NSDAP in bomb attacks.*

Uschla! Since that notorious scene during the World War, the Prussian Wagenknecht has continued to instruct the Austrian Sedlatschek, whose query is no longer just a linguistic one: "Herr Oberbombenwerfer, can I now throw a bomb . . . over . . . at them over there?"[3] To the extent that it was possible to catch any of those thus instructed, responsibility is now expressed through a combination of compulsively well-drilled denials and native mendacity, typically conveyed in such gruesome jargon as "So what!", "I dunno nuthin'!" and "My 'ands are clean!" They can't remember a thing and had no idea of the significance of a smoking fuse; it was only when they read the papers that they discovered it was an infernal device. It was not merely the sight of this rabble of nationalistic activists but a glimpse of their cultural breeding ground, revealed by the documents in the *Reichspost*, which really made the country's predicament palpable: to such trash the Austrian state has to devote its anxious defensive efforts! This is what demonstrates the futility of a satirical approach—it is mocked by the absurdity of events. Gruesome though these militant proles may be, the Machiavellis from the middle classes are even more repulsive. Even before awakening to the mortal danger of their politically orchestrated criminality, one's brain feels crushed by the thought of a society of fanatics jostling for jobs, disaffected philistines regurgitating the funny nicknames they pin on each other, bootlickers and money-grubbers, hogs fighting each other to get their snouts in the trough. Who could believe that such types control the means through which the world shall be healed? Here's how it is done:

> Let's concede that this third way is what they call a "*Jewish dodge*". But legally it is *permissible and incontestable*. . . . The purpose of the paper must be the moral improvement of our party comrades. . . . *Accordingly, it must preach a gospel.* Over and over again. It cannot be sequestrated, it cannot be suppressed, especially if it takes a *noble* line—in short, *as if it were a sermon in church*. . . . *Skilfully handled* in this way, it should be

> possible to *keep it going for* a number of weeks, perhaps even months. But in the present circumstances that is the main thing—*moral improvement is what our people need;* then they won't read the Jewish press.... The editor will have to go and see this minister and that minister, have a few friendly words with him *to set his mind at rest,* and *thereby deceive* him. For deception is our initial goal. That *there is also a clear link between this activity and a very useful "customer service"* need only be hinted at *in passing.*

But that's all it takes to identify the familiar cultural *mélange* of chocolate with garlic, cutthroats with guileless blue eyes, gangsters with haloes. From the jargon of this "brown study" one can more or less make out that Habicht wanted to bump off Proksch, for it's true Proksch had the go-ahead from Motz and Röhm (almost one of the best men we've got), but:

> *That's all the Habicht camp* was waiting for, to neutralise Proksch's influence on foreign policy *using the Uschla procedure.*

So *Uschla* signifies—apart from the lamentable German—a Committee for Investigation and Settlement which is less concerned with problems of language than with gangster underworld killings. To round out the picture the Wolff Bureau adds that it's not true that nothing was known, revealing that among these documents there are allegedly letters from the German Foreign Office. There are no plans to use cunning or force to blast the gateway to Austria open—what nonsense! Not the least vestige of truth in it, no illegal couriers, no economic sabotage, no "contacts with Siemens about intensifying the crisis", no use of the press as a "front", no ministerial espionage, no conspiracy against Austria, no legion of mercenaries at the gates. How could such a misunderstanding have arisen! One can only give an assurance that "of course there can be no question of conflict between Germany and Austria"—except what can be heard on the radio, perhaps. The German Embassy as an agency fomenting high treason against Austria? By no means! The documents

> were submitted for *examination* by the Embassy *in agreement with* the Federal Chancellery. *The Ambassador confirmed*

that he knows of nothing, and accordingly one does not enquire into one's partner's behaviour since the German language is perfectly capable of making the German case plausible. *Uschla!* Everything is plausible, no surprises anymore, indeed, if Austria continues to stir up trouble, Germany is perfectly capable of hauling it before the League of Nations! This is the ultimate sanction—thus Habicht's warning. On this occasion, they got away with it. Berlin can "confirm" that the matter "has happily been clarified, totally and swiftly"; albeit with the addendum:

> *It remains regrettable, however,* that Austria has felt it necessary to employ *such methods* against a *kindred state.*

Is Austria still stirring up trouble—by defending itself? The fiercest villain cannot live in peace if his God-fearing neighbour feels aggrieved.[4] How often has Hitler warned Dollfuss that "in politics, force achieves nothing"! No, there is a limit to the power of tyrants, and the *Völkischer Beobachter* is losing patience:

> If the responsible men in the government continue *to trample the rights of the people underfoot, a terrible awakening* will bring it forcibly home to them with indisputable certainty that, on the day of the coming insurrection, no one *will go unpunished for ruling a people through despotic acts and prohibitions.*

In Germany, a foreigner only gets two years imprisonment for writing a letter revealing "measures taken by the government against the Jews", thus making him guilty of the "most grievous abuse of hospitality", while the same horrendous punishment in Austria awaits any blood brother who has merely attempted to blow up the Jewish Quarter. And a further striking contrast:

> While Germany under *the rule of Adolf Hitler* is heading for an economic boom, Austria under the *despotism* of Herr *Dollfuss* is facing ruin.

Uschla. It's one long eulogy. Still, there is a sting in the tail: the disenchantment of a brother whose love knows no national bounds; his amazement and pain

> that *harmless tourists, visiting a kindred people,* are exposed to such treatment.

It's common knowledge that

> there is no true German who does not *love* Austria and its people *as if they were his own people.*

That even someone with a warrant out for his arrest is accepted as if he were at home. It's common knowledge that

> Austria has always been every German's heart's desire,

which even a 1,000-Mark tourist tax does not deter. Further repressive measures may be needed for this desire to be completely fulfilled, for

> the Rhine and the Danube are *equally precious.*

Which of course doesn't mean they should be linked up.[5] Far from it, for

> it is precisely what is uniquely Austrian that the Germans love about Austria and its inhabitants, and what draws them back to the Danube again and again.

Admittedly, whoever composed this mutual embrace with the title

> *Austria über alles:* Necessary clarifications

thought the matter somewhat suspect, so he clarified:

> Germany wants to remain at least inwardly linked to Austria, with which it is inseparably linked by *ties of blood. That's all.*

One surely cannot ask for more. Goebbels had already made clear in June that the attitude of the Reich's government towards Austria was "not determined by any party considerations"

> but *only by a desire to avoid incidents* which *might disrupt* the relationship between Austria and Germany.

What interest does Austria have in "aggravating relations"?

> From *a German perspective the opposite* is what we *desire*—that is surely beyond doubt.

Who could still doubt that my concept of "innocent aggression" already formulated during the World War offers the key to understanding this character type? If "the Four-Power Pact is not a suitable platform", this formula certainly is! And even better is the perception that they are not so much enforcing *Gleichschaltung* as switching over to something quite different: they are crushing opposition through their tribunal system for investigating and settling intra-party disputes. Their approach may be hands-on, but they have an ear for innuendo and formulate things accordingly. They stir up the dust until everything's settled and muddy the water to achieve clarity. That's *Uschla:*

> *What actually happened?* Aeroplanes *of unknown origin* have dropped leaflets, aimed against the *present* Austrian government, over various places in Austria.

That's all.

For them, the fuss kicked up over trifles by a hypocritical global conscience that totally fails to understand Germany is very small beer. However one reacts, it's the wrong way. When a certain Frau Jankowski collapsed following her treatment by SA men—no wonder, when a woman on her own is confronted by a dozen armed men—*The Times* was roused to write an article. But when it came to clarification by a member of the Reich Press Office:

> The Jankowski woman got what she deserved. You can safely say that I have cleared the matter up!

The Times took no notice. Nor did it report that, because she had been left permanently impaired by the incident, an investigation has been initiated accusing her of atrocity propaganda. When was it ever the case that a revolution felt obliged to clarify every unavoidable side effect? And what government would have so openly and persistently distanced itself from the individual outrages that form its bread and butter—although butter itself remains in short supply for the individuals concerned? The failure to appreciate the difficulties faced by the regime is all the more regrettable in light of the emerging tendency for it to soften its line on both major and minor issues, even a slight whiff of philo-Semitism—here without the worry that magnanimity might be taken for weakness. Enough is happening in both external and internal affairs for it to look as though psychopaths are open to reason. There has been a marked readiness to make concessions, starting from the Versailles Treaty, and although "the pulped grapes foam absurdly in the barrel" [6813], in the end it may be possible for a human life to be saved by a hundred-Mark note. On the other hand, interference in the economy is strictly regulated. The attempt to come to an arrangement with the Antwerp diamond merchants, though abortive, has no more escaped notice than the successful arrangement with the Jewish furriers in Leipzig. But visitors to the Trade Fair are promised the privilege of convincing themselves

> that the German nation as a whole has but one goal towards which it aspires: to live in peace and friendship with all nations. . . .

Jews, come on in!? Yet not only foreign Jews, no, even homegrown Jews are welcome. It may of course happen that the Berlin District Court rejects a Jewish shopkeeper's complaint that his shop was ransacked while the police looked on, on the grounds that it was his own fault, knowing full well that, on account of his descent, his business represented "an extraordinary provocation to the overwhelming majority of the German people" and that, accordingly, he should have reckoned with the possibility of its destruction at the outset as a normal business risk. Indeed, it is even possible that the same man will be sent to prison by the Special Court if he claims that "the Jews in Germany are having a hard time", for this would be to report alleged atrocities. But it is still possible that he would be made welcome at the Brown Fair. True, proof is required from the exhibitors that their firms are German. But

> this is *doubtless* to exclude *so-called non-Aryan firms* from exhibiting. But customers, *irrespective of nationality and race*, are to be given an opportunity to form a personal impression of the productive capacity and *indigenous specialties* of German industry.

Uschla. The only difficulty, notably for foreign Jews as yet unaware of it, is the prohibition on bathing which has just been announced (on the grounds that the water sometimes exudes a smell of garlic). But in the first place, this can be construed as a lie, and secondly, an exception can be made for especially deserving cases. The plan to introduce "Jews Only" coaches on the German Railways was discussed but shelved. Elsewhere, however, economic life has called for certain sacrifices to be made of a non-material kind. Thus, the executive has expressly indicated to subordinates—who so often create confusion in public life, especially during a revolution, through their egregious failure to recognise the difference between "mine" and "thine", as also, alas, between rich and poor, tarring all Jews with the same brush—that it is only Jewish employees in the public sector who are to lose their jobs. The procurement offices should "refrain from any kind of snooping". "Extensive investigations into who qualifies as Aryan", which "particularly in large public companies are almost impossible to carry out", are to be avoided at all costs; "the crucial factor is whether Germans are employed". It is not always possible to determine "whether the capital of an enterprise is German or not", and absolutely no attempt should be made to determine "the extent to which non-Aryan individuals are present, since this poses a far from simple set of problems", and "rash measures can sometimes cause damage to the economy as a whole". Furthermore, it is envisaged that with regard to the Adolf Hitler Endowment—donations to which are made on an entirely voluntary basis—and as a matter of principle, Jewish businesses in particular (without suffering any reproaches or disadvantages on that account) will participate on a large scale, failing which these firms would not receive their permits and would consequently not be protected from further local pressures to pay up, which often give cause for concern. As can be seen, the Jews live undisturbed—as long as their businesses are not being investigated—and their consciousness of being included in a system of blackmail which encompasses the whole nation offers a certain sense of satisfaction. Everything takes place on a gigantic scale, like a brilliant display of fireworks which draws attention away from the crisis on earth towards the heavens: pirates use pyrotechnics as a distraction, the people look on, irrespective of race, and get their money's worth. Measures to retrench the economy from a racial point of view have produced a certain amount of friction, but then again, it is astonishing what simple expedients can be found. An optical miracle has occurred at the General Electricity Company (AEG), where Jews have successfully been made invisible and are still retained. That this concern was founded by Walther Rathenau hardly helped, but taking into consideration that fifty per-cent of its production extends to countries averse to the Jewish boycott, a negotiated formula emerged—one which paid respect to reciprocal inalienable rights and the promotion of mutual understanding as regards national customs and traditions—which in practice sounds like cosmopolitanism, properly understood: a solution that forms a suitable platform. That is how it is explicitly designated in the firm's annual report, formulated as follows:

> A solution seems to have been found which *takes into account internal interests without giving offence to those abroad*. This solution consists of *most of the Jewish personnel remaining in the firm*, but *being withdrawn from contact with the internal public*. On the basis of this *agreement*, the NSDAP has *recognised AEG as a non-Jewish firm not dominated by foreign influence*. It will be treated no differently from other German concerns.

This is a first for *Uschla*, something in between the required ideal and the real world, a curate's egg—a bit off, but good in parts. Abroad, where prejudice leads them to disregard the racial factor, they can keep most of their Jews; internally, they remain under camouflage. Well, that's not "being in total control of circumstances", nor adapting circumstances to the Party programme, but a fifty-fifty agreement, made for reasons of expediency between the Nazi Party and AEG, at the same time that it signifies, in its simplicity, the solution to the Jewish Problem. It's not the fault of the Nazi Party, which makes such a good fist of investigating and settling disputes, if new ones emerge in the process, and neat solutions lead to further confusion. For in all these transactions, whether hostile or conciliatory, the malevolent world is inclined to misjudge a mind-set which remains totally oblivious of its nature and implications, right to the bitter end—a mind-set which in total naivety commits deeds that could normally only be invented by a caricaturist, exaggerated *ad absurdum*, as indeed they now are. It's a game, like when fairies get wind of "a leprechaun" and having caught Falstaff in the act, laugh at him all the way home.[6] Germany speaks a different language from that in which people laugh, so it doesn't hear it. Or it puts laughter down to the misunderstanding of the others, who are however fully informed, and who should therefore take a first step towards mutual comprehension.

Surely it can only be a matter of goodwill and doing justice to a divergent natural disposition, which reveals that there is another way of looking at things;

in Grillparzer's words: "in one language it's the word for bread, in another it means poison instead", and even more pointedly: "a pious greeting then appears a very curse to foreign ears, and it's that that leads to tears". But it continues, "So learn his language then . . . yours he'll never learn!"[7] Germany only understands German. Communication would at least begin to be somewhat easier if it were simply assumed that what is meant is the opposite of what is said, though even that is not certain. Do we really know how a lion sees things? We can only judge him by his deeds; if he suddenly started to speak, who knows what sort of communiqué would emerge, and how he might declare he had acted for the sake of his kingdom according to an ethic known to no other beast of prey. The secret way the Prussian digests impressions is hinted at but not revealed, especially not the infallible certainty that enterprises will be successful when they are doomed to failure. He never shrinks from employing any technical progress to demonstrate to those in the wider world with eyes to see and ears to hear what they are bound to dislike, while seeking their approval for contemporary phenomena they most likely despise. But let us assume that a majority of Germans—all of them God's creatures—are made equally uncomfortable by these natural loudspeakers, nature's loudmouths at whose mercy they have put themselves; let us hope that the expansion of the acoustic possibilities of the radio and the optical possibilities of the illustrated press make them conscious of the absurdity to which their cultural lives are now forcibly subjected. Does it not occur to the Germans—for it does to others—that not only does no other nation insist so often that it is a nation, but that in all the language spoken over a year throughout the whole world, the word "blood" does not occur as often as it does in a single day on German radio and in German journals? Blood and soil: as if they existed here only. And new, ever newer, definitions of all things German—masculine, feminine, and neuter—as if they had all just been discovered by a German expedition. Mammoth bones excavated from the native soil. "Der deutsche Mensch"—the German worker, the national people, the citizen of the Reich who belongs to the "Reichsvolk", and more of the same, none of which butters a single parsnip.

> Are human voices those that reach mine ear?
> At once my wrath is kindled, keen and clear.
> Aspiring forms, that high as Gods would soar,
> Condemned to be themselves for evermore.
> [8094 (after Bayard Taylor)]

> To me they look like pots of clay,
> Misshapen, coarse and flawed.

Wise men racking their brains survey
The fragments of a fraud.
[8219 (incorporating Williams)]

Surely at least these voices and faces should enlighten some mother's son, who hears nothing but the same stuff being barked out all day, and who observes monsters, like those in the chamber of horrors in Präuscher's Panoptikum, passing themselves off as exponents of high politics, simply because they once exerted a magnetic fascination on the small fry with their savings books; and certainly enlighten anyone who sees those vacuous faces we've come across in an Alpine inn where the annexe, evidently confused with annexation, is occupied by clog-dancers. Most extraordinary of all is that people are elated rather than depressed by the attempt to display in all its variants an uncongenial ethnic solidarity, supposedly rooted in the soil from Germany's northern shores to Upper Austria, with endless illustrations of the emergent "political elite constituted by race and blood". We know, of course, that these are the heroes who gave the order to spit in prisoners' faces; but why show their repulsive visages over and over again? The new Minister of Food has recommended "drowning those who are not fighting fit in swamps"—something hitherto only successfully attempted with Russians.[8] Such a project would demonstrate a devastating concept of eugenics, like honest Kent's outburst when facing his foes:

Sir, 'tis my occupation to be plain:
I have seen better faces in my time
Than stands on any shoulder that I see
Before me at this instant. [*King Lear*, II, 2]

So these are the ones who want to sterilise the others? And the onlooker doesn't find his stomach churning when a certain someone puts on a jovial public face and ingratiates himself especially with children?

His heart belongs to the young.

The great man is especially taken with the schoolchildren from Oberstaufen with their swastika flags.

This little girl in the waiting crowd called out to the Führer: "It's my birthday today", at which she was invited to coffee and cakes with Adolf Hitler and presented with his signed photograph. At left: Reich Youth Leader Baldur von Schirach.

Consider the scope of it all: this gigantic peacock's tail of popularity which eclipses all memory of a Bismarck; this insatiable Byzantine profusion of smiles and handshakes, of arms shooting up and down, royalty and rabble; the inexhaustibly monotonous rows of faces with their coordinated longing permeated by an enormous image bestowing its blessing on them all; this distorting mirror, its thousandfold facets reflecting both the earth and the skies, and everything that creepeth on the earth after his kind, and every fowl after his kind, every bird of every sort, not forgetting those votaries swooning in ecstasy as the camera clicks—who, with this view in his sights, would not fear for this people, and for mankind? One person wouldn't:

> He reads no books. Only life's practical problems interest him. . . . *His reading matter consists of illustrated journals.*

And they depict the Führer reading, alone or in convivial company with Goering, who shares his pleasure, dressed as a folksy war veteran. And that's what millions read, it's all spread out before them, and they see nothing. Even when there's a photograph of "Suffering Humanity" and a worldview that includes torture. For after all it's only self-inflicted Indian torture, the "hooks skewering the flesh on the back" in honour of the goddess, that's all, while conditions back home are illustrated by a spring idyll with a pair of lovers intoning a song of praise:

> Berlin—let's leave it behind us,
> Under apple blossoms they'll find us
> In Werder, we'll babble sweet nothings,
> So flutter your eyelids, stop blushing!
> The rest of the world doesn't matter a damn,
> So drink up, my poppet, come have a wee dram!

This carefree outlook, which often takes the form of not giving a damn—well now, it shows that happiness has to be pursued in a prescribed form.[9]

This strategy allows some people, so uninhibited that they ignore their own mistakes and misjudgements, to court the approval of those outside observers they feel hard done by and to counter brusque rejection by soliciting favours. The Führer expressed this insight early on:

> If the German nation wants to put a stop to the threat of being exterminated in Europe, it must not succumb to the same error it committed before the War and make an enemy of God and the world.

If it nonetheless succeeds in doing so, countermeasures must be taken, and it is generally acknowledged that this does not mean making people afraid. We present ourselves to the world as if nothing had happened, or only something that ingratiates us: fresh-faced and unaffected, like Wagner's (not quite so) pure fool; if the world is dumbfounded, it should be all the easier to win it over. Against all expectations, this strategy has been unsuccessful. Rosenberg's mission to gain public sympathy, obstructed by the efforts of the London police to provide protection, achieved the opposite of the intended effect, and it is understandable that, after so many questions about one unauthorised action after another, his patience was exhausted, and he unceremoniously sent his questioners packing, telling them that he couldn't be expected "to remember all that stuff!" Just how little honest striving for popularity is appreciated is proved by the fact that the British press was not even prepared to accept paid advertisements to promote German tourism—something that certainly need not have feared reprisals. But you must admit: Parsifal was a devious roué compared with the simpleton who, in the midst of the panic which gripped the world after the boycott of Jewish businesses, came up with the proposal:

> *to recruit friends worldwide for the German Idea underlying the national resurgence*, and *find those willing to collaborate with this new Germany.*

At a stroke, just as its greatest action had begun and was then called off. A week later shameless competitors saw their opportunity and seized it:

> The maxim "Germany is *the cheapest country in the world*" should play *a striking part* in this propaganda campaign.

Flair, tact, ethics—all working together in a joint effort. Now is the right moment: as when amid the gas clouds of the world war our own Moriz Benedikt exhorted commercial travellers to put out their antennae and get the feel of the market. "It remains to be seen" if this propaganda, brought into play at the right moment, should have "a purely economic slant"; but even if the economy is "the primary target",

> the important thing is still *to promote Germany's culture as such in the world.*

When, if not now? We must always insist at home and abroad

> that *in most cases* it is senseless to prefer *foreign goods and foreign culture* to Germany's own.

The propaganda should make special use of "placards and posters in the foreign language and the distribution of leaflets". Funds are available "to ensure"

> that the foreign press—*even if only* in the advertising section—draws attention repeatedly to what Germany can offer.

But even the advertising section proved disinclined to cooperate, while the main text then placed itself selflessly at the service of propaganda for Germany's culture, so extensively indeed that the world now knows for whom the bell tolls. And since, under the dictatorship of contingency nothing happens by chance, chatty reports about crimes follow right on the heels of the upbeat political coverage. So an eye that is alert to interconnections, and fascinated by every detail, perceives what the Berliner of 1933 is thinking: snatches from *Hamlet,* not simply "an offence so rank it smells to heaven", but its enactment: "for murder, though it have no tongue, will speak with most miraculous organ".

21

PROTECTIVE CUSTODY

The murderer, by contrast, is oblivious of the deed and its consequences and has a knack for making both sound all too human, which should surely gain people's sympathy. After all, everything was done in good faith, and the world should respond accordingly when it learns what actually happened in the case of Dr. Ernst Eckstein. This case was depicted abroad as one of the most gruesome of bloody deeds, after the spirit of the despairing victim was broken:

> Dr. Ernst Eckstein, *one of the first political functionaries* to be taken into protective custody,

—so, plainly an act of protection—

> *could come to terms with the conditions of his custody only with great difficulty*. . . .

It emerged that these conditions consisted of hard labour enforced by rifle butts, whiplashes to the face, force-feeding of castor oil, communal chanting, and other such misunderstandings. There were even occasional outings through town on a low cart, allegedly amid the jeers of nationalist fighters, while other onlookers wept in shock and horror.

> Only 14 days ago he was *working for* the concentration camp at Breslau.

Certainly not "in" the camp, at some desk job or other. Nor, to be sure, without being toughened up physically by the dynamic Heines, who had once set an example as a man of action and expected the same from those under his protection. One of these maintains:

> Eckstein had to cart heavy boulders, and when the rest of us could relax, he was ordered to clean the latrines. While scouring these, he was exhibited to visitors to the camp.

But as may happen in such cases, in spite of such distractions he succumbed to despondency, to which he was evidently prone. For during one attack

> of spiritual depression he attempted to commit suicide in his cell. He finally refused to eat, so that

—since they wanted to keep him alive—and working—

> he had to be force-fed.

They did everything possible. Doctors were summoned. They attribute his passing away

> in the *first* instance *to his losing the will to live,*

unfortunately preferring to die rather than to take on the more important tasks awaiting him. According to accounts of these fantastic atrocities, he had been taken from Breslau to Oels (the Crown Prince's residence), where "after an hour-long beating his lungs and kidneys were crushed"; he whimpered all night long; it was said that

> apparently he could no longer think straight. . . . He was brought to his unhappy mother. . . . She had him admitted to the mental asylum in Einbaumstrasse, where, soon after, he died.

The feeble resilience of the detainees often gives grounds for complaint. After spending no more than an hour or two in the camp, it is reported:

> They had to be taken to hospital.

Some prove "unfit for protective custody" even before they arrive and have to be rerouted to hospital—even if the journey had begun in an open vehicle and had to run the gauntlet of a jubilant crowd.

The judgement that someone has proved at this early stage to be "unfit for custody" is not without an element of reproach. In one such case, on the basis of statements by those escorting the prisoner, the following official report was issued (by the Bochum police):

> His body bears the marks of a number of wounds from beating. Periodic fainting and loss of consciousness were also noted. His condition is currently critical. *The circumstances under which the injuries arose have not yet been established, as the subject is still incapable of being interrogated.*

The authorities which carried out the arrest, and in whose hands the man remained throughout, were baffled; he didn't recover, and the case remains unsolved. The most conscientious investigation sometimes produces no result. As is well known, individuals active in the economic sphere must often be taken into protective custody "on suspicion of embezzlement", a most reprehensible characteristic; one such even demonstrated his unreliability while being transported, for he

> inflicted on himself injuries to his arm and his temple, which however were *not* life-threatening.

For that can happen, too. Politicians present a particularly difficult case. Some representatives who are not yet in protective custody, but merely on their way to the Reichstag, find themselves in need of hospital treatment. Such things are always reported with a degree of sympathy. A Bulgarian doctor released from protective custody, bearing traces of what had been inflicted on him—as a foreigner he only underwent treatment for three days, and besides, his wife was allowed to be present—well, he was collected by car and the person escorting him asked solicitously:

> Were you beaten? Oh, how dreadful!

Now and again it is reported, with a tinge of regret, that someone's state of health leaves much to be desired. To be sure, many cases have been observed of people simply feeling sorry for themselves. A Polish worker, for instance, yelled so loudly that the whole camp heard him; the reason was discovered later:

> he died of a weak heart; besides, he was stateless.

Most die a natural death. The diagnosis is often exhaustion; from time to time someone is overcome with faintness and plunges from the third floor into the courtyard of a police station, prompting his guard to deplore the man's carelessness in standing too close to an open window. Nor is a nervous breakdown uncommon, especially in travellers, in whose case suicide is then committed. As for this kind of death, it appears to be simply inexplicable if it takes place before the arrest, in which case the report can only say:

> Nothing is known about what motivated the deed.

In the case of Ernst Oberfohren, it is suspected that he took to heart a memorandum in his possession about the Reichstag fire.[1] Although the act was actually caused by horror when confronted with such a world, rumours stubbornly persist that his death originated from a different quarter, so it cannot fail to make an impression when we read:

> This is *indisputably* a case of suicide.

There was a similar explanation for one of the incidents at the Catholic Apprentices Festival in Munich, when a priest

> *as a result of becoming overexcited by an outbreak of street fighting,* succumbed to a *stroke.*

The following announcement should suffice to refute the suggestion that his death was due to unnatural causes—involving a fracture at the base of the skull:

> The police commissioners of Krefeld and München-Gladbach have given orders for *the use of rubber truncheons to be discontinued,* on the grounds that *this weapon* is *unworthy of a civilised nation.*

Meanwhile, Austria is old-fashioned enough to continue using truncheons against people who throw bombs.

A complete puzzle to the German authorities carrying out the investigation has been the discovery of the bodies of three drowned persons, chained together and weighed down with stones—which again seems to point to losing the will to live. Common to all versions in which such accidents are reported is a genuine note of regret that certain individuals, notably those in intellectual professions, have proved constitutionally unable to stand the strain of the great upheaval; or, again, that in this day and age so many people are afflicted by worries, alarms, and emotional instability as to cut short their natural span. But it is particularly regrettable that the meaning of protective custody is so often misunderstood, leading to expressions of vexation and impatience, though it is solely designed to protect the official or the private citizen against acts of violence that might affect his freedom: politicians against an enraged mob, lawyers and doctors against embittered clients and patients, controllers of radio stations against dissatisfied listeners. Never before has there been an age in which the state has pursued the protection of its citizens so assiduously with charitable intentions that surely deserve to be better appreciated. No one who understands the situation will deny that a Marxist past or Jewish origin in itself raises the suspicion of criminal activity. It is precisely to forestall such crimes that protective custody is used, although it is only approved after individual interrogation in the SA barracks is complete, the purpose of which is precisely defined by police regulations:

> Those arrested shall *first be brought before a branch of the national association* (SA). *The task* of the national association *is* to assist the political police by a *detailed preliminary interrogation* of those arrested regarding their offence.

Then it's off to the hospital, or if the person arrested is found to be fit for custody, internment in the camp, where treatment of the case is carried out within the framework of the community. From this it can be seen that exhaustive preparatory steps are in place, and thus how unfounded are complaints that alleged infringements on the part of SA activists might occur, without the approval of the relevant authorities. That the SA is contracted (as indeed are injuries to its victims) is meant to relieve and exonerate the political police, which has its hands full issuing false passports for murderers travelling to Austria, lifting the charge for a visa (deplored as excessive) in such deserving cases, and, finally, sustaining the assertion that none of the above is true. While these men expose themselves to the greatest danger across the border, the noxious parasites endangering the national uprising still enjoy protection. Misuse of this privilege can admittedly result in being shot while trying to escape—through the forehead, thus saving them from rashly repeating the attempt. It is true that representatives of the press, who were able to see for themselves the exemplary facilities of the camps, were not given a demonstration of such measures (which are only necessary in extreme cases), nor did they have an opportunity to attend other exercises, which are more of an internal nature. But they were permitted,

> after sampling the cuisine of the inmates' own kitchen, also to witness the release of several prisoners.

But what's the point of that? They'll be back! Shortly before going bankrupt the *Berliner Tageblatt* could still publish the sensational report:

> A considerable number of young people, who had already been released, *returned voluntarily* and asked if they might continue working in the camp. . . .

They couldn't care less about freedom after learning to appreciate the discipline of hard labour. While already capable of picturing such a camp as having facilities more fitting for concentration than distraction, one now discovers that, in addition,

> it is comparable to a *boarding school* with its rules and regulations, together with *religious services* and *classes in citizenship*.

It had been officially announced that such camps were "first and foremost educational institutions in accordance with existing regulations" and that the task of the press was to pursue the pedagogical line, for

> from the point of view of *internal politics*, the crucial question is whether *educational work* is *being carried out* in these camps.

And how!

> We know from experience that the question can be *answered unreservedly in the affirmative*

is the response of the press, which might otherwise have found its own activities subject to certain restrictions. And so it chooses a simple definition: a concentration camp is

> a *temporary restriction on freedom with educational aims*. Moreover, in many cases *one might* also speak of *a restoration to spiritual health*.

Indeed, one must! It was even discovered in Dachau

> that the communists, *who were sullen when they arrived in the camp*, after a while *began to enjoy good, patriotic songs once more. "Ich hatt' einen Kameraden"* was especially popular.[2]

In short, patriotic memories

> gain the whip hand

—provided it does not happen to be otherwise employed—and today the communists

> are *quite different people* than at the time they were taken into custody.

Meanwhile

> *fresh arrivals* are sulky, *stubborn*, and scared.

Of course, this does not mean that they felt fresh on arrival and later became stubborn, but just the opposite.

After an *educational programme* lasting a few weeks, they too will be different people. Sometimes a single day may suffice, though of course they can't comment themselves: in the first place because that's not permitted; then, too, because the psychic transformation, which often occurs slap-bang without warning, quite often leads to loss of consciousness or at least a clouding of memory, while the unexpected shock can cause speech disorders. However, one need only cite the gentlemen of the press, who assure us

> *that Germany has nothing to hide in this department either*, nor do the prisoners *have anything to complain about*.

The system runs like clockwork, it's money for old rope—if occasionally the hangman's. There's a time allocated for every task.

> Half past five: reveille; until six: bed-making.

It's true these are made of straw, that's obvious, but this is renewed at least once a week.

> Six o'clock: line up. Until half past six: *degassing and ventilation.*

Hygiene leaves nothing to be desired. Working parties, exercise, last post (9 pm) fill the daily routine; between times, there's the course of educational treatment and a striking variety of other treats and capers; lessons on citizenship from *Mein Kampf.* Here discipline still rules, while outside, where freedom reigns, it's all rather chaotic, everyone is leader and led at the same time, striking out wildly on their own. There, people are confronted by irrational forces, here in the camps they only face the supervisory staff. Here, the aim is to toughen up those who have lost their way so that they are once more fit to "become worthy members of human society"; those outside are not yet socially integrated. And so, since Dachau, Dürrgoy, and Sonnenburg do not merely resemble boarding schools but almost count as sanatoria (even if aiming more at *mens sana* than *in corpore sano*), it was decreed that, given the advantages that the state bestows on those in its care through such facilities, and because the expense incurred would otherwise be borne by the public purse, an appropriate fee should be imposed.

> Stuttgart, 23 June. Attention is drawn by the responsible authorities to the fact that *internees in protective custody are held jointly liable for the costs of their custody.* That is to say, *the liability of each individual in protective custody* for all *costs incurred by their custody. If the state exercises its pre-emptive right to do so,* it shall have *recourse* to *splitting the costs* between *the other detainees in protective custody.* Accordingly, to cover the *costs of protective custody,* orders to pay in the region of 100,000 Reichsmarks have now been issued against a number of *wealthy detainees in protective custody.*

If a wealthy individual entitled to Category 1 status refuses to sign a cheque, he is threatened with being downgraded to Category 3, but in general a grilling is sufficient to produce a signature on the cheque; after the required payment, release from the institution should promptly follow, albeit without any guarantee as to what happens after that. Evidently, from the perspective of a social policy that determines all measures taken by the state, this branch of the administration is also anxious to support those without means, whose stay in the camp, inclusive of food and treatment, is still provided free of charge, or at least at a reduced rate, at the expense of the rich who pay sanatorium prices. The representatives of the press are now satisfied that these are entirely appropriate for what is on offer. Whatever amount the inmates happen to have on them when they are admitted is changed into "camp money", with which they can purchase "snacks" in the canteen, nutrient substitutes and the like. These banknotes, with barbed-wire insignia, bear the signatures of three bank directors, cashing in on hunger and torture.

Another innovation that attracted considerable attention was the practice of continually transferring inmates between camps, the intention being to remedy grievances about the monotony of milieu, but above all to provide diversity for the staff and hence an opportunity to refine their skills by testing them out on the individuality of their charges. This is a practice that might admittedly turn the layman's stomach (easily done), seemingly spawned by the devil as one of the most ingenious products of the executioner's imagination. We read that Goering feels pity for animals and has forbidden vivisection, for "it can no longer be tolerated that animals are thought of as the equivalent of inanimate objects".[3] Those who breach this rule are sent to places where the procedure is carried out without an anaesthetic, not so much in pursuit of scientific knowledge as to amuse the medical orderlies. Frequently, what goes on there even seems to be linked to the world of music and recitals. The hangman lounges against the prison door, singing "Morgenrot, Morgenrot, leuchtest mir zum frühen Tod" (First flush of day, shall this sun rise / To light my way to early death? / The trumpet sound no sooner dies / Than I must take my final breath).[4] Feet are held to the fire until the Horst Wessel song rings out. Besides patriotic songs, hit tunes of the day are performed with instrumental accompaniment, and there's one number called "Playing the zither" or "Playing the gramophone" in which the person lying on the plank bed is the gramophone. Of course, there are not always such wild goings-on as there were at the start when even Count Helldorf came to have a look. That was the time when all of two hundred prisoners were blindfolded and stood to attention in the SA House in Annaberg, singing a variant on the song:

> *Where did I get those lovely black eyes?* From the SA. Oh, what a surprise!

On the other hand, there are reports from one camp that an Austrian, who had worked as chief stoker on a ship in Hamburg, was won over to the idea of Anschluss as follows:

> Every morning he had to empty and rinse the night-soil buckets from the cell and then line up with a Jewish merchant. Each of them had a match placed between the forefinger and middle finger of their right hand, which they then had to raise in the Hitler salute.

For half an hour the salute was accompanied by a lesson: "Chant clearly and distinctly", alternating the following maxims:

The Jew: "I—am—a—stinking—Jew!"
The Austrian: "And—I—want—to—become—a—Ger-man!"

Every time the chanting flagged, a German named Gaborinski intervened with his rubber truncheon, which is still in vogue up there. After a so-called "drubbing", from which his front teeth are still loose, the stoker managed to get deported thanks to the intervention of the Austrian consulate. He had come with 60 Reichsmarks in his pocket and some clothes and departed with just the suit he stood up in, retaining 22 Reichsmarks.

We shouldn't, however, for a moment imagine that the workings of the SA spirit are confined to straightforward thrashings; it is rather the idiosyncratic ways in which that spirit expresses itself which serve to refute the atrocity propaganda. For example, when one reads that prisoners have to pluck blades of grass with their teeth (by no means a metaphor), the said Heines, the beast of Breslau, murderer and police commissioner, has old men whipped and the former chief commissioner spat at by his officials, forcing him to sew the socialist campaign insignia on the seat of his trousers and then presenting him to visitors—all surely so improbable as to defy belief. Especially when the *Manchester Guardian* claims that the same Heines has internees taken to a pigsty and made to "shake hands with the pigs and address them as comrades", surrounded by whooping warders. One can surely understand why the *Neue Freie Presse* does not publicise such reports but prefers to concentrate on love affairs. Nevertheless, Europe has learnt via London and Paris that many prisoners in Dürrgoy, where these revels take place, have had their ribs broken; and every fourteen days they are

> taken under escort to Breslau and dragged through the streets. While marching they are *made to sing* . . . staggering along with hollow cheeks and blank expressions, starving, scourged, a procession of wretched figures no longer recognizable even to friends waiting to exchange a glance with them.

Lamentable figures such as Gerhart Hauptmann used to portray, an author now speaking up for Horst Wessel, about whom he has written a prologue.[5]

But what use does Europe make of this knowledge? And of Hitler's claim that "nothing in the Movement happens without my knowledge and without my willing it"? Or, as one state governor put it: "Nothing must happen with which the Supreme Leader cannot agree"? And ask America if, among the barely twenty cases reported, it has counted the death of the lawyers Günter Joachim [*recte* Joachim Gunther] and Alfred Strauss under torture, the butchering of the former Mecklenburg-Schwerin Prime Minister Johannes Stelling and the half-blind trade union leader Paul von Essen and all the witnesses of the massacre in Köpenick, especially the slaughter of a young girl.

Could it be that America has miscounted those consigned to the realm of the shades? And those sounds it must hear at night, "some shrill, some muffled, a ghostly hooting and screeching: tu-whit-tu-whoo, whoo, whoo"—former inmates who emerged as the ruins of God's creatures, who say they still start up from their beds convinced the voice bawling "Out!" must be directed at them? Cries of pain from those being beaten. Not to be confused with the bright sound of day, the spring chorus in Thuringia where a special procedure is in force. That's where there are high poplars that the chosen ones have to climb and sit on the branches until the last post is sounded. Then they're ordered to call out "Cuckoo!" But during this exercise, invented by nature lovers and enforced with a loaded revolver, the editor of a Social Democrat paper stands on a box and repeats aloud from morning to nightfall:

> I am a Jewish journalist pig and I wrote the following articles

while on the next box a freethinker recites the Lord's Prayer. And after every trace of Marx and Lassalle has been obliterated from their memory, could spiritual transformation be more completely realised than by what happens in Dachau, where the new believers were put to work raising a memorial to Horst Wessel? Doubtless, all this must seem incredible to the outside world, for it is incapable of visualising a German domain in which such primitive violence is unleashed with such inventive imagination, rich in ever more innovative forms of torture and humiliation. A Germany that romanticises the desecration of man seems inconceivable—until you experience and endure it yourself! And could the world go about its daily business, and sleep at night, if it were fully aware that these things are happening at the same time as it is trying to imagine them, and that they go on happening? That human beings lie unable to sleep, awaiting a beating and forced to count every blow? That there are possibilities of inflicting pain, and the anticipation of pain, of senseless and futile cruelty, compared with which ordeals and peril in time of war pale into insignificance? And does the world dare cast its eye on this Inferno, where all kinds of suffering, pain, and blood inflame the monstrous lust of these oppressors, like the hunting parties in Breughel and Hieronymus Bosch, escaped from the Middle Ages to make good here their earlier omissions? Does it look into the eyes of these tyros in the theatre of cruelty, whose youthful sexuality thrills with the mysterious mingling of torment and ecstasy—and thrives on it? For even here, even in this orgy of blood and excrement, nature plays its part, and a door to hell opens up from which there is no return for the voluptuary and no way of restoring the human dignity of his victims.

> As far as representatives of the German press are concerned, they have undertaken to report *their impressions frankly and truthfully.*

They have kept their promise. The concentration camps now being continuously expanded to meet the growing demand are not only an institution on which the world looks with envy, but one that—despite the German striving for uniformity—has ignited provincial rivalry, so that the Saxon Minister of the Interior has nevertheless declared Saxony to be far ahead of other parts of the Reich:

> *And so we alone have more than double the number of prisoners in protective custody than Prussia has, although it is much bigger!* We shall lock up anyone spreading discontent, *no matter what camp* they belong to.

Ultimately, all camps are concentration camps; the benefits accruing from the conversion and toughening up of malcontents have encouraged the Hamburg police to turn their attention to those active in water sports, which are often rumbustious affairs, and (since German authorities also enjoy their little joke) to threaten them with a concentration camp,

> so they *can be instructed in decent moral behaviour.*

These undeniable pedagogical successes have in turn prompted progressive Württemberg to open a concentration camp for women, too. This is meant not only to signal equal rights for women as a goal but also to counter the prejudice that women's only function in the Third Reich is to bear children—apparently a misunderstanding of the plan to expose childless married couples to public shame. It is true that this measure has proved necessary since we are short of soldiers, who need to be reared even more urgently, it seems, than culturally home-grown conductors who might erase the memory of Toscanini. One simply cannot allow couples who have been encouraged to marry to pocket the 1,000-Mark premium per child, only for the man to use it on an entry visa to Austria, say, instead of doing his patriotic duty. So the population policy of the Third Reich presents considerable difficulties, inasmuch as defamation of childlessness also to some extent contradicts the intention to take existing children away from parents in order to instruct them in the tenets of National Socialism—something colleagues in Chicago implement without using pedagogy as a pretext, and certainly without announcing it in advance. At the end of the day, the problem of human reproduction is a hard nut to crack, especially in Prussia, where young males accustomed to regimented sexual intercourse (*Gleichschaltung* by another name) generally lack the appropriate guidelines, so Grete misses out on what Hans hasn't learnt. This clinging to customs which enhance the heritage of Frederick the Great, but not the birthrate, also explains a certain conformity in appearance and apparel, which certainly marks both sexes as authentic standard-bearers of the movement but makes any erotic connection implausible. The encouragement of long hair in the demonstrably female contingent has met with surprisingly successful results in the shortest possible time; but whether a different norm will gain acceptance among Heroes from that which has won favour with Valkyries, only time will tell. The world of transvestites, which has congregated since time immemorial in the so-called male temples of Venus, retaining recognizably female sexual characteristics, is said to have suffered something of a setback. However, the urge which pairs off those in search of beauty in ritual dances, and prompts even elderly bachelors to play ladies' choice, is doubtless still alive. It is significant that, among the superabundant demonstrations of power which characterise the Movement in all its versions and perversions, acts of violation—namely of the other sex, which is after all the order of the day in revolutions and other warlike ventures—have rarely occurred. One can imagine what retribution might be extracted by a breed of men far removed from nature (in the SS barracks in Hedemannstrasse, for instance) when once unleashed—the type whose cultural interests in orderly times matched the proclamation:

> *Killing of a prostitute!*

or the professional censure of a boxer:

> *At first, Walter didn't quite get through to the region of the liver.*

But in the degradation of human life, in the disgraceful violence suffered since breaking and entering into people's private accommodations has become an organised activity, it has been noted that while brute force has been applied without respect of persons, even those campaigning against atrocities have not dared to claim that women's sexual honour has been affected. The opening of concentration camps for women—something mentioned again only in this context—surely proves that here too it is primarily the toughening up of this generation, rather than its reproduction, that is the aim. To cover every eventuality, guidelines have also been laid down in this sphere:

> The German woman *must become once more* the model *Germanic spouse*, and the German girl *must prepare herself for this honour*, to be one day worthy of bearing this name. *Little poppets* gadding about all

> dolled up in their war paint and makeup, thinking themselves fascinating and *simply the bee's knees,*

cannot be tolerated, so they'll be placed under supervision. That "the German woman does not smoke" is self-evident; if it is not, she will be reminded of her duties as a German woman and a mother. Once they've got that straight, attention will be drawn to the fact that gentlemen should prefer blondes—blondes with blue eyes, an open look, a rosy complexion, and a little mouth.

> *We demand* that the Aryan, *whatever the circumstances,* takes a virgin as his wife.

But instead of the Aryan giving the person issuing this demand a clip round the ear, his tendency to slavish obedience in such matters actually leads him to accept the further prohibition against lusting after the "Mediterranean type"

> with its characteristic negroid head and slim body *as well as her oval breasts.*

Instead of receiving another clout for lousy grammar, the custodian of racial purity feels obliged

> *to acknowledge, to his surprise,* that there are *still* some German girls who are not ashamed to appear in public with Jews.

That is why he not only feels he has to insert ironic inverted commas around "ladies", but also their names and addresses in the newspaper; and then add: "Taken into custody by SA and SS". They should

> *not be surprised* if one day they *are given a good hiding.*

But who would still be surprised at anything? Everywhere responsibility is shifted, and it is precisely the person handing out the beatings who deserves to be on the receiving end. It was the satrapy of Julius Streicher, from whose head the idea of a more comprehensive boycott sprang, that blazed this trail: a girl was led by six men in uniform through the taverns, her head shaven, so she could be spat at by the public. Somebody who witnessed this, on Sunday the 13th of August, reported it, and *The Times* adds that a notice was hung round her neck with her severed pigtails attached, together with the words:

> I gave myself to a Jew.

Stormtroopers surrounded her on the stage in every cheap nightclub, bellowing out the words and hurling further abuse. The girl, "slim, fragile, and despite her shaven head exceptionally pretty", was led past the row of international hotels.

> She stumbled once or twice and was dragged up onto her feet again by the squad, sometimes lifted up so those looking on from a distance could see her too. When this happened, she was shouted at by the public and mocked and for fun invited to make a speech.

The American Ambassador's children saw it happen; Europe heard about it. Nothing like it ever happened in a nightmare. Then it was reported that she had gone mad. Even if all thought of vengeance by a debased humanity had been turned to stone by the sight of the bloody spectre haunting it—for this deed, and the fate of this one girl, there will one day be flames of retribution.

22

SEXUAL HATRED, "UNFORCED" CONVERSATION, AND AN ACT OF DEFIANCE

What then occurred makes any comparison with the German Middle Ages blasphemous. A venomous witch's brew of sexual hatred and extorted confessions was spewed out between Nuremberg, Ingolstadt, Mannheim, Worms, and Cassel, and out of this journalistic filth a pillory has been erected day by day "to rehabilitate the race and cleanse nature of its pollution". A couple is driven through the streets in a car with placards round their necks:

> I dishonoured a German woman.
> I gave myself to a Jew.

Everywhere you could read, with names and addresses supplied, announcements like the following:

> She has the gall to appear in taverns on the arm of a Jew.
>
> She accompanied the Talmudic Jew on long journeys.
>
> If she is caught again, she can imagine what will happen to her and the Jew.
>
> We would not name her if this wretched female, having forgotten her racial origins, were from now on to *acknowledge the new age* in which we are living and break off relations with the member of the alien race. *She has not done so.* Her behaviour makes a mockery of all racial pride and national consciousness. That is why she deserves to be pilloried. *The whole neighbourhood* is shocked at this racial outrage, and *we welcome this healthy reaction.* Perhaps *some courageous German* will step forward and tell this Jew's whore *to her face* ... of her disgrace, and also *tell* the Jew as well *what's what.*
>
> ... threatened publicly to denounce any women who offend *against the pure-blooded community* ... a certain Thea D., who apparently deems it an honour to be the first to be mentioned ... we shall refrain from

> exposing her *this time.* If she is ever again seen with the Jew, she will be branded for what she is. We ask all racially conscious Germans to *look out for* any Christian girl who becomes a Jew's whore and to inform us of *her address and that of the Jew, including the facts of the case.*
>
> … the *fury* felt about this matter is widespread. *Girls in love with Jews* should regard these lines as *a serious warning* and be aware that their activities will not be tolerated for much longer.
>
> … has allegedly been caught in the act. *Further investigations have been initiated* and revealed that Fräulein Habermann was indeed seen with a Jew but that there were *no intimacies, let alone sexual intercourse … Der Stürmer will come back to the case.*
>
> The girl's *mother* has not done anything against the relationship, but allows it to continue. The girl, a Christian, *takes the view* that *the government has no right to prohibit the relationship either. In order publicly to expose these fine specimens to the population at large* and make them see *the error of their ways, SS Pioneers* drove *the Jew, his mistress, and her mother* through the streets of Cassel.

In Mannheim, the caption "You are looking at Jews' whores!" appears under photos with the question "Do you recognise her?" The scoundrel, claiming to be "conscious of our sacred mission", then sets out the following aims:

> The designation "German Woman" should no longer be applied to this fine lady, especially as the Hebrew comes and goes in her house whenever he wishes.
>
> Here are two more of the *little minxes …*
>
> It's for her own good, too, if she prefers emigration to Palestine to *the sterilisation awaiting her.*
>
> She has *betrayed her race* and has consequently cut herself off from the pure-blooded Aryan community.
>
> How it is possible *to take such a strong liking for these Asiatics,* is beyond comprehension.
>
> in a relationship with the Jew …, who is *still employed as a senior engineer* at the ASKA company …
>
> Perhaps one day the *police* will *take her under supervision.*

The article containing this list is written in a German of which any of the Jews denounced would be ashamed, and spiced with an Aryan irony that would make a worm squirm. The scoundrel, who signs himself with the pseudonym "Tiger", rounds it off with a threat:

> *If just one more* girl of Aryan blood *is caught with a Jew, forgetting her racial origins,* it could well happen that *the creature has her head shaved like a trollop* and *is exposed to the public gaze on Breite Strasse.* As for Jewboys, we recommend they work off their lust on *Rebeccas* of their own race from now on, otherwise the *Volk* might one day take bitter revenge.

Of course, here as elsewhere, the sacred mission of these racial bullies and pimps is to deprive people of their jobs, to which end it whistles for the police or the other irresponsible organised force (the SA):

> *On account of his lechery this Jew is known throughout the city.* Complaints about this Jew *to the management were made in vain. How would it be if the SA or the authorities took a closer look* at this peculiar "pure-blooded comrade"?

Postscript:

> *Summary dismissal.* In addition, the *police* are already *pursuing the matter further. That is also cause for celebration.*

The *Greater German News Agency:*

> In future the police will see to it that *these fellows* are reminded of their *duty,* namely with a few weeks in a *concentration camp.* What must surely be required of these young men and women, who never found it necessary to fight for the victory of the National Socialist coalition, is that they do not *sabotage the arduous work of building up the Movement.*

Sabotaged in bed! The Gestapo in Dortmund:

> The vast majority of the *Volk* have—*thank God!*—recognised the enormous danger inherent in any further mixing of *German blood with Jewish elements.* . . . The State Police is not prepared *to tolerate this state of affairs without taking action.* In future the police will take such irresponsible members of the *Volk* into *protective custody* and make them conscious of their grievous *offence against pure German descent.*

Police report from Worms:

> ... attempted to approach a Christian girl in an offensive manner. The man in question was ... *taken to the Osthofen concentration camp.*

Someone who got married and as a consequence was beaten up files a complaint and is officially notified:

> The Cassel Police Commissioner
> Cassel Police Headquarters
> Königstrasse 31
> Cassel, 16 August 1933
> To Herr.....
> With reference to complaint of the 12th of August 1933
> The matter at issue is *a justified outburst of national fury* that a *girl of German blood,* in this day and age, should still consort with *someone of an alien race.* That *the anger of the SS men in particular* was aroused by *your behaviour in marrying a girl of German blood seems to me only natural.* Such reactions *demonstrate a healthy instinct in the Volk,* and *accordingly* I cannot see that *any criminal offence* was committed. *Some hundreds of years ago,* racially conscious Jews stoned girls of their race for consorting with Christians (of alien blood).
> Signed von Pfeffer
> Certified:——illegible.
> Police Secretary.

Since then the Jews have abandoned this practice. In what jungle on earth could such things happen? From such events the underworld averts its countenance [3828]. The honorary president of the National German Jews is said to be annoyed. The Nazi Party Conference is taking place in Nuremberg, and the Deutsche Reichspost issued a pictoral telegram to mark the occasion bearing a large eagle and "the swastika beaming down on it like a sun breaking through dark clouds"; ever since the sun began to shine on this planet, it has never witnessed a darker shame. It was in Nuremberg that Wedekind gave me *Pandora's Box* in the summer of 1904. But not all German women are at risk of the chastisement portrayed in that play, most are already chaste, ill-disposed towards Jews and devoted to more earnest endeavours—allowing themselves to be enlisted in provincial associations, which are directly under the relevant Regional Womens' Association leaders (or *Gau-Frauenschafts-Leiterinnen*), who in turn are under the Reich leadership of the NS-Women's Association.[1] Is this not simply the end of the fairer sex? What nevertheless occasionally slips out, rises to an ardent climax:

> What a blessing he is, divinely inspired! . . . What a darling of the gods!! . . . And *this greatest of men—past, present, and future*—belongs—to us! *To us!!!* Can we ask for anything more? Have we deserved it? A blessing, pure and simple? *Maybe you'll laugh at me—I don't care*, go ahead, laugh! We're all laughing again now, *blooming, flourishing*, giving our sacred trust to him alone, our saviour and liberator—our very own Chancellor, our hero!

Such atrocity propaganda must be checked at the source. The evidence of one's own eyes is always the most convincing evidence, although cases where nothing actually happened offer the most effective rebuttal of accusations of harassment—which is still widely practised. For example, there was the recent affair of the secretary of a foreign legation who was detained in a normal investigation on suspicion of illegal business dealings—something that could happen before the great upheaval as well—and who was released when the suspicion proved unfounded—which happens even today. In brief:

> *Such are the atrocities in Hitler's Germany!*

National Socialist thought fascinates by virtue of its ability to make someone who tells the truth in one instance seem trustworthy when it's all lies; as when he makes the theft he—for once—didn't commit his alibi for a thousand murders. Perhaps even an eyewitness account of the (nonexistent) theft would not prevent it from being confirmed, who knows? But it's often enough to establish the truth by radio.

In my own case, for example, I heard "unforced conversational exchanges with detainees in protective custody", who personally gave all the information one could ask for—the programme actually bore this title, in itself enough to dispel any suspicion of something done under duress. "In order to counter the lies disseminated abroad", it consisted of conversations between the superintendent—a man who had obviously just seized the helm and was methodically testing it out on his charges; a representative of the Press Office; and genuine prisoners (certainly not actors playing the part), mostly former ministers from Baden, on whom—as was convincingly ascertained and heard by millions—there were

> *no outward traces* of any injury.

The prisoners—defenceless as this listener, who had previously only shared as a reader of written reports the sufferings inflicted on others—answered one after the other that they had nothing to complain about, a formula as stereotypical as the "November criminals"—so called on national radio, like the use of the title "the Jew X". The production wasn't entirely successful, sometimes the right answers had to be prompted rather forcefully as well as audibly, so that one also heard the noises off. In the final dialogue there was a perceptible bit of bungling, followed by a terrible silence (not the fault of the aether), then the person putting the question, whose way of speaking had up to then been that of a glib illiterate, started stammering. The unfortunate to whom the question had been put—enquiring whether he had been ill-treated, as claimed by hostile propaganda—sobbed and burst out:

> No, my ears—they didn't cut them off—but they destroyed—my whole existence—

The unforced conversation seemed to have come to an abrupt end. But it was repeated on a gramophone recording, with all the attendant shortcomings of improvisation, and it was this repetition that I heard. It surpassed anything one could imagine, either planned or actually carried out, intensified by the realisation that such horror, such monstrous propaganda, was actually designed to refute hostile propaganda! Faced with this attempt to manipulate the minds of the masses with a single godforsaken voice, one could only wonder whether the bungling was more active or passive, whether such a miscalculation was merely due to brazen devilry or to abysmal stupidity. It was transmitted from Stuttgart on 8 April 1933 between hourly doses of shrill sloganising and dance music; it trumped all other bestial impositions on the aether, on the ear, and on human dignity. A programme entitled "The Marxist Marriage", which was broadcast at the same time, was both contrived and convincing; but even more convincing was this "unforced" conversation. What German of the better sort would not have died of shame at the thought that listeners abroad, at whom it was aimed, might actually have heard it? Some evil spirit drives those in power from one blunder to the next. And since the refutation is conveyed in such a fashion, the propaganda it is contesting has in fact changed its tune, and is no longer primarily occupied with reports of atrocities, but only with the attempts to refute them, and never lets the least utterance of prominent Nazi spokesmen pass without reaffirming the "prejudice" they are intent on wiping out root and branch. To this end, the Nazis resort to the repeated assurance on the radio that these spokesmen are the "standard-bearers of truth", which is only now making itself heard. But one man's testimony is likely to mean two different things these days, so—as the proverb puts it—both must be heard. And indeed we hear more heartfelt pronouncements than we can really digest, where'er the German forked tongue resounds.[2] Thus Hans Frank—Frank II, as he's already called—has declared to the wider world:

> National Socialism is committed to the ideals of humanity!

But in all fairness we should also hear the other side of his argument, which continued as follows:

> All Jews without exception must be excluded from any form of legal existence!

As is well known, the reception he received from the emissary of the Austrian government on the airfield at Aspern was more clear-cut. Equally clearly, and without any partisan motive, I have to say—knowing as I do the intellectual impact when a well-placed form of words becomes a dramatic turning point in the action—that this word-become-deed pleased me more than any other since the foundation of the Republic, far more than anything from the realm of empty slogans which leave the political opposition only the disappointment of seeming to bite on jelly. After a period crippled by dutiful promises made and then betrayed, and given the flagging rhetoric of the opposition, what pleases me about this act of defiance—the decision to tell the visitor right there on the threshold that his visit was

> not very welcome

—indeed, what really impressed me was its novelty—a formulation to the point and unembellished, for once not mere words, the courage to do what has not been done before in politics, a breach of diplomatic conventions which surprised more than just the person addressed. For even if it was only a response to the very conventions being breached, the arbitrary infringement of people's sovereign rights to life and liberty, it still called for a gutsy display of energy—political courage as well as strong nerves—to reassert those rights. Imagine the scene: a Minister of the German Reich comes flying in on what, though not officially, is the first visit since world history was so rudely disrupted—and yet the Sirens sing:

> Banish hate and envy, rather!
> We the purest pleasures gather,
> Under Heaven's auspicious sphere!
> On the earth and on the ocean,
> We, with cheerful beckoning motion,
> Bid the wanderer welcome here. [7166 (Bayard Taylor)]

The author of that greeting is Federal Chancellor Dollfuss, the person who delivered it Assistant Commissioner of Police Skubl. It was such a simple phrase, it immediately acted as a dam, quelling the most powerful and destructive torrent that ever engulfed the established order. It marked the beginning of the end of this deluge in a most astonishing way, expunging the myriad marks of Cain with which a satanic will had covered the war-weary face of the land (the location at Aspern, scene of Napoleon's defeat in 1809, was singularly appropriate). I'm aware that even to acknowledge this pivotal action, unique in interstate relations, to applaud the conspicuous courage shown by Austrian ministers at the time and ever since, itself requires courage: courage when confronted with the obfuscation of politics by empty phrase-mongering and dogmatic stupidity, which denies the unmistakable benefit of an act that ultimately also serves the Social Democratic cause—and thereby risks advancing the cause of the mortal enemy. But I do not fear the censure of those socialist functionaries of freedom when I acknowledge the superior strategy which, for once, is being pursued by our government, for I have less to fear from being misconstrued than they have. In my role as accredited campaigner against official abuses and as a consistent adversary of this Austrian century, I remain committed to the positive outcome of its strategy, even if the powers of darkness were not its sole opponents. And as an artist, untouched by envy, I pay tribute to the excellence of an inspiration which, in a blunt, down-to-earth manner, makes short work of all political claptrap with, for once, a liberating expression of what everyone feels—in a realm where lying is the norm and utter humbug prevails under state or socialised control.

Is it not depressing to imagine personages as unwelcome as Hans Frank being admitted to diplomatic circles? To think that people abroad still "break bread" with them, however aware they are of the misery and disgrace such types have inflicted on their people—over and above the commiseration we rightly feel for those people, however questionable they may be as blood brothers? How can anyone tolerate the stench of blood—in the shedding of which such types were personally implicated—emanating from the country they represent? That there can ever be an exchange of views with violence, unforced conversational exchanges with jailers, discussions and meetings and all the rest of such nonsense (at public expense), all of which are mere preliminaries to something even worse! Isn't even the hobnobbing at the League of Nations in Geneva problematic—with envoys such as Goebbels—against whom, in addition to what is already proven, there is a strong suspicion of responsibility for the Communists starting the Reichstag fire? Success stories shouldn't be underestimated, like that of the Silesian Jew who, in a brave individual initiative, succeeded in getting the protection of minorities accepted.[3] Simply to disarm the honest German sleepyhead, who conceals a weapon under his nightgown, calls for "conferences" on a scale that Berlin theatre directors couldn't manage, even before they went broke.

How irrational that a diplomacy which connects the real world with a kingdom that is not of this world, that of the Vatican, was destined to confer prestige on the calamity![4] Equally irrational is the opposite extreme: a single-minded statecraft that bases terrestrial well-being on the most harebrained plans for the reconstruction of mankind. Far be it from us to pronounce on a Marxist system that is so far away, otherwise we might have to acknowledge that it destroyed fewer German workers than Russian peasants (upsetting Russian journalists and finally causing a degree of friction). Probably this is how things must be, and the salvation of the world demands that comrades Litvinov and Henderson should take a strong line at the conference.[5] Or perhaps the whole world is a blackmail victim when gangsters seize control of the coffers of the state. Then politics would be to blame for the situation, and to cap it all off mankind has got used to feeling that politics is beyond human control. And the astonishing thing about these matters would then be not so much that politics exists but that born politicians follow this calling and learn its language—a language remote from reality and yet with all too real consequences.

In the officially approved language there may be no expression for events that break the heart of God's creation, but it is surely not asking too much to be spared such honorifics as "putting out feelers" where nothing is felt; being "assured of attention" when no attention is paid; or to be committed "without prejudice" to a move that remains rooted to the spot, even when it consists of a social round that proves entirely circular; or the endless self-exhortations: "for this purpose it is essential", "we cannot wait any longer", "it cannot be too difficult"—namely to ensure that nothing happens. The thread of politeness does not even break when chaos presents its respects to the world in the guise of a hard taskmaster, and when the disruption of civilised behaviour plays its trump card by forcing the world to shut its eyes to the use of force. If a natural sound ever intrudes upon this rigid ceremonial, it comes as a shock. One wishes that postwar diplomacy, with its imperturbable patience and keen appetite, could experience that indescribable "unforced conversation" from the camp, for that would reduce it to helpless silence. Then at last it would become aware of the excruciating reality lurking behind those empty phrases!

23

DOLLFUSS AND THE SOCIAL DEMOCRATS

Declaring the embodiment of German diplomacy to be unwelcome in Austria is a decision that deserves to be supported, not impeded, by those who will ultimately owe it their continued existence as—essentially—"political pensioners". They know this but are such Pharisees that they profess the contrary, thus thwarting any effective measures against an evil they know themselves too weak to avert. This must be stated loud and clear—just as the boldness of that declaration was welcomed—even if this takes courage when faced with the mendacity of a supposedly "principled" stance which lacks any such courage. For if they had any, the Social Democrats would long ago have acknowledged the "harsh realities", so frequently cited in the past as alibis for failure; would have recognised that their power deficit derives from a surfeit of empty phrases; that a state of war leaves no scope for tactical manoeuvres; and that for the first time we find ourselves confronting a political reality that speaks of action and actually means what it slays.

Much of what once existed has gone. But one principle—an essential insight—needs to be preserved, once we recognise that the opportunity for reform in 1918 was bungled; that Social Democracy lost the peace and for that very reason must bear responsibility for this failure; that it became the scapegoat with only itself to blame; that the dying breath of freedom fades away and vanishes more swiftly than the sweetest music, defying all quantitative efforts to recover it; and that the word "struggle" has become an empty slogan with which expert diagnosticians of interminable party squabbles bore us to death. The essential insight is that the sleeping dog of freedom cannot be woken by the instruction to take to the streets under the banner of "Defiance", a cheap form of popular theatre that has had its day, and that the question whether the three arrows in the socialist insignia should point upward or downward, outward or inward, is irrelevant![1]

When the Reichstag was in flames, and all those who didn't set it on fire were already being skinned alive in protective custody, even a protest signed

"Long Live Liberty!"—Office of the Second International[2]

(which could not prevent the Third Reich, but rather promoted it) is as ineffectual as the solemn vow of the General Secretary, Friedrich Adler, to renounce Anschluss once and for all, though retaining the pipe dream of a "Greater Germany". Compare this with the plausible, indeed uniquely plausible, reassurance offered by the statement:

> *We're the same as we always were!*

In the exchange between the defiant Karl and the justifiably aggrieved Franz (the scoundrel), sounding like characters from Schiller's *The Robbers*, Franz, speaking in the vernacular, hits the nail on the head:

> Aren't we the fine fellows![3]

However, Karl's warning:

> Today the *struggle* is once more a *real* one, and every individual counts. . . . If we are attacked, we *defend* ourselves. . . . We will *not* be *intimidated!*

seems more reminiscent of the tailor Zwirn's even more homespun resolve in Nestroy's farce *Lumpazivagabundus*: "Once I get goin', cobbler, once I get goin'—but I ain't got goin' yet!" Perfectly honourable, for as a pacifist and a democrat he may well, and should, disapprove of violent methods. But to demand "discipline" in party assemblies for a decision which, thank God, we've been spared, having long since become used to having them made "without our involvement but over our heads"; to act as if, now more than ever and in spite of everything and though notwithstanding the fact that nevertheless, even if, and so on and so forth—up to the last breath of man and mountebank, sticking to empty phraseology whose content can only mean bloodshed, the blood that we cannot bear to see. . . . In the long run, the endless long run, this conjures up the image of a pitiable political figure who, for all the energy expended on phrasing and tactics, is still incapable of the strength of purpose to make a single short sentence come alive, one that has sufficient political objectivity, psychological assurance, and formal precision to break the spell. Standing at a distance from the cultural goal of both opposing worlds, but closer to what was socially planned (though not achieved) than to the content of many an emergency decree, it would be wrong for me to disguise or deny that the calibre of such party bigwigs, for all their rage and mockery, doesn't measure up to that of Dollfuss—the very antithesis of someone physically able to put the German colossus in his pocket, which in European eyes puts him head and shoulders above it. True, the magical motif of Walpurgis Night:

> A radiant dwarf! The like I ne'er did see [8245 (after Bayard Taylor)]

threatens to degenerate into toadyism. But from the dizzy flight through nether regions, where every kind of wisdom and warning can be found, the professional dissident can only cite the vulnerability of Homunculus:

> Such frailty is exposed to protean temptations,
> With symptoms of imperious yearning [8469]

But there is absolutely no danger that the most energetic force that Austria has seen in living memory could succumb if the protean Nazi leadership should tempt him with a charm offensive. It was only an unwelcome interlude when the Christian Social organ—between the end of the Zentrum Party and the guaranteed prospect of its own demise—was taken in by that unappetising enticement; when it seemed stupefied by the "change of tone" in the brigands' shameless praise for the Austrian police and was ready to welcome a figure who

> is *helping to make* Austrian National Socialism into *a factor* in Austrian politics. . . . The leaders of the Austrian government and their friends *would be the last* to refuse their support.

But the first to end up in a concentration camp. It was of course grist to the newspaper mill of those who tirelessly belittle the achievements of a man who, in spite of mentioning our "brother" to the north rather too often, has no intention of jeopardising the benefits of Austria's European position by such fraternising, and who is capable of resisting hostile compliments every bit as robustly as fraternal bombs. But he was spared another trial of strength the very next day, when, thanks to the principle of authoritarian irresponsibility and total disunity, the protean exponent of that "change of tone" had changed his tune again and the official offer of peace was retracted, to be replaced by the more official mission in which the brigands accused the police of abuse of the law. Well may the Sirens warn:

> Let them to descend be bidden!
> In the branches they have hidden
> Hideous falcon-claws they're wearing,
> And you'll feel their cruel tearing
> Once you lend them willing ear. [7161 (Bayard Taylor)]

Repeatedly turning a deaf ear to the fury unleashed by Nazism, and facing down daily attacks designed to plunge this country into the direst adventurism, requires circumspection, stamina, and courage, such as a representative of Imperial Austria would scarcely have mustered. When someone demonstrates such qualities, he deserves to have them recognised, however great the political pressure to demonstrate an oppositional stance, while respect for his actions inhibits the impulse to resort to cultural satire. Naturally, I don't enjoy seeing the man who achieved this allowing himself to be escorted by the Honorary President of the PEN Club (Felix Salten) as the national anthem rings out (since Dollfuss at least will be thinking of "Gott erhalte").[4] Nor can I endorse his declaration that there is nothing in Austria's past or present of which Austrians need to be ashamed, at least with respect to the period I have lived through. Of course, it depends on one's personal sensibility. At the turn of the century and during the final years of the Monarchy, the war period, and the Republic, it was never possible for me to shake off a sense of shame at the betrayal of Austria's cultural, human, and geographical patrimony to a mafia of political and journalistic opportunists, such as has never before been spawned and tolerated in any community. To the extent that I am inclined to grant the state any connection with underlying humanity, I feel drawn to it for the first time. It's not easy admitting as much, for it's hard to lay open to scrutiny the workings of one's own mind in forming impressions, yet a satirist who is sufficiently sure of his function can not only acknowledge a vigour and resolve unprecedented in Austria but also recognises the jokes this inspires from Social Democratic journalists as his own intellectual legacy. Joking aside! For jokes must yield to a sense of decency, indeed to respect for what has clearly been undertaken in the public interest and under constant threat of death. My polemic is more comprehensive: at present, disregarding norms and forms, it is confined to activities which make a mockery of both polemic and self-preservation. Indeed, I am incapable of any satirical response to Dollfuss—while in the course of these reflections my mind no longer goes altogether blank at the thought of Hitler. In spite of *The Last Days of Mankind*, I now spurn the use of mockery—something I have bequeathed to younger talents so that in this time of mortal peril they can utilise it against the country's saviour. All this may yet tempt them to turn their mockery against me. If so, they'll get the surprise of their life, watching me reclaim it!

In no way do I overestimate Herr Dollfuss apart from his manifest achievements in what really matters; but he undervalues himself when he compares the national emergency of today with that of 1914. At that time, Austria would have done better not to rise up but to remain as lethargic as ever; only now, twenty years later, is it entering into what the standard textbooks recognise as a "sacred defensive war". What threatens the country today, what threatens the working classes, is something their spokesmen know as well as I do, only they don't have even the glimmer of courage needed to admit it. They may well say that "being honest towards the masses is one of the most important tasks", but they don't practise what they preach. It is surely not surprising that I think fighting for the basis of "freedom" to be more useful—despite the sacrifices it entails—than the sham fights of those who have frittered it away, since as a commentator on public affairs I have devoted my whole life to facing the facts and above all to challenging those who deny them, and whose professional calling obliges them in newsprint to do so. Since facts in the real world unfortunately change from day to day and cause "contradictions", while stupidity is ingrained and can last a lifetime, my declaration of faith in Austria—though still without the least trace of any hope that Austria might declare its faith in me—in no way depends on a satirical stance that is reduced in the eyes of the public to mere "negation" (it is one of its most tedious platitudes). In truth, it has never been merely by demolishing destructive forces but also in a "positive" sense—by conserving more actively than is officially possible—that satire has helped to preserve intellectual and spiritual values, whose annexation by a barbarism that claims to share our language would be the work of the devil. Given such a self-assessment, satire remains both remote from the possibility of sacrificing its accumulated memories for a nonexistent socialist art and immune to being drawn towards the cultural interests of present-day Austria, which, I suspect, still aspire to the Christian-Germanic ideal of beauty.

I'm not talking about the life of the mind—I can take care of that myself! The real issue is to safeguard the basis of life itself, and that doesn't seem to me in any way impaired by a restriction on the freedom of the press. Nor even by the reduction of the number of titles, the curb on despotic opinions, and the taming of intellectual parasites. This audacious enterprise demonstrates more courage against the press than the conformity enforced on the press in Germany, where the regime evades criticism by exacting its own will. The forceful and beneficial measures in Austria, prefigured and acknowledged on every page of *Die Fackel*, have an impact that is reflected in the stifled market cries and teeth-gnashing frustration of those peddling such merchandise. If only newsprint were now confined to factual reporting, all would be well; if this had been done earlier, and globally, there would have been no war for the world to regret and no Hitler to fear. I share the progressive view that such measures were not possible either in liberal or in absolutist Austria. They required a determination that breaks the law of inertia without democratic scruples and, faced with calamity, demonstrates that it is actually still possible to do something. This observation in no way leads me into the sphere of politics but, on the contrary, into that of logic. Both the obvious objections to a nostalgic restoration of Habsburg traditions and the vigorous resistance to a system that would make the working classes pay for the sins of their bogus liberators must be set aside in favour of the fundamental aim: to save human lives. As to my own stance, now that I'm through with

Social Democracy, perhaps it will be attributed to a wish to gain favour with the Christian Socials. But the existential reason is that for the first time the primary interest of the individual, to preserve life and liberty of action, coincides with preserving the integrity of the state; and that a government which promotes this aim is doing a useful job—while a party that obstructs it with doctrinaire humbug lacks all sense of "realpolitik", to borrow a phrase from the country they used to regard with a wistful gaze.

24

CASTING OUT THE DEVIL THROUGH BEELZEBUB

However lamentable the decline of the Social Democratic Party for its followers, its inability to block the actions now so urgently needed is still an achievement. For the only thing the party inevitably achieves is that no one takes its stated aims seriously. Social Democracy is like the bad actor in Lutter & Wegner's Berlin wine bar, to whom a famous colleague tried to explain the reason for his flops, namely: "people just don't believe you" (even though he spoke quite well). "Go on, try to order a carafe of wine—the waiter listens to you, leaves, but doesn't come back with the wine—he simply doesn't believe you!" And we are expected to believe those who say they want to fight on the barricades, however loudly they proclaim it? The language is antiquated, it has no connection with the matter in hand, so it fails to come alive. Admittedly, National Socialism has thrived on a similar or at least an equally antiquated intellectual rhythm, while Socialism has been weakened by it. But the Nazis not only talked the talk, they also walked the walk; romantic through and through—and as a result better organised. Here: madness; there: merely a vacuum, from which Socialism wants to create its own unique reality. At a loss when the other camp takes up a rhetorical phrase and goes on to offer it to its readers:

> At the end of the day, the bright flickering flame will once more flare up into the sky.

Flare up it does, alas! The Nazi delusions may only have created delusionary figures, ruination, and death, but create them it did; it turned them into reality. But these incessant repetitions of "we for our part . . . whereas they", "on the one hand . . . on the other"—the litany fills every Social Democratic editorial—set the paper on fire when they write their inflammatory exhortations, yet every time they give their incendiary speeches, they stand by to douse the flames—a fire brigade that no one could mistake for a brigade of the SA! And while the poor German comrades in the Reichstag had to sing the national anthem, those standing on guard in Vienna, an exemplary body of men, still have the courage to maintain:

International capitalism has been rocked to its foundations.

But because Christianity turned the other cheek, and (even more crushingly) Russia thwarted hopes of a counter-Concordat—since the effects of politics are not guided by humanitarian concerns, and international horrors on the left blot out those on the right—there is consequently

only *one* power

whose enmity will endure

until the tyranny of the swastika *is overthrown*. That power is

Social Democracy![1] For until the tyranny overthrows itself—and surely only it can!—there will certainly be blood, but also paper, so that this kind of humour can help to dispel these baleful times.

If one pictures this natural catastrophe, the destruction of German Social Democracy, as the work of the Devil ("He blew with His winds and they were scattered"), then surely what has been—and will continue to be—glossed over with slippery words is beyond comprehension. And it is desolating to think how many hopes and disappointments were already twisted by lies, how many harsh realities by being lumped together and explained as "dialectical evolution", involving a guided tour through the ebb and flow of history, and by a makeshift intellectualism that even the experts would surely find too stupid were they not using it to stupefy the others. Never before have party leaders degraded such concepts as "struggle" and "power" into bureaucratic jargon, perverting them by tendentious typography. But when they fear to provoke proletarian impatience with such mockery, they switch to concepts such as isegoria, isonomy, and isotimia [equality in freedom of speech; equality before the law; equality of esteem/privilege] for a change—concepts that will supposedly facilitate the "free canvassing of opinions" and the "intellectual battle of convictions", so that everyone, including the Swastiklers, can go at it with both barrels, "canvassing support". After all, nothing should be more pressing than to oppose violence by democratic means, which violence can then be used to destroy democracy all the more effectively. This comes somewhere between swearing untenable oaths of solidarity (as in Schiller's *Wilhelm Tell*) and filing for bankruptcy, leaving us with the same old ticklish question: "Now the Party's over, what shall we do with the rest of the evening?"

Quibbles and squabbles, such as always emerge when fading passion fizzles out, have transformed an intellectual clique that reproduces itself by splitting into an international scourge. God created it in His wrath to represent the workers' cause—but these politicians are visionaries! Incapable of grasping the obvious, they project into the future, and each debacle is naturally only an episode in a gigantic revolutionary process:

> And for that reason: if we *have to return* to *forms* of the *struggle* that amount to a *setback for evolution,* and at the same time *move forwards* towards the *measures* required by the new age—*all of this combines to unify* the *great struggle* itself: its *past* origins, its *present* commitments, and its *future* orientation.

Stuff and nonsense! Who can make head or tail of it? Neither the proletarian reader, for whom the verbiage merely disguises their defeat, nor its author, who should be pressed to give a more detailed description of what he means by the "struggle", its "forms" and "measures", and especially how he distinguishes between them. Also what he imagines "evolution" to be, though one can indeed imagine the nervous strain it imposes on some female party official who has to carry the can. What one can readily imagine is the tragedy of a party whose history relies on the belated inspirations of its spokesmen, which by this time are Jewish jokes à la Pollak.

All that remains is the language in which party spokesmen convey their loss of power. No word is too grandiose or too far-fetched as a means of conveying their misfortune to the poor victims, who—to add insult to injury—still have to work out what it means. The evolution that *caused* the wrack and ruin, for example, rather than *was caused by* the wreckers—it is always this evolution that sets traps for virtue. No offence to the beautiful Helen of Troy if I compare her to Austrian Social Democracy, but by contrast with "the hand of Fate" that caused Helen's frequent sufferings, that to which the political innocents appeal is a veritable sledgehammer! But our fallen innocents are truly Helen and the Augurer combined.[2] For the day will come when Fate can close up shop and the game will be up for Evolution. Since there is an answer to every quibble, this too can be explained away:

> the small-scale struggles have seldom been as challenging as they are today; in the bigger picture, *never has victory been so certain.*

For what meets the Social Democratic leader's gaze, beyond the hailstorm beating down on his followers, is a cloudless azure sky; beyond any defeat there is always a triumphal arch erected, invisible to the rank and file, who have to take its existence on trust. The expected "reversal in the balance of power" can occur sooner than—well?

> sooner than many believe today, both *here and over in Germany,*

but this religious certainty,

> which *embodies* the supreme principle and *lodestar* of socialist thought and action,

requires preparatory measures for final victory, which have already been taken:

> But let no one come to us in the *perhaps not too distant future* with the saccharine assurance that, "actually", he had always been a Social Democrat!

Without question such a person will be turned away as surely as those who didn't "keep the faith"; those defaulters are the actual target, since as things stand they find it more logical to take their bearings from Dollfuss's "Patriotic Front" than from Social Democracy. Why shouldn't the Social Democrats also resort to a blacklist such as the National Socialists have introduced into "the free canvassing of opinions and intellectual battle of convictions"? Namely

> *the sharp eye* we are keeping—make no mistake about it!—on *anyone who breaks ranks* today or becomes *fainthearted*. . . .

I duly take note and for my part await developments, but I don't want to be thought of as one of the fainthearted. As for the perhaps not too distant future, I'm bold enough to believe that—if the Austrian Social Democratic Party, despite its efforts to the contrary, should succeed in avoiding the fate of its brother party, its diminished stature will simply become a matter of public record. Having been spared political realignment (*Gleichschaltung*), it should be content with mere elimination (*Ausschaltung*). Of course, one might still hope the working classes would ensure that their leaders, who have proved their worth over so many years, are suitably remunerated in retirement.

For as a result of passing the time with tactical squabbles, the working classes have lost almost all they gained in material terms from their wartime suffering, and all they gained spiritually as well—apart from the realisation (which their leaders avoid addressing) that, confronted by a danger of their own making, all thinking is reduced to the basic principle of political science: save your skin! The credit is due to Hitler, whose mission is "to restore even our most complicated fellow creatures to the natural simplicity of the *Volk*". The miraculous cure didn't work with Social Democratic intellectuals—but it was more successful in my case. They believe they can break his spell by recourse to the Austrian Constitutional Court, while he with his magic, and they with their cleverness, have made the likes of me into a patriot of a type that can be traced back to the years before my birth. The patriotism of that period reflected cultural blessings doubtless linked to Austria's exclusion from the German Reich—and lasted at most up to the turn of the century, when *Die Fackel* first appeared—not without justification.[3] But given the lying and cheating to which the advocates of freedom resort when faced with mortal danger, one could embrace any resource they dislike as long as it protects us from what we fear, for what we want is freedom from tyranny. Provided it doesn't enrich Germany through the 1,000-Mark tax, I'm even prepared to welcome the tourist trade as an economic last resort, seeing it as the most dignified resource that the state in its wisdom can deploy, an issue for intellectual debate in dour and simple times. Look to what I'm reduced! But why should one not go back to the twice-times table (an achievement, after all), when higher mathematics have led to the fall of man? Why not stand by the endeavours (whose practicality is self-evident) of a man accused of dishonesty by his adversaries, but with much less evidence than that of their own duplicity? Why not support efforts that actually work, which like all state activity impinge on one's own, no matter how distant the intellectual world of those who accomplish it? In no way does that mean siding with the democrat whose house has been burgled and who obstructs the police because they want to protect him under an emergency decree and not under the constitution, prompting him to give them a piece of his mind. (This analogy remains valid even though it has since been distorted by someone fond of borrowing my deeply held convictions.) The source of such basic insights is a problematic agitation for freedom that prefers to destroy itself in the conflict between phraseology and content, rather than allow its life to be saved by a decisiveness alien to its nature, preferring to peddle theories of peoples rather than tell the truth to the people.

There are parallels with the relationship to the Republic of the nostalgic monarchist, for whom ineffectual planning and vacuous speechifying have merely been equipped with principles. Let those who employ satire according to my precepts direct it against the tendencies towards restoration associated with the content of *The Last Days of Mankind.* Its author, now that the advocates of freedom have failed him, is open to any enterprise that could help avert an even greater horror today, whether actively or by affecting the public mood. I remain conscious of the antagonism that exists between symbols and aeroplanes and am unimaginably distant from the ideological creed of the front formed to combat the new Turkish threat.[4] I am no more susceptible to the magic of uniforms than to the sequined blouses of freedom. But in a world where typographically a cross is used by supporters of intellectual freedom merely to denote paid advertisements, praise be to the determined spirit who has confronted the crooked cross of Nazism with "the cross pure and simple".

Given the political emergency, it has to be said quite bluntly: there has never been anything more stupid since politics was invented (to mankind's detriment) than the behaviour of Austrian Social Democracy. Nothing more perverse than the attitude of a leadership showing its mettle by running headlong towards disaster, but without the heart to admit past mistakes. A leadership which—however regrettable the government's battle on two fronts—persists in conducting its own two-front battle verbally, thereby reinforcing the mortal threat without weakening resistance to it; which talks of being caught in the "crossfire between two equally dangerous, equally hateful forms of the counter-revolution", yet all the more resolutely impedes "Clerico-Fascism" in the real battle, about which it surely knows that today, under adverse circumstances, it even guarantees Social Democracy the possibility of "fighting" against it. And the height of dishonesty is that the Social Democratic press even finds room to publish the most deeply shocking documentation of the tragedy of its brother party, the unspeakable sufferings of those comrades in prison; and also for a statement by one who escaped: namely, that his Austrian comrades

> *enjoy the inestimable good fortune* not to be subjects of the Third Reich.

Thus Friedrich Stampfer, editor-in-chief of the erstwhile sister publication *Vorwärts*. Stampfer announced that the sad vote in the Reichstag, which the leader of the parliamentary party had to pretend was "free and unconstrained", came about

> after the government declared that the life of the nation was more important than *the lives of individual human beings*.

What firmness of principle it takes for a democracy operating far from the firing line to comment that under these circumstances a vote on this matter was "null and void"! But a party which has only had to save its skin from the petty tyranny of Bekessy cannot conceive of the phenomenal political pressure exerted by the Nazis on sacrificial victims compelled to affirm their free will. It knows that the German party, in order to save what remained of it from Hitler, would have allied itself to Death and the Devil, Reichswehr and Stahlhelm, longing for a return of the Hohenzollerns, in whose cause it had resolutely gone to war in 1914; it knows that in the final analysis the Austrian party itself would have sought Habsburg protection against the threat of the concentration camp. But it has the demagogic audacity to ironise the only rational choice as the "lesser evil" and to mock the plea of

> a liberal prayer circle: "Anything but Hitler",

as if that were not a better programme than its own, and as if it were strong enough to defy not only Hitler but all the other pressures too with consummate ease. The *Arbeiter-Zeitung*, whose reports from Germany are far more likely to break one's heart than its editorials to impress one's mind, publishes documents of such unmitigated horror and despair that one can only exclaim "Anything but Hitler"; and in truth no worker, no union leader, no party journalist could possibly react differently from that liberal prayer circle. For who could refrain from saying: "Anything but Hitler!" when they read how old comrades are hunted down by a rabid pack of pursuers until they collapse; are whipped in the face with steel rods while their wives are "forced to watch their contorted faces"; are defiled and martyred while their tormenters bray with laughter, till only a mass of wounds remains; and how the leader of the pack tormented the dying hero, who refused to repudiate his party, thus enforcing silence about the torture:

> So, Matties, you've got off lightly this time

and went on to become Justice Minister of Braunschweig![5] For if they've not read anything but the heart-wrenching account of what happened in Köpenick and the description of a funeral procession:

> There was no mention in the papers. Whoever passed on the news that the murder victims were being buried today could expect imprisonment with hard labour for spreading lies about atrocities. Whoever came, knew he was threatened with imprisonment. But they had come. The unemployed, after an hour-long trek, young people, old men with beards, stony-faced women dreadful to behold. Some hobbling on walking sticks, barely supported by tired limbs still swollen by the beasts' beatings. But they came;

and if they retained no more than this image:

> those who carried the coffin were themselves still all battered and swathed in bandages

—who could refrain from wishing: "Anything but Hitler!"?

The answer is: their own newspaper! The *Arbeiter-Zeitung* delivers a political message that diverges from its reports, mocking the cry of distress they provoke. That along with such hellish images has the courage to joke about the "evil Nazis" who are accordingly at most the lesser evil, overestimated by the others. But surely it could only justify this kind of thing morally (to itself, scarcely to the others), if it could convincingly argue that victory for the saviour of Austria threatens at least the same destruction. Or is the paper heroically determined to anticipate this and go straight for destruction by the external enemy instead?

The Ancients warned against sacrificing, for love of life, that which makes life worth living.[6]

Heroic, certainly, even if the Ancients (not to be confused with those who say "We're the same as we always were!") had not also given the advice "Live first, then find your way".[7] This might just be possible, up to a point, outside concentration camps, but one wouldn't want to take the Ancients at their word regarding the death of a hero and would spare him the need to prove it, faced with such an alternative. To lose what makes life worth living, if one has the very good fortune not to be a subject of the Third Reich! Unfortunately, the Social Democrats seize every opportunity to gamble their good fortune away, since they allow the Devil a democratic platform through the woeful misconception that we would be "casting out the Devil through Beelzebub".[8] Hence their determination to put this out of mind, reminiscent of Hamlet's "Methinks I scent the morning air".[9] Whatever Hitler's intentions for our democracy, it must stay intact to make it easier for him to destroy it. The Social Democrats are still firmly convinced that

> only people lacking all democratic principles and convictions

could willingly entertain the thought of taking action against a terrorist movement by dissolving its organisation:

> quite apart from the fact that *there is no legal basis for such measures.*

No, our Social Democrats would never acquiesce in antidemocratic methods which would permanently deprive them of the possibility of being taken into protective custody, and they will always obstruct those who try to save them, and everyone else, from such a fate. Not to mention that no death threat could possibly force us to vote otherwise than with our hearts! For their world of political ideas breathes free in empty space, where things don't clash with each other, and they resist the idea that the enemy is at the gates. They take it for granted that he too uses no more than set phrases. "Grandmother, what big teeth you have!" "All the better to eat you with, my dear!" Childhood in future—provided Hitler and his legacy permit its existence at all—will appreciate the full meaning of *Little Red Riding Hood* (also the riposte of the Grandmother). Social Democracy went looking for flowers in the forest, and our wing of it can think itself lucky if the huntsman comes to save it. An erstwhile minister when the Party was in power in Germany is today a victim of his complacency: when the growth of a movement that was already building barracks in front of his nose was brought to his attention, he replied that one could "keep an eye on them better" that way but that there was no "legal basis" for intervention. At a time when panic was already rife and discussion taking place about safeguarding the party archives, which two foreign legations were willing to take into safekeeping, another votary of legality coined the simple formulation, which is now going the rounds: Why, my friends, surely they're covered by a preservation order?!

No position could be more bomb-proof than the faith of democrats that the wolf they have nurtured will express its thanks, share their sense of legality, and reward their trust in democratic institutions. The most beautiful reminder of this is the issue of the *Berliner Tageblatt*, published when it was still free to say what it wanted, which "pinned Hitler down" to the Weimar constitution, on which he had sworn when he became a government official in Braunschweig: now he's taken the oath, that's an end of the matter; now we know that if he is still foolish enough to go ahead and found the Third Reich, his Justice Minister Hanns Kerrl will promptly have him arrested for high treason. Such sentimental touches confirm the inevitability of what followed, showing that the preservation order protecting German Social Democracy could not last. Its Austrian wing, still happily surviving, would be endangered if a party less concerned with legality had not made arrangements to preserve it as a curiosity. But its ungrateful followers will continue to thwart the government's efforts with raised fists (now really just a metaphor) and the cry of "Freedom!" repeated three times. How to dissolve organised bombers?

> Against political acts of terror there is a *much more effective* measure. *Genuine, vigorous, creative democracy—that is the only* effective measure against political terror.

Parliament is essential, the "political platform"—according to liberal theory an "outlet"—must be created to allow passions to be vented.

> That is why we cling to the Constitution.

Which has always proved effective against ammonium nitrate explosive so far—the very word "ammonite" is so suggestive of such magic that it cannot be repeated often enough. But our slogans belong to us. For when a "Nazi", law-abiding as they all are, criticised "the paralysis of the Constitutional Court", the question rang out in unison:

> And what is it like in Germany?

Orally, you can get away with it; after all, oral lying is not so blatant as lying in print. And here, like an exchange of blows, come the consequences that ought to be ringing in the ears of those leader writers, whose arguments the Nazis exploit:

> The last few weeks have seen yet more breaches of the Constitution.
>
> *Above all*, horrible Nazi crimes!

> The destruction of the *freedom of the press* is complete.
>
> And there have been *bombings!*
>
> *The ban on freedom of assembly* must be lifted. People *need an outlet.*
>
> *For bombs and hand grenades!*

And that is truer than the heckler thinks, for even if it were true that there are bombings because freedoms have been "crushed", there would definitely be even more if mouths and typewriters were unmuzzled. But once the National Socialists exploit our own platitudes, we come to our senses. We even get carried away, for one of our speakers

> deplores the half-heartedness of the measures against those who have imprisoned and tortured tens of thousands.

That is to say, antidemocratic measures—the subject of daily protests in the party paper—should go even further, and even martial law would not be so bad. But democratically sanctioned! For otherwise it would be against the law: one of the provincial heads of government has

> *banned a Nazi, a member of the* Landtag *government, from attending a cabinet meeting. He wants to debar the Nazi members from sessions of the* Landtag.

—all in bold type. What a climax, as in *Hanneles Himmelfahrt:* "He wants to deny her hallowed ground!" That's all we needed!

> If it is thought that the Nazis must be excluded from our parliaments *while the risk is particularly high—fine, we are prepared to discuss that.*

But first—for discussion precedes action—there has to be a new clause to the Constitution!

> Now more than ever.... Now more than ever.... Now more than ever.... Now more than ever....

a creative democracy has to prove its worth. Or:

> We fought.... Yes, we fought.... We must go on fighting

the good fight, what else did you think? Do you still remember, gentlemen, how, after protesting as a matter of utmost principle against the expulsion of our deadly enemies from the *Landtag* (where we so often fought shoulder to shoulder alongside them), we finally declared ourselves in agreement with breaking the law, provided it was legally sanctioned?

> *we have absolutely no intention of doing anything* that could *smooth the path* for the National Socialists *in their* struggle.

The Nazis called it a "declaration of neutrality", but one followed by the legal offensive, which the Social Democrats then called "the real deal". After that was completed, they held this up as an example to the Clerico-Fascists: That's how to do it! And raised such a victory cry that the geese in the Capitol were struck dumb, though the hens started clucking.[10] In bold type and under the title:

> *Freedom!*
>
> When the President declared the law passed, *Püchler called out into the hall in a stentorian voice: "Long live the democratic Republic!" Schneidmadl shouted: "Down with the brown plague!" The Social Democratic members rose from their seats and, with fists clenched, burst out cheering, crying "Freedom!" For some minutes the Landtag remained under the powerful spell of the Social Democratic demonstration against Fascism.*

What a spectacle! What a metaphor! But since they were now almost standing on the barricades, our Mayor seized the opportunity to burst out:

> In this Vienna of ours the old tradition of Konrad *Vorlauf has been revived,* of all the *mayors who did not yield,* defying brute force; the ideas of 1848 have come alive again, when Vienna stood firm against the united forces of reaction.

So I lay, and so I brandished my blade![11]

"Put that in your pipe and smoke it!" the *Arbeiter-Zeitung* might have said, doubtless recalling how they cowered before Bekessy. Instead, it recorded a protracted storm of applause, which drowned out the associations of the name Vorlauf ("full speed ahead"), which might all too easily have hinted at its opposite, or indeed at Leerlauf ("idling"). What a contrast with the brief report of a speech by Federal Chancellor Dollfuss, who at the moment appears to have very little to worry him:

> *He dealt mainly with the Nazis. . . .*

At the same time, the *Arbeiter-Zeitung* finds space for a report welcoming theatre director Max Reinhardt home like a long lost son, even though the collapse of his affairs has *left its mark on him:*

> *He must surely realise* that *his time has come* and that there are *undreamt-of opportunities for good theatre* in Vienna.

25

BETWEEN TWO FASCISMS: LANGUAGE BRINGS EVERYTHING TO LIGHT

This equivocation by Social Democracy is surely the most unnatural—if not the most dangerous—distortion of civilised life. For what could be more incongruous than to be intoxicated while stone-cold sober by incessant tirades, fanfares, and sonorous bombast, whose content—should it ever penetrate the noise being generated—demonstrates only the contradiction between the thinking at headquarters and the reality on the barricades? What could be more grotesque than the posturings of an equivocator who makes Fabius the *Cunctator* look like a veritable hothead?! There is no secret about the most ardent desire of Otto Bauer and his party functionaries, afraid as they are not so much of taking responsibility for their actions towards the enemy as for failing to act for their own members. Their dearest wish would be to lead a quiet life again on those nice, solid opposition benches. Beyond that, one can feel more genuine sympathy for the losses suffered by those who have been led astray, for which they have to thank the same functionaries. But why don't they finally admit they need the outlet for such passions provided by parliament, where they can still be channeled into speeches in the knowledge that the authoritarian measures of the government offer better protection against the Nazi threat? Why must there still be a "struggle", when every fibre of the party's being is drawn towards a pact? After all, between struggle and pact there is always the golden mean of the secret deal, and would not even that be more honest when (as has always been suspected) it is happening already?

> They say it's freedom that they fight to save;
> Look closer, and it's slave fights slave. [6962]

With our bare survival at stake, it seems important to put aside the problem of ideology (insofar as there is one)—but only "for as long as the particular danger lasts"; and when one flag in particular (whatever one's views on flags) happens to be prohibited: is it fitting to plant them on house-fronts and chimneys like crosses on a grave and play hide-and-seek with the police, who have a more serious danger to deal with? Has it not become a public nuisance comparable to those contemptible happenings that now keep the police constantly at full stretch, literally throwing them off the scent like dogs made to fetch a stick and then reporting derisively:

> The police are unstinting in their *grim acknowledgement* of the *singular audacity* with which the *mysterious rebels* attached the forbidden flag to places *only birds can reach*.... The two policemen *dealing with it took two hours* to take down three of the twelve flags....

while the onlookers "squinted up at them with a remarkably smug expression on their faces". It's hard to believe, but this childish prank formed a headline in the central organ of Social Democracy, sadly to be followed by another:

> *Policeman dies from over-exertion.*

Over-exertion suffered while averting, with unprecedented courage, a plot against life and property, day after day, night after night—while "mysterious rebels" are truly unflagging in their mockery of a vigilance that protects them, too, against bombs! The rebel mouthpiece reports:

> *For some days* District Inspector Friedrich Flassak *had hardly had time to draw breath*—on duty up to midnight. Three hours later—an emergency—on duty again. *There can be no doubt: he died from over-exertion.*

His death occurred after the perturbing discovery—such things now happen!—that the bomb was a "hoax". Not after hauling down a "hoax" flag—for which we would have no objection to overtime being paid either. For what looks like a textbook example of public nuisance is supposedly of service in the struggle for freedom—which its central organ associates with Giordano Bruno. Hoist away!—but without matching the record set by swastikas daubed on rock faces, which we naturally deplore as puerile pranks. But no, even here the Social Democrats repudiate the government's defensive measures. For since the authorities had the sensible idea of making those who share the Nazi ideology, and consequently share the blame, clean up afterwards (if the guilty ones couldn't be found or didn't give themselves up), those idiots dare to protest—on principle—that the use of "cleaning squads" is no different from the German tactic of taking hostages. Unimaginable! To place party chicanery, linked to responsibility for political agitation, on the same ethical footing as blackmail using innocent hostages! There is something sublime about this sense of justice, which springs to life precisely whenever "the violation of democratic liberties targets the enemy" and from which it's only a short step to the notion that the Nazis are as blameless as the Jews of Tarnopol, while the Austrians are as heavy-handed as a judge from Kolomea.[1] But if he thinks the gangs of daubers, who are not embarrassed when caught in the act and are always capable of more of the same, are "innocent" but still "have to pay the price", then he should surely at least suffer those who gloatingly sanctioned the deeds, having incited the flag gimmick in their editorials, to be held to account for having provoked the culprits. If such things were to cease, mankind would be spared much amusement but also the ominous consequences. A piece of dyed cloth means nothing individual when the crowd it requires to express its power foreshadows our doom. Till then, its effect is to make us feeble-minded and turn adults into children. And what of the dire consequences that the emblem of the enemy would bring?

When danger threatens the city in a thousand different guises, operating with ammonium nitrate, sulphuric acid, and wire cutters, tampering with telephone kiosks, postboxes, and tram lines, employing new tricks every day—then we read in bold type in the *Arbeiter-Zeitung* that our sense of living under the rule of law has been "deeply shaken". By what?

In Austria *thousands of people* are *imprisoned every day* by *decree*.

The same rhetoric that insists it "has absolutely no intention of doing anything that could smooth the path for the National Socialists", that laments the half-heartedness of the measures, that "finds it self-evident that a country in a state of war should defend itself"! Is not this way of thinking idcologically aligned with that regime which converts metaphors back into an original physical reality? The democrat who "stays the arm" of the police because they want to use an emergency decree to protect him from burglars—this actually happened! And with this mind-set, gyrating round a single fixed point, they still think themselves strong enough to reject Dollfuss's helping hand, despite the wretched daily betrayals of their May Day slogans. Yet who but a liar would have the courage to deny that emergency decrees don't merely save governments from defeat in parliament, since the worst social restrictions imposed by an angry adversary in dire circumstances are still more bearable than being sentenced to death? Who but a hypocrite could justify belittling at every turn the policies that prevent this, misrepresenting them by suppression of the truth, impeding them by malicious interventions? It surely takes ideological skill of a high order to insist on parading your socialist principles in times like this; to sabotage attempts at last being made to put an end to the iniquity that has seen poor suffering humanity at its wits' end; and to want to save the democratic ideal of freedom of assembly for enemies who would make more effective use of it—namely to bring about its most radical termination, conceding only the right to "concentration". As if anything would ever emerge from all this empty speechifying other than that we "want to fight" (if we could) and the no less contradictory assertion (given the relative strength of the parties) that there is absolutely no way we want to be "vassals".

> We were drawn to the German Republic. We don't want to find ourselves in a German concentration camp.

But everything the Social Democrats do leads in that direction. "We don't want" brown German fascism, they say, "but nor do we want" the black Austrian variety either. But what they really want isn't clear yet, so all they can do is let the latter save them from the former—that, at least, they do "want". For the time is not yet ripe for Austria to opt to become a "French colony" rather than a Prussian one, whose language is harder to understand. Until this time comes, it only remains for those who affirm ideals in which they no longer believe to sacrifice themselves for a Germanness notorious for feeling "threatened" the moment its own territorial and global demands are thwarted. If they had not at long last been forced to help drive Germanness from both houses of parliament, the Social Democrats would have supported it in loyalty to the constitution and voted with it against the "Clericals", as in the memorable shoulder-to-shoulder action with Sepp Straffner's Pan-Germans. For they will always demand freedom of speech for those who possess a capacity they lack: to convert it into freedom of action. This ultimately leads to the racial conundrum: How can Jews be so stupid?

That moment seems to have arrived. For what was unexpected even here, has happened: striving for democracy, the Social Democrats felt impelled to demand diplomacy as well—the height of stupidity, which cannot be topped by any red flag! The central organ of the party was grudging in its response to the undiplomatic reception of the emissary of the German Reich by the Austrian government—understandably, given its obvious success. But it subsequently voiced the specific objection that

> *more diplomatic means might* have been employed to avert the unwelcome visit of the gentleman and his still more unwelcome interference in our affairs, instead of having the Deputy Police Chief tell him at Aspern airport that *his visit was unwelcome* and *sending him a message* in Salzburg that was *tantamount to an expulsion order.*

Which it was—a response to the incitement by a minister of the Reich to Austrian citizens to disarm their country's police force; at which those who had grown up with diplomacy complained about the courtesy extended to the expellee, who was still allowed to pause for a snack before leaving Salzburg. But at this point it must also be conceded that many speeches by Austrian ministers, "containing decidedly unfriendly turns of phrase against northern Germans" (who no longer use such language themselves)

do not strike us exactly as masterpieces of diplomacy.

For their bluntness is indisputably put to shame by the star turn of these amateur diplomats, which promptly earned Austrian Social Democracy recognition on German radio and in the aligned press (which has continued on many occasions since). But such triumphant stupidity, assured of this kind of success, is still perhaps surpassed by one particular piece of arrogance which, though fully aware of its own deficiencies, dares to disparage one of the neatest and most incisive verbal exploits ever to have achieved its practical political goal. As a stylist, a choreographer of words, but above all one who grieves for a world reduced to lifeless writing, let me repeat: the greeting Herr Dollfuss sent to his guest from the Reich—one which diplomats of the Second International thought an offence against propriety—contains more political gravamen than all of their brains combined. But I would go further and praise the undiplomatic ministerial speeches too and declare (lest anyone suspect me of being motivated by a surge of Habsburg nostalgia)—that every speech by Herr Vaugoin seems to me a better, more objective, and more expressive summary of our deepest concerns than any by his predecessor, Herr Deutsch, or even by our beloved Theodor Körner ("O sword by my side").[2] Vaugoin is a veritable general in the fight for freedom, who in no sense repudiates the tone of my banqueting scene when demanding "Discipline, gentlemen" for decisions which the so-called enemy saves you gentlemen from having to take yourselves.[3] Moreover, other staunch custodians of reaction have shown courage through words and deeds directed against the greater, universal danger. And since Starhemberg has outgrown his awkward adolescent phase in ministerial office and defined many happy examples of political deception, it is no longer true that "what Starhemberg says / no meaning conveys". Least of all after his "J'accuse" speech—its sustained invective something no dialectician of evolution or reincarnation of Mayor Vorlauf could hope to match. (They might sooner compare themselves to Winkler and Schumy, the two eloquent engineers whose vague leanings towards a communal destiny with Germany also enjoy a degree of popularity among Social Democrats. Still, in order to achieve linguistic clarity all round, Herr Starhemberg should be reminded once more that his struggle

to *acquire* Austria anew

could be misinterpreted by opponents of the other fascism. They might suspect a participle implying Italy's participation; but Starhemberg surely didn't mean that Austria can be bought.)[4] Surely, I cannot be suspected of hoping for some consensus with the far right in these matters, or even thinking it possible, and I need hardly add that stocking school libraries in Austria with *The Last Days of Mankind* seems to me as unlikely as ever. Indeed, I'm not even disappointed when the work is disparaged by protagonists of the Austrian awakening—in many cases former Jewish blackmailers (including Sandor Weiss). By contrast, leading French intellectuals have acclaimed the play as a rehabilitation of Austria's reputation that restores the country's honour.[5] But how influential figures in Austria regard my achievement is less important to me than how I regard theirs, and my judgement on their speeches—irrespective of my hope to hear fewer of them one day—is measured solely by their practical effect in meeting current needs. They should not represent any personal interest, but nor should they reflect any intellectual or political opposition powerful enough to suppress recognition of what is (currently) needed, since that is (ultimately) conducive to everything one wants, fending off what one most fears. I am for many things that the Social Democrats "want" and am happy to see such things protected by their opponents against the worst that can happen. One feels their pain at what they have lost, whether caused by their own incompetence or willed by their adversaries: faced with the greater evil, the lesser evil offers them more than they lose. All I can think of is "Anything but Hitler!", for I can't summon up the internal resources of those who still want—or "don't want"—more, and I envy them the expansiveness which allows them to dance to one party tune at two blood weddings. Given that an opposition naturally opposes the government, and granted that "anti-social measures" are incompatible with the opposition's preeminently social bias; admitting, moreover, that it was a political error, through intransigence, to allow one's own fighting strength to be weakened—still, the sidelined Social Democrats would never be justified in hindering an action which was to their benefit, since they are always duty-bound to subordinate individual to general claims when the main issue is at stake.

The question is: who is "fighting" and who is being obstructive? The situation was illustrated as follows—guess by whom:

> An army has to retake a mountain range which it had to evacuate in the previous battle. If they took it, it would still be a long way from being the decisive victory in the war, but it would effectively strengthen their defensive position. At this point there is muttering in the ranks: "Why do we need to fight for the mountain range? Haven't we been up there before and don't we know it's not so special? And if we retake it, we still haven't won the war". *What do you do with people who talk like that in the middle*

> *of a battle?* According to the old *regulations in the Dual Monarchy: "Mow 'em down!" Rightly so.* For no army can take an enemy position if the men who are *ready to give body and soul* to conquer it are robbed of the belief, in the middle of the battle, that the position is worth fighting for.

Could not that have been written by some knight of the Maria-Theresa Order? "Rightly so". For after all, even a Social Democrat, for all his antipathy and with every reason to be embittered, could not deny (though he wouldn't admit) that this is someone ready to give body and soul, at this moment in time, to take an enemy position, or rather to hold it. True, he shouldn't begin by making figurative use of the military theme, since after all he's been going through the struggle in reality, and because such men really are compelled to turn against those who make speeches or mutter in the middle of a battle. But who is it that is using the struggle as a metaphor, and who would welcome something as effective as the service regulations of the Dual Monarchy, which would allow him to "mow down" the troublemakers? Herr Otto Bauer has lost the plot. The laboured naivety with which he uses the comparison demonstrates just how little it is based on experience. The "struggle" which he leads is defending democracy in the thick of resistance to Hitler; the troublemakers are partly those men of action who want to implement the leader writers' every word, though for the most part probably comrades of a more pragmatic cast of mind, who have come to think it stupid to interfere with what is beneficial; both are acting more logically than Herr Bauer. In making his absurd comparison he doesn't even realise that it belongs to the alternative reality in which his adversary operates—and to whom its use would be quite appropriate; nor that the socialist dog is ultimately chasing its own tail.

This instructive article shows exactly what intelligence is capable of; it appeared in the July 1933 issue of the journal, appropriately entitled *The Struggle*, in which the wily schemer opened up a new field of operations: to ensure that, in the struggle of the "Clerico-Fascists" against the National Fascists, the two sides are not driven into an alliance. But this won't happen, even though it is for this reason that we are fighting for democracy, "concentrating" our forces on the effort to "master" it. "Every day the news from Germany teaches us" what fascism is: so "is that not a sufficiently alluring, inspiring objective"—to fight for democracy and "by so doing" to ensure (as Dollfuss apparently cannot) that Austria, too, does not "slide into servitude"? At this one's head begins to swim, until finally clarity prevails—that the hour may come

> in which we have only the choice of shamefully capitulating or *boldly engaging in battle.*

Language brings everything to light.[6] Whereas the combatant is normally either victorious or defeated, here capitulation comes first, and the emotionally charged alternative falls in behind; alone the fact that "boldness" is merely one possibility, casually slipped in like "becoming rapturously excited should the occasion arise", already speaks volumes. Before the decisive moment arrives, there does, of course, remain the hope that democracy can be won back through speech-making, so that we have a functioning system of government monitored by parliament:

> *even if at first, for the time being, we can only monitor* this system of government *in parliamentary opposition.*

With opera glasses from one of the best seats! No more worries, then!

Immediately after this article by our leader there follow—under the title "Between Two Fascisms"—a series of Pollak-style Jewish jokes, pushing humour to audacious limits in such perilous times: jokes about the Jewish bourgeoisie "quivering with uncontrollable fear of the Nazis", while the editor looks them calmly in the face; about "Beelzebub", which can be used to dislodge me, at least, from my position, since I regard him as social democratic journalism's own creation; then a joke that already has a touch of gallows humour about it: "We shouldn't overlook" that "there is as yet no concentration camp in Austria", but this is small comfort when "we cannot overlook" the further fact (wait for it—no, nobody would ever guess) that there is "no parliament!" (The German comrades would doubtless be prepared to overlook this blemish today.)

The editor of the *Arbeiter-Zeitung* (quite unlike the editor of *Vorwärts*, who congratulated Austrian comrades on living in the "land of freedom") is already witnessing the total alignment [*Gleichschaltung*] of the calamity,

> with the *sole* exception of *physical violence* against the opponent.

But fortunately he can confirm that "the fighting strength of the Austrian proletariat remains intact", "its freedom of movement admittedly limited"—a contradiction which is resolved in the beguiling observation:

> *This strange situation,* whereby a party that is *as great as ever* has *temporarily ceased* to be a *powerful* one, *has had a very strong psychological effect.*

Golden words! A *single* success was achieved. What was that? There follows a Jewish joke so risqué one would hesitate to tell it in polite society:

> *Think* of the first of May

—as a success![7]

> the *only time* the party *did not succumb—the only success in all that time!*

The obscenity of it! It is reminiscent of that link between pride and modesty: "This is my bedroom and here's where my husband's retreat begins". Pollak is totally committed to changing tactics. He spurns making any deal with dictatorship, saying that's what they've always done, and all to no avail. Just as on the first of May, when no socialist celebration was permitted by the government even though there was no deal, so one must act in future:

> The party *must specifically declare that it is not prepared to enter into negotiations.*

One joke after another, but they are nonetheless seriously aware that "the party machinery is antiquated" and needs a good shaking to pep it up. Nowadays it's often acknowledged that in Germany "some social democratic leaders were bigwigs"—"although not all"; and now they're rummaging among the Left luggage here in Austria too. We've been "much too detached and 'statesmanlike'" up to now; our "appeal to people's imagination" has been found wanting. Where to find it? We must learn from our opponent, ruthlessly use "such power as we still have" and develop "the propaganda of crowd psychology". We could do with a Goebbels, and already speak like him:

> We need a comprehensive *ideological orientation*, a programme that reaches out beyond one single country at one moment in time.

What that may be, the ideologue doesn't actually know, but he gives us an inkling. True, there has certainly been no lack of ideological orientation up to now, but we need much more of the same. Our adversary, he proclaims, "has set us right back to pre-1918"—if you think about it, that is unfortunately true, but what to do?

> *Come now!* We *don't only want to return to 1918*, our struggle *points beyond 1918*, beyond the reconquest of republican democracy and *into the socialist future!*

A quite unequivocal programme of ideological orientation! There could be another way: tell the truth.

In any case, a reorientation would be advisable on both sides of the political divide. The *Arbeiter-Zeitung* would do well to write many (not all) of the *Reichspost* editorials, and the latter to heed the documentation in the *Arbeiter-Zeitung*. The Social Democrats have infinitely stronger evidence against Hitler, and in this regard "people believe them". But it is the Christian Socials who use it in a more practical and convincing way and whose commentary is more authentic. Compare that intelligent "Come now!", which is just as much at variance with lived experience as the order "to boldly engage in battle", with something Kunschak, leader of the Christian Social workers, said:

> But a new enemy of the freedom of our people and our fatherland has arisen. An enemy so ugly to our eyes, so painful to our hearts, because we recognise in him the features of a man from that community forged in the anguish of the trenches, we see in him the face of a brother and do not understand how it can have come to pass that German rises up against German, brother against brother, and above all the stronger against the weak and the enslaved.

The fact that this report wasn't headlined "Tumultuous Applause" but "Tumultuous Booing" is a measure of how effective it was—one looks in vain for something comparable in the phraseology of Social Democratic spokesmen. At the same time, one feels this proffering of a fraternal hand, this tribal nostalgia in the government press, to be feeble proof of intellectual life, just as frequent references to Austria's mission as a "mediator" ring hollow.

All in all, one would prefer not to have to choose between the simplistic implications of "Fatherland" and "Freedom" currently feeding an inflated rhetoric, both concepts becoming deflated by technological advances at the same rate that they are threatened with destruction by phosgene gas. But "as things stand", the decision has to be in favour of the popular refrain "Fatherland", which is validated by the emphatic alignment of words and deeds. Emotionally charged experience finds stronger expression in pamphlets and speeches than arguments that are merely conceptualised. I know how terribly difficult it now is, and how easily misconstrued, to prove that twice two is four and not, as people still hope, five. But the case has been conclusively proved. Since the political "evolution" of 1933 has turned everything on its head (for individual heads no longer count), the upshot is that Freedom is safer in the hands of the Fatherland than the other way round. And even if the situation is deliberately misconstrued, a language that speaks up for real qualities deserves priority, and traditional simplicity takes precedence over "creative democracy". Whatever else these adversaries may have said and done, their efforts in confronting a danger most directly faced by Social Democracy are more useful and effective than what Social Democracy does and says. However badly damaged it might be by the curtailing of workers' rights—something more fundamental than the loss of press freedom and freedom of assembly, and unlike these without justification as an emergency measure—surely only some suicidal urge, deceitful to the very end, could deny that it is better to save lives. Someone undeceived, who sees the world and the state differently from those in power—those who enable him to do so—cannot help but acknowledge that here in Austria, in the present circumstances, politics is for once not just vapid wrangling but a worthy trade, a fulfilling of one's "duty" by filling a depleted form with real content, so that for the first time one has the politically congenial impression of a government that deserves the name. For by calculating the atmospheric effects of the greater evil and skilfully disposing of the stench it leaves behind, it is at pains to meet our hope of escaping, here in Austria at least, the torment associated with the concept and the very word "Nazi". That goes for all of us, especially those in the forefront of the struggle for a freedom which up to now has only seen its flag prohibited by its adversaries—for lack of resistance to the enemy.

26

HEADLONG INTO SERVITUDE: WHEN MADMEN LEAD THE BLIND

What use is the addled brain, that malfunctioning mechanism, faced with a miracle of nature that bedazzles and stupefies us—the big lie of Nazism, which blatantly shifts its shape by the hour yet is never discredited, even when contradicting itself! Moreover, the times we live in make it possible for those who weave its deceptive web to start every day afresh, remembering nothing and ashamed of nothing—mocking some reproach that they themselves no longer understand, a position now abandoned and forgotten. Words spoken on the world stage cease to be true the moment they are regurgitated by liars. Or not, as the case may be—nothing can be proved, except that in the meantime people have bled to death; and even that crime cannot be made to stick, since imperious new decrees already demand new victims. The task of Sisyphus is child's play compared with the wearisome toil of depicting our age from one day to the next. But still one might persevere, were it not that the uncertainty principle on which the machinery runs facilitates this irruption of the irrational. The sheer perceptual overload, the very sight of which flies in the face of reason, creates confusions that are a heavy cross to bear—with knobs on! For this spanner in the works of our thinking processes would be confusing enough if it were self-contained but becomes infinitely more so when it contradicts reality and all the relationships through which we painfully perceive it. But by its very nature it is never what it seems, and by incorporating every possible antithesis it seems to be all the stronger when denying its intentions than when repudiating those of others.

By female arts, beyond our sharpest seeing,
They can divide Appearances from Being,
Claiming to be true Existentialists!
[10714 (after Bayard Taylor—with a nod to Heidegger)]

Even when they fall for this claim themselves, they can still count on its plausibility. Do we know, do even they know, the real content of the creed with which they torment us? No, they have no idea, they don't know what they stand for, nor even what they repudiate. "And so it is not open to us" follows logically from the realisation that it once was open to us, and still is. "It's not now a question of programmes and ideas", thanks to which the Nazi Party gained strength, becoming stronger still through their misuse, and strongest of all by betraying them.

> The ideas contained in the programme do not commit us to acting like idiots and destroying everything.

As if they ever committed the party to anything else! It's just that conditions are not yet sufficiently favourable to allow their ideas to be adapted and properly applied, and no one expects them "to be stupid enough" to put them into practice. The programme had such a strong impact that it is no longer needed; its legacy is a belief that all earthly goods are dispensable—a faith that, ultimately, moves mountains. That belief is no guarantee of power but forms a power consciousness; it gives courage to begin each day afresh and to inflict punishment and hardship, as if bestowing a privilege on a nation that exults in rushing headlong into servitude.[1] That applies to the world of politics just as readily as it does to the social sphere. When the Zentrum Party succumbed to its afflictions,

> *its liquidation followed as mutually agreed*

with the conqueror, and the deceased made a solemn vow "never to be outdone by anyone" in loyalty to Hitler. Jews wishing to leave Germany are "given permission" to finance the sale of German manufactured goods on the export market; and the "clemency" shown by the extortionist to his victims is enhanced by the ubiquitous, monstrous lie that they are acting "of their own free will". Everyone has to donate to party funds. Just when basic foodstuffs have become prohibitively expensive, "countless civil servants and other public employees", "countless workers", have not only contributed part of their salary or wages "as a voluntary donation in support of the national effort", but in addition

> *requested* their employer *to hold back*, until further notice, *an agreed* percentage of their salary or wages.

Otherwise they might find they are being held back themselves. And as delusion becomes the prevalent norm and chaos the order of the day, some place their faith in the miraculous turn of events while others are overwhelmed by it.

"How could it happen?" It could happen because a minority seized existing weapons with which to create new ones, and now as a majority it confronts the groups it vanquished as well as defenceless individuals. One might expect an end to the panic which has spread to the rest of humanity only after things have run their organic course, when the perversion of nature itself finally succumbs to natural law, and insatiable appetite turns against the thing that originally empowered it. In a community based on the notion that every individual has official status, permitting arbitrary actions against which official procedures normally provide protection, together with the seizure of property and spilling of blood, we sense that people will take revenge on those who authorised such things. We get an inkling of this in the directives we see emerging every day, as if from the nightmare of total impotence—the recurrent complaint that unauthorised factions "repeatedly interfere with the state apparatus", which could not have been created without them. This daily drumroll of slogans awakens fear in those who hear them but also stifles the fears of the drummers. Once it was possible to warn against communists, provocateurs, enemies of the national awakening, unruly elements carrying out the same actions in SA uniforms as their rightful owners. Those people would be harmless now compared with the danger presented by the real SA, who "continuously upset the economy by unauthorised interference", even attempting to "impose their own demands", and who are themselves now called unruly elements, enemies of the national awakening, even communists. If they were once the culprits, it was laid at the door of the others; now they themselves are to blame, albeit led astray by provocateurs. Those trolls meddle in every branch of the administration, they continue to drag the owners of department stores off to be tortured, they break into houses at night if they need money for petrol, they collect so-called voluntary donations, they set up private "racial protection" offices. And they are rightly astonished when told they shouldn't do such things, for no one has ever been able to make them understand that these unpleasant side effects are not the essential objective. And the more urgently this is explained to them, the less they are inclined to understand. No doubt about it: those organs that by nature are subservient to the Führer's will are threatening to exceed their designated role. "We want to push on further!" It had long been thought they could be kept amused by giving them free rein to assess racial purity or spill blood at will; now, increasingly, the signs are that this is not enough: they want more miracles. Some of them abandon the programme because they put private greed before public need, following the example of their leaders who subsequently lament that "personal interest shows through the outer idealistic trappings—that it's only human nature".

Others, however—and these are worse—are idealists who uphold appearances, want to abolish usury "and God knows what else". They are not content with achieving the nationalist goal, they demand the socialist one as well—aims hard to reconcile when they first appeared in the programme. Indeed, many think the nationalist goal, apart from its "immediate objective", the Jewish issue, has not been achieved yet either—the Treaty of Versailles needs to be rescinded as well (as if this had not to some extent already happened). Protective custody and the dissolution of their units is the lot of such malcontents, even a declaration by the Wolff Bureau that nothing of the kind has occurred. Nevertheless, the heresy that the programme has been betrayed casts a spell that raises it almost to the level of the programme itself. Countering it requires circumspection, such as has not previously been necessary. True, if one still doesn't know what one wants, at least today one knows what one doesn't want; and one realises that the socialist ideal, whose legitimate proponents have been butchered, would be a nonsense that would shatter the power structure established by such butchery. But since a refusal to contemplate socialism might open the door to a danger that has been averted, the danger of bolshevism, good advice is as hard to come by as butter.

As for the nationalist achievement, it doesn't appear to deliver what it promised, even if it allows scope for further advances. It rather created confusion with its insistence that Jews, Marxists, cyclists, those who accept the theory of relativity etc., etc., are responsible for all evils, including the outcome of the war. While—mainly on this issue—there is constantly reason to complain that other countries lack the understanding necessary to grasp what is going on in Germany, even the best intellects here have lost their nerve. Even a Hercules, faced with the choice between racial pride and increasing tourism, could not have taken on both. Success has crowned one effort, inasmuch as a German newspaper has consented to print (for payment) some fine words in English:

> Germany extends a cordial invitation to visit us this summer. In addition to all the famous attractions that Germany holds for tourists, there *can now be added the enchanting spectacle of the rebirth of a nation.*

It rightly goes on the say that Germany currently enjoys the distinction of being the most interesting country in Europe. Quite apart from the fact that everywhere order reigns supreme and security and comfort are assured, new ideas and a broader outlook than before await you, and (as with those sightseeing tours of battlefields) you will receive

> *indelible impressions* which will *haunt you* forever.[2]

Music fills the air, and nowhere else can the cultured traveller more readily

> *become acquainted with the good things in life in all their beauty.* Germany *now offers the complete realisation of a modern education for young*

> *and old alike.* It invites you to actively enter into the world of its *art*, its *science*, its *philosophy*, its *history, and above all to experience the fine art of living life to the full, ingrained in every individual citizen* in the Germany of today.
>
> Germany will play *mine host, extending a more authentically warm-hearted* welcome today *than ever before*. . . . In Germany, for a modest outlay you can *realise the dream of a lifetime.*

When honesty sings its own praises, the world cannot fail to be impressed. If only those here, after tasting blood, would see reason, calm down and carry on. "Are Britons here? As round the world they wheel, / they'd find here something worthy of their zeal" [7118 (after Bayard Taylor)].

So why haven't they been coming? Ah, there have been misunderstandings. Mine host, authentically warm-hearted as he is, doesn't browbeat foreigners, but sometimes, when they look too outlandish, he just can't resist the impulse. The advertisement said "Germany invites you", but when a visitor asks at the bar for orange juice, they'll reply: "No Jews served here" (not even freshly squeezed). Sometimes followed by an apology: it was all a misunderstanding, your appearance misled me, so not my fault. The explanation is accepted, but there's a lack of real warmth thereafter. Asiatics aware of their oriental appearance have long had misgivings about visiting Germany, but the West is now also of two minds. The greatest difficulty is that the world is not familiar with the customs of the country and is afraid of infringing them. Oblivious to the needs of German tourism, other countries have spread reports that Americans—unaware that you are expected to stand up for the Horst Wessel song and do arm-stretching exercises in front of flags—have been trampled underfoot. Then came one nationality after the other: English, French, Belgians, Dutch, Swiss. A Romanian engineer had his hands thrust into a fire "to force him to admit he was a Jew". A Briton, stopped and searched seven times in one hour, warns in *The Times* against visiting Germany: it would surely be helpful to all concerned if Thomas Cook simply distributed rules of conduct in good time. Natives could do with them as well: a landowner was foolish enough to call the Hitler salute childish: "portions of the population stand with their hands in their pockets while the Nazi standards pass by", obviously thinking this too will pass; a girl from Neuruppin had a placard hung round her neck declaring her a shameless hussy for not standing up for the Horst Wessel song. The population is fired with enthusiasm for the ideals but is difficult to educate, at least those outside the concentration camps. No one goes to the Schlageter exhibition, and a survey carried out by the theatre in Erfurt showed Offenbach to be more popular than Johst.

Nothing but bad luck, nothing but misunderstandings: the natives think the foreigners are Jews, the foreigners think the natives are barbarians, but the fact that the natives can't even distinguish among themselves is truly embarrassing.

What's to happen to Oberammergau when even Bayreuth needs a special concession, with the government buying up the complimentary tickets?[3] In Oberammergau a tragic conflict between tourism and a higher principle has flared up. People who rent out rooms and dress up as apostles are said to have converted to National Socialism and are allegedly conscience-stricken at having to portray Jewish types. So as not to feel the embarrassment of just play-acting, they went ahead and grew the long beards and kiss-curls needed for the Passion Play. What happens? Nationalist comrades come down from the north, see this, and tug at their—genuine—beards, in the mistaken belief they are really part of the costume. But they then deduced, in the face of such physical reality, that the Passion meant to be depicted is no longer just a play, and suggested trimming the beards back to a minimum and, instead of Christ's Passion,

> acting out the life of Hitler,

which was rejected, however,

> as it was thought such a theme would not attract any foreign visitors.

Finally, a happy compromise was reached—to retain the plays in their old form and merely brighten them up with repeated renditions of the Horst Wessel song. As for the actors, it was decreed that "the Christ figure could only be a blond man with blue eyes, with swastikas on his robe", and that the faithful disciples must be of the Aryan-Teutonic type, while the Judas figure should be played as "a pronounced Jewish type"—a reform the Propaganda Minister selflessly undertook in person, sparing no effort. However, the possibility of depicting the life of the Nazirene is to be postponed until such times as the outside world has been enlightened by appropriate promotion, should this not have already occurred naturally and in accordance with Goebbels's conviction

> that what we are doing today is blazing a trail for the whole civilised world: a national-socialist world. Even if it does not yet exist, in ten years' time it will be copying our laws. What we are doing today will in ten years' time be *a model for the whole world.* What we are doing today will *set the standard for all of Europe.*

It only remains to construct a system that will outlast future centuries and create an organisation that will endure even "if there should be a lack of talent". We must provide for future generations, and the altered repertoire for Oberammergau will come about of its own accord, for as Gauleiter Kube (of Pergamon Museum fame) said: "Adolf Hitler's mission is divine".

Could that mission be conceivable without the martyrdom so many have had to suffer in the cause? Have we not read about such martyrs, war veterans, also many a one whose body has only now been reduced to "a bloody mass from his back to the hollow of his knees"? To keep him conscious of his calling, they poured cold water over him

> and then extracted pieces of flesh from his chest with pincers.

And then the guardian of the faith took his burning cigar from his mouth

> and scorched a wreath of burns round the fettered prisoner's neck.

And spake the words:

> A necklace of red coral, as a reminder!

"We saw the man and his wounds", said someone at the Saarbrücken Refugee Office.[4]

Those in protective custody try to escape such tried and trusted methods as stabbing themselves with safety pins, sticking a pencil in their eye, smashing their head against the iron bed in their cell, and thinking up outlandish ways of curtailing even more outlandish forms of suffering. But the strict rites of protective custody outlive the faintheartedness of those fleeing from life; they exist thanks to the fanaticism of Nazi activists and—more significantly—because those who sleep easily in their beds have closed their eyes to what is happening. But if mankind finds such events inconceivable (because they are presented as a means of redeeming mankind), we should imprint the following firmly on our minds: the remembrance of all the martyrs who were compelled to pay the price, those trampled underfoot and those who emerged as incurable invalids: the executed Hamburg hero, whose mother heard the news on the radio and screamed as she plunged onto the street below; the woman in Cologne who, in mortal fear as they tortured her husband, jumped out of the window and was left lying on the ground, her legs broken; the cortege of auxiliary policemen in Krems, victims of the most cowardly murder imaginable; those killed and maimed in that Viennese jeweller's shop; the venerable rabbi subjected to a mock execution in Oberwiesenfeld, until it turned into the real thing; the child (they reported exactly what happened themselves) who ran howling after its mother when she was dragged through the streets of Pirmasens as a hostage, to make the father who had fled return to his killers. And the memory, too, of another of God's creatures:

> and they tried to set the wooden building alight with rags soaked in petrol.
>
> The night watchman's dog disturbed the arsonists at their work by barking. One of the Nazis then shot at the dog with his revolver, seriously wounding it. The dog was still able to run the hundred yards or so to the watchman's house and wake his master.
>
> When the watchman arrived at the clubhouse, the intruders had already fled. The man put out the fire with a few buckets of water.
>
> In the early hours of the morning the faithful dog, who had discovered the arsonists and suffered serious injuries, had to be put out of its misery.

People go out from their home and are returned to their family in a sealed coffin.

> Alas poor country;
> Almost afraid to know itself. It cannot
> Be call'd our mother, but our grave; where *nothing,*
> *But who knows nothing, is once seen to smile;*
> Where sighs and groans and shrieks that rent the air
> Are made, not mark'd; where violent sorrow seems
> A modern ecstasy; the dead man's knell
> Is there scarce ask'd for who; and good men's lives
> Expire before the flowers in their caps,
> *Dying or ere they sicken.*[5]

Such is Shakespeare's tremendous depiction of the turbulence in "this our suffering country under a hand accurs'd" ("Some holy angel fly to the court of England and unfold His message!")—only the choked sighs are not those of the indifferent bystanders. They know nothing; they don't believe it happened.[6] Yet it must mean something, something people only recognise when the Führer opens their eyes to it. It was symbolic when a group of young people from the home for the blind in Halle turned to him with the request:

> to be permitted to recognise him as their Führer and to call their room the "Adolf Hitler Room". The Reich Chancellor agreed to this in a specially written response and sent the young people a splendid photograph, signed in person.

Gloucester saw the Führer Principle for what it was: "'Tis the times' plague, when madmen lead the blind".[7] He was blind to its blessing; not all are equally worthy. That's why the German Society for the Blind expelled its Jewish members, but its counterpart in Austria acted as their communications centre. And in front of its Israelite equivalent it was someone with his sight intact who spelt out the inscription to his companion:

> Isra-elite-Insti-tute-for-the-Blind. I'll scrub that out in two ticks. The blind ain't seeing it anyway.

Whereas if you're targeting the Christian majority, you must hide your hand. For blindness is their fate, regardless of religion, and the more frustrated they feel by promises left unfulfilled, the more insatiably they are driven towards a destination shrouded in darkness.

27

OUT OF THE ABYSS: PRUSSIAN EAGLES AND PARCHED TONGUES

Everything that occurs helps to maintain momentum. Cynical careerists participate at least fleetingly in a wider world, revelling in a connection now finally established: that the historic migration of the Germanic peoples has

> instilled fresh Nordic blood into a global Roman empire made degenerate by racial miscegenation.

Let those Scandinavians who legitimately possess Nordic blood shudder with revulsion! Furthermore, Goering has discovered that Germany has finally turned into a super-Prussia, and accordingly ordered the old Prussian eagle to be reunited with sword and lightning, symbolising its desire to soar up to the sun and protect what is most holy to the last drop of its blood. This is more than a beautiful image, it is a symbol of the need to expand the Reich's Air Protection Corps, since Germany's aerial defences are now the top priority—to quell the storm of indignation at the shame inflicted on Germany by foreign aircraft, not to mention the commission paid by the aeronautical industry to its saviour for his contracts. Besides such a prospect, "the only comforting reassurance that can be given to all who are enraged or frightened" is "that every member of the Volk can and should see the government of the Reich as providing a firm guarantee that aerial danger, and protection against it, will be dealt with appropriately and with every hope of success"; moreover, with such vigilance that the incursion of foreign aircraft has been reported twenty minutes before nobody actually spotted them, while German planes are flying over Austria, supposedly only carrying leaflets. On the other hand, the allegation that Goering was responsible for disseminating news of the Communists having started the Reichstag fire a good hour before it happened is probably mistaken, since the fire itself broke out earlier than scheduled.

There has been trouble from the very outset caused by the overzealousness of subordinates, but where possible it has been kept in check. For instance, if Jewish doctors are still being arrested at this very minute, Aryan colleagues are in attendance to provide an exact diagnosis and ensure that no mistakes are made. When anyone has been roughed up, they also have strict instructions to issue an expert medical opinion stating that nothing untoward occurred, that the patient's body was still responding well, or that the corpse bore no traces likely to arouse suspicion. Such claims could at times be laughable. Even in Austria there have been cases where, in an emergency, doctors have themselves resorted to physical measures. Thus, one reads of someone suspected of having defaced a swastika being restrained by a doctor and thrashed by his son, who is still learning his trade. Some doctors take a more inclusive approach—shouting "Long live Germany!" during an operation, so insulting Dollfuss at the same time. If people in a Styrian inn start to "settle someone's hash", it's the doctor's duty to sprinkle pepper in his eyes. In Germany, priority is given to the economic interests of the profession, since one frequently reads that "Aryan doctors must refer their Aryan patients to other Aryan doctors, and vice versa", while Jewish doctors—if they still exist—are not to be consulted. All this is strictly regulated from one day to the next, and the marginalisation of Jewish doctors still continues long after they have all disappeared. The discovery that they were the very embodiment of dishonesty and deception opened the eyes of Aryan colleagues; it also opened up opportunities which the medical journals interpreted in different ways. Directly, for instance:

> *The disappearance* of Jewish doctors offers *a good opportunity for a German doctor to set up practice at a convenient location in* Neukölln. Enquiries to—

It is one of those cases where the autopsy incorporates a claim to the deceased's inheritance. Or indirectly, when a medical review prompts a doctor to ask whether the Führer,

> *for whom the title "Emperor" would in no way be too exalted,*

does not at least deserve that of "Duke of the German People" and issues his findings:

> In Adolf Hitler the German people have been gifted a man of such exceptional stature *that in millennia to come, in myth and history*, the people will *still* look upon him as *the greatest statesman and liberator of all time.*

While the master decorator F. Židek from Olmütz, on the other hand, came to the conclusion:

> Since I recognised during his probationary period that his technical knowledge lagged far behind his rhetorical skill and eloquence, I no longer required him to give me his personal data but dismissed him.

If a certain similarity to Christ were to come fully to light, and rumours of his Jewish descent from a certain Abraham Friesch in Polna turned out to be true, the result would be a global anti-Semitism that would leave the German model far behind.

But this is an example of fake news that is manifestly mistaken, since nobody could assimilate so completely to the Bavarian ethnic type, both in appearance and in speech—so turgid that it betrays a determined struggle with dialect:

> Deshtiny has tchosen me . . .

Listening to the radio or reading the *Berliner Illustrierte*, no one could possibly have any doubt about an accent so rooted in the soil—one hundred percent genuine, according to Goebbels, an authority in the field. Conversely, it is a bad habit of the Jews to claim everything as their own but regard belonging to a regional community as the ultimate disgrace. What good is all the genealogical snooping when it is swept away by a seismic eruption, as a simple creature "with monstrous effort struggles out of the abyss" [7570].

It is almost as if Hitler had sprung from the soil, self-taught and totally self-fashioned, and is now attempting to philosophise about a world he intends to conquer. How far this thinking is removed from the faintest particle of Jewish intelligence can be seen from a glance at his autobiography, for instance when it expounds this maxim:

> *Fundamentally*, all work has double value: one purely *material* and one *ideal*. The *material* value resides in the *significance, that is to say the material significance*, of work for the life of the community. *The more* members of the *Volk* benefit when a specific piece of work has been completed, *the greater* its material value should be judged to be. This assessment *in turn* finds *concrete* expression in the *material* wages the individual receives for his work. The opposite pole to this *purely material* value is the *ideal* value. It *doesn't* reside in the *significance* of the work done *as measured in material terms*, but in its *absolute necessity*. Just as the *material* benefit of an invention can certainly be greater than that of everyday donkey work, so it is equally certain that the community as a whole is just as dependent on this least significant form of work as it is on the most significant.[1]

No, this didn't spring from one of Abraham's children, nor will its author be restored to his bosom, but he shall cry in vain for his tongue to be cooled; for beside all this, between us and you there is fixed a great gulf: so that you who would pass from thence to us cannot.[2] Nevertheless, if it is given unto the simpleminded to produce a mystical effect denied to the more sophisticated, this passage illustrates its inordinate appeal. Its honest endeavour, using its own terms to think its way through to a platitude, is compelling. And the great disquisition about the principles of art and culture, which since the Nuremberg rally has acquired canonical status, again displays this groping for meaning, this simultaneous struggle for formulations such as educated people would use.[3] The defining feature of this worthy effort is the concept of "synthesis", the need for which the Führer so frequently emphasises, but also "the compelling reality of racial substance" along with "conspicuous display"; then there are the foreign words and technical terms such as "organic", "conglomerate", the "reorientation" inevitably ensuing from a worldview, the dominant influence of a distinctive racial core, racially determined constraints—all mixed together to form an overall picture of how life is expressed, the detachment currently required as well as the racially and ideologically based tendencies of an era which will also determine artistic trends and mentalities, the impact of its creative spirit, and, ultimately, the incarnation of the supreme values of a homogeneous nation. How moving in its sincerity, assuming this was not dictated by Goebbels! No wonder the *Völkischer Beobachter* felt impelled to declare:

> *As a singularly acute and lucid thinker Hitler ranks among the great German political philosophers, although few people* realised it. In this respect, *even the educated were astonished* by his two great Nuremberg speeches.

Well, well!, they said, when he spoke of the immutable laws of selective breeding and demanded a synthesis of tradition and renewal, and who would have credited him with so many foreign words! All his own work!

> This speech *marks a new departure in the history of German thinking.*

I must admit that from the very beginning I've evaded the influence exerted by *Mein Kampf*, being more concerned with struggles of my own, so a glance at it from time to time, or the occasional quotation, was all that was needed. It was also enough to learn that some of the Führer's findings were prophetic. For example, here's one which—as distinct from recognising the need to fool the people—still appears in later editions:

> The more the Movement has in its gift by way of readily accessible posts and placements, the greater the number of inferior types who will be attracted, until finally these casual labourers (in a political sense) overrun a successful party in such numbers that the honest foot soldier of former days no longer recognises the Movement as it once was, and the new-

comers emphatically repudiate him as an unqualified troublemaker. But when that happens, a movement's "mission" is done for.

If any participant in such a movement deserves to be pitied—apart from those murdered and robbed by the inferior types—it is the Führer, who wrings his hands for having called them to arms but now can't dismiss them.[4] Many guiding principles have proved themselves, many others been overtaken by evolutionary developments, which is why Goering (without whom these things would run more smoothly) issues a decree insisting that officials "shall no longer be unfamiliar with the essential thinking behind the Movement" and orders a new edition of *Mein Kampf*, so they can learn about "the most important aspects of national-socialist writing"—namely those that are no longer in force. That's his struggle, for even if he has a forty-room villa decorated to perfection à la Torquemada, he still wants to help out the tried and trusted SA. And so every day sees a change of scene and the slogans contradict each other, but it is nevertheless clear that evolution, supposedly the "safe bed" into which the torrent of revolution can be channeled, is gaining a turbulent momentum.[5] The call for the commissars to disappear because their "constant interference with the economy has become intolerable" seems to echo a demand made against a previous regime. As long as the regulation of economic life was based solely on Aryan firms paying an annual charge for the designation "A German Enterprise", the system functioned one hundred per-cent: a plaque or sticker showing "a radiant rising sun with a swastika, and a guardian eagle perched in front", the so-called "trade eagle", shielded you against the risk of some Jew or other making big bucks faster, earning quicker'n'slicker. But even if it meant paying more, experience shows that no trade eagle protects you against the vultures hovering over the firm, the spectre of bankruptcy. Then new regulations are continuously called for, not indeed telling you what you should do, but what you mustn't do. And, just at the right moment, the question of the primacy of economics over politics arises; since *Primat* could also mean "primates" in the jungle, this could be linked to the insight that we need a "politics of living space", rather than "economic illusions".

Those "ineffectual dreamers" who are still complaining should see the twenty-five points, which they think constituted a party-political programme, actually implemented.[6] But even that would be to no avail. When the Right doesn't know what the Left is doing, it gets ever more complicated if neither knows what they themselves should be doing, and promises made to the big industrialists are frustrated by a refusal even to discuss them, while "the workers who are now fully fledged members of the Master Race" can just hold their tongue. The ability to hold two contradictory opinions simultaneously means that filling employment vacancies "should not depend on which party you belong to"—for they are exclusively reserved for Nazi Party members! Next comes the proclamation that the struggle against capitalism will be conducted as a means of defeating bolshevism, while—to cap it all—socialism has been renounced in favour of a plan to erect a monument to German Labour, represented by four female figures, namely loyalty, justice, love, and truth—the core values of the German people.[7] Meanwhile, the following inscription is under consideration for the tombstone of leader figures:

> They were often harsh, they were hard, they were ruthless, but they were good Germans.

28

WHERE LAWLESSNESS MAKES LAW ITS INSTRUMENT

Certain irregularities appear in a different light the moment they are weighed against the administration of justice. According to guidelines established by the chief judge of a regional court and published in the *Deutsche Juristenzeitung*, a series of actions such as bodily harm, wrongful detention, and manslaughter are to be "determined by the national interest" and consequently exempt a priori from presumption of culpability, whereas hitherto the criminal proceedings first had to be quashed. There will be no repetition of the devious stratagem applied in the case of the Potempa murderers, whose lives hung by a thread while their official careers were set back by several months. What is required of judges is a certain independence when interpreting the law, to prevent them from going astray on such an important matter:

> In this he is also *following ancient Germanic custom. The enemy within* was outlawed by *our forefathers* and *became an outcast, deprived of rights and branded with infamy;* any member of the Volk could *openly kill* him, provided he had not sought refuge on sacred ground.
>
> The restoration of German honour requires *complete extermination* of the enemy within. The judge in a criminal case can contribute to this by a *generous interpretation* of the Criminal Code.

Experts expect that the imminent reorganisation of the Criminal Code will settle much that is uncertain and reassure anxious souls in the judiciary. It will be all the easier to implement since the judiciary will doubtless gain new recruits among champions of the nationalist movement who had been convicted of stabbing offences under the now-obsolete interpretation of the law, but have often advanced into top jobs in the police after knocking the stuffing out of their predecessors in office. It would, of course, be an exaggeration to claim that all officeholders had previous convictions. For instance, in the case of the Minister for Culture and Education, Bernhard Rust, who had never committed any acts of violence but had been implicated in a sex scandal under the previous regime, diminished responsibility (Article 51) was accepted as grounds for exemption from prosecution. Moreover, he was in the good books of the new masters, who otherwise look for more evidence of energetic personal initiative. Just how scrupulously the New Order observes the principle of reciprocity in international legal aid is shown by the fact that, despite the present political tension, even Austrian criminals, especially those who plant bombs, are given the same generous treatment and can claim asylum, provided they make radio broadcasts about the barbaric customs of their homeland. Considering how hard it is in general for emigrants to obtain employment, this concession by the German authorities is all the more remarkable: based solely on a warrant for his arrest issued by the Vienna police, they appointed a double murderer as a guard in Dachau. Of course, one mustn't overlook the fact that there is a moral obligation in this case, since the orders for the bomb attacks on Austria were given by the Munich chief of police.[1] On the other hand, in the case of those who have eluded German justice by fleeing abroad, confiscation of their assets serves mainly to pay for the damage caused in the course of the national upheaval at their place of residence, for instance when it proved necessary to wreck furniture and smash pianos, and articles of silver also went missing. It goes without saying, given the immutable belief that everything is to be done by the book, that rental demands must be punctually met by tenants who simply deserted their apartments, entrusting them to the care of SA men, and that they will likewise be served with regular tax demands. But overall there is a marked tendency towards ensuring the confidence of the public in the legal system, as demanded by various decrees; thus, not only are traditional prejudices broken down, but reconstruction work is also carried out, for instance when, during a break in a court case, Communist defendants are persuaded to make a full confession. In this way, the meaning of the national upheaval should gradually emerge—as a liberation from outmoded punitive measures, to the point where it is not life, liberty, honour, and rightful ownership that are considered matters and interests protected by law, but rather their abrogation. Unfortunately, consistency is thwarted even here by the rulings of individual office holders, such as the astonishing "measure to combat blackmail" which someone thought up on his own initiative. This asserted that irresponsible elements are exploiting opportunities for blackmail created by the national upheaval, "often enough successfully . . . attempting to extract" from wealthy individuals, by menacing or violent behaviour,

> modest sums of money or other assets by passing themselves off as accredited office holders, or as the powers behind the throne controlling the national upheaval, often enough by misuse of uniforms or other insignia. The police authorities will do their utmost to apprehend the perpetrators in all cases.

In the first place, it's not true—at least not as far as the modest sums of money are concerned. Moreover, the police authorities tend to avoid intervening in such cases, at best merely advising those concerned to pay up, and the incident is generally resolved amicably when the threatened party signs a declaration that nothing was demanded of them by the SA men, who in any case were not real SA men. A final point is that police interventions would touch a vital nerve for the movement, especially since it is often its frontline activists who would be affected. From the outset it was these activists who, to avoid the worst, have taken the reins into their own hands, while on the other hand, in case after case it was reported that those donors were more than willing to pay up, indeed to make sacrifices. Gauleiter Kothen, who has served Austria so well, recalls that when he arrived in Worms he was amazed to see comrades in classy private cars, and, upon making enquiries was told by a chuckling member of the old guard

> that the Jews, in order to implement the Jewish boycott more efficiently, *on demand* had *voluntarily put them at their disposal*, over and above which they had declared themselves willing to pay for a week's supply of petrol.

On another occasion, beyond this proof of sacrifice, he paints a picture of total fraternity between all classes, dependent as they are on one another:

> Food for prisoners is generously donated by Jewish firms in the main, who cannot resist friendly persuasion from our SA.

Observation of etiquette and common civility has gained ground everywhere, though its neglect can certainly have most unpleasant consequences. While the Jews are open to reason, the behaviour of the Stahlhelm veterans, once regarded as valiant allies of our brave SA and SS, has changed to such an extent that a local Gruppenführer had to be sent to a concentration camp for lack of tact, since he had

> by his behaviour drawn unwelcome attention towards SA and SS men on duty.

But unfortunately it turns out that they themselves give offence even more often by paying homage not only to the Führer, but "under the pretext of building up the party", to self-interest. When they are reprimanded for this blatant offence against the programme, they reply that that if everyone does it, the whole community benefits. By hook or by crook, aided by Krupp and Thyssen, the movement has reached the stage of "evolution", a foreign word (like "Reichspräsident") but one that does actually mean something, namely that unregulated greed should give way to rational planning. This innovation will not easily find favour, for if you can't steal things, how can you obtain them? The Führer preaches reason, yet it is the very men who have rendered such outstanding service to the nation who can't stomach the dictates of reason. With increasing frequency, their lucrative individual actions are hampered by irksome regulations, which really would regulate the situation but for the fact that there are further reasons for rescinding them.

From the very start of a revolution replete with sacrifices, one which should ultimately run its course without the spilling of blood, a certain degree of confusion was inevitable, which even the press coverage could not entirely rectify. We have seen the page proofs of this development made up and corrected, but the typographical errors of world history are prefigured in the press as if they were virtues, betraying a truth that might otherwise only be revealed to posterity. "Mine" and "thine" are easily confused, not only by proofreaders; and in a situation where it is never clear who should be "defended" and who "apprehended", it was only logical for Goering to appeal to the SA

> as loyal defenders of disturbances and excesses.

No less credible is Goebbels's declaration that the national revolution is intensified

> when viewed through the prison of fanatical popular conviction.

Meanwhile the German authorities characteristically "apply" the policy they "deny", namely

> energetically enforcing a mass exodus of German Jews.

In the process, everything conceivable is done to provide a legal basis for the altered living conditions, so that the courts become stamping grounds for well-drilled acolytes. The first community camp for a rising generation of judges has opened in Jüterbog, and while junior doctors arrest superiors who have tried to disguise racial flaws through their erudition, the trainee lawyers are relieved of their law books on entering their barracks in accordance with express instructions that field sports are more important than "cramming", while the course of justice is adequately served by "instruction in racial questions and the Treaty of Versailles" alongside lessons in cleaning and patchwork.[2] For "the days of judges lolling on the bench with their callow clerks" are past; now the judicial body needs to be toughened up and imbued with the spirit of the National Socialist state—a goal epitomised by a symbol reflecting the interests of the profession which is affixed outside the barracks: a gallows with a legal tome hanging from the noose, which, if the illustrations are anything to go by, the young legal eagles think is a scream. Moreover, since students of philosophy and, alas, also theology [354/356] are busy smearing swastikas on the fronts of Jewish businesses, all the faculties have now been pointed in the Right direction, all possess the right to expel the professors, who in turn spend the hours they would have wasted on their studies exercising in camps, setting a fine example on marches. But there are also many graduates already professionally qualified who find themselves no longer in post but in custody. Inspection of all facilities, in both community and concentration camps, is of course open to the German press, which has declared itself ready to report its findings faithfully and from which we can learn that camp inmates have nothing to complain about. On the other hand, foreign correspondents are no longer admitted—those

> who passed on the complaints they heard about living conditions in the camps to their papers.

An interference in the internal affairs of the state which is incompatible with its sovereignty and is rejected with feigned incomprehension.

Nor are differences between the German federal states in respect of the number of internees in protective custody of any concern to foreign countries. When the Prussian Minister of the Interior states that "all of Germany has 18,000, of which Prussia has 12,000", and the Saxon Minister of the Interior reveals, not without justified pride, that "Saxony alone has more than double the number of persons in protective custody than Prussia, even though it is much bigger", the first thing that clearly emerges from the source of these calculations is that it is an internal matter in each case. But the apparent discrepancy that Saxony has over 24,000 of the 18,000 persons in protective custody in Germany as a whole still leaves room for agreement with Prussia on one calculation, namely that—contrary to the assertion of one foreign telegraph agency—there are fewer than 100,000 persons in protective custody in Germany, and that this is the real issue. How even this number would be distributed among the federal states is up to them and them alone, and if German unity has not yet been achieved in this matter, it shows that each state, as a matter of honour, competes with the others to have as many persons as possible in protective custody, while claiming to have as few as possible in the eyes of the outside world.

One would be equally justified in finding fault with divergent conceptions of factors that cannot be calculated numerically. Opinions vary on how we should assess the phenomenon of extortion, although it is indisputably the lever controlling all internal and external political objectives, both material and ideal, with the material value residing in its material significance which in turn finds concrete expression in material wages. From jockeying for position to coercing hostages, from the confiscation of businesses by commissars to picking people's pockets, from voluntary disclaimers by victims of theft, or the signatures of those being tortured, to the measures against Austria—every breath of nationalist passion, every raised arm signalling the national awakening, is extortion. (For the more members of the Volk who benefit when a specific piece of work has been completed, the greater its material value should be judged to be, which is often the opposite of its ideal value—A.H.) Extortion—at home and abroad, from start to finish, underlying even the devious complicity at every turn between fraudulent acquisition of power and unnatural male bonding. Extortion, the element that nourishes and sustains us—with the exception at best of instances when the alternative "Your money or your life!"—as a concession to free will—seemed redundant, and prompt payment covered both options. And so, later, there was a sort of regression towards the Second Reich, when extortion became—theoretically—taboo.

We now witness a similar tendency to soft-pedal the problem of denunciation—certainly no less integral a component of national life. Here, too, restrictions were introduced. One fine day, it dawned on the Reich Chancellor that in many cases the incentive for taking the captains of industry to court wasn't the desire for justice; in short, the denunciations seemed to him to spring not from the moral awakening of a people but from their baser instincts, including the desire for revenge. But the legitimate grievances underlying such charges should never be overlooked, namely that they are a reaction against injuries inflicted years ago and all the more painful for that. The impulse derives from well-documented political positions, even if they were never explicitly expressed. That's why Goering, always alive to the way tolerance can cause bad blood, took a stronger line with a decree encouraging denunciation as a factor conducive to the well-being of the state, throwing his weight against attempts to inhibit it. On the other hand, there seems to be total agreement that corruption, and especially protectionism (of which there has already been more than enough), must be eradicated. Apparently with the sole intention of discovering whether such things can still exist, advertisements have appeared in the *Berliner Tageblatt* and the *Völkischer Beobachter* which must surely achieve the negative outcome envisaged:

> *Politician,* chief engineer, aged 40, *close current connections with top people,* seeks position of responsibility in industry or economics. Offers to—
>
> NSDAP. Are you a *leading member* with *extensive connections?* Respected firm seeks *ambitious gentleman*—Offers to—

Without doubt, what we're dealing with here is a purge, as it's been a long time since leading members with extensive connections were in need of a job. Goebbels's brother is provided for. The father of Frank II, guilty of some minor transgression, has been rehabilitated, Schirach's family taken care of, and each of them has at least promoted a cousin—if not prevented from doing so by his aunt (on account of a grandmother).

> These people have great reputations
> For favouring their own relations. [7748]

Is that from Walpurgis Night too? Everything is!

> The old tale—instances by dozens—
> In every region always cousins! [7742]

Of course, nepotism only accounts for a tiny fraction of the corruption—not the whole range of bribery, underhanded party-funding, or enrichment at public expense, which are open for all to see. This openness is a phenomenon which characterises totalitarianism and is evidence of the inner strength of National Socialism, distinguishing it quantitatively from the secretive cliques of financial backers in the former system. Even if one is continually struck with amazement, the total shamelessness (for instance, the gift of cars justified as promoting the automobile industry) also explains—as it were, necessarily—the implacability with which those who plunder the nation's wealth on a grand scale string up those they accuse, without justification, of minor theft. Somehow or other, it must be laid down in ideology that bandits who instigate the theft of pictures from churches can also make men, who have done nothing except draw a fair day's pay for a fair day's work, transport heavy boulders in carts. It would surely be neither a moral nor a technical headache to give to the upwardly mobile the jobs of a now dispossessed minority, at most a physical headache for their previous occupants who did not instantly acknowledge the old Germanic maxim: "Ôte toi que je m'y mette!" ("Get out of the way, and give me elbow room!") It's harder to deal with the many left empty-handed who begrudge the prosperity of others. Initially, an attempt is made to shut them up as follows:

> *Warning!*
> *There has been an increase in the number of cases* in which *suspicions* have been raised, *also by those in non-Marxist* circles, *against departmental heads, local authority chairmen, and others in administrative posts.* That being the case, I give explicit notice that I am compelled to proceed henceforth *with the utmost severity* against unfounded accusations.

But the problem remains of how to provide for the majority of serving members who have rallied to the "totalitarian" cause and who are still waiting for satisfaction, both ideal and material. Since ideal satisfaction cannot satisfy every craving, and quenching one's thirst for blood does not assuage one's hunger, the peaceful bed of evolution cannot guarantee a sound night's sleep. Unruly elements appear and trample on the plan. They shake the illusions that sustain the splendours of the state. To complete the nightmare, Faustian characters shaking their fists threaten to take over "where lawlessness makes law its instrument" [4785]. As a consequence—

> Still swelling like a tidal surge,
> Erupts the revolutionary urge. [4793]

And the hocus-pocus about of the Reichstag fire, a criminological conundrum surely unprecedented in the history of the world: to explain how the perpetrators could commission the courts to carry out the crime. They were supposed to play blind man's bluff while setting everything to rights:

> Accomplices are eager to defend
> The criminals who flaunt their evil deeds.
> Whereas the naïve innocent, who pleads
> For his release, will find himself condemned. [4795]

Fair enough: German justice often balances things out:

> A judge who will not punish crime
> Becomes a criminal in time.... [4805]

But German power demands more:

> In these wild days, how discords thicken!
> Each strikes and in return is stricken,
> And they are deaf to all commands....
> The mercenaries, no whit better,
> Impatiently demand their pay,
> And if we were not still their debtor,
> They'd start forthwith and march away.
> Deny them all that they demand
> And we would stir a hornet's nest,
> The Reich we pay them to defend
> Reduced to ashes and to dust.
> [4812 (Bayard Taylor plus a touch of Williams)]

And the international community?

> They give full rein to wild disorder,
> The world is splitting at the seams;

There are still kings beyond our border,
But not one country intervenes. [4827 (after Bayard Taylor / Luke)]

Internal affairs! The Lord Treasurer:

The gate of gold no more unlatches,
And each one gathers, digs, and scratches,
While we are left with empty coffers. [4849 (after Bayard Taylor)]

Reserve fund reduced to 7 per-cent:

We try to save day after day,
But still need more without delay. . . .
We've pawned the pillows from our bed
And have to eat leftover bread.
. . . .
Resulting from the global crash,
We're short of all things—not least cash! [4853/4889]

But there are still flags, festivals, fireworks:

It's Carnival, so let's enjoy the fun,
Knowing the day of penitence will come.
Till then, regale ourselves on beer and wine,
So every evening counts as party time! [5057]

Though not everything feels right:

He fails to see the threat that looms without,
So let him play the clown a little longer—
Until they terminate his knockabout.
The law is strong, but direst need is stronger. [5797]

Instructions: "Simply being a National Socialist is not enough for the economy. Work, performance, results: these are decisive, not ideology!" So that is what they were fighting for? The Führer coined the maxim that what we need now is a synthesis: between the idealism of National Socialism and the exigencies of the moment, that is to say, between the idealistic and the materialistic. The Führer is ready to make sacrifices: but he will "not capitulate except to reason" (which has hitherto capitulated to him). His followers think this attitude tantamount to desertion, but as for "synthesis"—he can whistle for it:

So this is now the latest thing,
A raucous throat, a twanging string
Form tones designed to harmonise.

The tinkling music that one hears
Is largely wasted on my ears,
Leaving my heart unsatisfied. [7175]

How does one deal with those true believers in all the promises, who now behave like creditors demanding their payoff?

They carry on regardless, just as fated,
You'd never know they had been educated. [7343]

The Sibyl whispers:

Those explorers I love best
Who make the impossible their quest. [7488]

It's growing dark. Care for a place in the sun?

Start on the race
To claim more space,
Work at full speed,
There's strength in the deed.
In peacetime conditions
We're making munitions,
Defensive resources
And arms for our forces! [7626]

"We have absolutely no intention of waging war":

Who can now save us?
We forge the steel
For chains that enslave us,
And yet we feel
That it's better to wait
For an easier fate. [7654]

The situation abroad is a mess, Goebbels tells us, and things are getting out of hand at home. Seldte has knuckled under, Hugenberg has sold his soul to the devil, and Papen is said to be up on his high horse:

Witches on broomsticks, all in flight,
Like the original Walpurgis Night. [7809]

Hindenburg is in the clear:

Let the general staff lead the attack,
That'll cover the Field Marshall's back. [10,313]

But the number of those dissatisfied with the implementation of the programme as broadcast is growing by the day. These are the "undercover Bolshevist elements talking of a second revolution at the very time the people and the nation are preparing" to build on the results of the first for the next century. At this time, the future is what matters, and inevitably "one well-meant theory or another won't get the recognition it deserves", though it remains valid for times past. The other ranks are overstepping the mark:

> Tread softly now! But to indulge yourself,
> Just go ahead and sneak things from the shelf. [7694]

They're avoided "as if they were toxic" by the party bosses, who are starting to be afraid of the "brown plague". So they introduce romantic distractions:

> Children love their knightly gear,
> The shining armour and the spear.
> That allegory is in vogue
> Really suits this type of rogue. [10,327]

And it really is the case that, from the age of ten, they can, and indeed must, come to class in uniform. "All my nine-year-olds are envious of Hans and Heinz. They both had to repeat a year; it normally counts as a black mark", said the teacher, "but the uniform compensates for that". Austria, too, has already addressed the problem of the education of the young, to the extent that there is no longer a divide between teachers and pupils, but both are working together as comrades making explosive devices, and in coeducational establishments it's often the case that the girls are the more proficient ones. Just as children once swapped stamps and marbles, now they swap detonator caps and ammonium nitrate explosives. According to one decree, "in future every primary schoolchild must be familiar with the landscape", which will stand him or her in good stead when bombs need burying. That explains the rising generation of SS troop leaders who planned to sprinkle petrol over the commodity exchange, until one of them "declared he had a better plan" and showed them the bomb he had brought along in a bag—and they saw that it was good. For allegorical as these rogues are, they are also practical and know the necessities of life. They're also trained on the physical side by the valiant pioneers Smasher, Grabber, and Hoarder. The first of these explains the rudiments:

> Let anyone give me the eye,
> I'll smash his face in with one hand!
> And if a coward runs away,
> I'll rip his hair out strand by strand! [10,331]

The second plunders everything unperturbed [10,337]. Fine, says the third, plunder is good, but keep some for yourself [10,342]. All three are having a great time:

> The booted foot enjoys inflicting pain,
> Crushing the necks of those who have been slain. [10,485]

Irrespective of Party; and even the Church's faith is shaken:

> The clergy's privileges we've crushed;
> Who cares if we have lost their trust! [10,616]

And yet Papen can announce:

> That day in Rome. The Pope still really cares
> And watches over you and your affairs. [10,447 (Williams)]

Then Smasher steps forward and describes what he did in Breslau:

> The man who shows his face to me, before
> He turns away I smash his cheeks and jaw;
> But if he turns his back, his skull is shattered,
> His brains hang down his neck, his hair all tattered. [10, 511]

Too close to the bone! Does the world still enjoy watching those who "harass others and shove them around"? [10,457]

> Onwards to victory, no holds barred! [10, 536]

But now avert your gaze! Mephistopheles has armed those just waiting for the signal to open fire—where that will come from, no need to enquire [10,553]. It's no longer just hot air. Once, "kings, emperors, knights ran the show" [10,559]:

> To revive the Middle Ages is the desire
> Of many a phantom in mediaeval attire. [10,561]

Now high-fliers drop bombs on those below. If the devil has filled them with phosgene gas, that toxin's effect is still first-class. [10,563]

> Banners in tatters, flags reduced to shreds
> Await the breeze to stir their drooping heads.
> Take heed! An ancient people's yearning for
> The chance of fighting in a modern war. [10,566]

Romanticism has caught up with chemistry. It's a last chance for a diversionary manoeuvre against those internal forces. However, "the boldest climbers grow confused" [10,723], indeed

Now confusion reigns supreme.

All warnings are in vain:

Among our troops he comes to grief
Who's both a soldier and a thief. [10,823 (Bayard Taylor)]

Have they forgotten their oath?

While loyal blood flows through our bodies still,
Our lives are subject to our leader's will. [10,963]

The leader's will remains firm, but as to his followers:

Drifting along, we've reached a turning point,
Uncertain whether this is what was meant. [10,847]

"Internal turmoil! Nation under threat!" They devastated the Reich with their "feuds and divisions" [10,392, 10,379]:

Turning against me, ready to rebel,
The fickle mob's been led astray,
Till in the flood they'll all be swept away. [10,379]

Playthings of every current, they bob up and down on the waves [10,733]; ultimately, in all these devilish diversions (when there are no more parties), hatred of the Party works best, says Mephistopheles, and is delighted to hear "horrid sounds of panic matching panic" [10,780]. For he has always known that

In the end we all are fated
To be in thrall to creatures we created. [7003]

Now everyone finds someone else to blame, and it's beginning to dawn on the Leader too:

The sins that burden me have an appalling weight;
Those sorcerers have left me in a sorry state. [11,033]

To the Devil with a movement whose banner—

has some kind of Cross stuck on it! [10,709]

29

PROPHETS OF DOOM AND THE TRIUMPH OF ARYAN TEUTONISM

So now I ask myself: how could I ever have swallowed the repugnance I naturally felt, and continue to feel, at embarking on this far-flung Walpurgis Night adventure, from which—when it has once put behind it that other, shameful, rallying cry "Jews, exterminate 'em!"—let Germany awaken! Its greatest poetic evocation, in Goethe's *Faust*, throws light on many of its mysteries, and the manifold visions conjured up by the Witches' Sabbath feature the best prophets of Germany's destiny, but also the worst. Its horrors even extend to Shakespeare's bloodiest vision, *Macbeth*. So now I ask myself how I was able to find my way through this dark labyrinth, while the German language—my language—was led astray by the hypocritical urgings of a mischievous will o' the wisp; stumbling over roots and snags even more treacherous than the linguistic minefield of the World War, while I was both encouraged and deterred by well-meaning readers demanding clear views as visibility deteriorated after the political landslide? Posing such questions to myself is to query in the same breath the moral justification of questioning the Nazi seizure of power, an event of elemental force whose workings provide a link between the press and my bias against it. Moral justification would come not only from my desire to reject this link, which is more ardent than my wishes concerning the press itself—wishes now granted with the victory of National Socialism. For the notion that I could ever feel this victory to be my own is as pitiable as the mentality from which it springs. My abhorrence for it does not prevent me from using it to rebuff those who supposedly take my side. Except that I go about this with a greater degree of responsibility and with insight into the connection between both evils. For National Socialism has not destroyed the press; rather, the press has created National Socialism. Apparently only as a reaction, but actually as a fulfilment of its true nature. Over and above the humbug with which they nourish their readers, it is, after all, journalists we are talking about. Those who write editorials in blood and features about fearless deeds. Troglodytes by nature, they have entered and occupied the cavernous void to which the printed word has reduced the imaginative powers of mankind. That they eschew all embellishment, or are unable even to fake it, can to some extent be construed as—for them—a cultural advance. Actions have escaped the control of flowery phrases, and it is pointless to use such phrases to adorn them, for the effect is simply grotesque. The mind remains unaffected. But if we regard the "alignment" of the press as a political act, it signifies no more than its final phase, the ultimate potential of an institution prevented by its true nature, prostitution, from evolving any further. The alleged degradation of the German press may well be problematic for a journalism free to express its opinions, as long as political power does not make a direct impact and masseuses advertising sado-masochistic services refrain from torture. But criminologically, when Nazi "commissars" force their way into a newspaper office and "lay their revolver on the editor's desk", the essential significance is that two revolvers now lie side by side.[1]

The idea that "culture" suffers a loss when the lower reaches of journalism are devastated is itself a form of shallow journalism. The existential factor, lamentable in every individual case, should be judged against the general public benefit of the profession thus depleted, and when a state of emergency has tyrannically put people out of work, even those outside the profession are likely to empathise with the fate of ruined doctors, rather than peripatetic editors. But even more journalistic is the idea that the victors' takeover of the news media could accord with my aversion to the journalists they have vanquished; that this horrific outrage could kindle some positive emotion in me, as an answer to my prayer, since the spirit of the Creation would no longer be under pressure from "intelligent stupidity" but from its inevitable sequel, a dumbing-down incapable of maintaining its purity of principle. As if one's insight into the depravity that appears every day but which, whatever its orientation, runs counter to the enlightening rays of the sun had not now found confirmation at the most fundamental level—to the point where ostensible opposites in this world of manufactured opinions coalesce in the "universal flux" of the verbal morass, which is fed by violent actions and generates still more. As if it were in any way significant for the inner world how political actors construe it; as if differences of opinion were of fundamental concern for the human spirit, rather than because of the suffering humanity that is trapped between them.

The problem, as recognised during the World War, is the simultaneous coexistence of slogans and weapons, which, irrespective of whatever alliances statesmen construct, accounts for the triple alliance of ink, technology, and death. If Herr Goebbels, the brains behind the upheaval, who provides his primitive entourage with its terminological foundations, had found timely employment with the liberal *Berliner Tageblatt* (which was his aim, not just ideologically), we would have been spared more than just the "alignment" of a newspaper. The alignment of my own work has unfolded between the two opposing worlds, which is why, hated by both, I can be claimed by either—something I find malign but to which I must resign myself. The descendants of the Wahnschaffes and the Schwarz-Gelbers take what they need for their purposes from *The Last Days of Mankind*—purposes categorically opposed to my own. The Wahnschaffes, whose children are running through their exercises today, speaking the dialogue I invented for them, are the more immediately threatening. Who could be more above suspicion when bearing witness against them than their creator, who through a process of familiarisation and long suffering has become the adversary of a mentality totally hostile to nature, one dedicated to the naked pursuit of material goods and the debasement of all higher intellectual and spiritual values? Who could be better acquainted with the vengeful violence that seeks to compensate for its inferiority by adapting methods from black-market trading to the realms of spirituality and language; that is busy interfering in everything that lies beyond its scope, harassing the competent authorities and hurling back in their face the spoils it has misappropriated and defiled? The real problem is how to be intellectually grounded, not rooted in a folksy tradition, one of blood and soil whose advocates feel only a vague urge to avenge their inborn sense of inadequacy, given their questionable intellectual endowments, and are motivated solely by envy of those who envy them. Just as I have absolutely no connection with those plagiarists of intellectual property whose mental powers match the grimy dregs of their impudence, so nothing, but nothing, connects me with the outbreak of pure stupidity which seeks to compensate for its inadequacy by claiming purity of blood and shedding that of others—an even more physical way of desecrating nature than the stupidity of those who manage to survive the martyrdom of the innocent. Wahnschaffes are more spontaneous. Admittedly, if I were protected from them and their sacrificial pyres because they failed to comprehend the German language in which my offensive—and my offence—is couched, there is still the possibility that the Schwarz-Gelbers would provide enlightenment. "To seek refuge in syntax / In times when language has disintegrated" (and actions are taking priority)—what good is that when language, too, is falling into the clutches of the barbarians?[2] And there was still so much that I intended to undertake against both groups! My position towards the parties fluctuates since I cannot take my bearings from the landmarks of the traditionalists but have no confidence in the progressive path to freedom. This explains my success in uniting deadly enemies in their distrust of me, while their occasional signs of appreciation are as starkly contrasted as they are to one another. For me to have influenced the representatives of all possible political persuasions, as is sometimes claimed, would have been casting pearls before swine, whereas my steadfast aim has been to protect myself from them.

How can I help it if my defence of mankind, campaigning for nature and spirit against the destructive powers of a warped intelligence and uncontrolled technology, was usurped by an Aryan Teutonism totally alien to me, as if my work not only served its interests but had that as its sole objective? After all these years it has surely become obvious that the notion of the inferiority of a "race" is one that I could only conceivably endorse if applied to the race that has succumbed to this insane ideology, which runs contrary to the purposes of the Creation. My credentials to repudiate the emergence and spread of such theories seem to have been confirmed by the movement's philosophical founder (Lanz von Liebenfels), who pioneered the idea of "selective racial breeding". His response to a questionnaire (in *Der Brenner*) is quoted here, twenty years later, not so much to satisfy my vanity as to indulge my liking for contrasts:

> KK's significance is all-embracing. Whoever sees only the phenomenal master of language, the bitingly vitriolic satirist and the brilliant and witty critic, does this genius less than justice. All these virtues and qualities are, for Kraus, merely the weapons and tools of his trade which he knows how to employ. What distinguishes him, however, is his great heart which plumbs the depths of humanity, suffering every injustice to others as a personal physical pain, and his incorruptible honesty. In Kraus, intellectual genius is combined with warmheartedness. In what he publishes he is ever true to his convictions, and a martyr in that cause. It is to this man we owe the fact—and here I can claim complete objectivity since scientific and religious matters are my field, and I am completely independent—that freedom of the press, which hitherto existed only on paper, but which in essence merely gave a free hand to literary freebooters, financial swindlers, and political tricksters intent on deceiving the people—it is to this man, then, that we owe the fact that press freedom has become a reality. He has drawn the teeth of the journalistic dragon that held sway over the whole world.—What emperors, kings, princes, parliaments, and governments didn't manage to do, with all their enormous power, this man did—this man alone and without any help, solely by virtue of his genius and talent. He has toppled that most recent and potent great power, the tyrant of our modern subhuman epoch, the rabble that is the press! The significance of this man is not only local and Viennese, nor yet Austrian, or even German; *this man has restored to the Aryan Teutons the right to be heard in public, he has enabled us* to raise our voice, to warn and to instruct, now that the problem of nation-

> alities is on the point of being solved and we are experiencing instead *the immense, the overwhelming spectacle* of the problem of race, which threatens to submerge Europe and its culture under its perilous yellow and black flood. He has *given us back the power of speech* and has silenced the yapping of the "journaille". So, whoever denigrates K.K. degrades himself and lowers himself to the level of the admittedly still too numerous horde of those who spread scientific and literary corruption—charlatans and parasites.

As can be seen, Right and Left are united in sensing a campaign with global consequences against Left and Right. What we have here, however, apart from fundamental ideological errors, is above all the mistaken—and exaggerated—view, that I had already succeeded by 1913 in neutralising the power of the press—which, on the contrary, had then promptly initiated and promoted the World War, emerging from it as the only victor, and with the unstoppable growth of its power to shape opinion by political provocation and manipulative techniques, culminating in the triumph of National Socialism. Of course, it must always be understood that in this evaluation of journalistic manipulation the ludicrous external concept of press freedom, with authorisations or restrictions imposed by a culturally impotent state, is quite irrelevant. Even the total alignment—or elimination—of the press in the service of politics is powerless against the destructive power of words dictated into a machine, whatever their ideological orientation. Let a hundred state prosecutors "muzzle" the press, it still functions with a certain freedom as long as no cultural censor terminates its very existence. Just how powerless the language of reason is to oppose this was already demonstrated in 1913. (To correct the notion that my work was directed against the yellow and black peril, it is sufficient to point out that I had published my satires on white racism, "The Chinese Wall" and "White Woman and Black Man", before that date.) But what seems today of prime importance is the assumption that I should be credited with restoring to the Aryan Teutons the right to be heard in public—which, were it true, I would consider extremely ill-judged. Since it has been asserted from such an influential quarter that this is the case, an author alleged to be a benefactor of mankind is entitled in his turn to be heard in public, though naturally dispensing with the further recognition that he is a martyr in the cause of loyalty to his published convictions. For this flattering opinion was an exaggeration both before and after 1913, given that I had only gained a reputation for campaigning against the wiles of the press, the spurns that patient merit of the unworthy takes, and the insolence of office.[3] So the right to be heard in public on Aryan Teutonism deserves all the more to be put to the test, now that the issue of the racial problem has swept all before it and we are in actual fact living through an "overwhelming" spectacle. Especially if my bitingly vitriolic satire is still in evidence, along with a great heart which plumbs the depths of humanity, suffering every injustice to others as a personal, even physical, pain. At all events, the intellectual barrier which fulfilment of my ideal would erect protects me against the possibility of becoming a martyr in the cause of loyalty to my published convictions. I maintain a secret relationship with the German language, which the nation is unlikely to recognise. But since I would not wish to claim any glory without also enjoying a contrasting effect, let it be noted (for reasons of incorruptible honesty, if nothing else) that the right to be heard in public, which I have enabled the Aryan Teutons to enjoy, also permitted them to make the following allegation:

> Kraus is part of a circle of Jewish literary figures, *partly* infected with syphilis, among whom the violation of females is an everyday occurrence.

Unfortunately the exact wording of this theatre review can no longer be ascertained, but the reservation relating to the infection, which did not preclude perverted sexual practices, may be regarded as fair comment; in any case, the critic had acted to safeguard certain legitimate interests, for which he was accordingly acquitted by the Nuremberg court, which did indeed later sanction harsher forms of pillory for such manifestations of degeneration. But one cannot be too careful when referring to someone's private life, as is demonstrated by the actions of communist agitators when compiling the biography of pioneering nationalists from that region: it was this very theatre critic they accused of child abuse, based solely on his activities as a teacher. It's true he was fined a small amount by the appeal court, "national provocation" being cited as a mitigating factor, for the bone of contention was my *Dream Play*.[4] For nationalist circles this represented "the greatest mockery ever seen on a public stage of all frontline soldiers who fell in the service of their country". But in those days it was also possible for a voice to be heard in Germany asserting that nothing demonstrates the spiritual and intellectual state of the country more clearly than when "a genuine, beautiful fanaticism imbues with truth and strength the face of a soldier now dead, discarded and forgotten", while on the following day the United National Councils of Bavaria rose up in protest against "the vilest mockery of dead frontline soldiers". It is as if proletarians were to protest against *The Weavers* "because they felt themselves mocked by this depiction of their sufferings".[5] (A possible interpretation which in fact the poet subsequently made good.) Unbelievable! As if the erection of a tomb for the Unknown Soldier should be seen as blasphemy. But it was all the more interesting when the same spokesmen, whenever it suited them to raise the racial issue, used analogous comments on the frontline soldier when peddling (albeit without permission) the Dialogue of the Hyenas from "The Last Night".[6] The satire on the Hyenas' contempt for the Dead Soldier surely has an exemplary significance, and yet it has been tendentiously suggested that my basic sympathies lie with the Hyenas, Fressack and Naschkatz.[7] The difficulty encountered by nationalist cultural criticism (and the other kind, too), not only because of divergences within *Die Fackel* as a whole but even within one and the same issue, means it is not inconceivable that I was simply overlooked during the cultural purge, which many suspected meant I had been identified with the Right and left alone.

And yet no one finds it more difficult to explain the language of Aryan Teutonism than the author who has allegedly "restored" it to them. He should at least be credited with making an honest attempt to understand it, without necessarily approving of it. That I do not approve of it should by now be obvious; that I have failed to understand it is the reproach which places me on the side of Europe, about whose civilisation I hitherto had serious reservations, although I would regard its "submersion under the yellow and black flood" as a far less horrifying prospect than the danger of being swamped by a tide of brown shirts. I know that this civilisation has its horrors even without the possibility of a blood-befuddled rabble seizing control; and sensitive as I am to symptoms, I derive war and famine from the use made of language by the press, its inversion of meaning and value, its diluting and dishonouring of every concept and content. Certainly, when it panders to heroic memory, the project assumes the shape of a nightmare:

An Austrian memorial to
BERNA cheese
the Unknown Soldier....

Shame on the newspaper guilty of this solecism through all the remaining days of its life! Assuming that the human race, barely conscious of such practices, has not yet seen its last days: a race about to sell its soul to a dictator who—"at the end of the day"—compels its spokesmen (in spite of all their daring initiatives and utter defeats) to welcome the day of their own demise. "Automatically" they seize upon that fateful formula which, like a last straggling moth when all the clichés have been caught in the flames, flutters towards the bonfire of a paper world. This world had space for the collusion of the press with the war, stretching from that actual Exhibition of Cheese (1914), through everything consigned to the worms, to this BERNA monument—space enough for every outrage against the Creation that civilisation is capable of, space for the triumph of barbarism with which a compromised reality has converged.

Even though the path has been paved by hollow words, even though the press may be a messenger of doom responsible for the message itself, we still must be grateful if it merely reports the calamity, so that with every attempt to interpret it our only thought is how to escape, our only feeling one of shared helplessness against what is being reported, our only question as to how long it will last. Eyes that are tired of witnessing murder, ears that are tired of being deceived, all senses in denial and revolt against the mixture of blood and lies, against the stream of shrill commands churned out by this pestilential regime, which further compromises itself through every conceivable measure: seizure of assets, deprivation of citizenship, cessation of the founding of new political parties, the licensing of casinos, the abolition of economic commissars, unregistered students to form no more than a third of the student body, compulsory membership of the Labour Front, incorporation of students into the voluntary workforce, banding together of musicians in a single organisation, compulsory registration of those afflicted with a hereditary disease, arrest of relatives of those who have fled the country, directives on when to raise one's right arm, shooting of prisoners trying to escape. How much longer?! The action has almost reached the point of no return: "Stepp'd in so far, that, should I wade no more, Returning were as tedious as go o'er. Strange things I have in head that will to hand, Which must be acted ere they may be scann'd ... but, for certain, He cannot buckle his distemper'd cause Within the belt of rule.... Now does he feel His secret murders sticking on his hands; Now minutely revolts upbraid his faith-breach; Those he commands move only in command, Nothing in love; now does he feel his title Hang loose about him, like a giant's robe Upon a dwarfish thief ... Methought I heard a voice cry 'Sleep no more! Macbeth does murder sleep!' ... And therefore ... Macbeth shall sleep no more! ... To be thus is nothing; But to be safely thus!"[8]

There are examples which show how such a rise ends up when each of the accessories, desirous of more than his share, seeks to seize the usurped throne for himself. Outwardly united, it will last for centuries: we are not a political party, we are a new worldview. Who dares spoil the myth by talking of hunger?

> We think in centuries.... Some have started to moan. There will be no moaning in Germany....

Diabolical word, that drags you down from Valhalla to a Hell that has been asphalted over! Are those thousand years guaranteed? Signs of despondency wherever you look. In Goebbels's diagnosis, the national press

> has failed almost a hundred per-cent in its feature articles, which is to say, in culture as a whole.

The task is to create the "new man", yet there is no full-time literary critic. Brückner says the revolution is not over yet, it is continuing. But there is no need to overreach yourself. They say the head of the SS, Reichsführer Himmler, with a view to establishing a National Racial Academy, has leased the castle at Schwabenberg for a mere 99 years. After that, it will be time to look further ahead. As a practical man of affairs, besides being in charge of security for Munich, he already reckons (albeit with reservations) that

> a new era has dawned which—*though this may sound* absurd—will last for over 20,000 to 30,000 years.

The SS will be based "on recognition of the value of blood"—the very special kind of juice in which Faust signed his pact with the Devil [1740]. When the first aeons have elapsed and stabilisation has begun, the SS may rise to join the ranks of the heavenly host. As for the SA—discontented and abandoned to the troubles of this world? Spiritual comforters appear, proclaiming that German Christians are the SA of Jesus Christ in the battle to eradicate physical, social, and spiritual suffering. But who will help the SA? In the Bürgerbräu (that's where the Movement started), someone tells of Hitler confiding to him that he sees subsequent developments as a miracle

> and thinks of himself as a divinely anointed instrument.

But the SA—what is its objective now? Something different from when it began? In no way different: exactly the same as when it began! Mission accomplished! It was the Communists—arsonists, larcenists—the Communists. When Communists are robbed or killed?—it was Communists who sullied the least bloody of all revolutions. Bit by bit a Communist uniform became the norm—till anyone in uniform is a Communist. At the end of the day, the terrifying revelation: they were all in disguise! Birnam Wood advances. "The face of the movement is clearly revealed". As it was in the beginning, for out of two characters that grew together to form a unique singularity, there gradually emerged the myth of German duality. From valiant Schweppermann, awarded two eggs instead of one, to the pathological Haarmann, whose appetite for human flesh and blood was even greater.[9] How that monster provoked us—and choked us! Was he born from the clouds of poison gas in the war, making new waves to stifle us completely? The poisonous spirit to which all minds succumbed threatens to withstand the Apocalypse. Shall the spiritually devout recognise in the heavens the divine rod punishing civilisation's misuse of its God-given gifts? At the point the earth has now reached, is there some comet, like unto a cross, of which the books tell that, twisted to the right, it signifies decline, ruin, death?[10]

An ill-starred people raise their right hand imploringly to their face, their brow, warding off the streak of bad luck: How long, O Lord!——Not as long as our memory shall endure of all those who suffered the indescribable things that were done here; the memory of all shattered hearts, all crushed wills, all violated honour, of every minute of happiness stolen from Creation, and every harmed hair on the head of all those who committed no crime, apart from being born! And only as long as it takes for the good spirits of this human world to rise up, seeking retribution.

> And may the Phantom, which against us stands,
> The self-styled Emperor, lord of our lands,
> The army's Duke, our Princes' feudal head,
> By his own hand be hurled among the dead! [10,469 (Bayard Taylor)]

NOTES

Foreword

1. Walter Benjamin, "Karl Kraus" (1931), *Selected Writings, 1927–1934*, trans. Rodney Livingston, ed. Michael W. Jennings, Howard Eiland, and Gary Smith (Cambridge: Harvard University Press, 1999), 2:438.

Translators' Preface

1. July 1934; see Sven Hanuschek, *Elias Canetti: Biographie* (Munich, 2005), 220–21.

Introduction

1. Brecht, *Letters* (London, 1990), 139–40.

2. Goebbels makes the same point as Kraus, mockingly: "The stupidity of democracy. It will always remain one of democracy's best jokes that it provided its deadly enemies with the means by which it was destroyed". See *Der Angriff: Aufsätze aus der Kampfzeit* (Munich, 1935), 61.

3. *Nineteen Eighty-Four* (Harmondsworth, 1974), 247–48, 171, 246.

1. Stunned by the Seizure of Power

This chapter corresponds to pages 9–20 in the original edition of *Die Dritte Walpurgisnacht* [*DW*].

1. Cf. "The tiger's tooth is the deadliest of its kind, but deadliest of all is when man loses his mind". "Das Lied von der Glocke", ll. 375.

2. One commentator interprets the "lovely home" as an ironic allusion to the concentration camps. See Jochen Stremmel, *"Dritte Walpurgisnacht": Über einen Text von Karl Kraus* (Bonn, 1982), 122–23.

3. Allusion to Emanuel Geibel's nationalistic poem "Deutschlands Beruf" (1861): "Am deutschen Wesen / mag die Welt genesen".

4. The concept of *Gleichschaltung*, the Nazi euphemism for enforced conformity, is repeatedly ironised in Kraus's text.

5. Kraus repeatedly ironises the unwittingly ominous use by journalists of the common phrase "letzten Endes"—"at the end of the day", anticipating "the end of days", "the bitter end".

6. Of the many adjectival derivatives of *Volk* (in this passage the *Völkischer Beobachter* is trying out *volkhaft*), only *völkisch*—the Nazi organ's titular appeal to nationalist sentiment, with its growing anti-Semitic message—established itself with proponents and critics alike.

7. *Fridericus*, an anti-Semitic broadsheet (films about Frederick the Great, such as *Fridericus rex*, were much in vogue); *Der eiserne Besen* was a journal of the Austrian anti-Semites.

8. Kraus's political drama *Die Unüberwindlichen* (The Invincibles, 1928) is a thinly disguised account of his failure to get the press baron (Bekessy), the police chief (Schober), and the financier (Castiglioni) into court for corruption.

9. "Es ist eine Lust zu leben" (It is a pleasure to be alive) is a quotation from the Renaissance humanist Ulrich von Hutten (1488–1523). This phrase was quoted by Goebbels during his speech of 10 May 1933 celebrating the book burning in Berlin.

10. *Menschheit* can equally be rendered as "Humanity".

11. Inverting the poet's insight in Goethe's *Torquato Tasso*, V, v.

2. The Satirist's Dilemma

This chapter corresponds to pages 21–29 in the original edition of *DW*.

1. See Glossary: Weiss, Bernhard.

2. See Glossary: Deutsch, Paul.

3. See Glossary: Bekessy, Emmerich: "chased out of Vienna"; Kraus dubbed Alfred Kerr "der grösste Schuft im ganzen Land", *Die Fackel*, 1928.

4. See Glossary: Reinhardt, Max.

5. Allusions to phrases attributed to Kaiser Wilhelm ("I didn't want this") and Emperor Franz Joseph ("I have considered everything carefully") during the First World War.

6. Allusion to the suicide in Schiller's *Maria Stuart* of Mortimer, her young admirer, which conveniently removes a witness from the scene.

7. Inverting Goethe's "Es bildet ein Talent sich in der Stille, / Sich ein Charakter in dem Strom der Welt" (*Torquato Tasso*, I, ii).

8. Allusion to one of the *Xenien*, freely translated here, in which Goethe and Schiller contemptuously dismissed the generation of German authors around 1800: "Aber der grosse Moment findet ein kleines Geschlecht".

9. See Glossary: Nobel Prize.

10. Kraus converted Mme de Stäel's evocation of "das Land der Dichter und Denker" (poets and thinkers) into "das Land der Richter und Henker".

11. Walther von der Vogelweide claimed he had learnt "singen unde sagen" in Austria.

3. And What about Culture?

This chapter corresponds to pages 29–40 in the original edition of *DW*.

1. Diebold's name occurs for the first time in *Die Fackel* of June 1924 (F 649–56,

35) with reference to Kraus's plays *Traumstück* and *Traumtheater.* In April 1932 Kraus published a scathing critique of the commercialisation of culture (including the culture of fascist Italy), for which he held Diebold responsible. See "Dieboldo", F 873–75, 44, with a facsimile tourist map of Italy from the *Frankfurter Zeitung* of 14 February 1932. See also Glossary.

2. "Zu neuen Taten, teurer Helde": Brünnhilde to Siegfried, Prologue, Wagner's *Götterdämmerung.*

3. Review of *Der Wanderer* by Joseph Goebbels in *Frankfurter Zeitung,* 11 June 1933.

4. "Und die Kultur?": *Frankfurter Zeitung,* 16 April 1933.

5. Goethe, *Torquato Tasso,* II, i: "Erlaubt ist, was sich ziemt".

6. Lines addressed to the spectators by Elpore (= Hope) in Goethe's *Pandora: Ein Festspiel.*

7. See Glossary: Brecht, Bertolt.

8. Kraus reprinted in *Die Fackel* the bellicose poems Kerr had published during the war under a pseudonym in order to expose Kerr's postwar attempts to play the pacifist.

9. *A Short Ethnology of the German People* (1929) by Hans F. K. Günther advocated a return of the German people to their Nordic roots (*Aufnordung*).

4. Goebbels, Manipulative Modernism, and Bucolic Jew-Baiting

This chapter corresponds to pages 41–51 in the original edition of *DW.*

1. This pen-portrait is a collage of motifs from a variety of sources, notably the speech of 8 May 1933 in which Goebbels defined his programme of steely romanticism.

2. Prince Friedrich Christian zu Schaumburg-Lippe became Goebbels's adjutant in 1933.

3. From Goebbels's speeches to Filmmakers on 28 March and to Theatre Directors on 8 May 1933.

4. The Cherusci, a Germanic tribe under the first German hero, Hermann, defeated the Romans in AD 9 in the Teutoburg Forest.

5. The Prussian soldier-king Frederick Wilhelm I formed an elite Guards regiment, known popularly as "lange Kerls" (long lads).

6. Bismarck's memoirs, *Gedanken und Erinnerungen* (Thoughts and Memories), appeared in 1898/1921; they are often approvingly cited in *Die Fackel.*

7. Hitler, addressing the founding congress of the Deutsche Arbeitsfront on 10 May 1933, echoing Bismarck's offer, at the Congress of Berlin in 1878, of neutral arbitration in the Balkan crisis.

8. Bismarck again, addressing the Reichstag on 6 February 1888: "Wir Deutsche fürchten Gott, aber sonst nichts auf der Welt".

9. Plausibly assigned to Johann von Leers—see Glossary.

10. Mecklenburg, the province where von Leers was born, was notorious for its sandy soil.

11. The robber-baron's celebrated response to the Emperor in Goethe's early play is: "Er kann mich im Arsche lecken!" (*Götz von Berlichingen*, III, xvi). In the German-speaking world the term *Götz-Zitat* (Götz quote) is a euphemistic way of expressing this vulgar sentiment.

12. "But apart from that, I decree"—a reference to Cato's insistence at the end of any unrelated speech that "Carthage must be destroyed".

13. Extract from a 1933 Hitler interview in the New York *Staatszeitung;* cited in N. H. Baynes, *The Speeches of Adolf Hitler* (Oxford, 1942), 1:727–28.

14. *Recte* "I will never again complain to the police". In fact, Dr. Michael Siegel survived—see Timms 2, 520–21.

15. Kraus reprinted it as the frontispiece of *The Last Days of Mankind* to epitomise the horrors of the First World War.

16. Nazi headquarters in Munich; subsequently so called in other cities as well.

5. Political Leadership and Artistic Transfiguration

This chapter corresponds to pages 51–54 in the original edition of *DW*.

1. "Imperial Court"—Hitler's aptly named headquarters in Berlin from 1930 onwards.

2. In Austria *damisch* is "foolish", so "foolish by name, foolish by nature".

3. A grotesquely inappropriate echo of the "difficult decision" (and unresolved riddle) in Beethoven's last quartet, "Muss es sein?", and its triumphantly life-affirming resolution, "Es muss sein!"

6. Heidegger and the Verbal Accomplices of Violence

This chapter corresponds to pages 55–65 in the original edition of *DW*.

1. In conversation with the historian Heinrich Luden, 13 December 1813.

2. Richard Wagner to King Ludwig II, 14–27 September 1865.

3. Richard Wagner, "Was ist deutsch?" (1865).

4. Richard Wagner, "Über Staat und Religion" (1864).

5. Quotations from Martin Heidegger's inaugural lecture as vice-chancellor of Freiburg University in May 1933: "Die Selbstbehauptung der deutschen Universität" (The self-determination of the German university).

6. See Glossary: Böhme, Jakob.

7. Kraus gave many public readings of *The Government Inspector*, calling it "the most powerful dramatic satire of world literature" (F 838–44, 127).

8. Germany's "black and brown" African and Asian colonies.

9. See Glossary: Disarmament Conference.

7. Gottfried Benn and the Sacrifice of Intellect

This chapter corresponds to pages 66–79 in the original edition of *DW*.

1. Close to Cologne, already from 1924 a centre of broadcasting.

2. *The Last Days of Mankind*, V, 42.

3. *The Last Days of Mankind*, I, 29, substituting "revolution" for "war".

8. Papen's Two-Faced Politics and the Military Tradition

This chapter corresponds to pages 79–86 in the original edition of *DW*.

1. The so-called *Hilfspolizei*, set up after the Reichstag fire, was disbanded in August 1933 after international protests that it violated the disarmament provisions of the Treaty of Versailles.

2. Unidentified; possibly connected with the *Wehrkatechismus* (Munich: C. H. Beck, 1934) of Eugen von Frauenholz.

3. In this speech, delivered to Stahlhelm military veterans, Papen cited the folk song "Kein schönerer Tod ist auf der Welt, als wer vom Feind erschlagen". *Deutsche Allgemeine Zeitung*, 14 May 1933, 2.

4. Hitler's first speech after being made Chancellor by Hindenburg on 30 January 1933.

5. Allusion to Hitler's Reichstag speech of 17 May 1933, which proclaimed Germany's desire for peace.

6. On 10 June 1933 the Congress of the Association of Catholic Artisans in Munich was violently disrupted by the SA.

7. See Glossary: Harzburg Front.

8. Setting of *Faust* II, Act 2, iii.

9. Quotations from the play *Schlageter* (1933) by Hanns Johst.

9. National German Jews

This chapter corresponds to pages 86–91 in the original edition of *DW*.

1. See Glossary: National German Jews.

2. See Glossary: Goering, Hermann.

3. Kraus doubtless knew Nietzsche's riposte to the Biblical saying: "den Schweinen wird alles Schwein" (to the swine everything is swinish). *Also sprach Zarathustra*, 3:14.

10. Turning Headlines into Lies

This chapter corresponds to pages 91–96 in the original edition of *DW*.

1. "Had it been shorter, the whole face of the world would have been changed"—Pascal's maxim, cited by Moriz Benedikt in one of the *Neue Freie Presse*'s more oracular editorials, obsesses its most gullible reader in *The Last Days of Mankind*.

2. See Glossary: Boycott Day.

3. *Kulturbund:* the leading cultural organization in Vienna—see Glossary.

4. Fritz Busch, whose contempt for the Nazis and sympathy for his Jewish colleagues was well known, was driven from his post as music director of the Dresden State Opera in March 1933.

11. Murder with Mendacity

This chapter corresponds to pages 96–99 in the original edition of *DW*.

1. Castor oil: a punishment well known for its use by the Italian Fascists.

12. Purveyors of Culture and the PEN Congress

This chapter corresponds to pages 100–110 in the original edition of *DW.*

1. *Antony and Cleopatra*, IV, 6.

2. See Glossary: Brückner, Helmuth. Mattern is the heroine's stepfather in Hauptmann's dream-play *Hanneles Himmelfahrt* (1893), which Kraus much admired (F 885–7, 17); she commits suicide.

3. The Austrian Grossmann had spent several years in Berlin but was abruptly expelled on the Nazi seizure of power.

4. The opening of Heine's "Nachtgedanken" from *Zeitgedichte* (1844).

5. Curt Goetz, *Hokuspokus:* hit comedy murder mystery (1927); film version (1930) dir. Gustav Ucicky, with Lilian Harvey, Willy Fritsch, Oskar Homolka.

6. See photo in Timms 2, 521.

7. Probably Franz Karl Ginzkey (1871–1963), who resigned from PEN as a protest against comments critical of Germany—and whom Kraus identified with the Ginzkey Carpet Company—cf. the joke in *The Last Days of Mankind*, II, i.

8. From Goethe's poem "An den Mond".

9. Salten was suspected of having written *Josephine Mutzenbacher: The Life Story of a Viennese Whore, as Told by Herself* (1906).

10. See photo in Timms 2, 499.

11. Offered diplomatic refuge after Schleicher's murder, he replied: "I am going home. They have killed my Chief. What is there left for me?"

12. *Greuel* signifies the German word for "atrocities" (*Gräuel*) pronounced with a French accent, perhaps evoking a Paris that was now crawling (*grouillant*) with exiles.

13. Verbal Imperialism

This chapter corresponds to pages 110–115 in the original edition of *DW.*

1. See Glossary for Nazi neologisms and acronyms.

2. As the Roman historian Suetonius said of the emperor Titus (and one of the Kaiser's generals described him—ironically—in *The Last Days of Mankind*, IV, xxxvii).

3. See Glossary.

14. Self-Refuting Rhetoric and the Price of Butter

This chapter corresponds to pages 115–121 in the original edition of *DW.*

1. Kraus despised the "Teutomania" of the Sudeten Germans (F 957–67, 74) and as a daily reader of the *Prager Tagblatt* had great affection for the Czech Republic.

2. *King Lear*, II, 4.

15. Rubbing Salt in the Wound

This chapter corresponds to pages 121–124 in the original edition of *DW.*

16. Poets and Barbarians

This chapter corresponds to pages 125–134 in the original edition of *DW*.

1. Mephisto taunts the aged couple: "Once violence has been overcome, / You'll settle in a pretty home" (V, 1)—it's possible that Kraus is referring to a concentration camp here.

2. Allusion to the "Black List for Purging Public Libraries", published on 16 May 1933 in the *Börsenblatt für den Deutschen Buchhandel*.

3. An amended figure of "131 authors" is given in Wagenknecht's edition of *Dritte Walpurgisnacht*, 144.

4. Friedrich Hölderlin, *Hyperion*, chapter 67: Hyperion to Bellarmin.

5. On 3 February 1936, Thomas Mann, already in exile in Switzerland, quoted the last lines in the *Neue Zürcher Zeitung*—"Weit klüger ist's, dem Vaterland entsagen, / Als unter einem kindischen Geschlechte / Das Joch des blinden Pöbelhasses tragen"—in an open letter marking his public rupture with Nazi Germany (hitherto postponed in order to retain his German readership until the Fischer-Verlag, his publisher, had moved to Vienna, and his application for Czech citizenship had been approved).

6. Friedrich Nietzsche, *Nachgelassene Fragmente* (Kritische Studienausgabe, 1988), IX, 395 & II, 511–12.

7. The jingle, signed "Dr. Hanns Heinz Ewers", was picked up by *Der Sturm* (vol. 5, no. 9) on 1 August 1914 with the following gloss: "This devil of a fellow with his pyjamas and ultraloud neckwear gives us a glimpse of the secrets of his *toilette*. The shock of blond hair that the poet's arm so often has to push back for the photographer deserves its gleaming fat-free sheen." The only prize Ewers ever won, his critics scoffed, was in a beauty competition. See also Glossary.

17. Translations from the Hebrew?

This chapter corresponds to pages 135–139 in the original edition of *DW*.

1. "Bin", meaning in German "I am", forms a source of ironic wordplay with the patronymic bin/ben meaning "son of". Emanuel bin Gorion (Emanuel Berdyczewski)—not to be confused with David ben Gurion—was the author of *Das Leben des Flavius Josephus* (Berlin, 1934–37).

2. Benn was keen to prove there was no bin/ben/Benn connection in the summer of 1933, after the NS Medical Association expelled him and Börries von Münchhausen called him a "pure-blooded Jew".

3. Around half of all books were still being printed in the "gothic" typeface *Fraktur*, defended by some as a typographical expression of the Nordic soul but banned from official use in 1941 when it became suspected of being of Jewish origin.

4. See Glossary: Goering, Hermann.

18. Soundbite-Hooks and Foreign Policy

This chapter corresponds to pages 139–156 in the original edition of *DW.*

1. "Tonfallstriche" is a triple pun, combining "Ton-Fallstricke" (sound traps), "Tonfall-Striche" (tonic constraints), and "Tonfalls-Tricke" (intonation tricks).

2. Toscanini was associated with fast tempi.

3. Iambic pentameter from *Wallensteins Tod,* II, 2: "Doch hart im Raume stossen sich die Sachen".

4. Emanuel Geibel, "Deutschlands Beruf" (1861).

5. That is, the Nazi version of the Blue Flower—for the Romantic generation the archetypal symbolic goal of longing, taken from Novalis's *Heinrich von Ofterdingen* (1800/1802).

6. Rolland's Open Letter appeared in the *Kölnische Zeitung* on 21 May 1933. The replies were republished in book form: *Sechs Bekenntnisse zum neuen Deutschland: Rudolf G. Binding, Erwin Guido Kolbenheyer, die "Kölnische Zeitung", Wilhelm von Scholz, Otto Wirz, Robert Fabre-Luce antworten Romain Rolland* (Hamburg, 1933).

7. See Glossary: Law for the Restoration of the Professional Civil Service.

8. Cf. *Der Heiratsonkel,* sold on the streets of Berlin in *The Last Days of Mankind,* V, 20.

9. See Jim Wilson, *Nazi Princess: Hitler, Lord Rothermere, and Princess Stephanie von Hohenlohe* [born Steffi Richter] (2011), which alludes to reports that she inveigled press baron Lord Rothermere into campaigning for the return to Germany of territory ceded to Poland.

10. Allusion to a line from Luther's hymn, "Ein feste Burg".

11. *Macbeth,* V, 1; II, 2; I, 7.

19. "When Jewish Blood . . ."

This chapter corresponds to pages 156–165 in the original edition of *DW.*

1. Cf. Goering's speech of 11 March 1933, published in *Reden und Aufsätze* (Munich, 1942).

2. See Glossary: Boycott Day.

3. Emanuel Geibel, "Deutschlands Beruf" (1861).

4. See Max Domarus, *Hitler, Reden und Proklamationen 1932–1945* (Munich, 1965), 1:312, and Timms 2, 509.

5. A reference to Kraus's leave-taking from his readers in October 1933, the poem "Man frage nicht" (F 888, 4)—see introduction.

6. Conversely, "Since acquittals were potentially dangerous, for the Gestapo could correct them with 'protective custody,' lawyers sometimes contrived to have innocent clients sentenced to terms of regular imprisonment, whose rigours were less lethal than concentration camps". Michael Burleigh, *The Third Reich: A New History* (Pan, 2001), 164, 198.

20. Austrian Independence and the Innocent Aggressor

This chapter corresponds to pages 165–183 in the original edition of *DW*.

1. To anticipate: an internal Nazi tribunal system, established by Hitler in 1926 to impose discipline and settle intra-party disputes.

2. Dollfuss's Notverordnung of 4 March 1933.

3. *The Last Days of Mankind*, I, 25.

4. Inverting "The very meekest cannot be at peace / If his most wicked neighbour will not let him rest" (Schiller, *Wilhelm Tell*, IV, 3)—also the source of the following reference to the "power of tyrants".

5. The Rhein-Main-Donau Kanal, begun under Charlemagne in AD 801, recently completed.

6. *The Merry Wives of Windsor*, V, 4.

7. *Der Traum, ein Leben*, I.

8. At Tannenberg they are driven into the Masurian swamps: "glug-glug, glug-glug as they choke to death". *The Last Days of Mankind*, II, 1.

9. Inverting Frederick the Great's maxim that everyone must find happiness in his own way.

21. Protective Custody

This chapter corresponds to pages 184–200 in the original edition of *DW*.

1. See Glossary: Oberfohren, Ernst.

2. "I had a loyal comrade", poem by Ludwig Uhland (1809), set to music by Friedrich Silcher (1825).

3. Law of 24 November 1933.

4. Traditional song adapted by Wilhelm Hauff, set by Friedrich Silcher (1824); the theme was popularised by a movie about heroic self-sacrifice entitled *Morgenrot*, released in February 1933.

5. This handwritten sentence from Kraus's proofs, omitted by Heinrich Fischer, has been restored here for the sake of continuity—see Glossary.

22. Sexual Hatred, "Unforced" Conversation, and an Act of Defiance

This chapter corresponds to pages 200–211 in the original edition of *DW*.

1. In 1933, Hitler appointed Gertrud Scholtz-Klink (1902–1999) Reichsfrauenführerin der Nationalsozialistischen Frauenschaft (NSF); a lifelong advocate of "Kinder, Küche, Kirche" (children, kitchen, church) as women's proper sphere, she also toured the concentration camps for women that Kraus so deplored.

2. Ironic allusion to a line from Ernst Moritz Arndt's patriotic song "Was ist des Deutschen Vaterland?" (1813).

3. Most likely Raphael Lemkin, whose speech on "The Crime of Barbarity" to the Legal Council at the League of Nations conference in Madrid (1933) led to the concept of genocide.

4. See Glossary: Zentrum.

5. The Disarmament Conference of the League of Nations (see Glossary) was presided over by former British Foreign Secretary Arthur Henderson; the Soviet delegation was led by Maxim Litvinov, an advocate of collective security; Goebbels represented Germany.

23. Dollfuss and the Social Democrats

This chapter corresponds to pages 212–218 in the original edition of *DW*.

1. Chosen in 1932 by the "Iron Front" of Social Democrats, Reichsbanner, and trade unions to counter the swastika, symbolising opposition to fascism, clericalism, and capitalism; the arrows point downwards and to the left.

2. See Glossary: Adler, Friedrich.

3. Signalling smug Viennese complacency. See Glossary: Schiller, Friedrich.

4. See Glossary.

24. Casting Out the Devil through Beelzebub

This chapter corresponds to pages 218–232 in the original edition of *DW*.

1. Moscow prohibited any tactical alliance between German Communists and Social Democrats.

2. In Offenbach's *La Belle Hélène,* reworked by Max Reinhardt and Erich Wolfgang Korngold (Berlin, 1931), the Augurer helps Paris win Helen by tricking Menelaus.

3. The first *grossdeutsch* solution failed in 1848 because of the incompatibility of a dynastic multinational state (Austria) with a single-nation state (the *Reich*), clearing the way for the *kleindeutsch* option under Prussian leadership by default.

4. See Glossary: Heimwehr.

5. See Glossary: Alpers, Friedrich.

6. "Propter vitam vivendi perdere causas"—Juvenal, *Satires*, VIII.

7. "Primum vivere, deinde navigare": Kraus is parodying the adage "Primum vivere, deinde philosophari".

8. Matthew 12:17.

9. And with it the "sulphurous and tormenting flames" awaiting Hamlet's father's ghost in purgatory (*Hamlet*, I, 5).

10. Juno's sacred geese warned the beleaguered Romans on the Capitoline Hill by squawking during the first Sack of Rome by the Gauls in 320 BC.

11. Heinrich Heine, *Romanzero* (1849).

25. Between Two Fascisms

This chapter corresponds to pages 232–246 in the original edition of *DW*.

1. Tarnopol: Galician town with large Jewish population that increasingly came under threat. Kolomea: a reference to the story *Don Juan of Kolomea* (1875) by Leopold von Sacher-Masoch.

2. See Glossary: Deutsch, Julius; Körner, Theodor.

3. *The Last Days of Mankind* concludes with Prussian officers denouncing Austrian incompetence at a drunken regimental rout.

4. In September, Mussolini agreed to supply Starhemberg with money and arms.

5. See Glossary: Nobel Prize.

6. Allusion to "The sun brings everything to light" ("Die Sonne bringt es an den Tag"), a ballad by Adelbert von Chamisso about guilt and retribution.

7. See Glossary: May Day.

26. Headlong into Servitude

This chapter corresponds to pages 247–257 in the original edition of *DW*.

1. "At Romae ruere in servitium consules, patres, eques" (Tacitus, *Annales*, VII).

2. Cf. "pious visits to the graves of heroes and war cemeteries will result in a lively tourist trade"—*The Last Days of Mankind*, V, 24.

3. Allocated to party members and war veterans—mainly reluctant attendees.

4. An echo of Luke 10:33–34. The Saar territory was under French jurisdiction from 1919 until the 1935 plebiscite, when it voted overwhelmingly for unification with Germany.

5. *Macbeth*, IV, 3.

6. *Macbeth*, III, 6.

7. *King Lear*, IV, 1.

27. Out of the Abyss

This chapter corresponds to pages 257–263 in the original edition of *DW*.

1. *Mein Kampf*, trans. Ralph Manheim (London: Hutchinson, 1987), 394.

2. Luke 16:23–26.

3. "Die deutsche Kunst als stolzeste Verteidigung des deutschen Volkes", speech delivered at Nuremberg on 1 September 1933. Cf. Thomas Mann's contempt for the pitiful style of this speech and its wretched synopsis of German culture, which he is astonished to recognise as Hitler's undoubted fixation, rather than the war-mongering of "Göhring [*sic*] and Röhm" (Mann's diary entry: 8 September 1933).

4. See Glossary: SA.

5. Hitler's speech of 6 July 1933 was attacked by Röhm as a betrayal of the revolution.

6. Hitler's Twenty-five Point Plan, developed in the 1920s, was promptly abandoned in 1933.

7. See Glossary: May Day.

28. Where Lawlessness Makes Law Its Instrument

This chapter corresponds to pages 264–279 in the original edition of *DW*.

1. Heinrich Himmler.

2. For a compelling first-hand account of the "corrosive power of comradeship" in Jüterbog camp, see Sebastian Haffner, *Defying Hitler* (Phoenix and London, 2003), chapters 36–40.

29. Prophets of Doom and the Triumph of Aryan Teutonism

This chapter corresponds to pages 280–292 in the original edition of *DW*.

1. "Revolverjournalismus" (derived from the revolving or rotary press, facilitating mass production) is a form of muckraking journalism designed to extort hush money by threatening adverse publicity or embarrassing disclosures.

2. "To seek refuge": from Kraus's wartime poem "Abenteuer der Arbeit" (F 443, 6).

3. *Hamlet*, III, i.

4. Kraus subsequently gave solo recitals of *Traumstück* (1922), his antiwar verse-play.

5. Gerhart Hauptmann's Naturalist drama *Die Weber* (1892), dealing with the unsuccessful uprising of the starving Silesian weavers in 1844.

6. The epilogue of *The Last Days of Mankind*.

7. *Fressack:* greedy pig; *Naschkatze:* compulsive nibbler.

8. *Macbeth*, Act III.

9. Schweppermann: German folk hero, rewarded by the Emperor for bravery in battle (1322): "Und jeder Mann bekommt ein Ei, / Der brave Schweppermann kriegt zwei". Fritz Haarmann: a "vampiric", homosexual Jack the Ripper figure whose serial killings terrorised Germany during the early 1920s, was a little man with a moustache.

10. The allusion is to the Emperor Constantine's vision of a radiant cross in the sky, which inaugurated the Christian era in Europe—but which has been blotted out by the swastika.

GLOSSARY AND INDEX

Bauer, Otto (1882–1938) Foreign Minister under fellow Socialist Karl Renner's chancellorship in postwar rump state of Austria, emphatic advocate of Anschluss with Germany as Austria's Schicksalsgemeinschaft or "communal destiny" (which Kraus opposed); resigned in 1919 over ban on Anschluss in Treaty of Saint-Germain; promoted socialization programme (which Kraus supported, though not the ultimate dismantlement of capitalism favoured by Bauer); co-leader and ideologue (in the Austro-Marxist journal *Der Kampf*) of Social Democrats during 1920s as permanent opposition, internally to Renner the tireless pragmatist, externally to the clerical faction under Ignaz Seipel. Kraus deplored the party leadership's hollow rhetoric, "dithering", and failure to prioritise a united front against Hitler. Bauer fled to Czechoslovakia after Dollfuss crushed insurrection of radical Schutzbund and Socialists (200 dead) in February 1934: 187, 193.

Baumbach, Rudolf (1840–1905) German poet, mainly of narrative verse, often celebrating the vagabond life: 38.

Bayreuth Festival 40f, 70, 113f, 203.

Beethoven, Ludwig van 23, 240.

Bekessy, Emmerich (Imre Békessy, 1886–1951) Established publishing empire in Vienna in partnership with the corrupt financier Camillo Castiglioni and became the most formidable of Kraus's antagonists. As a manipulative, unscrupulous newspaper magnate, he introduced sensationalist illustrated journalism in *Die Bühne*, *Die Börse*, and especially the seemingly progressive daily *Die Stunde*, which enjoyed some favour across the political spectrum. For Kraus's long, mainly solitary campaign against "Budapestilence" (1923–1926), to "rid Vienna of the rogue" (Hinaus aus Wien mit dem Schuft!), see "Sharks in the Danube" (chapter 16 in Timms 2:23): 22, 81, 113, 122, 181, 186, 238.

Benedikt, Ernst (1882–1973) Succeeded father Moriz as editor-proprietor of the *Neue Freie Presse* in 1920, after which Kraus's interest shifted from the liberal press, hitherto his main target, to Friedrich Funder's *Reichspost* and the increasingly antidemocratic line of the *Neues Wiener Journal* under Jakob Lippowitz in the late 1920s: 70.

Benedikt, Moriz (1849–1920) Kraus had portrayed the war-mongering editor-in-chief of the liberal *Neue Freie Presse* as the all-powerful Anti-Christ in *The Last Days of Mankind*, but the man who had wielded such influence in Habsburg Austria was a spent force in the new Republic: 145, 241.

Benjamin, Walter (1892–1940) xv.

Benn, Gottfried (1886–1956) The "scandalous" Expressionist poet (*Morgue*, 1912) briefly succumbed to communal intoxication in 1932–1933, fusing heroic myth with pseudoscientific jargon in a series of radio talks and articles. These diatribes drew Kraus's fire as epitomising *le trahison des clercs*, though Benn's "betrayal of intellect" in favour of escapist visions and a morbidly rapturous *nostalgie de la boue* was of long standing, his "opportunism" almost literally "mindless" ("Das Gehirn ist ein Irrweg"—the brain is the wrong track—*Ithaka*, 1914), the product of a mind at the end of its tether. Flattered by election to the Preussische Akademie der Künste in 1932, soon replacing Heinrich Mann, whom he venerated, as provisional head of its literary section, Benn coauthored a decree, commissioned by Hanns Johst, calling for suspension of all political activity by members "in view of the altered historical political situation." His public response to Klaus Mann's still conciliatory private reproach to *his* erstwhile hero was the infamous radio broadcast "Antwort an die literarischen Emigranten" (published in the *Deutsche Allgemeine Zeitung*, 25 May 1933), defending, in what Kraus construed as wilful self-deception, Germany's "tragic fate", while aestheticizing politics rather as Klaus Mann's father, Thomas Mann, had done in 1918.

Benn's past as a leading Expressionist poet weighed heavier than his defence of the conservative revolution. The "new biological type" he proclaimed in the essay "Züchtung" and the radio talk "Der neue Staat und die Intellektuellen" (24 April 1933) was envisaged as a spiritual and moral renewal, a far cry from the Nazi eugenic programme. His "Bekenntnis zum Expressionismus" (November 1933) was his nemesis, for this commitment attempted to define the Nazis themselves as "Expressionists" in his sense, provoking further accusations of *Kulturbolschewismus* and more questions about his racial origin (Benn / ben). Re-enlistment as an army doctor—"the aristocratic form of exile," he later proclaimed—provided a refuge for this lucky, or canny, survivor against attacks in the Nazi press. His poem "Ein Wort" (1941) might be seen as a response to Kraus's "Man frage nicht," quoted in the introduction: v, ix, x, 48ff, 82ff, 89ff, 94, 99, 118, 127, 240, 243.

Berchtold, Count Leopold (1863–1942) Austrian foreign minister (1912–1915), responsible for the deliberately unacceptable ultimatum to Serbia in July 1914; forced to resign in January 1915 when his attempts to conciliate Italy were frustrated, after which he took no further part in public affairs. In *The Last Days of Mankind* he is depicted as a controlling off-stage presence and is denounced by Kraus as a "demonic mediocrity" behind a jaunty façade: 51.

Berger, Baron Alfred von (1853–1912) Austrian professor of aesthetics and theatre historian, first director of the new Deutsches Schauspielhaus in Hamburg (1899–1909), director of Vienna's Burgtheater (1910–1912): 12.

Berliner Herold (1904–1935) Gossipy popular weekly that focused on the city's nightlife: 29.

Berliner Illustrierte With a readership of some 2 million, the first newspaper, from the anti-Nazi Ullstein press, to prioritise illustrations over text. It would be coerced into starting publication of Goering's World War I memoirs in March 1934, exacerbating his feud with Goebbels and ending Goering's influence over the press: 50, 209.

Berliner Lokalanzeiger (1883–1944) From 1916 part of the Hugenberg nationalist stable, published twice daily, enthusiastically supportive of the new regime from the start: 120f.

Berliner Tageblatt (1871–1939) the leading (Jewish-owned—by Rudolf Mosse) left-liberal Berlin daily. Kraus refused to forgive its wartime propaganda and pursued its editor/proprietor Theodor Wolff and theatre critic Alfred Kerr. Before final *Gleichschaltung* in 1936, it was permitted a certain independence to foster impression abroad of a free press. See also the Goebbels entry for an unexpected testimonial: ix, xxiii, 66, 151, 184, 218, 227.

Berliner Zeitung (founded by Ullstein in 1878) Developed into the *B.Z. am Mittag*, a hugely popular proto-tabloid, its newsflashes reflecting the celebrated "tempo" of the city: ix, 6, 26.

Berlin Radio (See Flesch and Braun) 108.

Billinger, Richard (1890–1965) Austrian writer of lyric poetry and darkly demonic Heimat dramas. Though homosexual (for which he was briefly imprisoned) and no Nazi, was able to thrive throughout the NS period: 38.

Binding, Rudolf (1867–1938) Served on western front and lectured fellow officers on the error of "supine inaction." A widely read German author in the 1920s and '30s, sympathetic to the "conservative revolution": 118ff, 244.

Bismarck, Otto von (1815–1898) xxi, 143, 239.

Blockwart Low-ranking Nazi functionary with oversight of 40–60 urban or rural households: 87.

Böhme, Jakob (1575–1624) Master shoemaker and influential visionary mystic within Lutheran tradition, envisaged the redeemed harmony of a fallen world through free will as God's greatest gift to man: 42.

Bonaparte, Napoleon (1769–1821) 92, 168.

Bonsels, Waldemar von (1888–1952) Enjoyed enormous success with *Maya the Bee* (1912)—a favourite of the Kaiser, among front-line soldiers, and in translation abroad—and fame in Weimar years with many further animal allegories, drawing resentment from some Nazis (especially Alfred Rosenberg) and initial blacklisting. As an outspoken anti-Semite of long standing, however, he ingratiated himself with Goebbels—his tract "NSDAP und Judentum," stigmatizing "the Jew as a deadly enemy . . . poisoning our culture", was carried by many papers on 10 May 1933—and he was accepted into the Reichsschriftumskammer under the protection of Hanns Johst: 98.

Book burning Purge of "un-German" literature in nineteen university towns on 10 May 1933, centrally coordinated by the Nazi students' organization, not directly by Goebbels, though he gave a famous speech at the Berlin event. SA, SS, and Stahlhelm also participated, along with duelling fraternities, in torchlight processions, notably in Heidelberg on 17 May: 14, 52, 86, 109, 238.

Börsenblatt für den Deutschen Buchhandel (founded Leipzig, 1834, trade journal of German book trade, Nazified from 1933) 243.

Bosch, Hieronymus (1450–1516) 156.

Boycott The boycott on Jewish small businesses and services in Germany (it was at least intended that the largest firms and department stores would be exempted as major employers, crucial to the economy)—an attempt to channel the uncoordinated anti-Semitic violence of the rank and file into concerted action—was declared on 29 March 1933 and came into effect on 1 April. Its almost immediate lifting was linked to the threat of a US boycott of German goods: xxi, xxiv, 9, 29, 33, 44, 63, 69, 79, 87, 126, 141, 145, 159, 215, 241, 246.

Braun, Alfred (1888–1978) Popular broadcasting pioneer, radio reporter, and film director during Weimar Republic and later. Like Hans Flesch, he facilitated Kraus's access to Berlin Radio, and given his Social Democratic background, along with Flesch experienced several months internment in Oranienburg and Moabit: 82.

Brecht, Bertolt (1898–1956) Kraus admired the young genius ("as though his *chosen* son" was Elias Canetti's surprised reaction in 1928 (see *Die Fackel im Ohr* (Frankfurt, 1982), 259), especially the dramatic effectiveness of his social-critical songs, use of music to break theatrical illusion, and shared passion for Shakespeare, and they enjoyed great mutual respect. Brecht addresses the silencing of Kraus's eloquence in two poems: "Über die Bedeutung des zehnzeiligen Gedichtes in der 888. Nummer der *Fackel*" (October 1933) (this is Kraus's poem cited in the introduction) and "Über den schnellen Fall des guten Unwissenden" (1934)—the latter a critique of Kraus's "well-meaning ignorance" of the consequences of Dollfuss's regime.

Brecht's 1928 poem "Die Liebenden" ("Cranes and Clouds") was incorporated as a duet in the Brecht/Weill opera *Rise and Fall of the City of Mahagonny* (1927–1930), in which context the back projection of a queue at a brothel, the prostitute's treachery, and her client's subsequent execution for insolvency rather undermine their fleeting idyll as lovers. Kraus, accompanied by Kurt Weill, included "Cranes and Clouds" in a Berlin public reading on 11 January 1932. His prophetic words on meeting the refugee Brecht in March 1933 in Vienna were: "The rats are boarding the sinking ship": xix, 22, 237.

Bredow, Ferdinand von (1884–1934) Major general and former head of the Abwehr (military intelligence) in Kurt von Schleicher's short-lived cabinet (December 1932–January 1933). An outspoken critic of Nazi foreign policy and actions against Jews, suspected of plotting the Schleicher faction's political comeback, he stoically shared Schleicher's fate in the Night of the Long Knives (30 June 1934): 82.

Brenner, Der (1910–1954) Literary journal edited in Innsbruck by Ludwig von Ficker, champion of Expressionism, especially Georg Trakl, who eulogised Kraus as the "white high priest of truth"—see Ficker's *Rundfrage über Karl Kraus* (1917). New Testament Christian in tone after the war, though still respected by the more Old Testament–oriented Kraus: 229.

Breughel, Pieter, the Younger (1525–1569) 38, 156.

Brückner, Helmuth (1896–1951) Provincial Governor and head of SA in Silesia, dismissed in 1934 on suspicion of association with Röhm and homosexuality (succeeded by Edmund Heines, "the beast of Breslau"): 234, 242.

Bruno, Giordano (1548–1600) 188.

Burckhardt, Jacob (1818–1897) 92, 95.

Bürgerbräu Munich beer cellar where Hitler made an annual speech commemorating the attempted putsch of 1923: 234.

Busch, Fritz (1890–1951) 69, 241.

Canetti, Elias (1905–1994) xvii, 237.

Christian Social Party Austrian Clerical party under the cassock-wearing Ignaz Seipel, supported initially by the liberal *Neue Freie Presse*, formed various postwar right-wing coalitions; by April 1927 it campaigned on the same "Unified List" as the overtly racist Pan-Germans and the fanatically anti-Semitic National Socialists, while itself equivocating on anti-Semitism. The Social Democrats' secularization programme under a predominantly Jewish leadership polarised positions, resulting in what some perceived as a virulent Kulturkampf between the Catholic provinces and "Red Vienna": 172, 175, 196.

Claudius, Matthias (1740–1815) Devout author of many of the nation's favourite poems—"Der Tod und das Mädchen", "Der Mond ist aufgegangen"—and much admired by Kraus: 118.

Cologne Radio 109.

Concentration Camp for Women Gotteszell (from March 1933; others followed) xxv, 158.

Conti, Leonardo (1900–1945) Head of Reichsärztekammer representing the medical profession, initiated the "eugenic" ("racial hygiene"; forced sterilisation; human experiments), later euthanasia, programme. Committed suicide at Nuremberg: 127.

Dachau Near Munich, the second concentration camp (opened 22 March 1933—the first was Oranienburg in February 1933), initially reserved for German anti-Nazis: 36, 47, 90, 92f, 152f, 156, 214.

Dalton, Hugh (1887–1962) 71.

Damisch, Heinrich (1872–1961) Music critic, co-founder of Salzburg Festival: 37.

Dawes Plan resolved international crisis in 1924 by providing for withdrawal of Allied troops from the Ruhr and staggered repayment of reparations: 115.

Demolirte Literatur, Die (1896/97) The demolition of Café Griensteidl, a favourite of the "Young Vienna" circle, prompted Kraus's satire on literary affectation. His targets were aesthetes such as Hofmannsthal, not the sharks of the newspaper and banking worlds he later confronted: 10f.

Denunciations 218f.

Deutsch, Julius (1884–1968) Leading Social Democrat, Austrian Defence Minister (1919–1920), Commander of the party's paramilitary Schutzbund: 191, 246.

Deutsch, Paul (1873–1958) Social Democratic editor-in-chief (1927–1934) of the well-regarded *Wiener Allgemeine Zeitung* (1880–1934), banned from his profession under the Schriftleitergesetz (4 October 1933, effective 1 January 1934); co-founder in 1945 of *Neues Österreich*. Kraus, *pace* Jochen Stremmel (*"Dritte Walpurgisnacht,"* Bonn, 1982), is probably not referring to Friedrich Deutsch (1902–1991) the music critic, who studied with Schoenberg and Webern before fleeing to France, emigrating to the United States in 1936, changing his name to Frederick Dorian and teaching music at the University of Pittsburgh: 12, 238.

Deutsche Allgemeine Zeitung (1861–1945) The "DAZ," owned by industrialist Hugo Stinnes (1920–1924), by late 1920s perceived as mouthpiece of Ruhr industrialists (*Ruhrlade*); supported Weimar Republic, but moved to right while trying, with great difficulty, to retain an independent conservative voice after 1933: 48, 93, 124, 241.

Deutsche Juristenzeitung Legal journal: 213.

Deutsche Reichspost German Post Office: 164.

Deutschösterreichische Tageszeitung (founded 1921) The "*Dötz*" pursued the Germanic ideal of "the elimination of price-cutting Jewish competition" (F 668–75, 149–51). A "Swastika sheet" whose contributors would prefer to use hand grenades (F 632–9, 30), it gleefully reported suicides by displaced eastern Jews under such titles as "Oh, if only they all did the same!" (F 838–44, 137): 37, 49, 70, 81, 114.

DHV Probably Deutsche Handlungsgehilfen-Verband: white-collar workers' trade union, whose leaders boasted of Christian allegiance and being the only "Jew-free" (*judenrein*) trade union; soon after 1933 absorbed into the Deutsche Arbeitsfront: 87.

Diebold, Bernhard (Bernhard Dreifuss, 1882–1945) Swiss theatre critic whose sympathies with the international avant-garde are reflected in his pioneering study *Anar-*

chie im Drama (1921). As the theatre critic of the *Frankfurter Zeitung*, he—it seems alone in Germany—was able to publish, on 16 May 1933, a staunch defence of Thomas Mann against the notorious "Protest der Richard-Wagner-Stadt München" denouncing Mann's controversial lecture "The Suffering and Greatness of Richard Wagner." However, he also appeared to endorse Goebbels's cultural politics in the paper, arguing, for example, that radicals who prefer Offenbach to Wagner (obviously with Kraus in mind) are responsible for "cultural confusion". His opportunism—unlike that of Hans Knappertsbusch, Richard Strauss, et al. in Munich—went unrewarded, for he was excluded from the Reichsschriftumskammer in 1935 on account of his Jewish origins. Protected from persecution by Swiss citizenship, he returned to Zurich to continue a successful journalistic career: 17ff, 23f, 26, 31f, 48, 238f.

Disarmament Conference of League of Nations (initiated early 1932, reconvened February 1933 in Geneva) Despite seeming recognition of Germany's great power status after the Four-Power Pact in July 1933, progress was blocked by Hitler's unforeseen and startling decision on 13 October to boycott the conference and withdraw from the League of Nations (supported in an—albeit manipulated—plebiscite on 12 November by 95 percent of German voters): xxi, 240f, 246.

Dollfuss, Engelbert (1892–1934) Devoutly Catholic, implacably anti-Marxist, member of Christian Social Party, elected Austrian Chancellor on 20 May 1932. Secured loan to stabilise Austrian economy at Lausanne Conference conditional on renunciation of Anschluss; suspended parliament (May 1933) and ruled through emergency decrees (hence his nickname "Millimetternich", on account of his diminutive stature). He outlawed and expelled Nazis (some 50,000 were convicted of political or criminal offences), suppressed Socialist insurrection (February 1934), and established a corporate state (Ständestaat). Kraus, disillusioned with the pro-Anschluss Social Democratic leadership and perceived failure of parliamentary democracy, broke silence and (to the dismay of many friends and readers) declared support for Dollfuss as "the lesser evil" and a courageous patriotic bulwark against the absolute evil of Hitler (the "little saviour from great danger," as he puts it in the 315-page essay "Why *Die Fackel* Does Not Appear"—written January/February but not published until July 1934—in which the terms "Austro-fascism" and "Clerico-fascism" always appear in scare quotes to distinguish authoritarian Austria from totalitarian Germany). Many Austrian Jews admired Dollfuss for protecting them against the twin dangers of Nazism and Bolshevism. His assassination on 25 July 1934 on Hitler's orders during the failed Nazi putsch all but silenced Kraus as a political commentator: vi, xxif, 71, 137, 170ff, 179, 193, 245f.

Dorsch, Käthe (1890–1957) German operetta soubrette and actress (in Vienna's Volkstheater from 1927); a hit in Lehár's *Friederike* with Richard Tauber (Berlin, 1928) and as Boulotte with Leo Slezak in *Barbe-Bleu* (Berlin, 1929) by Kraus's beloved Offenbach. She interceded with Hermann Goering, rumoured to be a former lover, on behalf of endangered colleagues, e.g., extricating the "Aryan" cabarettist Werner Finck, a thorn in (Goering's archrival) Goebbels's side, from Esterwegen concentration camp in 1935. Like Kraus, Finck pitched his satire above the heads of the brown and black uniforms in the front rows. See Finck's memoir *Alter Narr—was nun?* (Munich, 1972), pp. 59, 115: 23.

Dostoevsky, Fyodor (1821–1881) 107.

Dürrgoy (Breslau-Dürrgoy) Short-lived concentration camp: 153, 155.

Eckstein, Ernst (1897–1933) On left wing of SDP, Breslau city councillor, arrested after Reichstag fire on 28 February 1933 and subjected to hard labour in Dürrgoy, Edmund Heines's new concentration camp. After his death—probably suicide—in Breslau's sanatorium, his funeral was one of the last legal mass demonstrations of the working class against the regime: 147f.

Eichendorff, Joseph von (1788–1857) Arguably Germany's favourite Romantic poet; anticipated Kraus in his updating of "The Pied Piper of Hamelin" as a satire on the nationalist awakening of his own day. See National Harvest Festival below: 112.

Einstein, Albert (1879–1955).

Emergency Powers (Ermächtigungsgesetz, Enabling Act) Passed by the Reichstag on 23 March 1933, after intimidation, enforced absenteeism, and illegal exclusion of Communist deputies, with 444 in favour and 94 (all Social Democrats) against. By neutralising the office of the President, the Act—together with previous Reichstag Fire Decree—effectively transformed Hitler's government into a dictatorship: 10, 134, 171, 180, 189, 227.

Émigré intellectuals/refugees Those writers and other intellectuals forced into exile (Holland, Belgium, France; then generally via Spain/Portugal to UK and America). Thomas Mann's son, Klaus, became their leading spokesman in altercation with Gottfried Benn: 13f, 48, 55, 83f, 89, 90ff, 99ff, 117, 128, 204.

Epp, Franz Ritter von (1868–1947) Much-decorated professional soldier with prewar postings in Germany's colonies; created a personal Freikorps (members included Röhm, Hess, Frank, and Strasser) which helped crush the Munich Soviet Republic (Räterepublik) in 1919 before being integrated into the new Reichswehr, when he was promoted general (1921). He had already diverted army funds to purchase the *Völkischer Beobachter*, and became a prominent Nazi figurehead as Reichskommissar, then official Reichsstatthalter, for Bavaria (1928–1945). As Reichsleiter of the colonial office in the Foreign Ministry (5 May 1934) and head of the German Colonial Society, he was charged with regaining Germany's lost colonies: 133.

Essen, Paul von (1886–1933) Social Democratic trade union and Reichsbanner leader; like Johannes Stelling, a victim of the "Köpenick bloodbath"—his mutilated body retrieved from Berlin's Landwehr Canal on 1/2 July 1933: 156.

Ewers, Hanns Heinz (1871–1943) Had early success with sketches for Berlin's first cabaret, Überbrettl, as pioneer of German art film (*The Student of Prague*, 1913), and through fiction and reporting on his worldwide travels. Wartime propaganda work for Germany in the United States ended in imprisonment there; further disillusionment following return to the Weimar Republic and murder in 1922 of his close friend Walther Rathenau. Accused of triviality and eroticism while dabbling in satanism and the occult and dubbed "dämondän" (demonic/mondaine) by Kraus, Ewers was a lifelong nonconformist with an eye to the main chance. The novel, *Horst Wessel: Ein deutsches Schicksal* (1933) and resultant film satisfied neither Ewers's attempted verisimilitude nor the idealization that Goebbels, who commissioned it, demanded (it was shown later as *Hans Westmar* after cuts to scenes of violence no longer in fashion). *Pace* Kraus, the novel (lacking the necessary anti-Semitism) was banned even before the "decadent and pornographic" *Alraune* (Mandrake, 1911—a "femme fatale" horror story with echoes of *Frankenstein*) and all but one of his many books by the end of 1934. Ewers's support for Jewish equality took a more constructive turn after the Nuremberg Racial Laws of 1935, when he was instrumental in helping Jews to escape: 98, 105f, 243.

Fabius, Quintus Maximus Verrucosus, known as "Cunctator" (280–203 BC) Twice dictator of the Roman Republic, advocate of strategic patience, successfully used delaying tactics in the Second Punic War against Hannibal: 187.

Fachschaft (Reichfachschaft Film—RFF) The professional association within the Reichsfilmkammer which all those involved in film had to join: 87.

Faust (1808–1832) Quotations from Parts 1 and 2 of Goethe's play are followed in the text by line numbers in square brackets: viif, xviif, xxf, 28, 32, 43, 45, 120f, 171f, 219ff, 226, 233f, 241.

Feder, Gottfried (1883–1941) Early influence on Hitler's economic and financial thinking, and by 1931 head of Nazi economics council; his radical, anti-capitalist polemics against interest rates, *Kampf gegen die Hochfinanz*, and the Jews, *Die Juden*, appeared in 1933: 122f.

Fepo (Feldpolizei, formed 24 February 1933) Based in Berlin's Papestrasse (General-Pape-Strasse), blue-uniformed special branch of SA charged with investigating opponents of the regime and enforcing internal party discipline (Uschla): 87.

Fichte, Johann Gottlieb (1762–1814) 92.

Fischer, Heinrich (1896–1974) Kraus's literary executor: xix, 245.

Flesch, Hans (1896–1945) Physician and from 1924 broadcasting pioneer; as leading figure at Berlin Radio facilitated his friend Kraus's broadcasts (notably readings of Offenbach, and from 1930 such ambitious projects as *Madame l'Archiduc* and *Timon of Athens*) until he fell foul of the Nazis, and, with Alfred Braun and other "progressive" broadcasters associated with the Weimar "system", spent several months interned in Oranienburg concentration camp and Moabit prison: 82, 155.

Four-Power Pact (15 July 1933) Signed in Rome on Mussolini's initiative by Italy, Germany, Great Britain, and France (though not ratified by France), signalling tacit acceptance of Germany's great power status: xxi, 115, 138.

Franck, James (1882–1964) German physicist, winner with Gustav Hertz of Nobel Prize (1925). He resigned his post in protest at the treatment of numerous Jewish colleagues in Göttingen, though as a war veteran he qualified for exemption from the law of 7 April 1933 which provided for the dismissal of "politically unreliable" state employees: 76.

Frank, Hans (1900–1946; Kraus styles it "Franck") signed documents "Pg. [Parteigenosse / party member] Dr. Frank II" to distinguish himself from his controversial lawyer father. Member of Epp's Freicorps (1919), assessor on NS Uschla disciplinary committee (1927), Hitler's personal lawyer in over 40 court cases (1932–1933); appointed Bavarian Minister of Justice, charged by Hindenburg with *Gleichschaltung* of German justice. The cited speech was transmitted on Bavarian radio on 8 March 1933. His propaganda visit to Austria, along with Nazi fellow jurists Roland Freisler and Hanns Kerrl, was declared "not especially welcome" and the three effectively expelled by Dollfuss. Hitler responded on 27 March by imposing a 1,000-Mark exit visa to weaken tourism-dependent Austria and hasten the fall of Dollfuss. After a growing number of terror attacks, the NSDAP was banned in Austria on 19 June. Frank's subsequent career, finally as Generalgouverneur of Poland, led to his execution at Nuremberg: xxii, 60, 166, 168, 218.

Frankfurter Zeitung (1856–1943) Initially protected by Hitler and Goebbels for its prestige abroad; known especially for its feuilleton section, though Jewish contributors like Siegfried Kracauer and Walter Benjamin had to leave after the Nazi assumption of power. The only newspaper to retain Kraus's respect in his long-running battle with the press (F 827–32, 61): 17f, 23, 239.

Frederick the Great (1712–1786) 28, 158, 238, 245.

Freisler, Roland (1893–1945; Kraus styles it "Freissler") Rose quickly to legal prominence after Nazi assumption of power. Known as a virulent anti-Semite, proclaiming Rassenschande (race defilement) of "mixed-blood" liaisons to be treasonous. Later participant at Wannsee Conference (January 1942) and notorious chief judge of Volksgerichtshof (People's Court), in which he died during a US bombing raid: xxii, 60.

Freud, Sigmund (1856–1939) xix, 27.

Frick, Wilhelm (1877–1946) Nazi Minister of the Interior (1933–1943); he and Goering were the only two NS members of Hitler's first cabinet. Responsible for many *Gleichschaltung* laws consolidating the regime, later for Nuremberg laws, forced sterilisation and euthanasia programmes. Executed at Nuremberg: 60.

Fritsch, Willy (1901–1973) German actor and singer, star of some 130 films (often with Lilian Harvey) between 1921 and 1964; joined party under pressure but managed to avoid propaganda work throughout NS period: 36, 242.

Furtwängler, Wilhelm (1886–1954) Chief conductor of Berlin Philharmonic Orchestra (1922–1945, 1952–1954), whose gradual and unwilling accommodation with NS regime, which exploited his fame, is a divisive issue to this day. In his open letter to Goebbels of 10 April 1933 he deplored the regime's anti-Semitism, recognising only good or bad art, but more controversially maintained that what is "rootless," "kitsch," or of "sterile virtuosity" (all Jewish stereotypes) "cannot be pursued systematically enough". His many successful efforts to protect Jewish colleagues were somewhat undermined after he accepted the vice-presidency of the Reichsmusikkammer (under Richard Strauss) in the autumn of 1933, exclusion from which effectively deprived musicians of their livelihood. The most compelling case for the defence is made by his (Jewish) secretary Bertha Geismar in *The Baton and the Jackboot*: 76, 114.

Futterweit, Norbert (1898–1933) Died when his jeweller's shop on Vienna's Meidlinger Hauptstrasse was bombed by Nazis on 12 June 1933—one of the murders that led to the banning of the Austrian NSDAP: 134, 204.

Gau Nazi administrative district (roughly: a shire); the first of the planned thirty-two were established in the late 1920s: 164.

Gaukartei An index of NSDAP party members compiled by each Gau: 87.

Gaukulturwart Nazi "advisor" to public office holders on cultural matters: 87.

Gauleiter Paramilitary Nazi rank (in practice outranking the civilian administration, though the Reichsstatthalter or federal governors were increasingly party bosses) with authority over a Gau, subordinate only to the Reichsleiter (national leader). Further subdivisions were: Kreis (district, county); Ort (c. 1500 urban or rural households); Zelle (160–480 households); Block (40–60 households): 35, 48, 129, 204, 215.

Gausaf Gau-SA-Führer: 87.

Geibel, Emanuel (1815–1884) much-fêted poet, his aestheticism also receptive to patriotic fervour by 1870: 237, 244.

Gekawe Unidentified.

George, Stefan (1868–1933) A hero to many after the war and throughout the 1920s on account of the elegance of his diction, his "high style", and his refusal to compromise. Kraus thought his classicizing verse somewhat hollow and his reputation exalted, but seems to have recognised the uncompromising formal purity and rigour of rhythm and rhyme of his translations of Shakespeare's *Sonnets.* He was perhaps aware that Goebbels had offered the poet the presidency of the newly named Deutsche Akademie der Dichtung, though not of his (privately) contemptuous rejection of the "honour," followed by voluntary exile in Switzerland shortly before his death. Nor, seemingly, did Gottfried Benn know when writing his panegyric—published on April 1934 in *Die Literatur* (*Das literarische Echo*) XXXVI, 7—which aligned George's elevation of "form and discipline" with the new Movement. As the acknowledged Master of an elitist literary and intellectual circle (including Jews such as Goebbels's mentor, Friedrich Gundolf), George envisaged a spiritual aristocracy centred on the celebration of an ideal male figure totally at variance with the plebeian appeal of the Nazis. Nevertheless, the aloof and ascetic leader-figure who dreamed of a cultural "dictatorship" (*sic*—in a letter to Hofmannsthal), notably his adamant will to power, his dedication to heroism and self-sacrifice in a "thousand-year Reich", his evocation of "blood and soil"—all clearly appealed to National Socialist ideologues. Conversely, among his disciples was also Claus von Stauffenberg, whose last words before execution after the failed plot to assassinate Hitler on 20 July 1944 reaffirmed his faith in George's "Secret Germany" (George's poem, written a decade earlier, was included in *Das neue Reich*, 1928, and dedicated to Stauffenberg's brother): 48, 110.

German Christians Pro-Hitler Protestant fringe group under Pastor Ludwig Müller (1883–suicide 1945), thwarted—notably by the independent-minded Confessing Church—in its attempt to coordinate all 28 Protestant churches into a militant unitary Reichskirche: 234.

German Workers' Front (Deutsche Arbeitsfront) 94.

"Germany, awaken!" Deutschland, erwache! Juda, verrecke!—traditionally translated as "Germany, awaken! Perish Judea!"—was the most blatant of Nazi slogans, chanted on the streets of German cities. Our rendering as "Germany, awaken! Jews, exterminate 'em!" aims to accentuate both the genocidal message and the hypnotic rhythm—the Coué effect of auto-suggestion, here advocating collective chanting of uplifting maxims to relieve distressing symptoms by murderous aggression. As early as 12 September 1931, on the evening of the Jewish New Year, some five hundred SA men, chanting the slogan, attacked Jewish businesses on Berlin's Kurfürstendamm: v, xxiv, 6, 85ff, 226.

Gesiba (Gemeinwirtschaftliche Siedlungs- und Baustoffanstalt) Viennese agency with oversight over municipal housing development and building materials: 87.

Gestapo (Geheime Staatspolizei) German Secret State Police: 87, 163, 244.

Gott erhalte ("May God preserve") The Austrian anthem "Gott erhalte Franz den Kaiser," text by Lorenz Leopold Haschka (1797), as distinct from Hoffmann von Fallersleben's "Lied der Deutschen" (1841), the German national anthem from 1922 ("Deutschlandlied", also known as "Deutschland, Deutschland über alles"), which is also set to Haydn's melody: 172.

Gottsleben, Ludwig (1836–1911) A favourite Viennese comic actor in farces, monologues, and duologues: 117.

Grillparzer, Franz (1791–1872) Leading Austrian dramatist: 142.

Grossmann, Stefan (1875–1935) Established and ran the Freie Volksbühne "for workers" in Vienna (1906–1913), made his name as a journalist in Berlin, founding (with Ernst Rowohlt) and editing the respected radical journal *Das Tage-Buch* (1920–1927), before expulsion in 1933 and return to Austria, where Kraus disapproved of his sentimental articles about Vienna (F 608–12, 60–68). Reduced to public silence himself, Kraus took especial issue with Grossmann's attack, in an Open Letter of June 1933, on the venerable Gerhart Hauptmann, who had withheld support for Grossmann's Jewish colleague Max Reinhardt, failed to condemn the book burnings or the forced exile of prominent writers, and remained in the Prussian Academy of Arts alongside Hanns Johst. Grossmann contributed to the exiled Klaus Mann's monthly *Die Sammlung*, banned by Dollfuss: 77.

Grünwald, Alfred (1886–1951) Prolific operetta librettist: *Ball im Savoy* (1932), music by Paul Abraham: 25.

Grünwald, Georg SA victim: 43f.

Gulbransson, Olaf (1873–1958) Norwegian artist and renowned caricaturist on the satirical Munich journal *Simplicissimus*. He drew criticism from his colleague Thomas Theodor Heine, who suspected him of collaboration with the NS regime, as also from Klaus Mann: 76.

Gundolf, Friedrich (Friedrich Gundelfinger, 1880–1931) Distinguished literary scholar (*Goethe; Shakespeare*), part of the "George Circle" and inspiration to the young Goebbels at the University of Heidelberg: 27.

Gunther, Joachim (1900–1933) Berlin defence lawyer for Social Democrats and Communists, died from wounds after attack by SA auxiliary police: 155.

Habicht, Theo (1898–1944) Nazi "Landesinspekteur" in Austria. After Dollfuss's suspension of parliament in March 1933 and ban on Nazi organizations, Habicht, Hitler's principal lieutenant, was one of those responsible for Dollfuss's assassination on 25 July 1934. Hitler recalled him after the putsch failed (and thirteen of the murderers were hanged on Karl Schuschnigg's orders), while Mussolini sent four divisions to the Brenner Pass to stall any German attempts at Anschluss: 131, 135f.

Haid, Liane (1895–2000) Often described as the first Austrian film star, epitomising the "süsses Wiener Mädel"; made the transition from silent film to talkie to star in 1930s comedies with Heinz Rühmann, Hans Albers, et al., memorably singing "Adieu mein kleiner Gardeoffizier" in the fittingly titled *Das Lied ist aus* (The song is at an end, 1930): 36.

Hapag (Hamburg-Amerikanische Packetfahrt-Actien-Gesellschaft) Shipping company, founded 1847, motto: "Mein Feld ist die Welt." After merger in 1970, Hapag-Lloyd: 87.

offer employment to Jewish performers otherwise deprived of their livelihood and to provide segregated entertainment as well as to oversee the remaining Jewish publishing ventures: 19, 113.

Hirschfeld, Magnus (1868–1935) Author of the pioneering *Sexualpathologie* (3 vols., 1917–1920), after which he was relentlessly targeted by the Nazis, who finally destroyed his Institut für Sexualwissenschaft, burning its library on 6 May 1933. The sexologist was a friend of Hanns Heinz Ewers—fittingly, in Kraus's view: 98.

Hitler, Adolf (1889–1945) Is referred to approximately a hundred times, twice as frequently as Goebbels. Already identified in *Die Fackel* as a threat before the Munich putsch (F 632–9, 43), Hitler's sudden seizure of power [see Glossary] surprised Kraus, though he had no illusions about what was in store for Germany once he was in power, the hollowness of his promises of international reconciliation and an end to violence. In this Kraus grasped, better than those directly involved, the trickery of Hitler's seeming moderation in the negotiations of the Four-Power Pact and his staged outrage when announcing his intention to quit the Disarmament Conference and the League of Nations, thereby "taking back control": viii, xif, xviiff, 1, 3, 5, 11f, 23f, 28, 33, 35ff, 41, 43, 45, 48, 54, 60, 68, 71, 78, 92, 105, 112f, 116f, 119, 123ff, 127, 137, 140, 143, 154f, 165, 173f, 179, 181f, 192f, 195, 199, 202ff, 208ff, 234, 239ff, 244f, 247; "Führerprinzip" (One leads, the others follow): 88, 205.

Hölderlin, Friedrich (1770–1843) 103.

"Horst Wessel Lied" See Wessel, Horst.

Huch, Ricarda (1864–1947) Prolific, highly respected author—of pioneering studies of Romanticism and, during NS period, a voluminous history of Germany—but largely of historical novels about genuinely heroic personalities, among whom she could count herself when she refused to sign the loyalty oath demanded by the Preussische Akademie der Künste, from which she was the first to resign (over the exclusion of Alfred Döblin): 76.

Hugenberg, Alfred (1865–1951) Foremost newspaper proprietor, owner of UFA film studios, and leader of German National People's Party; helped Hitler become Chancellor and served in his first cabinet but failed in his aim to use him as his "tool": xxii, 61, 222.

Innocent aggression/Innocent victimiser In *The Last Days of Mankind* (III, 41), Kraus develops the idea of Germany as the "innocent instigator" of the war and Austria as its victim—an inversion of cause and effect equally applicable to the Nazis' aggrieved, self-styled victimhood at the hands of the "November criminals" of 1918 and the Marxist parties of the Weimar Republic: 7, 114, 132ff, 138, 245.

Jacobs, Monty (1875–1945) German literary historian and theatre critic for the *Vossische Zeitung*. In 1930 Kraus awarded him the "stupidity prize" among Berlin critics for his response to *The Invincibles*, Kraus's thinly disguised political attack on the pillars of bourgeois capitalism in Austria: the press baron (Bekessy), the police chief (Schober), and the corrupt financier (Castiglioni): 11.

Jelusich, Mirko (1886–1969) A leading figure in the Kampfbund. Kraus cites a *Deutschösterreichische Tageszeitung* article (20 March 1932) by Jelusich, a pseudo-intellectual "aesthete of the Swastiklers" admired by Mussolini despite having written *Der Zauber* *von Wien*, a story sentimentalising Vienna, and produced advertisements for beer. He was soon to emerge as one of the most prominent Austrian Nazis: 48.

"Jews, exterminate 'em!" See "Germany, awaken!"

Johst, Hanns (1890–1978) President of the Deutsche Akademie der Dichtung section of the Preussische Akademie der Künste, from 1935 of the Reichsschriftumskammer (the Nazi writers' union); and by 1939 Himmler's acolyte. He commissioned Gottfried Benn to issue advice to Academy members not to criticise the regime. Johst transformed the real-life *völkisch* nationalist Albert Leo Schlageter, executed for subversion in the French-occupied Ruhr a decade earlier, into a reluctant hero and proto-Nazi martyr. By far the most frequently performed play in Nazi Germany and a propagandistic triumph (its premiere celebrating Hitler's birthday a "national event," according to Bernhard Diebold, *Frankfurter Zeitung*, 23 April 1933), *Schlageter* featured a protagonist who rehearses objections to the inflammatory sentiments expressed by others, notably the commitment to blood, race, and sacrifice epitomised by the declaration "Wenn ich Kultur höre, entsichere ich meine Browning" (When I hear the word "culture," I release the safety catch on my pistol), a phrase soon widely attributed to Goering. Johst's intention had allegedly been subtly to "extend the hand of forgiveness and reconciliation" to the "Vernunftrepublikaner" in the audience who had embraced Weimar with their minds but not their hearts. The play concludes with an already familiar, unwittingly prophetic, call to arms: "Germany—awake! Turn into a flame, into fire! Burn—beyond imagining!": 18, 22, 62, 202, 241.

Jüterbog camp 216, 247.

Kadewe Kaufhaus des Westens, the country's most famous department store on Berlin's Wittenbergplatz. In 1933 the Tietz family were forced to sell it for a fraction of its value, and the store was "Aryanised": 87.

Kampfbund für deutsche Kultur (1928–1934) Overtly anti-Semitic, NS "battle front" to propagate "German culture." Founded by Alfred Rosenberg (renamed Deutsche Kulturgemeide in 1934 and known as "Amt Rosenberg"), it numbered some 38,000 by October 1933; its publication *Deutsche Kulturwache* (ed. Hans Hinkel, 1932–1933) attacked virtually all the established figures in the arts: 97, 113.

Kant, Immanuel (1724–1804) xix, 19, 48, 93.

Kerr, Alfred (Alfred Kempner, 1867–1948) Berlin's leading theatre critic (at the liberal *Berliner Tageblatt*), exposed by Kraus as "two-faced" for trying to restore his pacifist credentials after writing bellicose xenophobic verse (signed "Gottlieb") during the war. Accused of being anti-German by Kerr, an unforgiving Kraus resorted to protracted, inconclusive court actions and a mammoth issue of *Die Fackel* against the "scoundrel"—"der grösste Schuft im ganzen Land" (1928: F 787–94, 1–208): 11, 24, 60, 239.

Kerrl, Hanns (1887–1942) President of the Prussian Landtag and Prussian Minister of Justice, accompanied Hans Frank and Roland Freisler when expelled from Austria as "undesirables" by Dollfuss: xxii, 184.

Keyserling, Count Hermann von (1889–1946) Baltic German philosopher, who founded a "School for Wisdom" in Darmstadt in 1920 to promote spiritual regeneration and understanding of cultural diversity—a forum that attracted many eminent speakers (Jung, Hesse, Tagore). Keyserling's coinage of the term "Führerprinzip" in respect of worldwide intellectual elites (inspired by Plato's *Republic*) was predictably misread by the Nazis, who closed the school when Keyserling's vehement anti-militarism and anti-Nazi stance became better known: 53.

Killinger, Manfred von (1886–1944) SA leader involved in assassination of Matthias Erzberger (the main scapegoat as Germany's signatory to the Armistice); after Nazi assumption of power appointed prime minister of Saxony; fell from grace in Night of the Long Knives, but after rehabilitation represented Germany abroad in the United States, the Slovak Republic, and latterly Romania, enforcing anti-Semitic measures there: xxi, 45.

Koehler, Wilhelm (1884–1959) Art historian in Weimar and Jena, as champion of modern art clashed with Wilhelm Frick and the (since 1930) NS-controlled government of Thuringia; emigrated to the United States in 1934: 76.

Köpenick, Bloodbath of In this suburb of Berlin, the SA rounded up some 500 Social Democrats demonstrating between 20 and 26 June 1933 against the Nazi hounding of their party, killing 91 and torturing hundreds: 127, 156, 182.

Körner, Theodor (1873–1957) Distinguished war service on the Isonzo front, resigned as general after conflict with the Austrian Army Minister Carl Vaugoin over postwar reconstitution of Army; joined Social Democrats in 1924, helped Julius Deutsch run the Schutzbund until 1930. Subsequently in resistance, then postwar Mayor of Vienna (1945) and Austrian president (1951). Kraus also alludes to Körner's famous great-uncle of the same name (1791–1813)—poet, soldier, and national hero leading Lützow's Freikorps in uprising against Napoleon. His fiery patriotic lyrics include "Schwerdtlied" (Sword Song—"O sword by my side"—set by Weber), composed hours before his death in battle: 38, 246.

Kothen, Hans vom (b. 1894) unofficial German Gauleiter in Carinthia (1933), expelled from Austria and returned to Germany after liquidation of Röhm: 215.

Krauss, Werner (1884–1959) "A Nazi and a bastard, but a great actor" (Fritz Kortner), "a demonic genius . . . the greatest actor of all time" (Elisabeth Bergner)—Krauss dominated German stage and film from *Caligari* (1920) to *Jud Süss* (1940, in which he played six Jewish caricatures, a fact much cited in his postwar denazification process). Kraus's "demon of middling talent" may reflect Krauss's role as Napoleon in Mussolini's *Hundert Tage* at Vienna's Burgtheater in 1933, the Duce's congratulations swiftly followed by Goebbels's appointment of Krauss as acting president of the Reichstheaterkammer and figurehead for German culture: 78.

Krieck, Ernst (1882–1947) Liberal academic until joining the Nazi Kampfbund (1931), leading to his suspension as professor (1932–1933); as first Nazi Vice-Chancellor announced "cleansing" and *Gleichschaltung* of Frankfurt University; leading exponent of Nazi pedagogics (with Alfred Bäumler) who proclaimed "the end of the age of reason." Subsequently professor in Heidelberg (1934–1945) and SS informer; died in US internment (1947): xi, 104.

Krupp Main armaments manufacturer in Nazi Germany: 215.

Kube, Wilhelm (1887–1943) Ironically dubbed an "aesthete" by Kraus, presumably based on the 1933 revival in Detmold (under Nazi duress) of his *Totila* (1920), an oddity from the Expressionist period celebrating a Gothic king's sixth-century victory in Italy, locally hailed as "the first great dramatic Gestaltung of the National Socialist Weltanschauung" (*Lippische Staatszeitung*, 13 November 1935). In 1928, Kube became Gauleiter of the Ostmark (after Anschluss, Austria's official designation) and in 1933 was appointed governor of Brandenburg by Goering; after scandals, rehabilitated in 1941 as Generalkommissar of Belarus, where he both participated in the eradication of Jews ("What plague and syphilis are to humanity, are Jews to the white race") and controversially objected to the ill treatment by the SS of "culturally closer" German Jews deported to Belarus; his assassination in Minsk led to vicious reprisals: 35, 116, 204.

Kulturbund (Europäischer Kulturbund) Founded in 1922 by Anton (until 1918, Prince) Rohan and based in Vienna; attracted a veritable "Who's Who" of Europe's intelligentsia to its annual congresses in various European cities (their proceedings published in the *Europäische Revue*, 1925–1944), about whose posturings Kraus was scathing from the start. It numbered many of the conservative elite among its members, including Hofmannsthal and Seipel, and featured eminent speakers from abroad such as Martin Buber, Friedrich Gundolf, Paul Valéry, Leo Baeck, Thomas Mann, and André Maurois. Funded by both German industrialists and the Austrian government, its conservative, clerical, nationalist (if overtly internationalist) aspirations—in contrast to the liberal "ideas of 1789" associated with Geneva—were riven by irresolvable contradictions but became increasingly pro-fascistic, with Rohan himself joining Austria's illegal Nazi Party in 1935: 69, 241.

Kunschak, Leopold (1871–1953) Founder and head of the Christian-Social Workers' Association and anti-Semite; declared collapse of Austrian democracy under Dollfuss in a speech on 17 September 1933: 196.

Landtag A provincial parliament in the Austrian Federal Republic: 185f.

Lanz von Liebenfels, Jörg (Josef Lanz, 1875–1954) Erstwhile monk, founder of Viennese journal *Ostara* (1905) which propagated anti-Semitic and *völkisch* theories, subsequently its editor and sole author (1908–1931): 229f.

Lassalle, Ferdinand (1825–1864) 156.

Law for the Restoration of the Professional Civil Service One of the regime's most far-reaching decrees, passed on 7 April 1933. A misnomer, for its purpose was primarily to exclude Jews from state employment, defined (on 11 April) as having one or more "non-Aryan, particularly Jewish" grandparent. Exemptions—on Hindenburg's explicit insistence—were pre-war and war veterans and those who had lost a father or son in combat: 120, 244.

League of Nations xxi, 63, 115, 136, 168, 245.

Leers, Johann von (1902–1965) Anti-Semitic ideologue, whose prolific publications in the Nazi press, magazines, and radio broadcasts (some aimed at children), including *Juden sehen dich an* (Jews are looking at you, 1933), earned him considerable celebrity. Appointed professor of history at the University of Jena and made an honorary Sturmbannführer by the Waffen-SS. After the war, having converted to Islam, he broadcast anti-Semitic propaganda from Cairo: 239.

Lernet-Holenia, Alexander (1897–1976) Though the Austrian writer's two early poetry anthologies were praised by Rilke, Bahr, and Hofmannsthal, their over-indebtedness to Rilke, his idol, drew only the jibe "sterilke" from Kraus. Prize-winning success as a dramatist in the 1920s followed, while adventure novels with an anti-pan-German agenda ensured that his books did end up being burnt: 98.

Lessing, Theodor (1872–1933) Radical German-Jewish publicist, the thrust of whose book *Der jüdische Selbsthass* (Jewish self-hatred, 1932) Kraus repudiated. Lessing was murdered by Nazi thugs on 31 August after escaping to Czechoslovakia—probably the immediate reason Kraus decided not to publish *Die Dritte Walpurgisnacht*, since he did not want to risk his own life for a work he believed could have little effect at a time when Nazi words and deeds "embodied their own satire": 70.

Ley, Robert (1890–1945) Head of the German Labour Front, founded 10 May 1933, incorporated into the Nazi Party in October 1934 after the dissolution of the trade unions and abolition of the right to strike: 121, 128f.

Lichtenberg, Georg Christian (1742–1799) Mathematician, pioneering aphorist, and linguistic purist: a model "sceptic" prefiguring the "satirist" of Kraus's self-image. Quotations from *Vermischte Schriften* II (Göttingen, 1844), pp. 246, 251, 254: 111.

Liebermann, Max (1847–1935) Champion of Impressionism, initially opposed to Nolde and Expressionist abstraction, but conciliatory and inclusive as President of the Academy (1920). The essentially apolitical, much-fêted grand old man of German painting was elected honorary president on his retirement (1932). Already appalled by anti-Semitism, he memorably commented on 30 January 1933 in the down-to-earth language of Berlin: "Ick kann jar nicht soville fressen, wie ick kotzen möchte" (I can't gorge as much as I would like to puke), before resigning all official posts: 76.

Lippowitz, Jakob (1865–1934) Co-founder (1893) and editor of the *Neues Wiener Journal*, a populist "family" newspaper which recycled unattributed plagiarised stories along with notorious small ads—e.g., for "masseuses," a hypocrisy frequently attacked by Kraus. For this, the paper's support for the paramilitary Heimwehr, and the tendency of Jewish journalists to place an attractive gloss on fascism, anticipating an Austrian "Schmusolini" ("Schmus": Yiddish for "big talk" or waffle), see Timms 2, p. 466: 68, 70.

Litvinov, Maxim (1876–1951) Russian diplomat instrumental in American recognition of the Soviet Union, and its acceptance by the League of Nations: 169, 246.

Ludendorff, Erich (1865–1937) World War I general, figurehead of failed Nazi putsch in 1923: 122.

Ludwig, Emil (Emil Kohn, 1881–1948) Author of popular biographies (Napoleon, Goethe, Bismarck, Jesus, et al.) who enjoyed a wide readership, also in translation. He published *Talks with Mussolini* in 1928: 13.

Matuschka, Sylvester (b. 1892, Hungarian, imprisoned 1931, disappeared 1945) Caused many train derailments and deaths using explosives—motivation unclear: 134.

May, Karl (1842–1912) Author of wildly popular adventure stories, often set in the Wild West (notably *Winnetou*, 1893, featuring Old Shatterhand), which, it is well attested, was Hitler's favourite escapist—and inspirational—reading and helped form his world-view: xxiii, 27.

May Day In Germany, the traditional May Day demonstration of the labour movement's strength was granted public holiday status for the first time in 1933, but as a "coordinated" Nazi "Day of National Labour": the following day, SS and SA closed down all trade union institutions nationwide and imprisoned the labour leaders. In Austria, Dollfuss banned May Day parades to avoid violent demonstrations: viii, 189, 247.

Mayor of Vienna (Karl Seitz, 1869–1950) 186.

Meller, Maggie (1890–1971) Courtesan and, in 1917, mistress of future Edward VIII. She murdered her Egyptian husband in 1923 but was acquitted to avoid scandal: 134.

Metufa A Krausian coinage, fusing "meta" (beyond) with Hugenberg's UFA (Universum Film AG), suggesting that the flickering images on the screen, like the writing on the wall ("The Moving Finger writes, and, having writ, / Moves on"—Edward Fitzgerald's translation of the *Rubáiyát* of Omar Khayyám, v. 51), were metaphors of impending doom: 87.

Minister of Food (Richard Walther Darré, 1895–1953) a "blood and soil" ideologist and high-ranking SS officer, succeeded Hugenberg as Minister of Food and Agriculture in 1933: 143.

Mitterwurzer, Friedrich (1844–1894) German actor, star of Vienna's Burgtheater from 1871, where he famously played both Faust and Mephisto in Goethe's *Faust*: 78.

Moeller van den Bruck, Artur (1876–1925) Cultural historian, author of eight-volume *The Germans, our People's History* (1905), *The Prussian Style* (1916), and *The Right of Young Nations* (1919), who also published Elisabeth Kaerrick's first full German translation of Dostoevsky's works (1906–1922). A leading exponent of elitist "young conservative" thought, he was co-founder of the influential Herrenclub (formerly Juniclub) which helped Papen to the Chancellorship in 1932. He rejected Hitler, who sought to enlist him as party ideologue in 1922, as a "proletarian primitive", but the Nazis subsequently adopted both the title of his novel *Das dritte Reich* (1923) and its combination of nationalism (Germany) and socialism (Russia), though little of its idealistic spirit: 107.

Motz, Karl (1906–1978) Head of SS-Schulungsamt (1933), part of the Bauernschulbewegung that targeted sons of the soil as potential recruits: 136.

Mussolini, Benito (1883–1945) 13, 49, 247.

National German Jews (Verband nationaldeutscher Juden, 1921–1935) Under Max Naumann, desired total integration into the Volksgemeinschaft; ultra-patriotic anti-Zionists who favoured the expulsion of recent "inferior" Eastern European Jewish immigrants and came out in favour of Hitler. They rejected solidarity with the Reichsvertretung Deutscher Juden, established in September 1933 under the liberal and pro-Zionist Leo Baeck and Otto Hirsch. The book mentioned is *Die Greuelpropaganda ist ein Lügenpropaganda sagen die deutschen Juden selbst* [Atrocity propaganda is lying propaganda, say the German Jews themselves] (Berlin: Jakow Trachtenberg Verlag, 1933). The text is in German, English, and French; the preface, dated 15 May 1933 and signed by J. Trachtenberg, states: "May this book rehabilitate not only Germany's

operetta roles and in duets with his wife, the operetta diva Fritzi Massary, and under Max Reinhardt in Berlin's Deutsches Theater (from 1914) and at the Salzburg Festival: 78.

Pandora, Die Büchse der (1807/1808) Kraus thought Goethe's unfinished dramatic fragment in complex classicising metres (the opposite of *völkisch*) "the greatest and most unknown German poem" (F 868–72, 68)—one he had staged in 1905. The titanic energy of Goethe's youthful poem about Prometheus, bringer of fire and warfare, has receded behind the pastoral lament of Epimetheus remembering his lost wife, Pandora. In his many public readings and broadcasts (Berlin Radio, 1930; Radio Vienna, 1932) Kraus was urging his audience to understand the allegory as a choice between Goethe's humanism and the swastika (F 657–67, 3 & 6): 32, 108, 164, 239.

Pan-Germans Austrian movement represented by Sepp Straffner's Grossdeutsche Volkspartei. Kraus was consistently sceptical about the Anschluss movement—sometimes pretending to believe that Germany would be weakened by absorbing a territory "where not even muddle functions properly" (F 795–9, 17). When the Pan-Germans made an unholy alliance with the Social Democrats against Dollfuss's suspension of the constitution and introduction of government by decree, Kraus accused Social Democracy of "cowardice towards the enemy within" (F 876–84, 29): 111, 190.

Papen, Franz von (1879–1969) The anti-democratic Catholic aristocrat replaced the economist Brüning (who had to juggle his unpopular austerity measures with the support of the Social Democrats) as German Chancellor in 1932, appointing a "cabinet of barons." His emergency decrees removed Prussia's Social Democratic government from power in a coup, giving control of the police to Goering, and preparing the ground for Hitler. (Kraus complained that, as military veterans, the Social Democrats were too proudly patriotic and law-abiding to call a general strike, though this would have been difficult at a time of unprecedented unemployment.) After he brokered the Nazi takeover, Papen had "to sweat it out as Hitler's Vice-Chancellor". On Dollfuss's murder, Hitler felt obliged to replace his ambassador to Austria with the more emollient Papen: 58ff, 222, 224, 241.

Papestrasse (General-Pape-Strasse, Berlin) Headquarters of SA Feldpolizei (Fepo): 47.

Paudler, Maria (1903–1990) Versatile Austro-Hungarian stage actress and singer, star of Leopold Jessner's Preussisches Staatstheater, performing especially with Alexander Moissi and Paul Wegener. Also prolific film career in 1920s and '30s after discovery by Alexander Korda (1926), partnering Werner Krauss, Heinrich George, Adele Sandrock, et al.: 36.

PEN Club (Poets, Essayists, Novelists) At the first international congress in Dubrovnok after the book burnings, the German delegation walked out when asked to comment. The Austrian delegation led by Felix Salten and Grete Urbanitzky tried to block a resolution condemning the Nazi persecution of writers and was duly attacked by the *Arbeiter Zeitung* (28 May 1933). Salten responded by stressing indissoluble linguistic and cultural links between Austria and Germany "irrespective of political vicissitudes": 76ff, 242.

Pergamon Altar Showpiece (1930) of Alfred Messel's Pergamon Museum in Berlin—the reassembled temple and frieze with highly dramatic marble reliefs, excavated by Prussian engineer Carl Humann (1879/1904): 35, 116, 204.

Pfeffer von Salomon, Friedrich (Fritz) (1892–1961) Head of SA and SS in Cassel (1929–1933), then its Chief of Police (1933–1936): 164.

Piscator, Erwin (1893–1966) Avant-garde German theatre director, a Communist whose irreverent productions of the classics (Spiegelberg in *Die Räuber* becomes Trotsky—F 743–50, 88–9) Kraus, being averse to gimmickry, thought provocative of violent reaction "in the realm of the swastika." Nevertheless, Piscator's use of documentary dramatisation and film projections were clearly indebted to *The Last Days of Mankind*, which he unsuccessfully sought Kraus's permission to stage: 23.

Planck, Max (1858–1947) As leading German physicist, tried in vain to intercede with Hitler after the euphemistically entitled Law to Restore the Career Civil Service (7 April 1933) effectively excluded Jews from all posts. He avoided open conflict with the Nazis, however—one exception being his unsuccessful defence of the converted Jew Fritz Haber, the "father of chemical warfare," whom, it is ironic to recall, Kraus had pilloried in *The Last Days of Mankind* as Dr. Abendrot. Planck's quantum theory and Einstein's theory of relativity were soon bracketed by NS ideologues as "Jewish science": 76.

Platen, Graf August von (1796–1835) German neoclassical poet. Like Heine, a self-imposed exile (in southern Italy), champion of the oppressed (the Poles by Russia in 1830/31), and critic of German "barbarism." Platen's satirical comedy *Der romantische Ödipus* (1828) nevertheless prompted Heine's wrathful response *Die Bäder von Lucca* (1830—"Will der Herr Graf ein Tänzchen wagen. . . ."); their bitter feud featuring Platen's homosexuality and Heine's Jewishness was much lamented by Goethe (to Eckermann, 1830): 99ff.

Pollak, Oskar (1893–1963) Friedrich Austerlitz's successor as editor of the *Arbeiter-Zeitung*. Less respected by Kraus, who contrasts the hollow rhetoric of his editorials with the pragmatism of Starhemberg in defence of the Austrian "fatherland." After he claimed during the July 1932 election campaign (in which the Nazis made spectacular gains—37.4 per cent) an "indissoluble communal destiny unites the German working class on both sides of the border" (F 876–84, 1), Kraus's public broadside on 29 September, "Hüben und Drüben", condemned this "nationalistic slogan": 194f.

"Pollak jokes" Nazi anti-Polish humour: 178, 194.

Popper-Lynkeus, Josef (1839–1896) Progressive (utopian) social thinker, part of whose influential legacy was Vienna's Universal Food Services (1918–1938), co-founded by Fritz Wittels, author of *An End to Poverty* (1922): 11.

Potempa murderers In this Upper Silesian village, on 9 August 1932, five members of the newly legitimised SA openly trampled to death a suspected Communist, the Pole Konrad Pietrzuch. Hitler immediately acclaimed their "patriotic passion" and condemned the death sentence imposed on them. Chancellor von Papen, fearing a Nazi backlash after their success in the Reichstag elections in July, argued that the perpetrators at the time of the murder could not yet have learnt of his emergency decree authorizing the death sentence for politically motivated killing. They were released on 5 March 1933: 213.

Präuscher's Panoptikum Waxwork museum with a "chamber of horrors" installed in Vienna's Prater amusement park in 1871 by Hermann Präuscher: 143.

"Prayer to the Sun of Gibeon" (1916) Kraus's long declamatory poem based on Joshua's victory at Gibeon through miraculous intervention, when the sun "stood still" (Joshua 10:12). In *The Last Days of Mankind* (III, 14) the Grumbler compares German victories won by poison gas to "Jehovah's miracle weapons." Kraus's mythopoeic use of the Chosen People who are fighting with God on their side, and the equation of ancient Hebrew extermination of peoples who occupied the Promised Land with modern German expansionism, was too readily misunderstood as suggesting Germany had fallen under malign Jewish influence: 111.

Preminger, Otto (1905–1986) Austro-Hungarian protégé of Max Reinhardt at newly established theatre in Vienna (1924); directed first film (1931); director of Theater in der Josefstadt (1933–1935); emigrated to the United States (1936): 78.

Proksch, Alfred (1891–1981) Head of Nazis (Bundesleiter) in Austria, expelled by Dollfuss in August 1933: 128, 133, 136, 141.

Protective custody (*Schutzhaft*) The Reichstag Fire Decree of 28 February 1933 made emergency powers of protective custody permanent. It often "corrected" the courts' acquittals or mild sentences—Kraus repeatedly exposes the reality behind the claim that people have been interned "for their own protection": vi, 24, 91, 145, 147ff, 157, 159, 163, 165, 170, 201, 204, 217, 245.

Prussian Minister of the Interior (Hermann Goering) 217.

Püchler, Josef (1893–1971) Austrian Social Democratic MP: 186.

Puttkammer, Jesco von (1855–1917) Governor of Cameroon (1895–1907), whose brutal regime gave rise to the term "Putkamerun." A German colony until 1916, Cameroon was divided between France and Great Britain when the Treaty of Versailles brought an end to Germany's short-lived empire (1884–1919): 90.

Rathenau, Walther (1867–1922) Economic supremo during the war, a pillar of the German-Jewish elite, industrial magnate (General Electricity Company—AEG), and champion of technological rationalisation. As German Foreign Minister he negotiated the Treaty of Rapallo (22 January 1922) signifying rapprochement with Soviet Union and renunciation of a "Greater Germany"; assassinated by proto-Nazis who alleged a Jewish-Communist conspiracy and became a martyr for democracy: 141.

Reichfachschaft As part of the *Gleichschaltung* process, professional and other organisations—even lyric poetry, under a Reichfachschaftsleiter, one Herbert Böhme—were deprived of autonomy at every level: 87.

Reichsbanner Schwarz-Rot-Gold Organisation formed in 1924 by three of the coalition partners in the Reichstag—SDP (Social Democrats), the Catholic Zentrum, and DDP (German Democratic Party)—to defend Weimar democracy; banned by Nazis after their seizure of power.

Reichskulturkammer (1935–1945) Nazi writers' union: 246.

Reichspost Right-wing Viennese daily, its bellicose rhetoric and Catholic chauvinism were Kraus's principal press target (replacing the liberal *Neue Freie Presse*) throughout the 1920s when Christian Social leader Ignaz Seipel dominated Austrian politics with editor Friedrich Funder's vociferous, anti-socialist, and anti-Semitic support: 57, 59, 135, 140, 164, 195, 203.

Reichsschaft A nationwide "coordinated" organization, such as the Reichsschaft Deutscher Pfadfinder (German Boy Scouts): 87.

Reichstag fire The Reichstag Fire Decree (28 February 1933) introduced draconian restrictive measures against an allegedly imminent "German Bolshevik Revolution," notably empowering police to detain people in protective custody indefinitely and without court order. It effectively outlawed the Communist Party, which was finally banned after the election of 5 March: 43, 60, 109, 125, 130, 149, 154, 168, 170, 207, 220, 241.

Reichswehr (1919–1934) The German armed forces (officially restricted to 100,000 by the Treaty of Versailles). In February 1934, Röhm demanded they be merged with his much larger SA (some four million strong), but after liquidation of SA leadership during the Night of the Long Knives (30 June–2 July 1934), conscription was secretly introduced in March 1935 and the gratified Reichswehr renamed die Wehrmacht: 181.

Reinhardt, Max (1873–1943) Austrian theatre and film director, a dominant creative force since early collaboration with Richard Strauss and Hofmannsthal on *Salomé*, *Elektra*, *Der Rosenkavalier*, and the founding of the Salzburg Festival (1920); controlled the Deutsches Schauspielhaus and ten other theatres in Berlin in 1920s before returning to the Theater in der Josefstadt (1932–1933) until Austrian anti-Semitism finally drove him out of Vienna to America (1937). His outdoor production of *A Midsummer Night's Dream* in Oxford (where he was awarded yet another honorary doctorate on 14 June 1933, as reported by all German-language papers except Goebbels's *Der Angriff*) featured a malevolent, black-clad Oberon. Kraus was resistant to the extravaganza of Reinhardt spectacles, notably *Das Salzburger grosse Welttheater* (1922) set in a Baroque church ("The Great World-Theatre Swindle"—K.K.). His one-sided polemic against the most celebrated impresario of the age extended over thirty years, his verbal conception of theatre at odds with Reinhardt's visual, musical, and gestural focus (and such decorative touches as real trees and real grass on a revolving stage in his sensational 1905 production of *A Midsummer Night's Dream*). As a champion of Offenbach, Kraus found Reinhardt's grandiose production of *The Tales of Hoffmann*—with 35 soloists and 112 dancers—particularly disappointing (F 868–72, 6): 11, 13, 19, 23, 78, 186, 238, 246.

Richter, Steffi (1891–1972) 122, 244.

Robitschek, Kurt (1890–1950) Austrian cabaret artist, founder of the famous Cabaret of Comedians (*Kadeko*) in Berlin (1924–1932), which in 1926 could still mock Hitler as an easy target, an anti-Semitic buffoon, but was largely depoliticised by 1930/31 when Robitschek claimed that "satire was ineffective against him." He returned to Austria in March 1933, and after emigration in 1937, known as Ken Robey, produced vaudeville in America: 78.

Röhm, Ernst (1887–1934) Close friend of Hitler from 1919; led failed Beer Hall putsch (1923); co-founder of reborn SA in 1924, subsequently its leader when summoned back by Hitler from army advisory role in Bolivia (1928–1930); murdered with numerous other SA members on the Night of the Long Knives (30 June—2 July 1934) when Hitler, having won political legitimacy, sought to put an end to SA street violence: xxi, 136, 247.

Rolland, Romain (1866–1944) 118f, 244.

Rosenberg, Alfred (1892–1946) The leading Nazi ideologist, notably through his rabid anti-Semitism and propagation of a "Jewish-Bolshevist" conspiracy. Appointed head of foreign policy in January 1933, he became known as an inept administrator, a notable failure being his mission to London that year: 130, 145.

Rothermere, Lord 122, 244.

Rust, Bernhard (1883–1945) Sacked from a teaching post for allegedly interfering with a schoolgirl (1930) and considered mentally unstable, perhaps from a wartime head wound, Hitler appointed him Prussian Minister of Culture (1933), then Reich Minister of Science and Education (1934), in which post he introduced and as swiftly rescinded bizarre school reforms, purged universities of over 1,000 Jewish staff, and attacked "Jewish science" (Einstein et al.): 63, 213.

SA (Sturmabteilung) Initially informal postwar groupings of war veterans and beer-hall brawlers employed to protect Nazi gatherings and disrupt meetings of Social Democrats and Communists; banned in Bavaria after failed Beer Hall putsch but reorganised on Hitler's orders under Ernst Röhm as Nazi militia (1924/25). Membership of the SA grew—opportunistically—from 221,000 in November 1931 to some 4 million by spring 1934, their violence unleashed as "auxiliary police" after the Reichstag Fire Decree of 28 February 1933, until reined in by Hitler on the "Night of the Long Knives," 30 June–2 July 1934: xi, xx, 33, 44, 48, 59f, 65, 73ff, 87, 97, 104, 118f, 126f, 129f, 133, 139, 150f, 154f, 159, 163, 176, 200, 211, 214ff, 233f, 241, 247.

Salten, Felix (Siegmund Salzmann, 1869–1945) Member of the fin-de-siècle "Young Vienna" literary circle around Hermann Bahr and friend of Hofmannsthal and Schnitzler, whom he succeeded as president of the Austrian PEN Club (1927–1933). A frequent butt of Kraus's satire, notably as the author of *Das österreichische Antlitz* (1910), but himself its "two-faced embodiment": though a would-be moralist, he is thought to have written the anonymous pornographic tale *Josephine Mutzenbacher, The Life Story of a Viennese Whore, as Told by Herself* (1906); a keen hunter himself, he was also the author of *Bambi* (1923). Salten's popularity and journalistic versatility made him for Kraus the archetype of an irresponsible "demonic trickster". After his pro-Habsburg polemics during the war and Zionist equivocation over Jewish assimilation, Kraus took particular exception to his attempt to block a PEN resolution condemning the persecution of writers in Germany: 80f, 173, 242.

Samek, Oskar (1889–1959) Kraus's lawyer: xix.

Saxon Minister of the Interior (Karl Fritsch, 1901–1944) 157, 217.

Schaumburg-Lippe, Prince Friedrich Christian von (1906–1983) Ardent Nazi supporter, adjutant to Goebbels: 61, 239.

Schiller, Friedrich (1759–1805) In *The Robbers* (1781) Franz Moor, cursing his ugliness, conspires to disinherit his noble, outlawed brother Karl. The two never meet in the play, but Kraus has their modern counterparts fight for the soul of Social Democracy. Kraus had already made much of Schiller's *Wilhelm Tell* in *The Last Days of Man-*

kind, notably questioning which side in the war is symbolised by the idealistic Tell, and which by the tyrant Gessler; he sadly didn't live to see Goebbels belatedly banning the play from the school curriculum in 1941 over just such potential confusion: 2, 19, 22, 40, 86, 91, 171, 177, 238, 245f.

Schirach, Baldur von (1907–1974) Reichsjugendführer (National Youth Leader) and head of Hitlerjugend, then Gauleiter of Vienna: 34f, 143, 219.

Schlaffaria Club (*Schlaraffenland* = Cockaigne) Founded in Prague in 1859, the all-male, worldwide fraternal network survived the Nazis' dislike of its Masonic-style secrecy: 81.

Schlageter (1933) Theatrical work—see Hanns Johst: 202, 241.

Schleicher, Kurt von (1882–1934) General and last Chancellor of the Weimar Republic (December 1932–January 1933), who aimed to divide and rule the Nazis. Papen, who had been reluctantly dismissed by President Hindenburg on Schleicher's insistence, alleged that his successor was planning to depose the President, but Schleicher opposed an authoritarian military interim alternative to Nazism. He was murdered on orders of *his* successor during the Night of the Long Knives: 35, 242.

Schneidmadl, Heinrich (1886–1965) Austrian Social Democratic MP: 186.

Schnitzler, Arthur (1862–1931) After the scandal surrounding promiscuous relationships in *Reigen* (*La Ronde*) and denunciation by Ignaz Seipel of "a filthy play from the pen of a Jewish author" (11 February 1921), Schnitzler faced anti-Semitic demonstrations and, duly chastened, withdrew from public controversy: 80.

Schober, Johannes (1874–1932) Non-party politician; as Austrian Chancellor (June 1921—May 1922) initially enjoyed Kraus's support for standing up to military and acting against threat of a Communist putsch (F 514–18, 69–71), but not after the massacre of July 1927 when Schober, commanding the Federal Police Force, ordered police to shoot on demonstrators, killing 87, during which the Palace of Justice was set on fire. Kraus's poster campaign demanding his dismissal was supplemented by a mocking "Schober Song" that sold some 19,000 copies as a broadsheet (F 795–9, 27–9). Schober was Austrian Chancellor again in September 1929 with Heimwehr support, which Kraus dubbed "creeping fascism" under "a generalissimo parading the streets of Vienna" (F 820–26, 16; 811–19, 5), but after his proposals for a customs union with Germany and international successes (financial support from Britain and France in return for suppressing paramilitaries) he became a national hero, and Kraus, acknowledging the "lesser evil", effectively admitted defeat. As Foreign Minister in 1930–1931, Schober held the balance of power in a right-wing alliance known as the Schoberblock with Pan-Germans, Agrarians, and even a faction of the Nazi Party (prompting international furore at suspected Anschluss), and Kraus was shocked to see the Social Democrats joining the flag-waving—an "abomination in the sight of the Lord" (F 857–63, 1–4): 122, 238.

Schopenhauer, Arthur (1788–1860) the German philosopher suggested that King Nebuchadnezzar dealt too leniently with representatives of a people who gained their neighbour's land by pillage and murder, as their God had promised. See *Parerga und Paralipomena*, II, §174: 111.

Schumy, Vinzenz (1878–1962) Leader (with Franz Winkler) of the Austrian Landbund

(Country Party/Agrarians), briefly deputy chancellor (1929), Minister of the Interior (1929–1930, 1933): 191.

Schutzbund Founded in 1923 by the Austrian Social Democrat Julius Deutsch as counterweight to Christian Social Heimwehr. Banned, along with other opposition groupings and parties, on 31 March 1933, its continued underground resistance to now state-controlled Heimwehr led to civil war (February 1934): See Deutsch, Julius.

Schwarz-Gelbers Symbolic name for patriotic Jewish social climbers in *The Last Days of Mankind* (II, 33), black and yellow being the colours of the imperial Austrian flag: 228.

Seipel, Ignaz (1876–1932) Leader of Christian Social Party and Chancellor 1922–24 and 1926–29 in right-wing coalitions; known as the "Bloody Prelate" after he deployed the Heimwehr militia in support of police against Socialists during Palace of Justice demonstration (July 1927): See Christian Social Party.

Seizure of power (*Machtergreifung*) A term avoided by the Nazis themselves when describing Hitler's appointment as Reich Chancellor on 30 January 1933, since it smacked of an illegal putsch; they rather spoke of a legal "assumption of power", calling the coalition a "government of national renewal" or of "national uprising." The term became all too apt from February 1933 onwards, notably after the Reichstag fire and implementation (for the next twelve years) of emergency powers through the Enabling Act: v, xiv, xixf, 1ff, 37, 60, 117, 226, 242.

Seldte, Franz (1882–1947) Co-founder (with—or more often against—Theodor Duesterberg) of German Stahlhelm (1918) and its co-leader (1923–1933), helped create Harzburg Front, joined the NS Party on 26 April 1933 and became NS Minister of Labour (1933–1945): 222.

Seneca (d. 65 AD).

Shakespeare allusions and quotations xviii, 14; *Antony and Cleopatra*: 76; *Hamlet*: xxi, 11, 21, 146, 183; *King Lear*: xvii, 93, 120, 125, 205; *Macbeth*: xxf, 124f, 206, 226, 233f; *Merry Wives of Windsor*: 141; *Sonnets*: 109; *A Winter's Tale*: 90.

Shaw, George Bernard (1856–1950) 22.

Siegfried Line (Siegfriedstellung) A line of forts and tank defences built by Germany in northern France in 1916–17; demolished after the war in accordance with the Treaty of Versailles: 57.

Skubl, Michael (1877–1964) Deputy Police Chief in Vienna, conveyed Dollfuss's message to the Nazi jurists Hans Frank, Hanns Kerrl, and Roland Freisler on their arrival at Vienna's Aspern airport on 13 March 1933—that their visit was "nicht besonders erwünscht" (not especially desirable): 167f, 172f, 190, 197.

Social Democracy The Social Democratic Party (SPD) was founded in 1863 under Ferdinand Lassalle in Germany, replacing the liberals as the most popular political party before the war. Closely identified with the hated Weimar Republic, the Nazis hounded it until in a position to ban it, along with the Communist Party, on 14 July 1933. Its Austrian sister party, the Social Democratic Workers' Party (SDAP) was founded in 1889 under Victor Adler. After defeat in the 1920 election, the Austrian Social Democrats only enjoyed a lasting majority in "Red Vienna," an enclave of progressive municipal socialism in the most conservative country of Europe. Though enjoying warm relations with some of the Party's leaders (especially Friedrich Austerlitz) and its programmes (socialisation, but not its anti-capitalism or perceived slide towards embourgeoisement), Kraus became increasingly critical of the party's "dithering" and "zigzag" tactical compromises with the class enemy from the mid-1920s onwards. In violent street clashes, the Social Democratic Schutzbund also gave ground to the right-wing Heimwehr. Kraus's attacks on Otto Bauer and Oskar Pollak and his support for Dollfuss were largely a reaction to the Social Democrats' pipe dream of a Greater Germany: xxii, 170, 175ff, 181, 183f, 187f, 191, 196.

Sonnenburg (1933–1934) Concentration camp, a fortress on the Polish border, reopened in 1939 as a *Straflager* (punishment camp) for non-Germans: 47, 153.

Spengler, Oswald (1880–1936) His cyclical view of world history in *Der Untergang des Abendlandes* (The Decline of the West, 1918/22) was seized upon as further justification for a new vigorous politics to counter postwar "decadence." Heavily indebted to Nietzsche's bloodthirsty imagery and stoical fatalism (amor fati), he, like Stefan George, distanced himself from implementation of his ideas. *Der Mensch und die Technik* (Man and Technology—Munich, 1931), from which the quotations are taken, is imbued with a cultural pessimism incompatible with National Socialism. He rejected an offer from Goebbels to give public speeches: 47.

SS (Schutzstaffel) In 1923, Hitler's "Protection Formation" or Praetorian Guard; under Himmler from 1929, its black-shirted, elite "Aryan" squads were still subordinate to the mass-movement, brown-shirted, paramilitary SA; independent from 1930, then allied with Goering's Gestapo in April 1934 to resist Röhm's SA and liquidate its leadership in July: xi, 60, 74, 87, 158f, 162, 164, 215, 234.

Stahlhelm (1918–1935) Revanchist, monarchist, paramilitary war veterans' association, co-founded by Franz Seldte and Theodor Duesterberg (1918), intent on the destruction of Weimar democracy, supported by the Berlin Herrenclub and Mussolini, hence self-styled "German Fascists" rather than Nazis, though claiming to be "above parties." Numbering almost a million by 1933, the "field-greys" were enlisted by Goering as plainly junior partners in an auxiliary police force alongside the brown-shirted stormtroopers, until forcibly "aligned" with the SA by the end of May: 61, 129, 181, 215, 241.

Stampfer, Friedrich (1874–1957) Long-serving editor of *Vorwärts*, the German Social Democratic daily. He was forced to flee abroad in May 1933, first to Saarland, then to Prague and in 1939 to the United States, where he became a leading member of the German Labour Delegation: 181.

Standartenführer Highest field officer rank (c. lieutenant-colonel), later full colonel, subordinate to Oberführer (colonel) in SA and SS.

Starhemberg, [until 1918, Prince] Ernst Rüdiger von (1899–1956) A Catholic conservative, sympathetic to Mussolini, head of the patriotically Austrian wing of the Heimwehr and opposed to its pro-Nazi faction. He dubbed Police Chief Schober "Johannes der Täuscher" (John the Deceiver)—a play on Johannes der Täufer (John the Baptist)—after the massacre of rioting demonstrators at the Palace of Justice in 1927. At Dollfuss's request, Starhemberg coordinated various right-wing groups into a powerful Fatherland Front. Kraus generally approved of his pragmatism: 191, 247.

Steidle, Richard (1881–1940) Christian Social and leader of the radical wing of the Heimwehr, which threatened a putsch in 1929 (defused by Chancellor Schober with promise of more authoritarian government). Steidle struggled to build up the Heimwehr into a unified political movement and was succeeded by Starhemberg in 1930. He espoused corporate fascism as a patriotic Austrian, was subsequently imprisoned by Nazis and killed "attempting to escape" from Buchenwald: 134.

Stein, Walter Johannes (1891–1957) Austrian pioneer of anthroposophy: 76.

Stelling, Johannes (1877–1933) Former premier of Mecklenburg-Schwerin (1921–1924), like Paul von Essen victim of SA during "Köpenick bloodbath" on 21/22 June 1933, his mutilated body retrieved from a weighted sack in Berlin's Landwehr Canal on 1/2 July, together with those of twelve other Social Democratic and Reichsbanner functionaries: 156.

Straffner, Sepp (1875–1952) Pan-German leader, whose resignation on 4 March 1933 as co-president of the Austrian upper chamber of parliament paved the way for Dollfuss's takeover: 190.

Strauss, Alfred (1902–1933) Munich lawyer, taken into "protective custody" (27 March 1933) having crossed Hans Frank professionally, shot whilst "attempting to escape" from Dachau (24 May 1933): 155.

Strauss, Richard (1864–1939) Kraus (an interested follower of atonal innovation, unlike Strauss) was already a fierce critic of the man and his music (notably *Schlagobers*, 1924; *Intermezzo*, 1926) during Strauss's tenure as Director of the Vienna State Opera (1919–1926). When he replaced Toscanini at the 1933 Bayreuth Festival and became president (1933–1935) of the Reichsmusikkammer (with Furtwängler as vice president), he was beyond the pale: 114.

Streicher, Julius (1885–1946) Founder and publisher of rabidly anti-Semitic, populist newspaper *Der Stürmer* and organiser of first boycott of Jewish businesses. Convicted of crimes against humanity at Nuremberg and executed: 159.

Stunde, Die (1923–1938) Hungarian press magnate Bekessy's Viennese daily, epitomising the new sensationalist *Boulevardjournalismus* (cf. *Berliner Illustrierte*) with text subordinated to photographs. Allegations and retractions featuring a touched-up photograph of the young Kraus on 25 March 1925 culminated in Kraus's eventual legal victory over "Budapestilence" (1926): 122.

Sturmbannführer Rank of major in SA and SS.

Stürmer, Der (See also Julius Streicher) 162.

Swift, Jonathan (1667–1745) viii.

Thomas Cook Prominent travel agency: 202.

Thyssen Primary manufacturer of steel in Nazi Germany: 215.

***Times* (London)** 9, 139, 159, 198, 202.

Tolstoy, Leo (1828–1910) 107.

Toscanini, Arturo (1867–1957) Cancelled participation in 1933 Bayreuth Festival (replaced by Richard Strauss) in protest against exclusion of Jews from German cultural life, having also refused to conduct fascist anthem "Giovinezza" at La Scala, then in Bologna in 1931, when he was assaulted by Blackshirts. Kraus responded in both prose and song, adapting verses from Offenbach (F 857–63, 67 & 70–1): 70, 114, 157, 244.

Tucholsky, Kurt (1890–1935) The most formidable left-wing critic of the unloved Weimar Republic. Though sharing many targets and "certain pugnacious merits" (F 827–33, 75),

Kraus became suspicious by the mid-1920s of his ability to write under pseudonyms for the "Vossischen" (the liberal *Vossische Zeitung*) and the "Mossischen" (Rudolf Mosse's liberal *Berliner Tageblatt*) while moving steadily leftward towards the communist "Russischen" (*Die Weltbühne*—F 847–51, 78). After presenting Hitler as a pawn and underestimating his charismatic appeal and the revolutionary drive of the Nazis, Tucholsky published nothing between 1932 and his suicide in Swedish exile: 15, 21f.

UFA See Metufa.

Uhland, Ludwig (1787–1862) German Romantic poet, academic and moderate liberal delegate to the National Convention in Frankfurt's Paulskirche. His speech of 26 October 1848 in the debate on German unification favoured the "Greater German" solution, i.e., including Austria (the sticking point being whether with or without its non-German components): 50, 245.

Ullmann, Ludwig (1887–1959) Austrian journalist and author, pre-war contributor to *Die Fackel*, after World War II editor and critic in the United States: 54.

Ullstein Publishing house: 118.

Undset, Sigrid (1882–1949) Norwegian novelist and Nobel Prize winner (1928—Kraus had also been nominated that year). Her conversion to Roman Catholicism in 1924—"scandalous" in Protestant Norway—chimes with Werfel's conversion and with the pious background of Barbara in his novel of that name (based on Werfel's nanny): 98.

Unruh, Fritz von (1885–1970) A German general's son, who had early fame with antimilitarist plays *Offiziere* (a hit in 1911 under Max Reinhardt at Berlin's Deutsches Theater), *Louis Ferdinand Prinz von Preussen* (1913, banned by the Kaiser), and the moving prose narrative about Verdun (*Opfergang*, 1919); further antiwar plays were produced by Reinhardt in 1920s. Joined anti-royalist, anti-Nazi, and anti-Communist Eiserne Front (Iron Front) in 1931—an initiative of the Reichsbanner in opposition to the Harzburger Front. Although he signed the Academy's loyalty oath on 19 March 1933, his books were burned and he was excluded from the Academy by Gottfried Benn on 7 May 1933. Emigration followed: 23.

Urbanitzky, Grete von (1891–1974) Austrian novelist, whose work dealt critically with bourgeois morality and attitudes to homosexuality; co-founder of Austrian PEN (1923). After confrontation at international Dubrovnik congress in 1933, moved to Berlin and identified with NS cultural policy and authors: 81.

Uschla (Untersuchungs- und Schlichtungsausschuss) Internal Nazi tribunal system, established by Hitler in 1926 to enforce discipline and settle intra-party disputes: 87, 134ff, 140f.

Vaugoin, Carl (1873–1949) Austrian Army Minister (1921–1933), succeeded Ignaz Seipel as leader of Christian Social party, briefly Chancellor (1930): 191.

Verdhandi The Norns in Norse mythology—female spirits who spin, weave, and cut the thread of life—form an obscure source of Nazi ideology, though also familiar from Wagner. See the reference to Hitler as "designated by the Norns" in a speech by Hermann Burte, "Intellectuals must belong to the people"—*Sieben Reden von Burte* (Strassburg, 1943): 9.

Versailles, Treaty of (1919) 47, 115, 117, 133, 139, 201, 216, 241.

Völkischer Beobachter (1920–1945) Official Nazi newspaper, banned in Austria by Doll-

The Austrian author Karl Kraus (1874–1936) was the foremost German-language satirist of the twentieth century. As editor of the journal *Die Fackel* (The Torch) from 1899, he—singlehandedly after 1912—conducted a sustained critique of propaganda and the press through polemical essays, satirical plays, pungent aphorisms, and resonant poems.

Fred Bridgham is the author of *The Friendly German-English Dictionary* and wide-ranging studies in German literature and history of ideas. His translations include Hans Werner Henze's *The Prince of Homburg* for performance by the English National Opera, Imanuel Geiss's *The Question of German Unification*, and *After Expressionism: Five Plays by Georg Kaiser.*

Edward Timms, Professor of German and founding director of the University of Sussex Centre for German-Jewish Studies, is best known for his two-volume study *Karl Kraus—Apocalyptic Satirist.* The title of his memoirs, *Taking up the Torch*, reflects his long-standing interest in Kraus's journal. He died shortly after the completion of this volume.

FB and ET were awarded the Scaglioni Prize by the Modern Language Association of America for the first complete English translation of Kraus's *The Last Days of Mankind.*